John Power Lacroix, Adolf Wuttke

Christian Ethics

Volume II: Pure Ethics

John Power Lacroix, Adolf Wuttke

Christian Ethics
Volume II: Pure Ethics

ISBN/EAN: 9783337023256

Printed in Europe, USA, Canada, Australia, Japan

Cover: Foto ©Lupo / pixelio.de

More available books at **www.hansebooks.com**

CHRISTIAN ETHICS.

By Dr. ADOLF WUTTKE,
LATE PROFESSOR OF THEOLOGY AT HALLE.

WITH AN INTRODUCTION
BY DR. W. F. WARREN.
OF THE BOSTON UNIVERSITY.

TRANSLATED BY
JOHN P. LACROIX.

VOLUME II.—PURE ETHICS.

EDINBURGH:
T. & T. CLARK, GEORGE STREET.
MDCCCLXXIII.

Entered according to Act of Congress, in the year 1873, by

NELSON & PHILLIPS,

In the Office of the Librarian of Congress at Washington.

NOTE OF TRANSLATOR.

This second volume contains the first of the three forms under which Dr. Wuttke treats of the subject-matter of Christian Ethics. It embraces and occupies the entire ethical field. Its aim is to treat each phase and bearing of the moral life from a normal or ideal stand-point; in other words, to present the moral life as God originally willed, and yet wills, that it should be. It involves in its scope, therefore, all the essential principles of the system of the author, and constitutes a whole in and of itself.

As to the scientific character of the work, and as to whether it answers wants which are but very imperfectly met by any of our present English treatises; in a word, as to whether the work of Dr. Wuttke finds before it, in the English-reading world, a comparatively unoccupied and yet very important field, I beg leave to refer the reader chiefly and ultimately to the work itself, but also, preliminarily, to the special *introduction* to this volume, for which I am thankfully indebted to Dr. W. F. Warren, of the Boston University. Frank and earnest words like these from this distinguished scholar and theologian will, I am sure, not fail to arrest the attention of whoever thirsts after clear and truly Christian views on the great problems of human life.   J. P. L.

INTRODUCTION.

No literature is richer in native productions in the field of Ethics than the English. It probably presents more original, representative systems of moral philosophy than any other. This at least would seem to be the verdict of a distinguished French philosopher, and French philosophers are not often afflicted with "anglomania" in any amiable sense. In the nineteenth Lecture of his Introduction to Ethics, Jouffroy pays this high tribute to his neighbors across the channel: "How has it happened, you may ask, that all these moral systems, which we have been considering, were of English origin? The explanation of the fact is this very simple one, that moral philosophy, properly so called, has been infinitely more cultivated in England during the seventeenth and eighteenth centuries than in any other part of Europe. In France, for example, the Cartesian era produced only one eminent moralist, Malebranche; and Malebranche belonged neither to the class of selfish philosophers, nor to that of the sentimental philosophers. Cartesianism was followed in France, in the middle of the eighteenth century, by a new philosophy, but this was the system of materialism in metaphysics and of selfishness in morals; and called to choose between Helvetius and Hobbes, I could not but prefer Hobbes. Much the same might be said of the philosophy of Germany, which has always been more metaphysical than moral, and has never exhibited any forms of the selfish or instinctive systems, which have obtained such a European celebrity as those of Hobbes, of Smith, and of Hume." That this fertility of Anglo-Saxon mind in the department of ethical speculation was not limited to the centuries named, is clear from the bulk of our more recent ethical literature. Its full stream has never subsided, and is to-day pouring on past Bain and Barratt, in England, past Hickok and Hopkins in America.

But while this department of our literature is almost immeasurable, and certainly invaluable, it is sadly deficient in works written from a distinctively Christian stand-point. One large portion of our treatises are purely philosophical. Another, perhaps still larger, wretchedly confuse and mix up the ethics of philosophy with the ethics of revelation. Scarce one author has attempted to present in an independent scientific form the whole ethical system of Christianity. It is much as if we had innumerable treatises on what is called natural theology, but as yet not one on the doctrines of the Christian Revelation. Didactic theologians have occasionally included in their Bodies of Divinity a brief account of the "Morals of

Christianity," but thus far no one has yet done for Christian Ethics in our literature, what Danæus and Calixtus did for it in the Reformed and Lutheran Churches of continental Europe. The Science of Christian Ethics is with us almost unknown. Too many of our least suspected manuals, written by honored and able evangelical divines, presuppose and continually imply a Socinian anthropology, and a worse than Romish soteriology.*

Whatever may be the true explanation of this grave deficiency, it certainly is not due to an oversight of the essential difference between philosophical and Christian Ethics. Not a few of our evangelical writers have pointed out the incompleteness and comparatively imperfect basis of the former; but, with the exception of Wardlaw, scarce one has done any thing to supplant or to supplement it. John Foster, in the Fourth of his "Essays," has some excellent thoughts on the impossibility of ignoring such revealed facts as Human Depravity, Redemption, the Mission of the Spirit, Immortality, and Future Judgment, in any comprehensive and thorough presentation of the system of Human Duty. Richard Watson enumerates five grave mischiefs, which result

---

* Twenty years ago, when a mere college lad, the present writer addressed a letter to Dr. Wayland, respectfully and earnestly inquiring in what way certain statements in his "Moral Science" could be harmonized with evangelical views of human depravity. His answer was a curiosity. I would give not a little to be able to present it here.

from the attempt "to teach morals independently of Christianity." The writer of the essay on the Science of Christian Ethics in the work, "Science and the Gospel," (London, 1870,) a writer who acknowledges his great obligation to "the lucid and admirable WUTTKE," calling him "one of the most deservedly distinguished ethicists of modern times," "a Christian ethicist of superlative merit," expresses this sentiment: "The propriety of discussing moral questions apart from their natural and immediate implication with Christian Truth, admits of the gravest doubts." Wardlaw goes even further and asserts that, "The science of morals has no province at all independently of theology, and it cannot be philosophically discussed except upon theological principles." Watson's final definition of the relation of the two systems or methods is less extreme than this, and accords very nearly with that given by WUTTKE in section fourth of his Introduction.*

But whatever may be thought of philosophical ethics, or of the exact relation of the two branches to each other, no believer in Christian Revelation can for a moment call in question the legitimacy of specifically Christian Ethics. No Christian believer can possibly speak his whole mind respecting man, the ethical subject, or God, the author of our ethical relations, or our destiny, the result of our ethical action, without stating or implying all the fundamental doc-

---

* See "Institutes," Vol. II, bottom of p. 474.

trines of Christianity. Indeed, no man can elaborate any ethical system of any considerable completeness without definite and most important theological implications. As a matter of fact, most of our accepted text-books are thoroughly Deistic. They give us not the Morals of Christianity, or of Judaism, or of heathenism, but simply the ethical system of Lord Herbert, or Theodore Parker. We are glad to possess them, glad to see just what ethical consequence Deism carries with it; nevertheless we must repudiate their claims to an exclusive occupancy of the field, and especially their claims to represent the ethics of Revelation. Their use in Christian schools is at least of very doubtful expediency. Let every theological system, even those of the heathen, develop its supplementary ethical system, only let it not attempt to palm off its own ethical implication for those of wholly different systems.

The value of any elaborate system of ethics is largely in proportion to its fidelity to the theological views and principles of its author. If we study an atheistic system, we desire to ascertain precisely what the logical results of atheism are in the field of morals. This is the only special benefit we can hope to gain from the study. So a modern Jewish, Mohammedan, or ethnic system is valuable in proportion as it gives us the true ethical results of the particular religion from which it springs. Thorough ethical treatises are, therefore, to be welcomed from whatever theological stand-point they may be written. If thorough, they will serve the cause of truth. In the way of *reductio ad absurdum* they will often evince the untenableness of the theological principles upon which they rest. So far as they spring from correct theological conceptions, they will mutually complement and confirm each other.

The same thing may be said of systems of Christian ethics written from different confessional stand-points. Their value, too, is usually in proportion to their logical consistency. One of their most important uses is to throw light upon the necessary ethical consequences of their respective types of doctrine. In this respect the most strictly confessional are the most useful. In the interest of universal Christian theology, therefore, we greatly desiderate a thorough and active confessional cultivation of this field. The more clearly and constantly conscious of his distinctive doctrinal stand-point, the better service the author will render. Nothing is gained, much lost, by mixing up essentially Romish and essentially Protestant definitions. In like manner Augustinian ethics are as eternally distinct from Pelagian as are the theological systems so named. If Methodist theology be true, no consistent Calvinist can ever write a system of ethics acceptable to a Methodist, and *vice versa*. Romanism, Calvinism, Lutheranism and Methodism as much need distinctive treatises upon ethics as upon Christian doctrine. Each has the same right to the one as to the other. Nor will they thus aggravate and prolong the dissensions and divisions of the universal Church; they will rather accelerate the coming of the day when each great branch of Christendom will have matured its distinctive thought and perfected its distinctive life, preparatory to a higher and grander synthesis. Even before that day comes, each type of ethical inculcation will have its essential and characteristic excellences, and so effectively supplement all other types.

Especially welcome to the English reader must be a thorough scientific presentation of Christian ethics from the Lutheran stand-point. Hitherto none has been accessible. The whole theological literature of Lutheranism in the English language is deplorably meager. Considering the historic interest and present relations of this great Church of the Reformation, the deficiency is almost inexplicable. In this country the actual numerical proportions of the communion, its rapid growth from immigration, the close affinities of its best theology and best life with the dominant theology and life of the country, conspire to render its teachings and spirit a study of great interest to every intelligent American believer. Nor can the unedifying controversies and schisms which have hitherto so excessively characterized the body, or even the high-churchly self-complacency of such representatives as the author of "The Conservative Reformation and its Theology," effectually prevent the Christians of neighboring folds from cherishing a growing interest in their ecclesiastical life, and in that of their confessional and ethnological kindred in the Fatherland.

An English translation of Wuttke's great work on "Christian Ethics" ought, therefore, to be warmly welcomed on many accounts. First, for all the excellent reasons suggested by Dr. Riehm, at the close of his special preface to Volume I of this translation.

Second, because as a work on *Christian* Ethics it will contribute to the supply of what is perhaps the gravest and most unaccountable lack in the whole range of English theological literature.

Third, because it will have a tendency to stimulate American and English moralists to a cultivation of their science from evangelical, and possibly from strictly confessional, stand-points.

Fourth, because by means of it the English student will now, for the first time, have an opportunity to see in full scientific form the ethical implications and inculcations of modern evangelical Lutheranism.

For all these reasons, it affords the writer unfeigned pleasure to bid the new-clad work God-speed, and to commend it to the faithful study of all lovers of Christian truth and holiness.   Wm. F. Warren.

Boston University, School of Theology, *October*, 1872.

CONTENTS.

	PAGE
§ 50. Classification of Christian Ethics	1

PART FIRST.

PURE ETHICS; OR, THE MORAL *PER SE* IRRESPECTIVELY OF SIN.

Introductory Observations.
I. Notion and Essence of the Moral, § 51 5
  § 51. The Good 5
  §§ 52–54. The Moral 8–14
II. Relation of Morality to Religion, §.55 15
III. Scientific Classification of Ethics, §§ 56–57 ... 23–29

CHAPTER I.

THE MORAL SUBJECT, § 58.

I. The Individual Moral Subject, Man, § 59 36
  A. Man as a Spirit, § 59 36
    § 60. (1) The Cognizing Spirit 41
    § 61. (2) The Volitionating Spirit, Freedom of Will ... 45
    § 62. (3) The Feeling Spirit 49
    § 63. (4) The Immortal Spirit 51
  B. Man as to his Sensuously-corporeal Life, §§ 64–66 .. 59–64
  C. The Unity of Spirit and Body, § 67 67
    § 67. (1) The Stages of Life 67
    § 68. (2) Temperaments and National Peculiarities ... 71
    § 69. (3) The Sexes 74
II. The Community-Life as Moral Subject, § 70 76

CHAPTER II.

GOD AS THE GROUND AND PROTOTYPE OF THE MORAL LIFE AND AS THE AUTHOR OF THE LAW.

§ 72. (1) God as Holy Will 82
§ 73. (2) God as Prototype of the Moral 85

	PAGE
§ 74. (3) GOD AS UPHOLDER OF THE MORAL WORLD-GOVERNMENT	87
§ 75. (4) GOD AS HOLY LAW-GIVER	90
I. THE REVELATION OF THE DIVINE WILL TO MAN, § 76	92
(a) THE EXTRAORDINARY, POSITIVE, SUPERNATURAL REVELATION	92
§§ 77–78. (b) THE INNER REVELATION AND THE CONSCIENCE	96–99
II. THE ESSENCE OF THE MORAL LAW AS THE DIVINE WILL, § 79.	107
§ 79. (a) THE FORM OF THE LAW (COMMAND, PROHIBITION, "OUGHT")	107
§ 80. (b) SCOPE OF THE LAW (REQUIREMENT, COUNSELS)	112
§ 81. (c) RELATION OF THE LAW TO THE PERSONAL PECULIARITY	118
§ 82. THE ALLOWED	122
§ 83. MORAL PRINCIPLES OR LIFE-RULES	133
§ 84. DUTY	136
§ 85. RIGHT	139

CHAPTER III.
THE OBJECT OF THE MORAL ACTIVITY.

I. GOD, § 86	145
II. THE CREATED, § 87	149
§ 87. (1) THE MORAL PERSON HIMSELF	149
§ 88. (2) THE EXTERNAL WORLD	151
§ 89. EXTERNAL NATURE	156

CHAPTER IV.
THE MORAL MOTIVE.

§ 90. PLEASURE AND DISPLEASURE	159
§ 91. LOVE AND HATRED	161
§ 92. ANTE-MORAL LOVE	163
§ 93. MORAL LOVE	168
§ 94. LOVE TO GOD	169
§ 95. GOD-FEARING	171
§ 96. GOD-TRUSTING AND ENTHUSIASM	173
§ 97. HAPPINESS	175

CHAPTER V.
THE MORAL ACTIVITY, § 89.

SUBDIVISION FIRST: THE MORAL ACTIVITY *per se* IN ITS INNER DIFFERENCES, § 99	180
I. MORAL SPARING, § 100	182

	PAGE
II. MORAL APPROPRIATING, § 101	186
(a) IN RESPECT TO WHAT ELEMENT OF THE OBJECT IS APPROPRIATED, § 101	186
§ 102. (1) NATURAL APPROPRIATING	187
§ 103. (2) SPIRITUAL APPROPRIATING	190
(b) IN RESPECT TO HOW THE OBJECT IS APPROPRIATED, § 104	191
(1) GENERAL (UNIVERSAL) APPROPRIATING, COGNIZING, § 104	192
(2) PARTICULAR (INDIVIDUAL) APPROPRIATING, ENJOYING, § 105	194
III. MORAL FORMING, § 106	198
(a) IN RESPECT TO WHAT ELEMENT OF THE OBJECT IS FORMED, § 107	200
§ 107. (1) NATURAL FORMING	200
§ 108. (2) SPIRITUAL FORMING	201
(b) IN RESPECT TO HOW THE OBJECT IS FORMED, § 109	203
§ 109. (1) PARTICULAR FORMING	203
§ 110. (2) GENERAL FORMING, ARTISTIC ACTIVITY	205
§§ 111, 112. APPROPRIATING AND FORMING AS MORALLY RELATED TO EACH OTHER	210–212
SUBDIVISION SECOND: THE MORAL ACTIVITY IN RELATION TO ITS DIFFERENCES AS RELATING TO ITS DIFFERENT OBJECTS:	
I. IN RELATION TO GOD, § 113	214
(a) THE MORAL APPROPRIATING OF GOD, FAITH AND KNOWLEDGE, § 113	214
§§ 114–117. PRAYER AND SACRIFICE	218–221
(b) THE MORAL SPARING OF THE DIVINE, § 118	232
II. IN RELATION TO THE MORAL PERSON HIMSELF, § 119	236
(a) MORAL SPARING, § 119	236
(b) MORAL APPROPRIATING AND FORMING, § 120	237
§§ 120, 121. (1) OF THE BODY BY THE SPIRIT	238–242
§ 122. (2) OF THE SPIRIT ITSELF	247
III. IN RELATION TO OTHER PERSONS, § 123	252
(a) MORAL SPARING, § 123	252
(b) MORAL APPROPRIATING AND FORMING, §§ 124–126	254–262
IV. IN RELATION TO OBJECTIVE NATURE, § 127	264
(a) MORAL SPARING, § 127	264
(b) MORAL APPROPRIATING.	
§ 128. (1) SPIRITUAL	266
§ 129. (2) ACTUAL.	267
(c) MORAL FORMING, § 130	271

CHAPTER VI.

THE FRUIT OF THE MORAL LIFE AS MORAL END.

	Page
§ 131. Good	274
§ 132. The Highest Good	275
I. The Personal Perfection of the Individual, § 133	277
(a) Outward Possessions, § 134	270
(b) Inner Possessions, § 135	280
§ 135. (1) Wisdom	280
§ 136. (2) Bliss	283
§ 137. (3) Holy Character	284
(c) The Good as Power, § 138	289
§ 138. Virtue	289
§ 139. The Virtues	291
§ 140. The Piety-Virtues	297
II. Moral Communion as a Fruit of the Moral Life, § 141	302
(a) The Family, § 142	304
§ 142. Sexual Communion	304
§§ 143. 144. Marriage	304–306
§ 145. Parents and Children	313
§ 146. Brothers and Sisters, and Friends	318
§ 147. Blood-Relationship as Bearing on Marriage	319
§ 148. Family Property and Family Honor	323
(b) Moral Society, § 149	324
§ 150. Honor, the Moral Home	330
(c) The Moral Organization of Society, § 151	332
§ 151. Right and Law	332
§ 152. Church and State, Theocracy	334

CHRISTIAN ETHICS.

SECTION L.

THEOLOGICAL Christian ethics, as distinguished from philosophical ethics, has an historical presupposition—the redemption accomplished in Christ. But redemption presupposes sin, from the power of which it delivers man; and sin presupposes the moral idea *per se*, of which it is the actual negation. Hence the knowledge of Christian ethics, as resting on the accomplished redemption, presupposes a knowledge of the moral state of man while as yet unredeemed, as in turn this knowledge presupposes a knowledge of that ideal state of being from which man turned aside in sin. Christian ethics has therefore a threefold state of things to present:

(1) The ethical or moral *per se* irrespectively of sin,—the moral in its ideal form, the proto-ethical, that which God, as holy, wills.

(2) The *fall* from the truly moral, namely, *sin*, or the guilty perversion of the moral idea in the actual world,—that which man, as unholy, wills.

(3) The moral in its *restoration* by redemption, that is, the regeneration of moral truth out of sinful corruption,—that which is willed by God as gracious, and by man as repentant.

These three forms of the moral or ethical stand, in relation to humanity, not *beside* but *before* and *after* each other,—constitute a moral *history* of humanity: the first stage is *pre*-historical; the second is the substance of the history of humanity up to Christ; the third is the substance of that stream of history which proceeds from Christ and is embodied in, and carried forward by, those who belong to Christ.

As in Christianity all religious and moral life stands in relation to the redemption accomplished in Christ, that is, to an historical fact, hence Christian ethics must also, under one of its phases, bear an historical character. Man is Christianly-moral only in so far as he is conscious of being redeemed by Christ; hence in this Christianly-moral consciousness the above-stated three thoughts are directly involved. Only that one can know himself as redeemed who knows himself as sinful *without* redemption; and only he can know himself as sinful who has a consciousness of the moral ideal. The classification of ethics here presented is based therefore in the essence of Christian morality itself. The first division presents ideal morality as unaffected as yet by the reality of sin,—morality in the state of *innocence;* the second presents the actual morality of man as natural and spiritually-fallen,— morality in the state of *sin;* the third presents the *Christian* morality of man as rescued from sin by regeneration, and reconciled to and united with God,—morality in the state of *grace.* The first part is predominantly a steadily-progressive unfolding of the moral idea *per se;* the second belongs predominantly to historical experience; while the third, as a reconciling of reality with the ideal, belongs at the same time to both fields. The historical person of *Christ* is, for all three spheres of the moral, a revelation of the truth that is to be embraced; in relation to ideal morality Christ is the pure moral prototype *per se*—the historical realization of the moral idea; in relation to the moral state in the second sphere, he manifests the antagonism of sin to moral truth, in the hatred of which he is the object; in relation to the third sphere, he is the essentially founding and co-working power, and manifests the antagonism of holiness to sin.

To present distinctively-Christian morality alone would be scientifically defective, as, without the two antecedent forms of the moral, it cannot be properly understood. To present ideal morality alone is the task of purely philosophical ethics,—usually, however, instead of the proposed pretendedly ideal ethics, the result is simply an artfully disguised justification of the natural sinful nature of unredeemed man. The ideal morality of our first division is in itself fully sufficient only for such as do not admit an antagonism between the actual state of humanity and the requirements of the moral idea, or who explain it into a mere remaining-behind the subsequently to-be-attained perfection, instead of conceiving of it as an essentially perverted state. The fundamental thought of *Christian* morality is this, namely, that the natural man is not simply normally imperfect, but that he is, guiltily, in an essential *antagonism* to the truly good, and that he is in need of a thorough spiritual renewing or regeneration. That this is the case is not to be proved *à priori*, not to be developed scientifically, but to be recognized as a fact. With the reality of sin the moral life becomes essentially changed, and an ethical treatise which should make reference to sin only as a mere *possibility*, as is the case with purely philosophical ethics, would, for this reason, be insufficient for the actual state of humanity. The history of humanity has become in all respects *other* than it would have been *without* sin, and hence a complete system of ethics cannot have merely a purely philosophical, but must have also an historical character,—must grapple with the entire and dread earnestness of *real* sin. If it ended at this stage, however, it would present but a dismal panorama of woe, utterly unrelieved by a gleam of comfort. But divine love has interrupted the history of sin by an historical redemption-act, and founded a history of salvation inside of humanity,—has given to man the possibility and the power to overcome sin in himself, and to rise up from his God-estrangement toward the moral goal. This is the third sphere, that of distinctively Christian morality, which, while it has indeed its prototype in the ideal ante-sinful form of morality, is nevertheless not identical therewith, inasmuch as its actual presuppositions and conditions are entirely different,—namely, no longer a *per se* pure, and spiritually and morally vigorous, subject, and no longer a *per se* good, and, for all moral influences, open and receptive, objective world, but, on the contrary, in both cases an obstinate resistance; it is in both respects therefore a morality of incessant *struggle*, while that of our first division is rather the morality of a simple *development;*—it is also not a mere pressing forward out of an, as yet, incomplete and in so far, imperfect state, but a real overcoming of actual immoral powers; and the earnestness of the morality, as well as of the ethical system, rises in proportion as we more deeply comprehend the inner and essential difference between the above-given three divisions of the subject-matter of ethics, as well as at the same time their inner and historical connection.

This our distribution of the subject-matter of ethics, though manifestly very accordant with the Christian consciousness, has been assailed on many sides; and especially have some writers manifested great concern as to whence in fact we could have any knowledge of this ideal and strictly-speaking non-realized morality. Such an objection ought at least not to be urged by those who think themselves able to construct a system, even of Christian ethics, upon the mere facts of the consciousness, or indeed upon a basis purely speculative. But certainly all who conceive of sin as a something absolutely necessary, will of course have to regard our first division as a pure product of a dreamy imagination; we contest, however, to writers holding such an opinion, the right to deny to a system of *Christian* ethics—which is throughout inspired with the thought that sin is the ruin of men [Prov. xiv, 34] and an abomination to the Lord [xv, 9]—the privilege of treating upon and discussing that which God, as holy, requires of his good-created children. As to whether for such discussion we have also a source of knowledge, will appear as we proceed.

PART FIRST.

THE MORAL *PER SE* IRRESPECTIVELY OF SIN.

Introductory Observations.

I. NOTION AND ESSENCE OF THE MORAL.

SECTION LI.

The moral idea rests upon that of *purpose* or *end*. An end is an idea to be realized by a life-movement. Whatever answers to an idea is *good* relatively to that idea. Whatever answers to, and perfectly realizes, a rational, and hence also a divine, idea, is good absolutely. All divine life and activity has a divine purpose; whatever God brings to realization is therefore absolutely good,—is in perfect harmony with the divine *will*.—A nature-object is good *per se* and directly, in virtue of the creative act itself; and whatever is implied in it, as an end to be attained to by development, is actually realized in fact by an inner divinely-willed necessity. The essence of a *rational* creature is *per se* likewise good; but its full realization as that of a truly rational being, that is, its rational end, is not directly forced upon it by natural necessity, but is *proposed* to it as to be realized by its own rational, and hence *free*, activity. The goodness of a merely natural being lies in the necessarily self-fulfilling purpose of God *in* the creature; that of a rational creature lies in the free, self-fulfilling, through it, of the *will* of God *to* the creature. The divine will is, in the latter case, not merely an end for God, it is also a conscious end *for* the rational creature. The good in general, in so far as it is a conscious end *for* a rational creature, is *a* (concrete) *good*. In as far as this good is unitary and perfect, and hence perfectly answering to the divine will as to the creature, it is the *highest* good,—which consequently must also be absolutely *one* and, for all rational creatures, essentially the same, namely, their fully attained rational perfection. Hence all rational development of a rational creature aims at the realization of the highest good.

As far back as in ancient Greece, philosophers have engaged in the discussion of the notion of the good, and of the highest good, and have proposed various definitions thereof,—those of Aristotle being in the main correct. In and of itself the question is quite simple; it becomes difficult only when we look upon the actual condition of man without fully taking into account the antagonism of his reality with his ideal, and are for that reason unable clearly to distinguish in human aspirations the abnormal from the normal. As to the notion of the *relatively* good, there is no dispute; it is always the agreement of a reality with an idea or with another reality, and hence is based on the thought of a mutual congruity of the manifold.—The simple and true notion of the good is indicated in Gen. i, 3, 4, 31; [comp. 1 Tim. iv, 4]. God speaks and it comes to pass; the reality is the perfect expression of the divine thought and will, and hence, of its own ideal. We have here the notion, not merely of the relatively good, but of the absolutely good; relatively good is every harmonizing or congruence of the different; absolutely good is a harmonizing with God. Hence, first of all, *God* himself is *good* and the prototype of all good [Psa. xxv, 8: lxxxvi, 5; Matt. xix, 17],—good relatively to himself, as being in perfect harmony with himself,—good relatively to his creatures, in that He sustains them in the form of life which He gave them, that is, in their true peculiarities and autonomy, and constantly manifests himself to them as their loving God and Father [Psa. xxxiv, 9]. A creature is good in so far as it is an *image* of God,—namely, such a revelation of the divine as is conditioned by the normal peculiarity of the creature,—and, from another point of view, in so far as its actual state is in harmony with its essence, its ideal, and hence also (since all creatures are created for each other) with the totality of creation. Every thing that God created was "very good" also in this respect, namely, that the different creatures constituted among themselves a perfectly concordant and harmonious whole; "it was *not* good that the man should be alone," seeing that a finite creature is, in its very essence, not a mere isolated individual, but should constitute a member of a community. Hence the expression טוב has also the signification of κάλος, *gratus, jucundus, suavis;* we attribute this quality to an object as bearing upon ourselves in so far as it harmonizes with and reflects our own peculiarities,—in so far as we feel an affinity for it and are enriched and furthered by it in our life-sphere and activity. Hence, that is truly good for man which contributes to the attainment of his true, divinely-intended perfection, and hence, in the last instance, this perfection itself. Now, a mere nature-object possesses the good within itself as a necessary law, and cannot but realize it; but a rational creature has it within itself as a rational consciousness, as a *free* law, as a *command*, and it may decline to realize it. In a nature-object the end fulfills itself; in a rational creature it is fulfilled only by the free will of the same. Nature-objects *are*, in and of themselves, an image of God; but man was created not only *in accordance with* the image of God, but also *unto* it,—has this image before him as a goal to be attained to by free action, as a rational task.

Whatever is good is good *for* some object, and is for the same, in so far as actually appropriated by it, *a good*. That only can be a true good which is good absolutely, that is, divine; all true goods are from God [James i, 17], and lead to God. The idea of the *highest good* we propose here to determine, preliminarily, not as to its contents, but simply as to its form. It cannot belong exclusively to any *one* phase of man's being, but must consist in the symmetrical completion of his life as a whole; hence it cannot be simply the perfection of his isolated individuality as such, but only as a living member of the living whole. Nor is the highest good a merely relatively higher among many other less high goods, otherwise the sum total of the former together with these latter would amount to something higher still; on the contrary all goods collectively, as far as they are really such, must be single elements of the highest good; and the simple fact that a particular object which I desire, and which hence seems to me as a good, is adapted to be a manifestation or an element of the highest good, is clear proof that it is a real, and not a merely seeming, good. Whatever a man aims after appears to him as a good; whatever he shuns, as an *evil;* and rationality consists in the fact that he aim not at the seemingly, but at the really, good, and, in each single good, at the highest good; and this aiming is itself *good*. The highest good is, consequently, the highest perfection of the rational personality, or the perfect development of God-likeness, or, in other words, the perfect agreement of the actual state of man's entire being and life with his ideal, that is, with the will of God,—which all are, in fact, only so many different expressions for the same thing. Whatever contributes to this highest end is good; whatever leads from it is evil.

SECTION LII.

In so far as a rational creature realizes the good rationally, that is, with a consciousness of the good end, and with a free will, it is *moral*. The *moral* is the good in so far as it is realized by the free will of a rational creature; and, in this manifestation of rational life, both the will, and also the action and the end, are moral; and true morality consists in the complete harmony of these three elements. *Morality* is therefore the life of a rational being who accomplishes the good with conscious freedom, and, hence, works the harmony of existence,—as well the harmony of its own being with God as also (and in fact thereby) the harmony of the being in and with itself and with all other beings, in so far as they themselves are in harmony with God. Morality, therefore, embraces within itself two phases of rational life: on the one hand, it preserves and develops the normal autonomy and peculiarity of the moral subject,—does not let it vanish into, or be absorbed by, God or the All,—for there is harmony only where there is a distinctness and individuality of the objects compared; on the other hand, it does not permit this difference to become an antagonism or contradiction, but preserves it in unity,—shapes it into rational harmony. The moral is therefore the *beautiful* in the sphere of rational freedom,—is rationally self-manifesting freedom itself. To be rational and to be moral is, in the sphere of freedom, one and the same thing.

Moralness bears the same relation to the goodness of mere nature-objects, as conscious freedom to unconscious necessity. The goodness of creatures is not their mere being, but their life, for God whose image they are, is life; God is *not* a God of the dead but of the living. Hence the goodness of rational creatures is essentially life also, and in this life morality realizes the good. With this view of morality we may properly enough speak also of a morality of *God;* the fact that human morality is really a progressive development of the image of God, even presupposes this; moreover the Scriptures positively express this thought, and there is no good ground for explaining it away. God is *good* [טוב] and *upright;* [ישר; Deut. xxxii, 4; Psa. xxv, 8]; hence our German hymn: "O God, thou upright God!" is strictly Biblical. God, as the absolutely holy will, is perfect morality itself, inasmuch as his entire being and activity are in perfect accord with his will and essence, and inasmuch as his infinite justice and love establish and uphold the harmony of life in the created universe. God's morality is his holiness. For this reason God is also the perfect prototype and pattern of all morality; " ye shall therefore be holy, for I am holy" [Lev. xi, 45]; also virtue, ἀρετή, in the strict sense of the word, is attributed to God [1 Pet. ii, 9; 2 Pet. i, 3]. Hence, man is moral not merely in general, in that he makes God's will the law of his life, but more specifically, in that he makes God's morality his pattern. In God all good is also moral or holy; in the creature, all that is moral is also good, but all that is good is not also moral.

Rothe objects to the more common notion of the moral, because it embraces only the idea of the *morally-good*, but not that of the moral in its secondary sense; in his view a definition of the moral should include also the morally-evil. It is evidently proper, however, to confine a notion primarily to the normal manifestation of its contents, and to treat the contrary manifestation as an abnormal perversion. Surely, for example, it would be too much to ask that the notion of the rational be so conceived as to embrace also the irrational,— that of organism, so as to include also disease. In fact the objection of Rothe has weight with him, chiefly for the reason that, in his system, evil is viewed not as a merely morbid phenomenon, but on the contrary as a necessary transition-state of development; in which case, of course, a definition of the moral would have to include also evil.

SECTION LIII.

Though morality, as the free realizing of the good, appears essentially in the sphere of the *will*, yet as this will is a rational one,—the expression of a consciousness and of a love to the object of that consciousness,—hence, morality embraces the whole life and being of the spirit in all its forms of manifestation, as knowing, feeling, and willing. Moral *knowing* is *faith*, not only religious, but also rational faith in general; moral *feeling* is *pleasure* in the good, and *love* of it, and, on the other hand, displeasure in the non-good; moral *willing* is a *striving* after the realization of the good. Morality itself, however, is not one of these three, but always and necessarily the union of all three of these phases of the spirit-life.

These three phases of the spirit-life are severally and collectively an expression of the union of the subject with objective being, with the All in general,—in the final instance with God. The subject itself becomes also to itself an object, and only thereby attains to its truth. The mere isolatedness of a being is *per se* evil, is the opposite of true existence and life, the ruin of life, that is, death,—is a dissolution of the unitary collective life into indifferent ultimate atoms. The individual exists in its truth only in so far as it comes into union with the All; this union is not its annihilation but its preservation, its recognition *in* the All as an organic member of the same; it is a mutual, vital relation, a unity in diversity; and this is in fact the essence of life, namely, that both the individual being and the collective whole, in all its parts, stand in relation to each other, and that, in this relation, the individual is, on the one hand, as a member, quite as fully at one with the whole, as, on the other, it is an integral being of itself.

In actively knowing, man brings the object into relation to himself,—takes it up, in its idea, spiritually into himself; in feeling, the subject brings himself in this spiritual appropriation into relation to himself,—embraces the appropriated object as in harmony or as in disharmony with his own being and character, that is, as pleasing or displeasing; in willing, the subject assumes an active determining relation toward the approvingly or disapprovingly received object; hence, the will rests on feeling, as in turn, feeling on knowledge, though the latter may be obscure and only half-conscious. In each of these three respects the spirit may be more or less free or unfree; in so far so it is free, it is also moral. It is true, knowing and feeling are primarily unfree,—they press themselves directly upon the essentially passive subject without his voluntary co-operation, and in so far as this is the case they are as yet extra-moral; but the moment they appear as freely willed they enter into the moral sphere, and this is their higher, rational form. Knowing is moral when we *will* to know *rationally*, that is, when we embrace isolated being, whether that of objective nature or of ourselves, as not existing *for itself* in its isolation, but on the contrary, when, passing beyond its isolatedness, we conceive it as having ultimately a divine ground,—in other words, when we associate all individual being with the infinite being and life of God, and thus conceive all existence as unitary and as established by God. Now, this passing beyond the individual object is not an unfree process; the object does not force us to do so, much rather it arrests us at its own immediate reality; but it is our rational nature that induces us to *will* to pass beyond. Knowing becomes moral when it becomes a *pious* consciousness,—assumes a *religious* character; and this pious associating of the finite with the infinite is *faith*, which is in its very essence religious. Faith can never be compelled by a presentation of arguments; in all its forms it is a voluntary matter; and from the simple fact that faith is a *moral* knowing, and hence includes within itself willingness and love, it is consequently not a *mere* knowing, not a mere holding-for-true; hence it may be, and is, a moral requirement. Without this *willingness* to find and acknowledge the divine in infinite objects, there is no knowledge of God, and hence no real rationality of knowledge. Though faith is essentially religious, nevertheless, springing forth from this source, it overflows and fructifies with its moral potency the entire field of rational knowledge. By virtue of this faith we have confidence in the truthfulness of the universe,—confidence that truth is discoverable, that the laws of our mind and the impressions made upon us by the external world are not untrue and defective, that divine order and conformity to law, and hence conformity to reason, pervade the universe, so that, consequently, we may rely on this order and this conformity to law. Without such a faith, without such a confidence independently of all presentation of evidence, there could be no knowledge—no possibility of a spiritual life in general. Without this confidence we would be unable to avoid suspecting poison in every cup of water, in every morsel of bread,—we would tremble lest, at every step, the ground might give way beneath our feet. Fondness of doubting presupposes depravity; skepticism proper, like the arts of sophistry, is an immoral dissolution of rational knowledge; under the skeptic's eye, both the spiritual world and the realm of nature fall apart into lifeless ultimate atoms.

In so far as *feeling* is simply a direct consciousness of such an impressed state of the subject, it is as yet extra-moral, because unfree; it becomes rational and moral through freedom on the basis of the religious consciousness,—namely, when I do not *permit* myself to be determined by finite things in an absolutely passive manner, but, on the contrary, when I subordinate all my states of feeling to the power of faith or of the religious consciousness,—in a word, when I rise so far into the sphere of freedom as to have pleasure only in that which is God-pleasing, and displeasure only in the ungodly,—when my love to finite things is only a phase of my love to God.

The *will*, the more immediate sphere of the moral, is in itself likewise not as yet moral, but must first become so. *Free* will, as distinguished from the unfree impulse of the brute, is primarily as yet devoid of positive contents,—is only the possibility, but not the actuality, of the moral. It becomes a *really* free and, hence, a moral will only by coming into relation to faith, namely, in that it ceases to be a *merely* individual will determined solely by the isolated personality of the subject,—for, as such, it is as yet simply irrational and animal,—and furthermore in that it imbues itself with a positive faith,—determines itself by its God-consciousness and by its love to God,—so that thus, passing beyond mere finite being, it bases its outgoings on a rational faith in the infinite. This is so wide-reaching a condition of the moral will, that even an evil will (which also lies within the sphere of the moral) is determined by a certain faith-consciousness, seeing that such a will is a rebelling against its God-consciousness; "devils also believe" in God's existence "and tremble" [James ii, 19]; the degree of guilt is strictly determined by the degree in which God is known. Hence the will is morally good when it rests on faith,—when it strives to realize the God-pleasing because of its God-consciousness and of its love to God; and it is morally *evil* when, *despite* its God-consciousness, it aims at the ungodly,—seeks to divorce finite beings, and especially its own, *from* its union with God. Hence in general terms, though morality has its essential sphere in the will, yet it also embraces, as intimately involved therein, the spheres of knowledge and of feeling.

SECTION LIV.

As the life of a rational spirit is continuous, namely, a continuous *free* activity, hence it bears continuously a *moral* character. Morality is not simply a succession of single moral points, it is an uninterrupted life, and every moment of the same is either in harmony or in antagonism with the moral end,—is either good or evil. In the entire life of man there is not a single morally *indifferent* moment or state.

Man is God's image only in so far as he *lives* this God-likeness, for God is life, and all life is continuous; a real interruption of the same is its destruction,—is death. Sleep is only a change in the manifestation of life, arising from the union of the spirit with material nature, but not a real interruption of the same. Spirit sleeps not; also the slumbering spirit is moral,—may be pure or impure; the soul of the saint cannot have unholy dreams; dreams are often unwelcome mirrorings forth of impure hearts; when Jacob rebuked his son Joseph for his supposed ambitious dream [Gen. xxxvii, 10], his moral judgment was quite correct,—simply his hypothesis was erroneous. Any assumption that there are morally indifferent moments in life is anti-moral. And that there are, in fact, in the natural life of man middle states between life and death,—for example, swoons,—is of itself a fruit of depravity, and in the same sense that death is such. Morality is the health of the rational spirit; and every interruption of health is disease. God's will is incessantly binding; there is absolutely nothing conceivable which would not either harmonize with, or antagonize, it.

II. RELATION OF MORALITY TO RELIGION.

SECTION LV.

The religious consciousness,—which expresses the conditionment of our being and life by God, and which, as a state of heart, is *piety*,—is necessarily and intimately connected with morality, so that neither is possible without the other; yet they are not identical. Religion and morality, both, bring man into relation to God. In religion, however, his relation is rather of a receptive character,—he permits the divine to rule in him; in morality he is more self-active, he reflects forth the God-pleasing from within himself. In religion he exalts himself to communion with God; in morality he *evidences* this communion by developing the divine image both in himself and in the external world. In religion he turns himself away from finite individuality and multiplicity, and toward the unitary central-point of all life; in morality he turns himself from this divine life-center as a basis, toward the periphery of created being,—from unity toward multiplicity,—in order to manifest the former in the latter. The two movements correspond to the double life-stream in every natural organism, and hence they are simply two inseparably united phases of one and the same spiritual life; and the very commencement of spiritual life involves the union of them both. In religion and in morality God glorifies himself no less than in creation,—in religion *for* and *in* man, in morality *through* man; and the moral man, in that he fulfills God's will in and for the world, actually accomplishes the divine purpose in creation,—the free moral activity of man being, in fact, the divinely-willed continuation and completion of the work of creation.

The consciousness that we, as separate individuals, have no absolutely self-sufficient and independent existence and rights, as also that we are not simply dependent on other finite powers, but, on the contrary, on an infinite divine first cause, is of a religious character; and the spiritual life that develops itself on the basis of this consciousness is the religious life. In so far, however, as it is a disposition or *state of heart*, that is, in so far as it expresses itself in the feeling of love to God and in the thence-arising habit of will, it is *piety*, —in which form it assumes directly also the character of morality. A pious life is *per se* also a moral one; and morality is the practical outgoing of piety. Religion and morality are therefore most closely and inseparably associated; as morality rests on the recognition that the *good* is either the actual state or the final destination of all existence, and as this recognition, even in its rudest forms, is of a religious character (since the "good" can have no meaning save as the divine ultimate destination of creation), hence morality without religion is impossible, and its character rises and falls with the clearness and correctness of the religious consciousness. He who despises religion is also immoral; and the immoral man is also correspondingly irreligious; all immorality is a despising of God, since it is a despising of the good as the God-like. As now, on the other hand, religion is a *believing*, and hence a free, *loving* recognition of the divine, and as it places man in a living relation with God, hence all religion is *per se* also moral, and religion without morality is inconceivable.

Thus, whatever is moral is religious, and whatever is religious is moral; and yet these two are not identical; every religious life includes in itself a moral will, and every moral action contains a religious element,—implies religious faith; "without faith it is impossible to please God" [Heb. xi, 6]. This looks like a contradiction utterly irreconcilable save by making religion and morality absolutely one and the same thing. Things, however, that are indissolubly associated, as, for example, heat and light in the rays of the sun, need not for that reason be identical. In the religiously-moral life two things are always united: our individual personality as a relatively self-dependent legitimate entity, and the recognition of God as the unconditioned ground of our entire being and life,—that is to say, an affirming and also a relative negating of our separate individuality, an active and a passive element. Both are equally true and important; the one calls for the other, and either, taken separately for itself, would be untrue; the two must exist in harmony and unity. The passive phase—the emphasizing of the being of God in the presence of which individual being retires into the background and appears only as conditioned and dependent—is the *religious* phase of the spiritual life; the active phase—that is, the emphasizing of the personal element by virtue of which man appears, as an initiative actor with the mission, as a free personality, of carrying farther forward in the spiritual sphere the creative work of God—is the *moral* phase. The religious life is, so to speak, centripetal; moral life, as radiating out from the middle-point, is centrifugal; the former corresponds, in the spiritual life, to the functions of the veins of the body; the latter is more like the arteries, which, receiving from the lungs, through the heart, the vitalized out-gushing blood, distribute it nourishingly and productively through the body, and ramify themselves out toward the periphery, whereas the veins conduct it back from the outermost ramifications toward the center. In correspondence to this figure, the separate outgoings of the moral life are more manifold than are the center-seeking manifestations of the religious life. Hence piety, by its very nature, tends to a communion of pious life-expression, to the social worship of God; but in morality the person comes into prominence more in his self-dependent individuality: in the sphere of morality, moral communion rests more on the moral individuals; in that of piety, the pious personality rests more upon pious communion and upon the spirit which inspires this communion. In the moral sphere, Christ says to the individual: "*Go thou and do likewise;*" in that of religion he says: "Where two or three are *gathered together* in my name, there am I in the midst of them." Secret prayer does not conflict with this, for it is only one phase of piety; the piety of the recluse is simply morbid.

Religious life is only then genuine when it is at the same time also moral,—when it does not in Pantheistico-mystical wise dissolve and merge the individual into God; the one-sidedly religious life which lightly esteems outward morality entangles itself inevitably in this quietistic renunciation of personality. Moral life is healthy only when it is at the same time also religious,—when the person does not assume to live and act as an isolated being from an unconditioned autonomy of its own independently of God; it is, however, as distinguished from the religious life, essentially a virtualizing of liberty. The one-sidedly moral life, that is, the attempt to virtualize personal freedom without religion, leads to the reverse of the morally-religious life—to haughtiness of personality as of an absolutely independent power, to an atheistic idolizing of the creature, and, in practice, to a throwing off of all obligation that conflicts with personal enjoyment. The moral life is therefore true and good only when the virtualization of the freedom and independence of the person is rational, that is, essentially religious; and it becomes morally evil so soon as it asserts its freedom as unconditioned and apart from God.

Piety and morality consequently mutually condition each other,—develop themselves in no other way than in union *with each other*. It is true, the first beginning of the religiously-moral life is, in so far, the religious phase, as all religion rests upon a revelation of God to man, that is, upon a receiving, and not upon a personal doing; but this revelation is only then our own, the contents of our religious spirit, when we *embrace* it in faith, and this embracing is a free, a *moral* activity. Hence even the first incipiency of the rational, the morally-religious life includes in immediate and necessary union *both* phases of the same, so that, though in logic we may speak of the one as being antecedent to the other, yet in point of reality we cannot so speak. Should this seem enigmatical to the understanding, still it is no more enigmatical than is the nature of all and every life-beginning; and just as little as we can deny the reality of the beginning of man's natural life, for the reason that it is absolutely hidden and mysterious—so that we can neither say that the material being of the same is *antecedent* to its spiritual power nor the converse,—even so little can we hope to solve the mystery of the beginning of the religiously-moral life, by assuming the one or the other of its phases as the first and fundamental one. The plant, in developing itself out of its embryo, grows upward and downward almost simultaneously; if it is insufficiently rooted it fades; if it cannot grow upward it decays; the sending out of roots corresponds to religion; the development into foliage and fruit, to morality. Also in the further development of the rational life these two phases are constantly associated, and in their associated unity and harmony consists the spiritual health of man. We are religious in so far as we recognize that God is the unconditioned ground of our being and moral life; moral, in so far as by our free life we confess *in acts* that God is for us the absolute rule of action,—that we are free accomplishers of the divine will. In religion, God is for us; in morality, we are for God; in the former God is manifested *to* us; in the latter God is manifested *in* and *through* us. "I live, yet not I, but Christ liveth in me" [Gal. ii, 20]; this is the essence of Christian morality. "As many as are led by the Spirit of God, they are the sons of God" [Rom. viii, 14]; that is, religion is the *vitality* of morality, and morality the factive life-manifestation of religion, and consequently of divine sonship. "Fear God and keep his commandments, for this is the whole duty of man" [Eccl. xii, 13; comp. Deut. x, 12]; hence the fear of God is the ground and beginning of moral wisdom; "this is the fear of God, that we keep his commandments" [1 John v, 3]. According to the uniform tenor of Scripture, religion and morality go always hand in hand; this is aptly expressed by Luther in his Catechism: "We should fear and love God, in order that," etc.; the fear of God necessarily involves the keeping of the commandments, and this fear is itself of moral character, as is implied by the very word "should"; "if thou doest not well, sin lieth at the door" [Gen. iv, 7]. Hence the usual Scripture expression for morality is: "to walk *before* God" [Gen. xvii, 1; xxiv, 40], that is, to act out of a full consciousness of the holy and almighty One, in full trust and love to Him; or: "to walk *with* God" [Gen. v,

22, 24; vi, 9], to "keep the way of the Lord" and "do justice and judgment" [Gen. xviii, 19], "to walk in God's ways," "to serve the Lord" and "to keep his commandments and statutes" [Deut. x, 12]; and God's exhortation to the progenitor of the Israelites is: "I am the Almighty God, [therefore] walk before me and be thou perfect" [Gen. xvii, 1].

The glorifying of God in religion and morality is the completing of his glorification in nature. In religion, God permits the man who comes into living communion with Him, to behold his glory; in morality God permits men to show forth his glory—to let their light shine before others that they also may praise the Father in heaven. The will of God in creation was not as yet fulfilled at the conclusion of the creative act. "Let us make man in our image, after our likeness,"—but this image is God-like, not in its mere being, but only in its rational, moral life. God created the world for rational creatures, in order that for them and through them his image might be manifested in creation,—that is to say, in the interest of moral development. Hence sin is treachery against God, an infringement on his honor. Morality looks to the honor, not of man, but of God; it is *per se* a serving of God, and all divine service or worship is a moral act.

The relation of religion to morality is often stated quite differently from the view here presented. The more important of these views are the following four:

(1) *Religion and morality are totally identical.* In developing this view, the one is necessarily reduced to the other. (a) *Morality* is entirely merged into *religion*—the view of all consistent mysticism; man has nothing to do but to give himself entirely over to God; and wisdom consists not in acting, but, on the contrary, in renouncing all practical activity (Eckart, Tauler, Molinos). (b) *Religion* is entirely merged into *morality*. Morality is directly in and of itself true religion; to be moral is identical with being pious; outside of virtue there is no piety which is not only not simply associated with virtue, but which is not, in fact, itself virtue;—the view of the worldly-minded in general, and, particularly, of the "illuminism" of the eighteenth century.

(2) Religion and morality are in their entire nature radically

different, and hence entirely independent of each other; the one may exist without the other. This is the view of all the naturalistic systems of recent date. It is at once refuted by the simple fact that the different religions have given rise to correspondingly different systems of morality.—In approximation to this view, Rothe affirms (Ethik, I, Seite, 191, sqq.) at least a predominant *non-dependence* of the two spheres on each other.

His position is as follows:—Morality and piety, while not entirely different, are yet relatively independent and self-based. Each has indeed a certain relation to the other, and there is no morality which is not, in some degree, also piety; both have the same root, namely, the personality; but the two form, nevertheless, independent branches strictly coetaneous. The consciousness of this relative independence of morality belongs among the inalienable conquests of recent culture,—namely, the consciousness that an individual human life may be relatively determined by the idea of the moral, nay, even by the idea of the morally good, or, more definitely, by the idea of human dignity and of humanity, *without* at the same time being determined by the idea of God,—and indeed in such a manner that it shall possess this idea of the moral as *not* derived to it from the idea of God. The Christian moralist cannot refuse to recognize this consciousness. The misconception, that morality can rest on no other basis than the religious relation, would at once vanish, could moralists determine to keep distinct the moral *sensu medio*, from the morally-good. For, that there can be moral evil on a basis other than a religious one, will of course be questioned by none. It is true, when strictly *understood* or *comprehended*, the idea of the moral cannot arise *apart from* the idea of God.—These last two statements of Rothe undermine his entire position; for the question here is not at all as to evil, but exclusively as to the morally-good; and it is hardly possible that any one would argue thus: Because evil can exist without religion, therefore also the good can exist without religion. Moreover, in admitting that without religion man can be morally-good only relatively, but not truly, Rothe implicitly admits also that morality is in fact *not* a something existing alongside of religion and in real independency of it; consequently the above-assumed morality that is independent of religion, is but mere appearance.

(3) Religion is the *first*, the *basis*, also in point of time; while morality is the *second*, the *sequence*. This is the most usual, also ecclesiastical, view; and as applied to *Christian* morality it is also undoubtedly correct, since here the question is as to being redeemed from a presupposed immoral state; in which case, of course, the religious back-ground forms the basis of the renewal, from which, as a starting-point, the moral will, in general, must rise to freedom. Where, however, the moral life does not presuppose a spiritual regeneration, there no moment of the religious life is conceivable in which it does not also contain in itself the moral element,—thus absolutely precluding the idea of a precedency of one to the other; moreover, even in the spiritual regeneration of the sinner, the process of *being* morally *laid hold upon* by the sanctifying Spirit of God, issues directly into a willing, and hence moral, *laying hold upon* the offered grace of God.

(4) Morality is the *first*, the basis, while religion is the *second*, the sequence, also in point of time; the moral consciousness of the practical reason is the ground upon which the God-consciousness springs up;—so taught the school of Kant, and in part, also, Rationalism. This view, in its practical application, coincides largely with that one which merges the religious into the moral. It is true, appeal is made to the passage in John vii, 7: "If any one will do his will," etc.; here, however, the question is not as to the religious consciousness in general, but as to the recognition of Christ as the Messenger of God. But whoever purposes to do the will of God, must have a consciousness of God already.

From the intimate unity of religion and morality, which we have insisted upon, results readily the solution of the question, as to how and whence we can have a knowledge of the moral condition of humanity as pure and unfallen. The sources of a knowledge of *religion* are at the same time, also, the sources of an acquaintance with *morality;* and religion throws light not only upon what has transpired and now is, since the fall, but also upon what preceded all sin. Thus we have for morality in general, as well as for the consideration of morality *irrespectively* of sin, the following sources of information:—1. The rational, morally-religious human consciousness, both as it is yet extant even in the natural man, and also, as it is enlightened by divine grace in the redeemed.—2. The historical revelation of God in the Old and New Testaments. Although as bearing upon the moral sphere Revelation relates predominantly to the actual sinful condition of humanity, yet it contains also, at the same time, the holy will of God to man *per se*. The moral law of Christ, "Thou shalt love thy God," etc., is in fact absolutely valid, not only for such as are as yet implicated in sin, but also for man *per se*, and irrespectively of sin; moreover, it is not difficult for the Christian who has become acquainted with the divine economy of grace to distinguish, in the divine precepts, that which is intended for the chastening and discipline of the sinner, from that which is morally binding *per se*.—3. From the personal example of Him who knew no sin, from the holy humanity of the Redeemer.—So much here merely preliminarily.

III. SCIENTIFIC CLASSIFICATION OF ETHICS.

SECTION LVI.

The usual distribution of the subject-matter of ethics into the doctrine of *goods*, of *virtues*, and of *duties*, does not answer the nature of this science, as these are not different parts of the whole, but only different modes of contemplating one and the same thing,—modes which are so intimately involved in each other, that such a classification inevitably involves, on the one hand, an unnatural severing of the subject-matter, and, on the other, manifold repetitions of the same thought. All the various articulations of this science into the mere discussion of virtues, duties, and goods, according to the different classes and subdivisions of particular virtues, duties, and goods, come short of exhausting the subject-matter, and must therefore involve the throwing of other important ethical considerations into an introduction or some other subordinate position.

Among the various classifications of the matter of ethics, the above-mentioned is in recent times the more usual; it is adopted by Schleiermacher, though only in his Philosophical Ethics, and it is applied by Rothe to Theological Ethics also. In both of these writers, the importance of such a classification lies in the thought of the working of reason upon nature, in which morality is by them made to consist. The goal of this working, namely, the positive harmony of nature and reason, is the *good;* the *power* of reason which works this good, is *virtue;* the mode of procedure for working the good, the directing of the activity toward it, is *duty*.* This view, irrespectively of the so-strongly emphasized thought of Rothe, of the good as a harmony of (material) nature and reason,—which is utterly inapplicable to Christian morality,—is in fact valid also for Christian ethics (Schwarz). In Christ's words: "Seek ye first the kingdom of God and his righteousness, and all these things [temporal goods] shall be added unto you" [Matt. vi, 33], are comprehended both the highest good and the single goods, duty and virtue,—the latter being embraced in "righteousness," though righteousness is indeed more than virtue. There is a difference between the goal to be reached, the way or movement toward it, and the power of the subject which conditions this movement; still it does not follow from this that the entire subject-matter of ethics can be organically and exclusively distributed on this basis. The antithesis of duties and goods could be most easily carried out, since the producing activity and the produced result are clearly distinguishable. But even here the difficulty arises, that true good, and hence, of course, also happiness (as Aristotle very justly remarks), is not an inert result but an activity; but every activity, if it is rational, must be the expression of a moral idea, the realizing of a duty; so that we are brought to the at

---

* *Schleirm. Syst.*, p. 71 *sqq.; Grundlinien*, 1803, p. 175 *sqq; Üb. d. Begriff des höchsten Gutes, Werke III,* 2, 447 *sqq.* Comp. §. 48.

first strange-seeming conclusion, that dutiful acting is itself a part of the being and essence of the good,—is in one respect itself a good. The family, the church, the state, etc., are goods; but these all are conditioned not merely on dutiful acting,—they themselves are a purely moral *life*,—consist, strictly speaking, in a collectivity of moral actions, although not *solely* therein. If we once abstract these actions, there remains neither family nor state nor church; these are not mere empty spaces in which moral acting takes place, but they are themselves incessantly generated by this acting, and without it would *not* exist,—just as the fiery ring of a revolved torch is not an entity *per se*, but exists alone by virtue of the motion. Hence the visible embarrassment of the ethical writers in question as to where they shall treat, for example, of family and political duties, whether under the head of duties proper or of goods.—Still more embarrassing is it in the discussion of the virtues. That virtue is *per se* a good, being an end to be acquired by moral effort, is perfectly evident, and is so admitted by Schleiermacher (Werke, III, 2, 459); also in the above-cited utterance of Christ, righteousness appears as a goal of effort, as an element of the essence of the kingdom of God [comp. Phil. iv, 8]; we *aim at* virtue, and we *possess* virtues; but every possession is a good. Now as goods are of course not merely objective,—as indeed the highest good of Christians, the possession of the kingdom of God, comes not with outward observation but is of a strictly inward character [Luke xvii, 20, 21],—hence it is plain that virtue is also a good; as indeed the kingdom of God consists "in power" [1 Cor. iv, 20], and hence by its very nature includes in itself virtue. Hence the doctrine of goods cannot be discussed without treating also of virtue. On the other hand, a merely dormant power is in reality nothing at all; the reality of a power is its outgoing,—the reality of virtue is moral action, that is, the fulfilling of duty. It is not possible, therefore, to discuss the virtues without at the same time treating of all the duties, and *vice versa*. Hence the distribution of ethics above-mentioned can be adhered to only so long as the discussion lingers in generalities and avoids the particular.

Schleiermacher and Rothe, in fact, admit that the three

divisions, goods, virtues, and duties, are not, in reality, different parts of, but only a three-fold manner of viewing, the same object,—yet in such a manner that in *each* of the three the other two are included, if not expressly, at least substantially. The doctrine of goods, of virtues or of duties, embraces, either of them, according to Schleiermacher, when fully developed, the *whole* of ethics (Syst., p. 76 *sqq.*). The classification in question can therefore be carried out only by arbitrarily leaving some of the divisions imperfectly discussed. Particular goods, says Rothe, do not spring from the working of a particular virtue and through the fulfilling of a particular duty, but on the contrary no single one is realized otherwise than through the co-working of all the virtues and through the fulfilling of all the duties, and each single virtue contributes to the realization of all the goods, and is conditioned on the fulfilling of all the duties, and each particular virtue contributes in turn to every dutiful manner of action (i, 202). Irrespectively of the fact that the latter declarations are too sweeping,—seeing that, for example, the family may often exist as a good without the virtue of courage, of industry, etc., and that courage may exist apart from the fulfillment of the family duties, etc.,—still it is quite evident that if either of the three divisions in question were really and completely, and not merely in general, carried out, there would remain nothing for the other divisions save a few general observations. The family, for example, is a good only in so far as it has domestic love for its basis, and, in point of fact, Rothe treats of domestic love among the goods; but what remains then to be said of it in treating of the virtues and duties? The remarkable scantiness of Schleiermacher's discussion of duties is itself evidence of an erroneous classification. And Rothe obtains for his discussion of duties (in fact confessedly finds any occasion whatever therefor) simply because, as he says, reference is there to be had to *sin*, so that the discussion of duties becomes essentially the portrayal of struggle. But this admission destroys the very basis of the classification;—were it not for sin, a discussion of duties would not be possible, whereas the basis of this classification has not the least reference to sin. If Schleiermacher, after speaking, in his first part, of chastity and unchastity, had then in his second part spoken of chastity as among the virtues,—which his plan required of him, but which he does not do—and in his third part fully discussed the duties of chastity, then in order to carry out his classification he would have had to reiterate the same matter three times.—Rothe speaks in very strong expressions against those who do not adopt this classification, affirming that all previous ethical teaching and phraseology have been erroneous, and have ignored the fact that even every-day parlance makes a difference between *being* virtuous and *acting* dutifully;—as if common usage does not, just as frequently and just as correctly, speak also of *acting* virtuously and *being* true to duty! Oddly enough it seems, in the face of this so-deemed "imperishable desert" of Schleiermacher in regard to this classification, that Schleiermacher himself—clearer-sighted here than Rothe—does not apply it to his own *Christian* Ethics; and not only that, but he even declares it inadmissable here,—seeing that a description of virtue and a description of the kingdom of God as the highest good, cannot possibly be kept separate, inasmuch as virtue is simply a "habitus" generated by the Holy Spirit as indwelling in the kingdom of God; nor can Christian ethics, in his opinion, be treated under the head of duties, seeing that no one duty can be discussed save in and with the totality of all the duties, and hence in connection with the idea of the kingdom of God (Chr. Sitte., p. 77 *sqq.*). And the same might also be said against the application of this classification to Philosophical Ethics.

If this classification of general ethics into the doctrines of goods, of virtues and of duties, is practically untenable, much more is it inapplicable to *Christian* Ethics, since it lacks one essential Christian thought, that of the divine *law*. Schleiermacher presented no discussion of the law, as he wrote wholly irrespectively of the idea of God; and for this reason alone his classification would be inapplicable to Christian Ethics. For duty is not identical with the law. The law is objective, duty subjective; the law is the moral idea *per se* in its definite form, as thought, as universally valid—the will of God in general; duty is the subjective realization of the law for a particular individual under particular circumstances,—relates *per se* always to the strictly particular, the actual. The law is valid always, and under all circumstances; duty varies largely according to time and circumstances; the very same mode of action which is to-day my duty, may be to-morrow, contrary to my duty;—to-day my duty is silence, to-morrow I must speak. The law is categorical, duty is usually hypothetical; the former is the expression of divine morality, the latter of human. So also is the relation of *goods* to *virtue;* the former are more the general, objective phase; the latter is more the particular, personal, subjective phase; virtue is the subjective possession of a moral power the product of which is objective good. In the Old Testament the moral life-movement went over from the divine objective will, namely, the law, to the human subject in order to bring the latter into possession of the highest good; in the Christian world the moral life-movement goes out from the subject as being already in union with God, and already in possession of the everlasting good, and directs itself to the objective realization of God-like being,—from the inward possession of the kingdom of God to the objective manifestation and realization of the same.

Of other scientific classifications, we will say but little. The older popular division of the subject-matter of ethics according to the *Ten Commandments*, was a form very well adapted for popular Christian instruction, and, indeed, by giving a large construction to the more immediate scope of these commandments, it admits of the treatment of all evangelically-ethical thoughts: it does not, however, suffice for a scientific development of Christian ethics, seeing that this series of commands was constructed primarily for merely practical purposes; very essential points, such as the moral essence of man and of the good, and (as parts of the latter) of the state and the church, would have to be thrown into introductory or collateral remarks.—The classification according to our duties to God, to our neighbor, and to ourselves, while in fact embracing the whole circle of duties, yet requires likewise too much of the essential matter to be thrown into an introduction.—Harless makes the divisions, the good itself, the possession of the good, and the preservation of the good; but by "good" he understands rather the antecedent condition than the goal of the moral life; by "possession," more the obtaining and preserving of the possession; and by "preservation," rather its actual manifestation. This, as well as Schleiermacher's theological classification, relates only to distinctively Christian ethics.—A very common classification is, into general and special ethics,—the latter treating of the special circumstances and relations of the moral life; but such a system can be carried out without violence only when the first division is reduced to a mere general introduction.

SECTION LVII.

Morality is life, and hence, activity or movement, and more definitely, rationally-free movement. Herein lie three things: the subject that moves, the end toward which the movement goes out, and the movement-activity itself. The subject goes out from its immediate condition of being *per se*, through movement, over into another condition which lies before it as an end. But the *moral* subject is not a mere isolated individual; on the contrary, it is the freely self-developing image of God as the primitive ground and prototype of all morality, and it lives only in virtue of constant inner-communion with God. The holily-ruling God becomes, as distinguished from man, the eternal, holy proto-subject of the moral life; and there is no moment of the moral life in which the human subject, strictly *per se* and without God's co-operation, works the good.—The *goal* toward which the moral movement directs itself is also of a twofold character. Man finds himself already in the presence of an objective world different from himself; and even where he makes himself his own object, this, his reality, is, primarily, a gift conferred upon him without any moral action on his own part; this conferred existence (world and self) is the working-sphere of his moral activity—the most immediate object and end of the same. But man is not, in his activity, to throw himself away upon this objective world—to merge himself into it—but he is to shape it by his own power, and in harmony with the moral idea,—to make the possibility of the good into real good, to realize a spiritual end in and through the objective world. Hence the goal of the moral activity is to be considered under two phases: (*a*) As a pure object untouched as yet by the moral activity,—as a mere platform, as material given *for* the moral activity in order to be spiritually dominated by this activity so as to become a spiritually and morally formed real good. (*b*) This object itself, as morally fashioned, as having become a good,—existing primarily only as an idea, a rational purpose, but afterward as a result of moral activity, as a fruit realized,—that is the *ideal goal* proper, or the *end* of the moral activity. In the first case, the object is, for the moral activity, a directly-given reality, but it is not to remain as such; in the second case it is primarily not real, but exists only in thought, but it is ultimately to *become* a reality expressive of the thought. —The third phase of the moral movement, namely, the *moral activity* itself, is, as spiritually free, likewise of a twofold character; on the one hand, it is to be considered from its *subjective* side, that is, in respect to how it is rooted in the subject himself, and from him issues forth,—the subjective motive of the moral activity, the source of the stream; on the other hand, it is to be considered as a *life-stream*, sent forth from the subject and directed upon the object,—that is, the activity proper itself as having become real and objective in its progressive development toward the attained goal in which it ends.

The subject-matter of ethics falls, therefore, into the following subdivisions:

1. The moral *subject*, purely in and of itself considered.

2. God as the *objective ground* of the moral life and of the moral *law*, and also as the *prototype* of the moral idea, and as *co-working* in the moral life.

3. The given *objective* existence upon which, as material to be fashioned, the moral activity exerts itself.

4. The *subjective* ground of the moral activity, the personal *motive* to morality.

5. The moral *working* or *acting* itself, the moral life-movement toward the moral goal.

6. The conceived *object* of the moral activity, its *goal* or *end*,—the *good* as an object to be realized.

While Dogmatics sets out most naturally from the thought of God, Ethics takes its start from man, the moral subject, inasmuch as morality in its totality is simply the rational life-development of man,—God coming into consideration here not so much in his character as Creator as rather in that of a Lawgiver and righteously-ruling Governor. Should we, however, divorce Ethics entirely from Dogmatics, we would, of course, have to preface the moral discussion of man by a presentation of the doctrine of God.

The idea of the moral subject, of the rational personality, is the foundation-thought of ethics,—the root out of which all the other branches spring. But man is a morally rational person only in so far as he conceives of himself, not as an isolated individual, but as conditioned by the divine reason and the divine holiness. Hence the idea of the moral personality leads out beyond itself to the thought of God, as the eternal fountain and the measure of morality, as the holy and just Lawgiver; the prototypal relation of God to the moral has its personally-historical manifestation in *Christ*, the Son of God; the moral idea becomes in Christ an actually-realized ideal. The doctrine of the moral *law* belongs not in the sphere of the human subject, but in that of the divine, for the law is not man's but God's will.

In the notion of the moral subject considered as an individual being, there lies implicitly also the notion of an objective world different from the same. Morality, as active life, has this world before it as its theater of effort; the activity in its outgoing comes into contact with a reality independent of itself, which, though because of the unity of creation it is not antagonistic to the subject, is nevertheless primarily foreign to the same, and not in any wise imbued with or dominated by it. But to be a spirit, implies in itself the dominating of the unspiritual, the entering into harmony with all that is spiritual. It is the task of the moral subject to bring about this domination and this harmony. Moreover, in so far as man finds himself in a simply given, and not as yet spiritually-dominated and cultivated condition, he becomes to himself his own object, his moral activity being directed upon himself.

The modifying activity as exerted upon this given existence is not, however, of a purposeless character, but it has before it, in the rational end, an ideal object the realizing of which is to be effected by the activity as moral. In an ethical discussion which follows the actual order of the moral life, this moral activity will have to be considered first, although with constant reference to the moral end. This activity, as a spiritual outgoing from the subject, has, on the one hand, its fountain in the moral subject, on the other, it has also a development-course as a stream. Each is to be considered separately, so that we have here again two subdivisions. The consideration of the subjective origin or ground of the moral activity—its *motive*,—has to do with the *why*. The existence of the law and the encountering of an external world by the subject, do not suffice to explain why man should enter upon a course of moral activity; there must be found, as distinguished from these, a motive in the subject himself that prompts directly to moral activity,—that sets the subject into movement. The mere "*should*" is not enough to move us; we may remain indifferent and emotionless in the presence of every "categorical imperative" and of every, however well-grounded, command; if there is not some *impulse* to activity *within* us, all and every command will fall back powerless from us; and this impulse must be of a rationally-free,-a moral character.

The moral activity itself, which is occasioned by this inner motive, is to be considered primarily only in its essence and in its general forms of manifestation, and it involves only the general, but not the special, discussion of the doctrine of duties. By far the largest scope of special activity comes under the last division of our classification; for the true essence and real worth of moral *good* lies in the fact that it is not a dormant possession, but that, on the contrary, it unfolds continuously new and richer life,—just as a natural fruit is not simply a product in which the life of the plant ends, but is also the germ of a new life;—with this difference, however, that the fruit of the moral activity is not merely the germ of a new life that simply repeats its former self, but rather of an enriched, spiritually-heightened life. In the attained moral *good* the moral life-movement rises to a new, higher circulation; the person in possession of this good has become richer,—is a spiritually higher-developed personality; the previously existing moral-subject has become more exalted and spiritualized,—is, in fact, the already attained moral good itself; and the moral activity gains thereby ampler and more ennobled contents; with the acquired good springs up new duty.

In elucidation of the classification we have given, compare the passages Deut. x, 12 *sqq.*; xi, 1 *sqq.*; xii, 1 *sqq.* Here we may consider as the moral subject the people of Israel,—the moral mission and activity of whom cannot possibly be understood save in the light of their historically-moral peculiarity. Jehovah is the sovereign, requiring moral obedience to his will; the people's sinful hearts [x, 16], the heathen country and inhabitants [x, 19; xi, 10 *sqq.*; xii, 2 *sqq.*], and the national life of the Israelites, form the sphere, the theater, of the moral activity; thankful love to the merciful, long-suffering God is the moral motive [x, 15, 21 *sqq.*]; willing obedience, the walking in the ways of God, is the moral activity; and the approbation of God and his blessings are the moral end [x, 13–15; xi, 8 *sqq.*; xii, 7 *sqq.*].

In consideration of the thought that there lies at the basis of all moral activity an end to which the activity directs itself, it might seem more correct to consider this end, namely, the good, *before* discussing the moral activity itself; however, on the other hand, as the realization of the good presupposes the moral activity, and as we are to consider the good not as simply conceived, but as realized, and, inasmuch as out of the realization of one good a new field of moral activity arises in turn before us, hence it is clearly more natural, in fact, to place the discussion of the end or the good (as being actually the last in the order of the moral development) in the last place; for, it is in fact quite evident, that we cannot speak of the family, the church, and the state, without having first examined the moral activity *per se*. To begin with the discussion of the good would be the so-called "analytical method," whereas ours, on the contrary, is the "synthetic;" —the course of the former is, so to speak, retrogressive; while the latter proceeds forward, more in the actual course of the moral development, and hence is the more natural.

The first three subdivisions of our classification embrace, it is true, only the antecedent conditions of the moral activity itself; but it does not follow from this that their subject-matter is to be thrown into an introduction. Free rational life, as an object of ethics, cannot be treated as a *mere* activity without taking into consideration also the active subject, as well as the law by which the subject is governed, and the field upon which it acts; he who describes vegetable life, must surely speak also of the organs of plants. In any case, a controversy as to whether this consideration forms only an introduction to the subject-matter, or is a part of the subject-matter itself, would be very unprofitable.

CHAPTER I.

THE MORAL SUBJECT.

SECTION LVIII.

The moral subject is the personal spirit, in a stricter sense, the created spirit. Between the different grades of spiritual beings, there is, in respect to the moral life-task, no essential difference; and, hence, for the individual spirit, the life-task never comes to a definitive close. The basis of the moral life is the *individual* moral person; but in so far as a plurality of persons constitute themselves into a spiritual life-whole, such a collective totality becomes also itself a moral subject with a peculiar moral task.

In the widest sense of the moral thought, even God himself, as the holy One, is a moral subject. But in so far as ethics has regard not to an absolutely infinite, eternal Being and life, but to a task accomplishing itself in time, it considers only the created spirit as a subject of morality. But all created personal spirits without exception are moral subjects, and that too with an individual task that never comes to a close; the blessed spirits, angels included, have not only, like earthly men, constantly to accomplish morality, but so soon as we leave sin out of view as an abnormal reality, their moral task is essentially the *same* as that of man; and Schleiermacher is wrong in limiting moral acting, and hence also ethics, to the, as yet, militant life, and in excluding them from the perfected life of the blessed (*Syst.*, p. 51, 61). Unless we are to conceive the blessed as spiritually dead, then they must have a life-activity answering to the divine will,— that is, a moral one. Were this not the case, then Christ's holy life would be moral only so long as he had to do with an opposing world; and only the earthly, but not the glorified, Christ, as also not the saints in heaven, could be looked upon as moral examples for us. It is true, the manifestation-form of the morality of a blessed spirit will be different from that of the yet militant; nevertheless the essence remains the same.

The distinguishing of the moral collective subject from the individual subject is a point of essential importance; for, the moral activity of the two is by no means the same. For the member of a moral community, there arise special moral duties that fall to him, not as a moral individual but as an organic member of a whole, and which he is to fulfill not in his own name but in that of the totality. The action of the individual is, of course, the first, the presupposition of the other; the moral community is always the fruit of a precedent moral activity of the individuals.—is itself a realized-good, which, however, at once becomes in turn itself a morally-active subject, unless indeed it is to cease to be.

I. THE INDIVIDUAL MORAL SUBJECT, MAN.

SECTION LIX.

Man as created after God's *image* is, as spiritualized nature, both spirit and nature, and also the real unity of the two.

A. As a *spirit* he is a rationally-free, self-determining being, attaining to his full, peculiar reality through free activity. The basis and essence of this spirituality is personal *self-consciousness*. Only in so far as man is self-conscious can he be moral, and by virtue of this self-consciousness he is answerable for his life,—his life becomes to him a moral one, and is *counted to* him. But he is conscious of himself as a *personal* individual, that is, he distinguishes himself from others not merely by his *being*, but by a to him exclusively-*peculiar*, determined being,—by his peculiar *personality*, which in this peculiarity does not belong to him directly from nature, but is acquired only by personal, moral activity, and hence constitutes character-peculiarity. The individual being of man is distinguished from that of nature-objects by the fact that it has inherent in itself, as an inner rational power, the destination not to remain a mere individual unit, but to become a personality,—in a word, man is from the very beginning not a mere specimen of his species, but is called to become a peculiarly-determined being.

The Christian idea of man is summed up in the thought of the *image* of God, and hence presupposes dogmatically the development of the idea of God. The great emphasis which is laid in Scripture on this idea of God-likeness [Gen. i, 26, 27; ix, 6; 1 Cor. xi, 7; James iii, 9; Col. iii, 10; Acts xvii, 28, 29] shows of itself that we have not to do here with a mere poetic figure. All that is created is *good*,—is an expression of the divine will, and hence is an image of the divine thought; but the rational creature, as the crown of creation, is the most complete expression of this goodness,—is the *image* of God, bears upon itself the most perfect impress of the Creator. Now as God is essentially a *spirit*, hence, man is God's image more immediately only as a rational spirit, whereas the body merely bears on itself, like other nature-objects, the *trace* of the Creator, but not his perfect impress, and it becomes an image of God only, mediately,—namely, in so far as it is progressively transfigured by the spirit into its own perfect expression. In the Scriptures Christ is called by pre-eminence, the true image of God; but man is called to become like this image [Rom. viii, 29]. Christ is this image not merely as the eternal Son of God, but also and especially as the true Son of Man, who historically and visibly reveals the divine [Col. i, 15]; and as such he is the "first-born among many brethren."

The rational spirit stands in contrast to mere nature-existence. A nature-entity determines not itself, but *is determined* by a nature-force not lying within its own consciousness,—is even in its activity predominantly unfree, whereas that which constitutes the essence of spirit is, to be free, to determine itself in its peculiarity, to be active toward conscious ends. The brute has not purposes, but only impulses. There is indeed reason in the brute; the brute does not, however, have the reason, but the reason has the brute. The reason that is in nature is only objective rationality; whereas spirit is a subject possessing reason as a consciousness. This consciousness is rational, however, only as self-consciousness, wherein man becomes to himself a real object,—comes into spiritual self-possession, and in this self-possession distinguishes himself from all other objective beings. By virtue of self-consciousness man remains ever *in the presence of himself*, and at one with himself; and only in virtue of this continuous sameness of the personal spirit, is it morally responsible.

But a spirit is more than a mere numerical individual; nature-creatures differ from others of their species, not by essential peculiarities but by their mere separate being and by outward fortuitous determinations,—are mere essentially-similar specimens of the same kind, mere repetitions of the same existence. But each individual personal spirit has, as distinguished from other personal spirits, a determined peculiarity of its own, which raises it from a mere numerical existence into a determined personality. In self-consciousness man knows himself not merely as *a* man, but as *this* particularly-determined man. He bears, therefore, a personal *name*, the significance of which is, that it is his destination to be something different from others,—to possess in his being something which others neither have nor can have in the same manner. The name is, with man as well as with God, an expression of personal peculiarity—of that which inwardly distinguishes one determined personality from others [Exod. xxxiii, 12, 17; Isa. xliii, 1; xlv, 3, 4; lvi, 5; John x, 3; Rev. iii, 5]; this personal peculiarity the spirit does not have from *nature*, nor yet is it generated by merely natural development; but the child has from the very beginning the *capacity* for, and hence the *destination* unto, such a personality-constituting peculiarity; nor is this capacity a merely conceived possibility, on the contrary it is a real germ; but this germ can come to development only by moral activity. This germ of personality which lies in the very essence of the rational spirit does not contain within itself the determined peculiarity; it simply requires development, but as to *how*, and unto *what* peculiarity it becomes developed, that depends on the free moral activity of the person himself. That this personal peculiarity does not come from nature, but belongs to the life of the free spirit, is clearly implied in the custom, prevalent among almost all nations and tribes, of *name-giving*. Nature gives to man at birth his individual existence; the spiritually and historically formed society, or family, gives to him his personal name,—designating thereby either the goal of this personality or its already acquired peculiarity [Gen. iii, 20; iv, 25; v, 29; xxi, 3; xli, 51, 52; Matt. i, 25; Luke i, 60, etc.].

This thought of the moral quality of the personality is not so uncontested as might be supposed. Schleiermacher, in his Philosophical Ethics,* holds that moral individualities differ *primitively*, before all moral activity, and hence do not merely become different. While preceding moral systems, and especially that of Kant, either overlooked the special peculiarity of the person, or even ignored it as something illegitimate, Schleiermacher emphasizes justly enough the moral significancy of this peculiarity, but he also rushes to the opposite one-sidedness, and magnifies the difference into a primitive, determined, ante-moral one,—a sort of moral atomistics, which, in order to escape the difficulty of the notion of free self-determination, assumes a much greater incomprehensibility. In a system, sprung up from essentially Pantheistic soil, this view is not inconsequential, inasmuch as here the notion of a really free self-determination is out of the question; but at the same time also the notion of moral personality is precluded, and ethics is reduced to a presentation, not of how man as a free individual *should* conform himself to a moral idea, but of how he *must* develop himself in his strictly naturally-determined idiosyncrasy. But a spirit that is absolutely determined by the All (conceived here as

---

* *System*, p. 93 *sqq.*, 157, 172; comp. *Christl. Sitte*, p. 58 *sqq.*, and *Grundlin. einer Kritik*, etc., p. 79 *sqq.* (2 ed., p. 57); *Monologen*, 4 *Ausg.*, p. 24 *sqq.*; *Reden*, 2. ed., 129.

strictly impersonal) could not essentially differ from a mere nature-creature; even brutes have unfree spirituality. We admit that men, even had they not sinned, would not have manifested perfect similarity, but would have been in some respects differently attuned from nature itself,—as, for example, in the peculiarities of sex, of temperament and of nationality, (see § 67,) but these natural differences affect not the personal essence itself,—do not make of the individual a being strictly *personally*-different from *all* others, but are only different traits of entire clans or groups,—are not so much differences of individuals as of races. The fact that in the present condition of mankind, each individual has inborn within him the germ of determined moral peculiarities, of particular vices and the like, is simply a result of his illegitimate abnormal state, and is very far from justifying us in merely cultivating and developing our inborn peculiarities. But Schleiermacher is very erroneous when he regards this original difference, even in spiritual and moral respects, as something necessary and contributive to the æsthetic beauty of the All,—as, for example, when he says: "Some [of the phases of humanity] are the most sublime and striking expression of the beautiful and the divine; others are grotesque products of the most original and fleeting whim of a master-hand; . . . why should we despise that which throws into relief the chief groups, and gives life and fullness to the whole? Is it not befitting that the single heavenly forms should be glorified by the fact that thousands of others bow themselves before them? Undying humanity is unweariedly busy in reproducing itself and in manifesting itself under the greatest variety of manner in the transitory phenomena of finite life. Such is the harmony of the universe, such the great and wonderful simplicity in its eternal art-work. What indeed were the monotonous reiteration of a *beau ideal* in which, after all, the individuals would be (time and circumstances substracted) strictly like each other—the same formula with the coefficients varied?—what were such a monotony in comparison with this infinite variety of human peculiarities? . . . This individual appears as the rude animal part of humanity, affected only by the first infantile instincts of the race; that other one, as the finest sublimated spirit, free from all that is common and unworthy, and with light wing rising above the earth;—but all are there in order to show, by their existence, how the various forces of human nature operate separately and in detail." (Reden, 2 ed., p. 130 *sqq.*). Such language outdoes even the Greek distinction of man into barbarous and free-men, and is, as a consistent expression of a purely naturalistic view of the world, in most direct antagonism to the Christian thought of a moral world-order upheld by a holy God.—Rothe (*Ethik* i, § 120 *sqq.*) adopts the view of Schleiermacher in a somewhat different, though less consistent form.

SECTION LX.

The self-conscious personality unfolds its life under a variety of forms.—(1) Man is a *knowing*, a cognoscitive, spirit,—he takes objects spiritually, that is, according to their idea, into himself, and thus makes them his enduring possession. The object of knowledge is *truth*, and the knowing spirit is capable of attaining thereto. Knowledge is in itself *true* and does not deceive, for God's created universe is good, and hence true and in perfect harmony with itself. As a *rational* spirit, man knows not only the created world but also its divine source,—in fact the essence of rationality consists in the knowledge of God in his existence, his nature, his government, and his will. This God-consciousness, resting upon a self-revelation of God to man, is indeed, as finite knowledge, not capable of thoroughly comprehending the infinite essence of God, yet, with a full consciousness of its own limits, it is nevertheless a true, real, and well-grounded knowledge of the divine, and as such it is the presupposition of morality.

The human spirit is an image of the *eternal* divine life, though in the form of a temporal life. God, in his eternal life, is eternally self-begetting, self-knowing, and self-loving,

—absolutely his own object; and the finite spirit, reflectively manifesting the life-development of God, has a threefold object upon which its life-movement is directed, namely, itself, the external world and God. Man is God's image in this threefold relation,—in willing, in knowing, and in feeling; but as, primarily, his reality is *given* to him, as already existing without his co-operation, hence these three activities appear in another and chronologically different order of succession, as knowing, feeling, and willing. Thus the finite spirit knows (takes cognizance of), feels (loves) and wills both itself, the objective world and God; and, as the life of a created being is a progressive development whose spiritual significance lies before it as a goal or purpose,—as something not as yet fully real, but rather as to be won by effort,—hence the threefold life of the spirit has also a threefold end, namely, truth, happiness, and the good; and it is only in the perfect attaining of this threefold end that the image of God in man perfects itself,—that the highest good is realized. But as the perfection of created things consists in the fact that they perfectly correspond to the divine creative idea, so the perfection of knowledge, feeling, and willing, and consequently of truth, of happiness, and of the good, consists in their so relating to God that all finite objects are known, willed, and loved only in God and as relating to him. God himself *is* the truth, the good and love, and whatever falls under this threefold notion, does so only in so far as it is rooted in and in harmony with God.

Man, as created good by God, must have the capacity perfectly to attain to this good state which is divinely proposed to him as his life-goal. Hence his knowledge cannot be deceptive, but must have the truth as its contents. The world would not be good, would not be in harmony, if the intellectual images of objects in the knowing spirit were not true to the originals,—if the thought as objectively real were essentially other than the subjective one. What Christ promises to his followers: "Ye shall know the truth" [John viii. 32], must also be fully applicable to man *per se ;* redemption is in fact essentially a restoration of the lost perfection; God wills that all men should "come unto the knowledge of the truth" [1 Tim. ii, 4]. The destination of man to know the truth is expressed in Gen. ii, 19, 20. God brought the beasts to Adam in order "to see what he would *call* them," that is, how he would distinguish them from himself and from other objects,—form of them a definite, generically-characterizing notion; the name is an expression of the obtained notion;— and whatsoever he severally called them, "that *was the name* thereof;"—this is not a mere experiment on the part of God, but, on the contrary, a divine guaranty for the truthfulness of human knowledge, and at the same time for the freedom of the same. God himself brings before man the outer world; thereby he guarantees to him that his knowledge is legitimate, true, and reliable; and it is not God who gives names to the objects; man himself does it, and freely; the knowing (taking cognizance) of the truth is a free, and hence a *moral* activity; and this calling by name, this definite, distinguishing knowing, is sealed by God as truthful,—"that *was* the name thereof;" man's free knowing is not to be mere empty play, but to have a reality as its contents; and the spiritual significance of things is to find its goal only in its being spiritually appropriated by man. Our knowledge of the objective world is not to remain a mere sensuous beholding, as with the brute, but is to rise beyond that stage into the sphere of ideas; this is for us a moral duty, and one which has a divine promise. Thus the first man takes cognizance of, and names, also the woman, his created helpmeet [Gen. ii, 23]; and Eve, as well as Adam, recognizes the divine will and distinguishes it from her own as owing obedience to the former [Gen. iii, 2, 3]; in the one case as well as in the other, there is manifested at the same time a definite self-consciousness as different from the objective consciousness.

The relation of our knowledge to *God* is of course quite different from its relation to the world. While all worldly being may, as created, be also ultimately fully known and comprehended by man, on the contrary the infinite and eternal being and essence of God is, for the essentially limited human spirit, a thought never fully to be grasped; and the *incomprehensibility* of God [Psa. cxlvii, 5; Isa. xl, 28; lv, 8, 9; Job xi, 8; Rom. xi, 33] is a Christian doctrine by no means to be rejected. But this incomprehensibility does not preclude a very essential and true knowledge, otherwise were all God-likeness in man a mere empty rhetorical phrase. Even as the eye is unable to take in the entire ocean, and nevertheless has a very definite intuition of its existence and peculiarities, so likewise is the finite spirit unable to take in the infinite, to fathom it in its bottomless depths, and yet it is able with constantly increasing clearness to attain to a true knowledge not only of the existence but also of the nature of God,—not, however, by means of the *understanding*, which relates to and is exclusively occupied with the finite, but by means of the *reason*, which relates essentially to the infinite. As all created being is a reflection of God, and as man is his image, hence the type leads directly to an (imperfect it may be, but yet) true knowledge of the prototype [Rom. i, 19, 20; Col. iii, 10]. The assumption that man can know of God only *that* he is, and what he is *not*, but not *what* he is, is self-contradictory and unbiblical; a merely negative knowledge is no knowledge at all, and of that of whose nature I know nothing I cannot affirm even, that it is. The Evangelical Church very strongly emphasizes primitive man's capability of attaining to a knowledge of the truth, even in relation to the divine nature; the *Apologia* (i, § 17, 18) ascribes to him *sapientia et notitia dei certior*, "a correct and clear knowledge of God." Skepticism may readily find excuse for itself outside of Christianity, but what holds good of man as estranged from God, does not hold equally of him who is in communion with that God who is himself the truth; and hence within the Christian world, skepticism has no longer any reason of existence. Also the assertion of Kant, that the object *per se* remains hidden from human knowledge, and that all knowledge of reality has, in the sphere of pure reason, only a formal and subjective validity, is in direct contradiction to the Christian world-view, which expresses a much greater confidence in the harmony of the universe. The perfect man and the Christian can do more than "conjecture and presume;" for, "the spirit of man is the candle of the Lord" [Prov. xx, 27].—That man's first God-consciousness should rest on an objective self-revelation of God, was a necessary condition to his spiritual education toward finding the truth for himself.

SECTION LXI.

(2) Man is a *willing*, a volitionating, spirit; the goal of his life-movement is for him a conscious *end*. He is not impelled unconsciously and by extraneous force toward that to which he is to attain, but he knows the end, and himself directs himself toward it,—he *chooses* the known goal by virtue of a personal will-determination,—that is, in his willing he is *free*. The end of rational willing is the *good*, and, in so far as this is to be realized by freedom, the *morally-good*. That which in nature-objects takes place by necessity, becomes, in the sphere of the moral will, a "*should;*" that which in the former case is natural law, becomes here a moral precept; that which is there natural development, becomes here *moral life*. But the will of the created spirit differs from the prototypal will of God by the fact that its development in time is not unconditioned, but is always conditioned on free self-determination, so that consequently there exists the possibility of another self-determination than that toward the true end,—that is, in a word, by the fact that man's freedom of will, as distinguished from the divine (which is, at the same time, eternal necessity), is *freedom of choice—liberum arbitrium*. The finite spirit can, and should, attain to the good as the purpose of its life, but it can also—what it should not do—turn away from this good; and it attains to the good only when it freely *wills* to attain to it. Man, as created good, has this freedom in the highest degree, so that it is not limited or trammeled by any *tendency* to evil inherent in his natural non-perfection, as, for example, by his sensuousness. It is incumbent upon ethics to describe and explain the

development of the natural freedom of the, as yet, undetermined will, into the moral freedom of the holy will.

The moral freedom of the will is distinctly presupposed in the Biblical account of primitive man. "And the Lord God commanded the man, saying, Of every tree of the garden thou *mayest* freely eat; but of the tree of the knowledge of good and evil, thou *shalt* not eat of it" [Gen. ii, 16, 17]. God's injunction addresses itself to the free will of man, and requires of him moral obedience. When, now, man nevertheless actually did that which was forbidden, he simply did the opposite of what God's holy will was; and he thereby demonstrated in fact, though to his ruin, the reality of human freedom of choice. Scripture knows absolutely nothing of any other view of the true nature of man than that he was capable of freely choosing good or evil. For this idea of freedom of choice, however, Scripture has no specific expression; for ἐλεύθερος, ἐλευθερία, originally used in a legal sense, designate the condition of man as emancipated by Christ; the idea of man's freedom of choice is expressed rather as a "choosing between good and evil;" for example, in Isa. vii, 15, 16, where the time of the spiritual maturity of a man is called the time when he "shall know to refuse the evil and choose the good" [comp. Deut. xi, 26 *sqq.*], or when he can do "according to his pleasure" [Esth. i, 8], or that which is "good in his own eyes" [Gen. xvi, 6; xix, 8]. The view of freedom of choice as presented in the book of Sirach xv, 14, holds good in its full sense evidently only of man as free from the bondage of sin. In the New Testament, man's freedom of choice is implied by θέλειν (for example, in Matt. xxiii, 37; whereas the "power over one's own will" mentioned in 1 Cor. vii, 37 refers more to our moral discretion).

In the Christian church the full moral freedom of choice of man *before* the fall, has been uniformly admitted; and the notion that human actions are necessarily determined, just as uniformly rejected [comp. *Apol.* i, p. 52, 53; *Form. Conc.* ii, p. 580, 677]. The "supralapsarian" predestinarianism of Calvin has never been ecclesiastically sanctioned, nor in fact does even it deny freedom of choice as a principle, and expressly, but only actually. Entirely different from this teaching of Calvin is the *fundamental* denial of freedom of will in all Pantheistic systems since Spinoza. In Pantheism there is no place for freedom, and what appears there under this name is something entirely different from that which the consciousness of all nations understands thereby. Where conscious spirit is not the ground, but simply a product of the collective development of the All, there the individual spirit is in its entire existence, essence, and life, absolutely determined; and its single life-manifestations are quite as absolutely determined as is its being itself;—in which case the rational spirit can never have a consciousness of freedom, but only a "sense of absolute dependence," and hence there can be no room for any moral responsibility. The seemingly moral life is as immediate and necessary a manifestation of the "all-life" as is the growth of plants, and it differs from the nature-life only in the fact, that man has a consciousness of that which he does necessarily, in fact, but which he *fancies* he does freely. The will differs from unconscious nature-impulse only by the consciousness which attends it, but it is, in fact, quite as absolutely determined and unfree as is the latter. This view is expressed most clearly, simply, and consequentially, by *Spinoza;* and it is neither in the interest of clearness nor of scientific honesty, when more recent systems, based on him, make free use of fair-sounding words about human freedom. In essential agreement with Spinoza, Schleiermacher, in his "Discourses on Religion," rejects the freedom of the will. The essence of religion is a sense of the absolute unity of the universe and the individual existence,—a consciousness that our whole being and activity are the being and activity of the universe itself, and are determined thereby.—Schelling, who subsequently attributed to the idea of the personal will a very high significancy, held as yet in his "Lectures on Academic Study" (1803) to the unconditional necessity of all apparently free phenomena. History is quite as fully an immediate and necessary manifestation of the absolute, as is nature; men are but instruments for carrying out that which is *per se* necessary, and they are, in their reality and peculiarities, quite as fatally-determined as the actions themselves. Actions *appear* as free or arbitrary only in so far as man makes a necessarily-determined action specifically *his own*, but this action itself, as well as its result in good or evil, and hence also man in all his life-manifestations, is but the passive instrument of absolute necessity; all that which is apparently free is but a necessary expression of the eternal order of things. Subsequently (1809), Schelling sought to rise above Pantheism, and, in some manner, to comprehend the freedom of the will, but he did not rise beyond wide-reaching contradictions. The assumption of an ante-mundane fall into sin was intended to reconcile freedom with necessity (*Phil. Schr.*, 1809, i, 438 *sqq.*, 463 *sqq.*). On this we remark here simply, that from an ethical stand-point it makes no moral difference whether free self-determination is precluded, for our whole *mundane* life, by an absolute natural necessity, or by a pretended *ante*-mundane free determination of man himself, but of which he has not the least consciousness. Where there is no continuity of the consciousness, there there is also no unity of the person; and a pretended free act which *I* am supposed to have done, but of which *I* know absolutely nothing, is not my act but is absolutely foreign to me; and a fettering of my freedom by a, to me entirely unknown, timeless act cannot be regarded from a moral point of view as other than a simple being-determined by unconditional necessity.—Hegel has left the idea of freedom, in many respects, in great uncertainty; he is very fond of talking of freedom; but his system itself is compatible only with a universal all-determining necessity; freedom is nothing more than "the not being dependent on another, the sustaining relations to one's self;" in its full sense, however, this is true only of the spirit as absolute; individual spirits are only transient manifestations of the collective life, and are determined by the same.— More recent philosophy, wherever it deviates from strict Pantheism, uniformly attempts to bring personal freedom of will more clearly before the consciousness. There is here no possibility of a middle-ground, and ambiguous rhetoric can no longer deceive. Where God is not the infinite eternal Spirit, but comes to self-consciousness only in man, there the thought of a real freedom of will is impossible. The infinite domination of the All leaves no place for the free movement of the individual spirit; the misused freedom of a single creature would throw the collective universe into disorder, for the unfree All affords no possibility of preserving moral order as against the free actions of individuals. On this ground there remains a freedom only for thoughtless contemplation; and this would then, of necessity, lead to the ethics of an unlimited self-love which can seek and find in the bedlam of individual wills nothing higher than itself. Freedom is possible only where a free Spirit rules in and over the All. The personal God is able, in almighty love, to create free spirits, and to guarantee them in their freedom, namely, in that he lovingly withdraws his direct activity from the sphere of will-freedom, and thus preserves the created spirit in its spiritual essence which is freedom itself; and such a God is able in the midst of the diversity and multiplicity of free actions, and even of ungodly ones, to preserve the moral order of the universe.

(The question of freedom of will has of late been much discussed, mostly from the stand-point of recent philosophy and in relation thereto. Daub: *Statement and Criticism of Hypotheses Relating to Free-Will*, 1834; Romang: *On Free-Will and Determinism*, 1835 [starting out from Schleiermacher's stand-point, he attains only to a semblance of freedom]; Matthias: *The Idea of Freedom*, 1834; [since Hegel] Herbart: *On the Doctrine of the Freedom of the Human Will*, 1836 [critical, rather than furnishing new matter]; Vatke; Passavant: *On the Freedom of the Will*, 1835; K. Ph. Fischer, in Fichte's *Zeitschrift*, iii, 101; ix, 79; Zeller, in the *Theologische Jahrbücher*, 1846; and others).

SECTION LXII.

(3) Man is a *feeling*, a sensitive, spirit,—becomes conscious of himself as standing in harmony with, or in antagonism to, other being; and, inasmuch as in the primitive unperverted creation, goodness, and hence harmony, is an essential quality, and a real disharmony therein inconceivable, hence while man —as self-developing, that is, as seeking after an, as

yet, unrealized goal—has a consciousness of something yet lacking to his ultimate perfection, still he knows nothing of any real antagonism of existence, and hence he has no feeling of pain, but only of *joy* in existence, arising from his consciousness of an undisturbed harmony of universal existence with his own personality,—that is, in a word, the feeling of *happiness*. In so far as this feeling expresses at the same time the recognition of this existence in its peculiar reality, it is *love*. Bliss and love to God and to his works are not two different things, but only two different phases of the same spiritual life-manifestation,—the former being rather the subjective, the latter the objective phase,—inasmuch as in bliss and love man is, in fact, perfectly at one with the objective universe.

Feeling is not peculiar to the rational spirit; it becomes rational only in so far as it is an expression of self-consciousness; and as self-consciousness is rational only in being a consciousness not of mere individual being but also of a God-likeness in the peculiarity of the person, so also is rational feeling not of a merely individual nature, but it is excited by the traces of God which shine forth from all created existence, and hence it is, at bottom, always a love of God. The goodness of created existence is embraced by rational feeling not as being good merely for the feeling individual, but as a being-good *per se;* the rational spirit feels not merely that this or that entity stands in harmony with itself, but it feels *itself* as standing in harmony with the *totality* of existence,—feels the harmony of God's world as such. In the same degree that spirituality rises, rises also the vividness and compass of feeling. The unconscious nature-object is affected only by the very few things that come into immediate contact with it; the brute shows so much the more extended and more lively a sympathy with external existence the higher and nobler its rank. Emotionlessness, blunt indifference toward external objects, is always, save where it is artificially superinduced by false teachings, a sign of deep moral degradation. The Biblical account of the primitive condition of man uniformly represents the destination of nature to be, to procure to the rational spirit the feeling of joy, of happiness. Man is placed in the garden of Eden, and thereby brought into the immediate presence of the full harmony of the created world; in it God causes to grow "every tree that is pleasant to the sight and good for food;" and the full feeling of happiness, as springing from his love to that which harmonizes with him, is procured to man (to whom it is not "good" to be alone) by the creation of woman,—in whom he at once recognizes that she is bone of his bone and flesh of his flesh, —a being other than, and yet of, himself.

Feeling is the presupposition of all activity, and hence also of the moral; and the most real feeling of all—that which relates to the moral—is not an un-pleasure feeling, as is often assumed in antagonism to the Biblical world-view, but in fact a happiness-feeling. It would not imply a "good" creation, nor indeed any God-likeness in man, were it a fact that man were incited to activity only by un-pleasure, that is, by pain, while yet happiness were the end of the active life. Even as God is not prompted to activity by any feeling of want, but rather in virtue of his eternal and absolutely perfect bliss, so also can the true moral feeling of man, who is God's image, be no other than the feeling of happiness and love; but the consciousness of a yet to be won good is *per se* by no means a feeling of unhappiness, on the contrary it in fact awakens a direct pleasure in seeking.

SECTION LXIII.

(4) Man, as a rationally self-conscious spirit, is personally *immortal;* only as such is he a truly moral being,—has a moral life-task transcending his own immediate individuality. Faith in immortality is the presupposition of true morality; for the moral life-task is one that is incessantly progressive, ever self-renewing, and at no moment perfectly brought

to a close; and, as the perfect realization of God-likeness, it can only be accomplished through an uninterruptedly-continuing personal life.

We have to do here, not with the scientific demonstration of the doctrine of personal immortality, but only with its moral significance. In recent times, especially since Kant, the notion has frequently been maintained, that morality is entirely independent of a belief in immortality, nay, that it evinces its purity and genuineness by the very fact of entirely leaving out of view this belief, and that a man is not truly moral so long as he allows himself to be determined in his moral activity by this belief. It is true, Kant deduces from the idea of the moral, the idea of personal immortality as a rational postulate; the moral idea itself, however, is with him independent of this postulate,—calls for its fulfillment absolutely and unconditionally. There is in this some degree of self-contradiction; if the "categorical imperative" demands morality unconditionally, and utterly irrespectively of immortality, then this immortality cannot be embraced in it as a postulate, but must be merely associated thereto from without. In the endlessness of the life-task, however, as it is presented by Kant, there actually lies, in fact, the thought of immortality as included in the moral idea itself,—so that his express dissociating of the two ideas is illegitimate and unnatural. Schleiermacher goes further; and, even in his Dogmatics, he is unable entirely to rise above his previous express denial of immortality. In his Discourses on Religion he places the religiously-moral life-task proper in an actual disregarding of the idea of this immortality. "Strive even in this life to *annihilate* your personality, and to live in the One and All; strive to be more than yourselves, in order that you may lose but little when you lose yourselves;" the immortality to be aimed at is not that of the personality, not above and beyond the earthly existence, but it is an ideal immortality in each and every moment; men should not desire to hold fast to their personality, rather "should they embrace the single opportunity presented to them by death for escaping beyond it."* Even in his Dogmatics Schleiermacher holds,

* *Reden üb die Rel.*, p. 174 sqq., 2 Auf.

that the purest morality perfectly consists with a "renunciation of the perpetuity of the personality,—that, in fact, an interestedness in a recompense is impious. In the Hegelian philosophy morality is absolutely independent of immortality; this idea in fact can nowhere find footing in the system; the religion of the "this-side" which sprang from this philosophy, affects to give point to its rhetorical flourishes on morality by its seemingly magnanimous renunciation of all expectation of eternal life.

The pretended disinterestedness of moral actions performed without reference to immortality, is mere appearance. All moral activity looks to an end, and this end is a good; and personal perfection is for each individual an essential part of the highest good, or, in fact, this good itself; hence not to wish to obtain any thing *for one's self* by one's moral activity is simply absurd; the first and most necessary of all goods, and the one which is the presupposition of all morality, is in fact existence; to desire to renounce personal existence, or to regard it as indifferent, is equivalent to renouncing moral life, and is consequently not unselfish, but it is immoral. It is true we cannot claim for the so-called *teleological* proof of the immortality of the soul, full demonstrative power; this much, however, it does prove, namely, that the highest moral perfection would be impossible without immortality; for, as man can never arrive at such a perfection of the moral life as that he can advance no further, so that consequently his farther existence would be purposeless, but in fact, on the contrary, every fulfillment of one moral duty gives in turn birth to new ones, and there is absolutely no point to be found where the moral spirit might say, "thus far and no farther, there remains nothing more for me to do,"—hence also moral perfection cannot be realized save in an unbroken perpetuity of personal life. To say now, that the moral life-task does not consist in obtaining entire moral perfection, but only a limited degree thereof, would be *per se* immoral. And in fact should we for a moment concede some such limited degree of the moral, then there would be no conceivable rule for fixing this degree, and each would be at liberty to narrow the limits of his morality at pleasure, without that any one would be justified in blaming, or less esteeming him therefor.

In all moral systems, even those of heathen nations, morality is *more precious* than temporal life, and that person is regarded as ignoble and contemptible, even by pagans, who clings to his life at *any price*, for example, at that of failing in his duty to his country, to his family, or to his own honor. This moral sentiment of honor we have no wish to weaken. It is conceivable, on the assumption of the prevalence of sin, that one's moral duty, as, for example, that of speaking or confessing the truth, or of fidelity in love or obedience, cannot in some conjunctures be fulfilled save at the sacrifice of temporal life. Now, to one's existence in general one has an unlimited *right;* it is his first and most natural right. In the *absence* of immortality, however, the sacrifice of one's life for a moral duty would not only not be a moral requirement, but it would be downright folly and sin: for morality can never require the giving up of the first condition of all moral activity, namely, personal existence. The first, the most immediate and absolutely unconditional duty, is self-preservation, and other duties are binding only in so far as they do not radically interfere with this one. As it would not be a moral action, but on the contrary a proof of insanity if one man should really choose* eternal damnation for the sake of another, just as little is any being whatever at liberty to purchase for others any temporal good, however great, at the cost of personal existence; and in the absence of immortality there can be none other than temporal goods. Man may sacrifice any one good only for the sake of a higher good; but in renouncing existence he obtains no good whatever. The sound and unsophisticated judgment will find, on the denial of immortality, no other rule of life-wisdom than simply to take advantage of the short span of life here allotted to us for enjoying the greatest possible happiness. Happiness is in fact an absolutely necessary phase of human perfection, and an essential expression of the highest good: to strive after it is not only not selfishness, on the contrary, it is a requirement of reason and of moral duty; and it is not possible that in a world of rational order morality should work any thing else than happiness. Were it otherwise it would be a plain

---

* It is only seemingly so that Paul expresses such a willingness in Rom. ix, 3.

proof of the non-existence of a rational, moral world-order, and in that case it would be totally absurd to speak further of moral duty at all, for duty is itself a part of a *moral* world-order. If there is, now, no eternal blessedness as a highest good, then it can be only after temporal, earthly happiness, that man has to seek, and by which consequently he is to measure the morality of his acts. If it is true that all morality necessarily renders happy, then on the above hypothesis only that can be moral which procures for us earthly comfort, temporal enjoyment; the teachings of the Epicureans would then be the only rational theory, and no valid objection could be made to the moral rule: "Let us eat and drink, for to-morrow we die" [1 Cor. xv, 32]. Foolish then would he be who did not recklessly seek as much enjoyment in his earthly life as in any way he possibly could. It is, of course, not necessary that this system should lead simply to groveling sensual enjoyment; the ancient Epicureans knew well enough that riotous intemperate indulgence works much suffering, and the modern ones also know equally well, that by unrestrained wantonness they bring themselves into shame and contempt in the eyes of the morally-taught masses; this, however, does not in any degree ameliorate the essence of this morality of the "this side." The outwardly-respectable life of many a denier of immortality rests in reality on the power of public opinion, and on custom as grown up from Christian ground. But the case is quite otherwise where unbelief becomes *fashionable* in wider circles of society. Let vouch for this, the utter immorality and depravity that prevailed in the circles of the French and of the Gallicized German free-thinkers of the last century. In the lower walks of society where a simpler logic prevails, and where respect for position and for public opinion has a less controlling power, the practical inferences from a naturalistic philosophy are more speedily and consistently drawn; and the ringleaders in depravity among the lower classes of the present day are, for the most part, deeply imbued with the conquests of "free thought," and are able thereby admirably to justify their wantonness; and there is scarcely conceivable a more absurd *rôle* than that assumed by the "respectable" among the free-thinkers, who presume to preach morality to their more-free-thinking and more logically reasoning brethren.

He who is without belief in immortality cannot act from an unconditional moral idea, but only from empirical external fitness, from circumstantial need; he *cannot* make moral duty his life-task, and his moral life sinks to a merely higher-cultured animal life. The question as to whether *Christian* morality is possible without a belief in immortality would have to be rejected as trivial,—seeing that a belief in Christ's and God's express word is certainly included in Christian morality,—had it not been expressly affirmed by some. The word of Christ, however, is a sufficient answer. "He that loseth his life for my sake shall find it," and "He that loveth his life shall lose it, and he that hateth his life in this world shall keep it unto life eternal" [Matt. x, 39; Luke ix, 24; xvii, 33; John xii, 25; x, 17; comp. 1 Cor. ix, 25; Phil. i, 21]. We emphasize in these passages, not the expressly pronounced affirmation of a life after death, but simply the express requirement to *sacrifice* one's life in the interest of a moral duty. But a world-government in which the realization of the good is possible only by the destruction of him who has for his life-task to realize the good, would be *per se* in a state of utter anarchy, and would have no right to impose moral duties. The simple undeniable fact is this, that the Christian heroes who literally fulfilled the above word of Christ, had joy in so doing *only* because of that living faith that enabled them to pray amid the tortures of death: "Lord Jesus, receive my spirit" [Acts vii, 59]. But between the Christian martyr's *joy* in death and an unbeliever's defiant *contempt* of death, there is a world-wide difference. Cases are not unfrequently seen of hardened criminals and atheists meeting death with undaunted courage and great coolness; this is, however, but another form of the cold defiance with which other persons blow out their own brains; and whoever has the assurance to compare such blind hardness, even in the remotest degree, with the joyousness and peace of soul of the Christian, surely shows himself utterly incapable of appreciating the true nature of morality.

When Schleiermacher and others, after him, declare it as unpious to be interested in a recompense,—understanding by this assertion that there is wanting a pure and immediate seeking for piety and morality themselves, and that both are desired merely as means for attaining to perfect happiness in a future life,—there is indeed some ground for their position, but only in so far as the subject should regard morality *merely* as a means to happiness, and that too as a *meritorious* means even in our present state of sinfulness, while the happiness should be considered as a justly claimable reward. But so soon as the objectors presume to reprehend the seeking after happiness as an essential and necessary phase of the high st good, and to brand as unpious the striving after the same as an actual life-purpose in general, we must reject their position as one-sided and untrue. Every good and hence every moral end produces happiness; and it would be a strange requirement, to permit the seeking after the good but not the seeking after the happiness therein contained. When Christ and the Apostles hesitated not to base all moral sacrifice on the promise and confident hope of eternal life, it does not seem very becoming in a Christian to stigmatize this as immoral self-seeking. When appeal is made to the Reformed divine Danæus, who (in his *Ethica Christ.* i, c. 17) represents the honor of God as the sole motive, and that for the sake of which we should be in duty bound to take upon ourselves eternal death, were it required of us, and who stigmatizes it as mercenary to act morally for the sake of eternal happiness,—we may reply, on the one hand, that it could never occur to one who is a Christian and conscious of redemption by grace to regard eternal blessedness, as a reward due for his virtue-merit,—which, in fact, is the sole view that Danæus rejects [*fol.* 78, *ed.* 3],—and, on the other hand, that this somewhat rash and readily misunderstood declaration has quite a different sense in the mouth of Danæus, who held fast to personal immortality, and in the mouth of those who see in the thought of immortality only a "dogma" without significance for the religious life, and which it is well to vail as much as possible in ambiguous phraseology. And in fact it doubtless forms a part of the moral honoring of God, that we believe in his promises, and love and thank him for them, and also act piously from this loving thankfulness. For the moral life is genuine only when it is a full and true expression of the filial relation of man to God; and it is not only illegitimate, but also a sinful disregarding of God, to require that we should keep only one phase of this relation in view, and violently throw aside and forget the other,—that we should see in God only the Sovereign and not also the lovingly promising Father. If God has gifted man with immortality, if he has promised to the Christian eternal life, then neither can nor should man, as moral, have any *other* moral goal than that which answers to this promise; if man, in his moral life, ignores that this life is the way to *eternal* life,—that God has placed before him an everlasting goal,—such conduct is an immoral rejecting of God's love. Whoever does not act from love acts immorally; now, for the promise of eternal life we owe God thankful love; hence there is no true morality which has not this loving thankfulness for its motive.

Against this view,—which is surely in perfect harmony with the general Christian consciousness,—indignant warning has been made,* as if it were an ignoring of the inalienable "conquests of recent science," and even appeal has been made to the Old Testament, in which, as an actual fact, it is asserted, the doctrine of immortality is not presented as a moral motive. Now, if the conquests of modern science are to consist in going back to the Old Testament stand-point, for which, on other occasions, the objectors are not in the habit of showing any very high esteem, we may well allow ourselves to deem it a *progress* beyond said conquests, to come back to the stand-point of *Christ* and the *Apostles*. What the wise educative purpose of the said Old Testament peculiarity was, we have elsewhere inquired, and we do not hesitate in the least to claim that *Christian* morality stands higher than that of the Old Testament, and that also in *moral* respects "he that is least in the kingdom of heaven is greater" than the greatest of the Old Testament saints [Matt. xi, 11], though indeed the latter also had, in their faith in the divine *promise*, in their hope of a future glorious goal for *all* the children of God, a powerful moral motive that was in no wise opposed to a belief in immortality, but on the contrary

---

* So especially Alex. Schweitzer in the *Protest. Kirchenz.*, 1862, *Nr.* 1; Fr. Nitzsch in the *Stud. u. Krit.*, 1863, II, 375.

implicitly contained it. Whether those who in recent times decline, with such professed disinterestedness, the application of faith in immortality as a moral motive, seek their moral glory in quite as unconditional a submission to God's revealed Word and guidance as did the saints of the Old Testament, seems to us, after all, quite questionable. We do not doubt but that there may be *some* sort of morality without said faith; but the question is as to *true* morality—that which embraces the whole man, appropriates to itself *all* truth, and is *of* the truth. The pains which some persons give themselves to prove that there may be a moral life without faith in immortality, reminds us very much of the recently made experiment of a naturalist:—he scooped out with a spoon the brain of a living dove, and the poor bird actually continued to live for six several weeks, and even partook of food in the mean time! Very interesting experiments may be had by performing similar amputations on the living body of the Christian faith,—and some of our theologians are quite busy at the work,—but whether the patient prospers very well under the operation is another question.

B.—MAN AS TO HIS SENSUOUSLY-CORPOREAL LIFE.

SECTION LXIV.

The natural body, as the physical basis on which the spirit develops itself to its full reality, has not a purpose in and of itself, but only for the spirit, namely, to be the perfectly-answering and absolutely-subserving organ of the spirit's relations to nature. This embraces three points:—1. The sensuous corporeality is, despite its seemingly trammeling power over the freedom of the spirit, *per se* absolutely *good*, and there is neither any thing *evil* in it nor is it the *cause* of any evil whatsoever; and as the body must, in so far as it is normal, be in harmony with the spirit and with nature, hence there is in it no sort of ground for any *trammeling* of the spiritual life—for any *pain*.

The moral significance of the sensuous nature, the corporeality, of man is a very important point in the Christian world-theory, and can in no wise be regarded as non-essential. It is, in fact, one among the living questions of the day,—questions which are being warmly agitated even outside of the church, and in relation to which the bearing of the Christian consciousness is, in many respects, entirely misunderstood. As early as the fourth century there infected the Christian church (partly under the prompting, or at least the countenance of non-Christian influences) a spiritualistic view of the naturally-sensuous,—a practical disesteeming of the same in comparison with the spiritual; and the Middle Ages followed in general the same tendency; the Reformation returned to the primitive Christian and biblical view. The recent rationalistic philosophy of the understanding developed, in contrast to the Middle Ages, the theoretical rather than the practical phase of spiritualism, and conceived the sensuously-corporeal life, not merely as the cause of sin, but as *per se* and originally a trammeling of the spiritual life,—as the real source and seat of sin, and hence as a mere transitory and soon entirely-to-be-thrown-off evil,—and interpreted, utterly erroneously, the New Testament term, σάρξ, referring it to the natural corporeality. Death, which had previously been viewed as the wages of sin, was now regarded as the emancipator from the seductive and spirit-burdening corporeal life,—as the divinely appointed normal beginning of the untrammeled life of the spirit. Sensuousness is here the not inherited, but innate, and not guilty, but guilt-generating *malum originis*—an evil, the origin of which was not free responsibly-sinning man, but the divine creative will itself; in getting rid of corporeality therefore man gets rid at the same time also of his (so-regarded) scarcely-imputable sinfulness. Sin consists essentially in the predominating of the sense-life over the spirit; the spirit *per se* would have little or no occasion for sin. The doctrine of a resurrection of a glorified body is rejected as belonging to a crude, unspiritual world-view; it is only the pure disembodied spirit that is free and perfect. In opposition to this view, the more recent and now spreading irreligious *Materialism* has exalted the sensuously-corporeal nature *above* the spirit, and conceived of the spirit as merely a transient force-manifestation of organized matter.

The evangelically-Christian view is neither the above spiritualistic nor this materialistic one. Christianity, though so often charged by worldlings with a one-sided spiritualism, places in fact a much higher moral worth on the corporeal nature than was ever done by heathenism. The body is destined, it is true, to absolute subserviency to the spirit; but it has precisely in this, its perfect service, also a share in the high moral significancy of the spirit,—it is not only not to be discarded as a trammeling of the spirit, but is a very essential part of the moral person. As the eye cannot say to the hand: "I have no need of thee" [1 Cor. xii, 21], neither also may the spirit thus speak to the body. As the nature-side of man, corporeality mediates the action of the spirit upon nature, so that nature becomes thrown open to the spirit as an object both of knowledge and of action. The spirit stands in living relation not only to spirit, but essentially also to nature, and virtualizes also therein its God-likeness.

The normal relation of the body to the spirit cannot be directly inferred from the present actual state of humanity; for if we assume, even preliminarily, the possibility that the moral spirit of the race has fallen away from its harmony with God, we yet thereby render it unsafe to infer that relation from the present state of things, since from the disturbed harmony of man with God follows also the disturbance of his harmony with himself, and especially of that between spirit and body. The true original relation can be educed only, on the one hand, from Scriptural declarations and from the living example of Christ, and, on the other, from the Christian idea of creation. The simple fact that all that God creates is *good*, is itself proof that the corporeality created for the spirit can neither be a trammeling nor a natural source of suffering for the same. Suffering and pain are indeed means of educative chastening for man as sinful, but for the unsinful their presence would be the reversing of all moral order. In God's good-created world, men, were they unfallen, would receive their moral training through manifestations of love, without the intervention of suffering and pain; to deny this would be to deny either God's love or his power.

The sensuous corporeality in its uncorrupted primitiveness can disturb neither the moral life by really immoral appetites, nor the feeling of happiness by pains and sickness,—the *aequale temperamentum qualitatum corporis* (equipoise of the qualities of the body) of the *Apologia* (i, 17);—in that which was created good there can be no antagonism between the life of the spirit and that of the body, nor between the body and nature; but every suffering, every pain, is evidence of an antagonism, of an evil in its subject. In the Scriptures all bodily sufferings are expressly traced back to sin [Gen. iii, 16, 19; Rom. v, 12–21]; this is the only possible "theodicy" in regard to human suffering. The body of the rational spirit is under the dominion of that spirit, and not under that of unspiritual nature; and the spirit is under the power of itself, and not under that of a nature-bound body; and it is only such a spirit as is free in every respect,—one that is not rendered unfree by a hampering corporeality,—that is in a condition to fulfill the whole of moral duty. In proportion as the now actually spirit-hampering sensuous corporeality is held to be the normal condition, and to answer to the divine creative idea, in the same proportion must the moral life-task also be lowered. And when Rationalism finds the true freedom and moral emancipation of the spirit only in the freeing of the same from the body, there is at least this much of truth in the position, namely, that it is an admission that the present bondage of the spirit under the manifoldly-hampering power of the body is *not* in harmony with the true life of the moral spirit. But whereas the evangelically-Christian consciousness refers this antagonism in God's world to the guilt of man, Rationalism casts the responsibility for this condition (which itself admits to be in contradiction to the moral idea) upon *God*, and thereby, in fact, undermines the Christian idea of God, and hence also the unconditional obligatoriness of moral duty. *Ultra posse nemo obligatur* (Obligation does not transcend ability); this is an ancient truth valid not only in the sphere of jurisprudence but also in that of morality.

SECTION LXV.

2. The body mediates the relation of the objective world to the personal spirit, through the *senses;* and this mediation, as being established by the divine creative will, is a *truthful* one. On the other hand, the body mediates the *active* relation of the spirit to the objective world, and, in subserving the spirit, it thereby mediates the morally-essential *dominion of the spirit over nature,* and is, hence, the necessary and adequate *organ* of the moral spirit in its relation to the external world,—and not that of nature for its dominion over the spirit.

If the created spirit has surety of ability for knowing the truth, this of itself implies that the knowledge mediated by the senses must be real and true,—that sense-impressions *per se* do not deceive us. "The hearing ear and the seeing eye, the Lord hath made even both of them" [Prov. xx, 12]; but God is a God of truth; and the solemn exhortation: "Lift up your eyes on high, and behold who hath created these things!" [Isa. xl, 26], is at the same time a guarantee of the reliableness of the senses. If the senses deceive us, then God deceives us. Just as without faith in God there is no morality, so also, without confidence in the truthfulness of the divinely established world-order—which of course includes the vital relations of creatures to each other—a complete morality is impossible. Man cannot be under obligation to be truthful, if creation is not so. The matter is therefore not so morally indifferent as at first glance it might seem. If God is to be seen in his works [Rom. i, 20] then must these works speak truthfully to us. If sense-impressions have only subjective truth, then they have none at all, and hence no worth whatever,—then we sustain no moral relation to the objective world, inasmuch as under such circumstances it would have *for* us no existence. There could then be no further question save of a moral duty of man to himself or to God. Skepticism on this point is therefore no less anti-moral than impious. Deceptions growing out of false *judgments* as to *per se* true sense-impressions, must of course not be confounded with the deception of sense-impressions themselves; it is not the *eye* that sees the sky touch the earth at the horizon, it is only a premature judgment that leads to this deception. Real sense-deceptions spring of disease, but disease does not exist in a state of moral purity.

The spirit is to dominate over nature, not directly, however, by a mere magic-working will, but by the instrumentality of its own dominated body. The destination to this domination is expressed even in the build of the human body: erect, with upturned look, with hands planned for the most manifold activity, the human body bears upon it the impress as well as the reality of dominating power. While Materialism subordinates spirit to nature, the Christian world-view subordinates nature to spirit; and as the spirit is entirely master over its body, so is it likewise master over nature by means of the body. A childish, morally-unripe spirit cannot, it is true, dominate nature at the will of its irrational whims, —but we speak here only of the rational spirit, and in this sphere the words, "the spirit is willing, but the flesh is weak," have no application; in normal man the flesh is also willing and strong. Even as through the senses nature is open and unlocked for the cognizing spirit, so is it also through the bodily organs for the volitionating spirit. If the facts seem otherwise in the present reality of things, if the body is no longer an absolutely obedient medium for the dominion of the spirit over nature, but on the contrary is much oftener a mere instrument of nature for her dominating over the spirit, this is simply because the right and primitive relation has been disturbed, and has given place to the enfeebling influence of sin.

SECTION LXVI.

3. The incipient limitation of the freedom of the normally self-developing spirit by the body in consequence of the dependent condition of the latter on external nature, is only the corresponding normal expression of the still existing unfreedom of the, as

yet, unmatured spirit, and is therefore also the protection of the same against its own immaturity,—a divinely-intended means of discipline for the same. But this primarily limiting relation of the body to the spirit is only transient, and is not a real trammeling. The body, while following in its own development the growth of the spirit in rationality and freedom, passes gradually over from its at first predominantly determining and conditioning character to that of being predominantly determined and conditioned by the spirit; and in its ultimate perfection,—as corresponding to the full moral maturity of the spirit,—it becomes perfectly spirit-imbued and spirit-appropriated,—the absolutely subservient organ of the emancipated spirit,—becomes a perfectly spiritualized and transfigured body, which latter, as being developed by a regular growth out of the original unfree nature-body, is conditioned neither on a violent death of the nature-body nor is subject itself to death, seeing that it is simply the necessary and normal organ of the immortal spirit.

It would be an injustice in the Creator, and a God-repugnant defect in creation, were the essentially free and morally matured spirit bound in unfreedom by a *per se* irrational nature; and the anti-scriptural notion, that the rational spirit has been banished into a body, as into a prison, in punishment for the sins of a previous life, would then be the sole possible justification of the Creator. But the conditional unfreedom of the spirit such as we must admit also for the unfallen state, namely, that it is limited by the natural alternation of sleeping and waking [comp. Gen. ii, 21] by the natural wants of food, etc., [comp. Gen. i, 29, 30], is not against but for the spirit. It reminds the personal spirit of its belonging to the *per se* unitary and law-governed All, its regulated connection with nature; it protects the, as yet, inexperienced spirit from unwise presumption, from arbitrary irrational meddling with the divinely-established order of the world,—teaches it to submit itself to the divinely-willed and ordered laws of existence, teaches it humility, and brings to its consciousness its dependence on God's power, thereby impressing upon it the lesson that it can attain to true freedom only by a free and cheerful self-denial in relation to the will of God. Hunger, *e. g.*, is the most powerful stimulus to activity, and hence to the development of the spirit, and ever *since* the entrance of sin into the race there has been no other so sure and effectual a means of stirring up the spirit out of its slothful indolence [Prov. xvi, 26, in the original]. In the present state of man hunger is not only of significance for the individual, it is a world-historical power, the first and most persistent stimulus to civilization. Unfallen humanity, it is true, knows nothing of any hunger-*stress*, but it knows it as a want requiring satisfaction; and it is not a feature of the suffering but of the true humanity of Christ, that he also felt hunger.

That which was a disciplining beginning, however, is not to be permanent; but it is not the body, but only the limiting power of the same that is to pass away. The view that the body is not a permanent condition of the spirit, but only a prison-house destined to destruction,—a merely useless burdening incident of the spirit,—is a very favorite one, it is true, but it is a very un-Christian one. What God does is done well, and he has given the body to the spirit for perfect service, and not for a burden and a clog. Of the notion that the original body is only a worthless case or husk, to be cast off like the chrysalis of the butterfly, the Scriptures know nothing;—the dissolving of the earthly house [2 Cor. v, 1] applies only to the body of sin and death [Gen. iii, 19];—the body is originally, on the contrary, the divinely-established *permanent* condition of true life, though indeed not an absolutely necessary condition of the life of the spirit in general. Christ, the perfect man, shows in his own person what the human body signifies and is; Christ's resurrection is a stone of stumbling for all one-sided spiritualism. Christ lives on, not as a mere bodiless spirit, but in his now *glorified* body, and he will transfigure our sin-ruined body that it may be like unto *his* glorious body [Phil. iii, 21]. This transfiguration, though *without* death—not a being unclothed, but a being clothed upon [2 Cor. v, 4]—is the original purpose of the body given to the immortal spirit as its subservient organ. The spirit's body is in fact, as such, no longer a mere nature-object, but, as the exclusive possession of an immortal subject, it is also itself raised above the perishableness incident to all mere nature-objects.—*Death* is in the Scriptures uniformly referred back to *sin;* and the great emphasis which the New Testament lays upon the resurrection of the body indicates what the original body was to have been. If it is the moral destination of the spirit to be free, to dominate by reason over the merely natural, then death, as a violent interruption of life, comes into direct antagonism with this destination; it indicates a complete ascendency of unconscious nature over spirit, the impotency of the spirit in the face of nature—a condition of the real bondage of spirit to nature. Were this wide-reaching antagonism between the actual state and the moral nature of the spirit the original condition, and were it included in the nature of things or in the creative will itself, then the nerve of all morality would be paralyzed, and all moral courage broken. To struggle against too great odds is folly; if irrational nature is more powerful than the moral spirit, then the latter can rationally take no better course than to yield to superior force, and to place its own sensuous nature higher than its spiritual.

C.—THE UNITY OF THE SPIRIT AND THE BODY.

SECTION LXVII.

In virtue of the union of spirit and body into one personality, the spirit is manifoldly determined also in its moral life, and it appears in consequence under different phases of existence, which occasion also correspondingly different manifestations of morality.

1. *The stages of life.* The spirit is dependent in its development on that of the body, not absolutely, however, but only relatively; the development-stages of the moral spirit—which do not entirely coincide

with those of the body, but only in general and partially run parallel therewith—are the following:— (*a*) The stage of moral *minority*, childhood. Here the body is as yet master over the spirit; the spirit is as yet in most things essentially unfree—dependent on outer, sensuous, and spiritual influences,—is more guided than self-guiding.—(*b*) The stage of *transition* to majority,—still wavering between freedom and unfreedom; morality appears essentially under the form of free *obedience* toward educators.—(*c*) The stage of moral *majority*. The person has come into possession of himself,—is actually master over himself as regards moral self-determination, is able by his moral consciousness to guide himself independently; hence he is fully morally responsible, and is in process of developing an independent *character*.— A relapsing of the morally matured into a state of moral irresponsibility, a becoming childish, is not conceivable in a normal condition of humanity, though here there would doubtless, indeed, be a greater turning away from merely earthly things, and a growing preoccupation with the supernatural, —in the stage of moral *old age*.

The development of a spirit as united with a body, consists in one of its phases in the fact that it more and more throws off its primarily normal greater dependence on the corporeal life,—that it becomes freer, ripens toward maturity. Although we cannot conceive of the first created human beings as beginning life in a state of unconscious childhood, still the above-mentioned stages of life, seeing that they are implied in the very nature of self-development, must hold good, at least, of all succeeding generations; and even the first man could not appear at once as a perfectly mature, morally-ripened spirit, but had to pass through similar stages of development. According to the naturalistic view, the spiritual development is exclusively and absolutely conditioned on that of the body —is only the bloom and vigor of the same. This assertion, as well as the theory on which it is based, is refuted by the simple matter of fact that spiritual development often far outruns that of the body, and in fact in a normal development must do so, and also that in persons of precisely equal bodily development, the spiritual ripeness may be very widely different. In an as yet unmatured body there may be a mature spirit, in a weak and ailing body, a strong spirit; this would be inconceivable on the naturalistic hypothesis. But especially the *moral* development may come to ripeness of character much earlier than the corporeal life; growth in knowledge is much more dependent on the development of the body; the understanding does not outrun the years, and children that are early ripe intellectually, are usually morbid phenomena; but a very youthful soul may acquire a real and firm *moral* character. The proverb, "Youth is without virtue," in so far as it is meant to be an excuse, is absolutely immoral and perverse.

In consequence of the normal super-ordination of the spirit to the body, the spiritual development-stages do not coincide, in point of time, with the corresponding bodily stages, but precede them somewhat. The first stage is that of childlike innocence, where the child as yet knows not how to distinguish between good and evil [Isa. vii, 16], where, as yet, the moral consciousness slumbers, and the life-activity does not spring from a will conscious of a moral purpose, but, on the contrary, from unconscious feelings which are directly excited by external or sensuous influences; hence an accountability proper cannot as yet be presumed. The child has indeed propensions and aversions, love and anger, and other states of feeling, but it does not have them intelligently,—is not as yet in spiritual self-possession. Obedience is, as yet, a mere scarcely-conscious *following*, taking its rise simply from natural feelings and from the instinct of imitation, and which is indeed a germ of morality, though not, as yet, actual morality, but is, in fact, also found to some extent among domesticated animals. The typical character of children as presented by Christ [Matt. xviii, 3] does not relate to any moral perfection in them, but only to their receptiveness for moral impressions, to their innocence, to their consciousness of need, and their readiness to believe.

The stage of transition, or youth, is the time when the person can distinguish between good and evil, and where, consequently, there exists a real moral consciousness, though not one that is thoroughly formed and in every case self-determining, but only primarily a consciousness of good and evil in general, and the particular application of which in single cases is, for the most part, not left to personal free self-determination, but to the guidance of educators. The boy has the definite law, as yet, only in an objective manner, in the will of his parents; his moral consciousness sketches only general outlines,—for the more definite traits and shades it is as yet dependent on some other, to him objective, consciousness. Hence the most characteristic form of the morality of this period is obedience; and the greatest danger to morality, so long as this partial uncertainty yet remains, is the tendency, readily resulting from the incipient consciousness of moral self-determination, to wish to determine one's conduct in particular cases directly and immediately from the, as yet, only general and indefinite moral consciousness,—that is, the tendency to premature freedom, the pleasure in an unregulated enjoyment of freedom, in arbitrary self-determination. This in fact was the danger to which our first parents fell a prey.

The stage of moral maturity, in a normal development, far more than overtakes that of bodily ripeness. While civil law fixes the civil majority, that is, the time of ripe understanding, at the period of full bodily maturity, the *moral* community, the Church, declares man as *morally* mature much earlier (confirmation); also the state fixes full moral responsibility much earlier than the civil majority. These distinctions rest on well-grounded experience. The young man knows not merely moral duty in general, but he is also capable of conforming his life thereto in particular. Obedience to parents or guardians assumes now the form of obedience to the moral law, which latter indeed includes the former, but no longer as an essentially unconditional obedience, but simply as one that is to be *subordinated to* the moral law. But a morally mature person can come into an actual conjuncture where it is necessary to refuse obedience to parents, only on the presupposition of a morally disordered state of humanity; and also civil law finds in such obedience, after years of moral majority, no excuse for criminal acts.

The becoming-childish of the aged would be a very weighty reason for doubting of personal immortality, were it a normal phenomenon of old age. When, however, we consider that even in the present sin-disordered condition of the race, this becoming-childish is by no means a necessary and universal phenomenon, but that, on the contrary, the fruit of a morally-pious life—even in far advanced age, and despite the otherwise slumber-like obscuration of the intellectual faculties—is a *heightening* of the religious and moral consciousness, and that even the better forms of heathenism consider reverence for the moral wisdom of the aged as a high virtue,—we can readily, then, infer from this, how little room there would be for a real becoming-childish in any respect whatever in an unfallen state of humanity. Precisely *what* would have been the characteristics of normal old age in a sinless state, we know not; this much, however, we do know, that the life of an immortal spirit, as being destined to a higher ennoblement or transfiguration, and as not subject to a positive violent death, could not be liable to a return to a state of moral minority,— at the farthest it would only have prepared itself for this freely self-accomplishing ennobling, by a greater turning away from earthly things. All senility of age we can regard only as an absolutely abnormal sin-born phenomenon, seeing that it stands in manifest antagonism to the nature and destination of the personal spirit.

SECTION LXVIII.

2. Differences of *temperament*—the different tempers of the spirit in its bearing toward the outer world, as determined by differences of bodily peculiarity. These differences are—as an expression of that manifoldness of being which is necessary to the perfection of the whole—*per se* good, and give rise to a vital reciprocalness of relation among the members of society. As mere natural determinations of

the spirit they have primarily no moral significance; they receive such, however, as conditions of the moral life. They do not constitute moral character; on the contrary, they are, in their disproportionateness, to be controlled by the character, and trained into virtue.—Related to the temperaments are the normal differences in the natural peculiarities of *nations*.

From a naturalistic stand-point great importance is attributed to temperaments, as if they were original *moral* determinations. But that which is original and merely natural is not as yet moral; it is only the antecedent condition of the moral. Moral character is not determined by nature, but only by the free action of man himself; in proportion as we consider the moral as determined by nature, we destroy its very essence. While the ancients considered the temperaments rather in their purely corporeal significance, in recent times emphasis is often given rather to their spiritually-moral significance, to the detriment of morality. On this point there has been much fallacious speculation, and the inclination is in many respects manifest, to attempt to comprehend man in his moral peculiarity from mere nature-circumstances, rather than honestly to look into his moral nature—to search his heart; and men are very ready to excuse their moral foibles and vices on the score of temperament; this course is naturalistic, and, in fact, materialistic. Temperament is, essentially, simply the normal basis on which morality is to develop itself; it does not, however, itself determine the moral life-task, but only has influence in throwing it into its peculiar form; he whose character is shaped only by his temperament has no character. The moral character stands *above* all temperament; and where there are different and opposed temperaments like moral characters may be formed, and the converse. Temperaments are not *per se* a peculiarity of the *spirit*, but are based in that of the corporeal life, and pass over upon the spirit only by virtue of a kind of *communicatio idiomatum*. It is usual to distinguish four temperaments,—according to the susceptibility for external influences, and to the active bearing toward the outer world: (1) that which is very open for outward impressions, and is at the same time more acted upon from without than self-active—the *light*, sanguine temperament;—(2) that which is very open for outward impressions, but is at the same time rather self-active, initiatively working, and influencing the outer world—the *warm*, choleric temperament;—(3) that which is less receptive for outward impressions, and at the same time rather inactive, indifferent—the *cool*, phlegmatic temperament;—(4) that which, while equally feebly-receptive for outward impressions, is yet more active, storing up in itself what it receives—the *heavy* melancholic temperament.—The types of temperament, however, do not usually appear under these pure forms; generally they are commingled and toned down. Nor does a temperament always remain the same, but it changes with the outward relations and age of the person.

As the moral person is not to permit himself to be determined by the irrational, but should himself freely determine himself on the basis of the moral consciousness, hence he is all the more moral the more he subordinates his temperament to his moral will,—not cultivating simply those virtues which are more congenial to his temperament, as, for example, friendliness in the sanguine, patience in the phlegmatic, courage in the choleric, etc. Morality consists rather, on the contrary, in the inner harmony of all the different moral phases, and must consequently counteract the one-sidedness of any particular temperament. The light temperament tends to frivolity, the warm to passionateness and revenge, the cool to indifference and indolence, the heavy to selfishness and narrowness. He who leaves his temperament unbridled, cultivates not its virtue but its defect; for virtue is never a mere nature-proclivity. As a peculiar endowment, temperament, like every other endowment, must be morally shaped, and hence brought into proper harmony with the moral whole of the life. No sin finds a moral justification in temperament; and, on the other hand, only that course of action is morally good which springs *not* merely from temperament, but from the moral consciousness.

The differences of natural *national peculiarities* are related to the difference of temperament. Also in a sinless state, a diversity among nations, a difference of taste, etc., arising primarily from differences of country, would be perfectly normal and necessary [Acts xvii, 26]. As the mountaineer is different in his entire bodily and spiritual temper from the dweller in the plain, the inhabitant of the North from him of the Tropics, etc., so there arises therefrom a diversity of forms of the moral life-work,—which, however, cannot come into hostile antagonism with each other, but in fact constitute a stimulating diversity, from which arises an all the greater and more vital harmony of the whole. Labor and enjoyment, the family-life and the life of society, will necessarily assume different forms; and the proper development and preservation of the normal peculiarities of nations form an essential feature of general moral perfection. It is not as a progress of spiritual and moral culture, but to some extent as a perversion thereof, that we must regard the tendency manifested in recent times to sweep away, to a large extent, the peculiarities of nations, and to bring about the greatest possible uniformity. Manifoldness of language and spirit is not confusion, and it has, as opposed to a bald, lifeless monotony, its legitimate moral right. The sons of Jacob, as differing in character, imparted also a normal difference to the tribes in Israel; nevertheless *one* spirit could and should have pervaded them all.

SECTION LXIX.

3. The difference of *sex* conditions a correspondingly different peculiarity of the moral life-work. Man represents the outward-working, productive phase of humanity, woman the receptive and formative,—he more the spirit-phase, she more the nature-phase; in him preponderate thought and will; in her rather the feelings, the heart; to man it is more peculiar to act initiatively,—to woman rather, morally to associate herself. The moral life-work of each is different in the details, but in both it is of like dignity; it is simply two different mutually-complementing phases of the same morality. The

morality of both sexes consists, in fact, in especially developing that phase of the moral life that is peculiar to each,—not as strictly the same as, but as in harmony with, the peculiarity of the other.

The antithesis of the two sexes is the highest spiritualized manifestation of that primitive antithesis of the operative and the reposing, the active and the passive, that conditions all earthly life,—that assumes an endless variety of forms, and appears in each single phenomenon of the world under some of its many forms of combination. Nowhere do we find mere force, nowhere mere matter, but every-where in nature both are united; and yet they are not the same. What this primitive antithesis is in nature,—what the greater antitheses of the light and the heavy, repulsion and attraction, motion and rest, sun and planet, animal and plant, arteries and veins, etc., are,—this is, in highest refinement and perfection, the antithesis of man and woman in humanity. That the nature-phase is somewhat more prominent in woman than in man is evidenced also by the earlier physical development and maturity of the female sex, and by the greater dependence on nature and on the changes of the seasons in the entire female sex-life. The higher intellectual power is undoubtedly with man, and the moral subordination of woman to man in wedlock and in society is an unmistakable law of universal order. The difference of the two sexes is not to be toned down, but to be developed into moral harmony. As an effeminate man or masculine woman is offensive to the esthetic sense, and a hermaphrodite repugnant to uncorrupted feelings, and a sexless form expressionless and unnatural, so also, in moral respects, it is the duty of man to cultivate his manliness, and of woman to cultivate her womanliness; and any assumption by one party of the peculiarities of the opposite sex, is not only unnatural but also immoral.

II. THE COMMUNITY-LIFE AS A MORAL SUBJECT.

SECTION LXX.

Man is not simply an individual being, but, by virtue of his moral rationality, which seeks everywhere to reduce the manifold to unity, he effects also a moral community-life, a community of persons, to which the individual is related as a serving member, and which has in turn itself a definite moral life-purpose, to the fulfilling of which the individual members are indeed called, though this moral life-purpose, that is to be carried out by the individual, is not identical with the life-work which he, as a personal individual, has to fulfill for himself. A plurality of persons constitutes a moral community-life only when, in virtue of a real common-consciousness, and a common moral life-purpose, they are molded into a life-unity, so that the individual members bring not only the whole into active relation to themselves, but also and essentially themselves into active relation to the whole; and the moral life of the individual is the more perfect the more it develops itself into a life of the whole; and the ultimate goal of moral development is, that all humanity become a *unitary* moral community. The true morality of the individual assumes therefore always a twofold form: one that is personally-individual, and one that is an expression of the moral life-purpose of the community-life, and in the name of which it fulfills that purpose; neither is subordinate to the other, but they stand in vital reciprocity of relation.

The notion of the community-life as a moral subject is of very great significance for ethics. Heathenism attained to it but very imperfectly, inasmuch as the thought of the unity of mankind was entirely wanting, and as where the community-life was most prominent—in China—there only a naturalistic, mechanical world-theory prevailed, and as, on the contrary, where the personal spirit came into prominence—in the Occident—there it did so only in the form of the strong individual will,—that is, the will did not appear as general but as individual and arbitrary, so that the community-life itself bore the impress of the individual will. In the Israelitic theocracy we find, in virtue of the divine disciplinary purpose, only the embryonic beginnings of the community-life; as yet, the morality of the individual prevails over the collective morality. But to the idea of the latter itself there is very clear allusion. The words, "I will make of thee a great nation; . . . in thee shall all families of the earth be blessed" [Gen. xii, 2, 3], are not a mere blessing, but they imply also for Abraham a moral duty, namely, that he live not for himself, but also for his people, and through them for the whole race,—that he work and act not merely as Abram but as Abraham, as the father of nations [Gen. xvii, 5]. Christianity brought the great idea to realization; the truth that makes man truly free rendered again possible the founding of a true moral community,—primarily as the Church, but then also as the Christian state. The idea of moral *communion* becomes here at once a fundamental one. Personal communion with the personal Son of God and of Man as chief, creates the true, vital moral community-life; the individual lives for the community and the community for the individual, and both through Christ and for Christ. This circumstance is very suggestive as to the moral destination of humanity as sinless.

The moral activity of the individual person as such is clearly to be distinguished from the moral activity of the same as an embodiment of the public morality. The mere circumstance, that in a state of sinfulness these two forms of morality may appear in antithesis and contradiction—that a man may perform his duty as a citizen to a certain degree of serviceableness, while his personal morality stands very low—shows that in the thing itself there is a real difference. What I do as a vital member of the moral community—as it were out of the spirit of the same, and to some extent, in the name of and as representing the same, that is, what I do, not because I am a moral individual, but because I belong, as a part, to a moral community,—that must of course, under circumstances of moral maturity, be in entire harmony with my personal moral disposition; but harmony is not identity. As representing the moral community-life and the common consciousness, my personal individual will retires essentially into the back-ground, and the public spirit possesses me and guides me,—rules sovereignly in me, and thrusts aside even my otherwise legitimate individual weal. The warrior, in fighting for his country, acts not from his personal individual will; he seeks, in case he enters into it morally, nothing for himself, but every thing solely for his country; he sacrifices his personal right to domestic happiness, to quiet labor, to legitimate enjoyments, and even his life itself, for the community, —not as a personal individual, but as a vital member of the nation. The morality of the individual bears more a masculine, that of the community more a feminine character, inasmuch as in the latter case there is a predominancy of yielding to influence, of self-associating, of devotion even to sacrifice. The moral honor of a community is other than that of the individual; when the soldier defends the flag of his regiment, it is not, or should not be, his own honor, but that of the entire body, that prompts him; and where there is honor, there there is also morality.

The distinction of this twofold morality presents itself, under one of the special forms of the second phase, namely, *official* morality, as recognizable also outwardly. What the clergyman, the soldier, the judge does officially, is also morality, but it is not by any means identical with his personal morality, as is shown even by the fact of the different degrees of censure incurred for violations of duty in the two spheres. An untruth, a deception, perpetrated in official activity, is much more severely punished, and deserves also severer moral rebuke, than a like act done in non-official life. He who is acting in a public capacity is not at liberty to overlook an offered indignity, while his very first duty when insulted in a private capacity, is, to manifest a readiness for reconciliation. The moral community often expresses this difference in the fact that those who act principally and professionally in its name, wear a special official garb, so that the entire external appearance and bearing of such public persons are not governed merely by their personally free self-determination, but bear the impress of that which transcends the individual will, namely, the community-life; personal character, while realizing public morality, falls back behind the character of the community-life. Nevertheless it is true that the *whole* moral activity and life of the individual contributes essentially to the honor or shame of the family and of the community to which he belongs [Lev. xxi, 9], so that consequently this distinction of a twofold moral sphere of activity does not amount to a real separation.

CHAPTER II.

GOD AS THE GROUND AND PROTOTYPE OF THE MORAL LIFE AND AS THE AUTHOR OF THE LAW.

SECTION LXXI.

As morality is connected with religion in an indissolubly vital unity, hence the God-consciousness is the necessary presupposition and condition of morality, and the character and degree of the morality is consequently also conditioned on the character and degree of the God-consciousness, although a higher degree of the latter does not *necessarily* work also a higher degree of morality. Hence true morality is only there possible where there is a true God-consciousness, that is, where God is not conceived of as in some manner limited, but as the infinite Spirit in the fullest sense of the word. Only where the moral idea has its absolutely perfect *reality*, in the personal holy God, has morality a firm basis, true contents, and an unconditional goal.

If morality is in any manner conditioned by religion, then is also the *quality* of this morality different in different religions. We have already shown that morality is not conditioned by the mere God-consciousness, but only by it as having grown into religion, for a God-consciousness which does not become a religious one, but remains mere knowledge, cannot become a moral power; and this is the simple explanation of the fact, that while a feebler God-consciousness cannot produce a higher degree of morality, yet a higher God-consciousness does not necessarily create also a higher degree of morality,—namely, when it does not develop itself into a religious life-power. When it does so develop itself, however, then it is unconditionally true that the degree of morality perfectly corresponds to the degree of God-consciousness;—otherwise we would be forced to modify our previously assumed position, that religion and morality are two indissolubly united and mutually absolutely conditioning phases of one and the same spiritual life. Where God is conceived of as merely an unspiritual nature-force, as in China and India, there morality cannot rest on the free moral personality of man, but, on the contrary, it must throw the personality into the back-ground as illegitimate; where the divine is conceived of only in the form of an antagonism of mutually hostile divinities, as with the Persians, there the moral idea lacks its unconditional obligatoriness, and in fact the contra-moral has its relative justification; and where the divine is conceived of as a plurality of limited individual personalities, there the sphere of morality is invaded by the pretensions of the arbitrarily self-determining subject, and moral action lacks a solid basis. It is only where there is a consciousness of the infinite personal Spirit that both the moral personality is free, and the moral idea absolutely unconditional and sure. The heathen do not really *have* the divine law; they have only, lying in the very nature of the rational spirit, an unconscious presentiment of the same [Rom. ii, 14, 15].—Though Polytheism is with us no longer in fashion, still we are all the more infested with Pantheism, or such a form of Deism as differs therefrom only by an unscientific arbitrary inconsequence,—not, however, by any means with that vigorous and comparatively respectable Pantheism of India which drew, with moral earnestness, the full practical consequence of its world-theory, and presented in an actually-carried-out renunciation of the world the very contrary of our natural and legitimate claim to happiness,—but, on the contrary, with a Pantheism that is in every respect morbid and characterless, and which, greedy of enjoyment, delights itself in a world robbed of God. Pantheism lacks the *antecedent condition* of all morality, namely, personal freedom; with the universal prevalence of unconditional necessity there is no place for choice and self-determination; it also lacks a moral purpose, seeing that it knows no ideal, reality-transcending goal of morality, but, on the contrary, must acknowledge the real as *per se* the fulfillment of the ideal, that is, as good,—and for the reason that that which appears as a goal of life-development, is, in fact, realized from necessity; it lacks also a moral *motive*, for the sole causative ground of the absolutely necessary life-development is, as unfree and as unfreely-acting, non-moral,—is only a conscious nature-impulse. On the assumption that the entire being and activity of the individual is simply a necessary expression of the existence and life which God generates for himself in the world, it follows that each and every being is fully and perfectly justified in whatever nature and activity he may chance to appear, and no one can reproach another because of any seeming moral depravity. The moral tendencies of Pantheism, and of the therewith essentially identical Naturalism, must not be judged of from individual instances of men who are still unconsciously imbued with the moral spirit of the community, but rather from the effects that result where this world-theory has taken hold on the *masses*,—as at the time of the Reign of Terror in France, and in the bearing and aspirations of our more recent demagogues of reform, nearly all of whom are imbued with Pantheistic views.

SECTION LXXII.

The personal God is the basis of the moral, (1) in that He, as *holy will*, is the eternal fountain and embodiment of the moral idea. The good is not a mere object of a *possible* willing, not merely *ought* to be willed, but *is* eternally willed by an eternal will, and is nothing other than the contents of this will itself; God is the absolutely moral spirit, the *holy* spirit—perfectly at one with himself in his free personality, and eternally self-consistent,—and who as such guarantees to the moral life-task of his free creatures, full truth, unconditional and permanent validity as God's requirement, and unshaken certainty, and perfect, constant unity and consistency.

Outside of the Christian God-consciousness the moral idea lacks all certainty and strength. It is easy to say, that we should do the good for its own sake, that the moral law presents itself as a "categorical imperative," but in the reality of life such generalities will not avail. For a mere idea without any sort of reality, no human heart can grow actively warm; here there is at best only an intellectual interest, but not a morally-practical one. The validity of the moral idea must have a deeper basis than a mere intellectual process. Before I can do the good for its own sake, I must love it; before I love it, I must with full certainty know it. So long as I am in doubt as to what is good, or as to whether there is any good, I have no object of love. The essence of the good, however, implies that the same is not my merely subjective opinion, but that it is universally valid—good *per se*. Now, should I leave the God-consciousness out of sight, then there would remain for me, in order to determine the unconditional validity of a supposed moral precept, and to avoid the possibility of a mere arbitrary judgment, no other resort than the impracticable test of Kant.* Suppose, however, that, apart from religious faith, there were in fact a scientific source for a certain knowledge of the moral law, still this would not yet answer the purpose;—not every one can be a philosopher, but all are required to be moral. Hence the moral consciousness cannot be based on mere scientific demonstrations, but must have a basis available for all rational men; now just such a resource is the God-consciousness. So soon as I know that a mode of action is *God's* will, then am I perfectly certain that it is *good*, that it has universal and unconditional validity;— I have not to infer that because it is universally valid, therefore it is God's will, but the converse. Without certainty of moral consciousness there can be no moral confidence; in this connection all doubt works ruin. The question is as to certainty of moral consciousness, and hence essentially as to God's will's becoming known to me.

So soon as there exists a consciousness of God, *all* good must be referred absolutely to God's will; whatever God wills is good, and whatever is good is God's will. The

---

* Namely: "Act so that the maxim of thy conduct shall be adapted to become a universal law for *all* men."

divine order of the world assumes, in the sphere of the free will of creatures, the form of a moral command; the "must" becomes a "should;" this is not a lowering, but an exalting of the law, for freely realized good is higher than the unfreely realized, seeing that God himself is freedom. If a moral duty is God's will, then I am also further certain that it cannot be in real conflict with other moral duties. This is the high *moral* significancy of faith in the living God, namely, that it alone can give a full unity and certainty to the moral consciousness; with every limitation of the idea of God the moral consciousness also becomes uncertain and doubtful. Hence the Scriptures, even in the Old Testament, attribute such high significancy to the unity and unchangeableness of the holy and almighty God as moral law-giver, and base thereon, in contrast to heathenism, all morality,—as, for example, in Gen. xvii, 1; Deut. vi, 4 sqq.; x, 14, 17. In the first passage God's omnipotence is emphasized in order to awaken in man a consciousness of his dependence; inasmuch as *all* existence is absolutely in God's hand, therefore *should* also man's free activity subordinate itself to Him,—therefore also is the sinful effort to be independent of God, that is, to be equal to God, unmitigated folly. Hence also he, who walks *before* the Almighty, has the assurance that he will attain to his goal; thou canst, for the reason that thou shouldst, for it is God who places upon thee the "should."

But the certainty of the moral idea is only one of its phases, the other is its actuating *power*. It is true, the idea itself of the good should move the will; but its power is immeasurably greater when it is itself the expression of a holy will than when it merely speaks *to* the human will. It is the sacred awe of the Holy One that lends it this power. In a mere idea I can have pleasure, but it cannot inspire me with awe. The command that emanates from the Living One, gives life; a mere idea pre-supposes life as a condition of its efficacy. The moral idea becomes truly influential on the personal spirit only by its being the actual will of a personal God. "The statutes of the Lord are right, rejoicing the heart; the commandment of the Lord is pure, enlightening the eyes" [Psa. xix, 8].

The question: is a thing good because God wills it, or does

God will it because it is good? contains for us no contradiction. It would do so, however, if the first clause meant, that it is accidental and arbitrary that God declares this or that to be good, and that He might also just as well have declared good the very opposite (Duns Scotus, Occam, Descartes, Pufendorf). God cannot will anything else than what is God-like—corresponding to his nature; this "cannot" is a limitation only in the form of expression, in reality it is the highest perfection. A being that can come into contradiction and antagonism with itself, is not perfect. If the good is that which corresponds to the divine nature, and if God's will is necessarily an expression of his nature, then, whatever is good is good because God wills it, and God wills it because it is good. God's declaration: "I am that I am" [Exod. iii, 14] is valid also for his holy volitions. The idea of the good is not something existing without and apart from God, it is a direct beam from his inner nature.

SECTION LXXIII.

God is the basis of the moral, (2), in that He *reveals* himself in his universe as the *Holy* One,—discovers himself to man as the *prototype* of the moral, as the personally holy pattern after which man should form himself. In this consciousness of God as prototype of the moral, man conceives morality as *Godlikeness*, and himself, in his true moral dignity, as God's *image* and as a child of God.

The idea of a *moral* self-revelation of God is of wide-reaching moral significancy. Heathenism knows nothing of such a self-revelation; it is true, in the higher heathen religions, moral laws are referred to a divine origin, but this signifies simply either a revelation of the general laws of world-order, or, at best, a revelation of the divine will *in regard to* men, but not of the real moral nature of God. According to the Christian world-view, the good is not merely *to be realized*, but it exists already in full reality from eternity; morality is not to create something absolutely new, but only to shape the created after the model of its divine Creator; the free creature is to become *like* the holy God,—to come into free harmony, not simply with a naked idea but with an eternal reality. As a consequence of this, morality has an incomparably higher certainty and vitality than if the moral law appeared merely under the form of an idea. There can be no more convincing logic than the word: "Ye shall be holy, for I the Lord your God am holy" [Lev. xix, 2; xi, 44, 45; xx, 7; comp. Deut. x, 17 *sqq.*; 1 Pet. i, 15, 16; Eph. v, 1]; and Christ himself repeatedly presents the moral essence of God as the true pattern for man, both in general and in particular [Matt. v, 48; Luke vi, 36]. Even as in education there is no better moral instruction than that by personal example, so is there also in the moral education of humanity no more deeply influential moral revelation than that of the holy personality of God; and as the child naturally seeks not so much to realize a lifeless law as to become like a beloved and revered personal example, so is it likewise the case in the moral development of humanity in general; and this is not childlike immaturity, but rational truth; and herein also is the child a proper example. In realizing morality man does not present himself in the All as a solitarily-shining star, but as a God-loved and God-loving image of the invisible God,—as a human resplendence of His holiness.

A much deeper impression than that made by the revelation of the holy personality of God through speech, is made by the revelation of the same by actual reality in the *person of Christ*. We cannot answer here the oft proposed question as to whether the Son of God would have become man even had not sin entered into the world; the Scriptures give us on this point no decision; and even those who affirm it do not place the advent of the perfect man at the beginning of the race. Hence, even in this view, the coming of Christ is not held as a necessary condition of the moral life. But as Christ is in fact not merely the Redeemer *suffering* for and through sin, but also the true personal manifestation of the perfect image of God—the absolutely perfect prototype of human morality,— hence, *for us*, who are no longer in the condition of original sinlessness, the knowledge of pure morality is essentially conditioned on a knowledge of Christ. The first sin-free human beings needed not *this* historically-personal example in order to have a truthful moral consciousness, and to be able to realize morality; but we need it—we who have had to be redeemed from the curse and power of sin; we need, also as a help to a knowledge of the morality of unfallen man, this example that did not rise *out of* sin but stood above it. In a much higher degree, in fact, than Christ is the example for the redeemed, is he the true criterion for a knowledge of unfallen human nature; for there is much in the moral life of the Christian for which Christ's own life cannot be a direct example; for instance, the continuous struggle against the still-remaining sin in the human heart,—in Christ there was no such struggle; to him every thing that was sinful was foreign and external, but never inward and personal. On the contrary, there could be nothing in the moral life of unfallen man which could not be directly connected with the person of Christ, though indeed, not all the *special* phases of human morality could have their particular expression in the life of Christ. Thus we have occasion here to make at least allusion to Christ.

SECTION LXXIV.

God is the basis of the moral, (3), in that, omnipresently ruling and judging in his universe, He wisely, lovingly, and justly guides and furthers toward its eternal goal the moral life of his creatures, without, however, interfering with their moral freedom. This consciousness gives to the moral life full confidence and joy in the fulfillment of the divine will, and the proper fear of all that is ungodly.

The thought of a merely impersonal moral world-order may seem in itself simple and attractive; for real life, however, it is of no efficiency. Even the proud equanimity of the Stoic is unable definitively to find any better remedy for the antagonism of the reality of existence with his self-conceived ideals, than suicide; and those who, in recent times, assuming that the Christian world-view is gloomy and unhumanitarian, prefer to it the domination of eternal impersonal necessity, and explain away all evil and anarchy as mere appearance, gain after all from this pretended self-explaining and all-reconciling view, little other profit than a complacent satisfaction with themselves and with their own system. So long as man cannot rid himself of his consciousness of freedom and of the possibility of its misuse, as well as of his consciousness of the reality of evil in the world, just so long will the notion of a world-order unembodied in a personal God prove to be powerless. The Greek had a much higher world-theory than that of ordinary Pantheism, and yet he could not explain away the antagonism that exists between the moral life and non-moral fate, or the excess of real evil; and he gave utterance, in his noblest intellectual productions, either to a melancholy lament over the mysterious tragedy of life, or to a blank hopelessness as to the triumph of the good. Greek tragedy is, by far, more moral than the anti-Christian Pantheism of recent date. To feel and bewail the antagonism of existence even with out-spoken hopelessness, approximates more nearly the truth than to explain it away with delusive sophistry. In a world where the misuse of moral freedom may create evil and disturb the harmony of existence, there can be hopefulness and confidence in moral effort only in virtue of a firm faith in the personally-ruling almighty and holy God; without this there is for the rational spirit no possibility of an unshaken conviction that a truly moral conduct will, in fact, bring real fruit, and not prove to be a useless vain undertaking, an empty play of a restless activity-instinct.—We are here as yet not dealing with a world actually disordered by sin; but also for the unfallen state all moral effort becomes impossible, becomes even idle folly, so soon as we assume even the *possibility* of a disturbance of the harmony of the world,—unless there exists at the same time the consciousness of a holy God freely ruling *above* all creature-life, and conducting the moral order of the universe. But the possibility of such a disturbance through the misuse of freedom, is directly implied in the idea of freedom. Hence the notion of a merely general world-order without a personally-ruling God does not suffice, even for the unfallen state, to give to moral effort the necessary confidence. The question is here as to a certainty not merely that the moral efforts of the individual will bear the expected fruit for himself,—though we must consider this also as a perfectly legitimate claim,—but also, in general, that his moral efforts will not be in vain for the furtherance of the perfection of the whole,—will not be counteracted by the possibly interfering power of evil. Without the confidence that by virtue of the all-potent wisdom of the personal God, *all* truly moral effort will bear legitimate fruit, and that evil can never prevent him who continues faithful, from reaching the last and highest goal of the moral, and that consequently the anarchy that evil brings into the world will fall only on the heads of the evil-doers, while even the "prince of this world" can effect nothing against the just [John xiv, 30],—without this confidence, the courage and vitality of all morality are paralyzed. Also in the unfallen state human knowledge must still be limited,—must be unable to see into the ultimate depths and ends of existence, and least of all into the future. Hence, without confidence there is no means of rising above doubt as to the success of moral effort, and consequently also of a degree of discouragement in the same. The true moral courage is not a blind defiance of fate, but a rejoicing in the consciousness that all things work to the good of those who love God [Rom. vii, 28], and that "in Him we live and move and have our being" [Acts xvii, 28],—that God, the ground and source of all morality, is not far from any one of us, but works in and with us for the accomplishment of his holy will. —And as effort for the good can be potent only through *confidence* in God, so also is the moral dread of evil effectual only through the *fear* of God. Not as if a mere fear of punishment were to restrain man from evil, but rather a *holy* awe of the holy and all-knowing God. This is also fear,—not, however, slavish, selfish fear, but moral reverence, befitting shame in the presence of the pure and holy One. To say that man should shun evil even irrespectively of God, is empty talk; if he believes in God, then he *cannot* leave Him out of thought at the sight of evil; and if he believes *not* in God, then he believes also not in the holiness of the moral command, and he will in fact not shun the evil,—he will simply deny it, as modern observation proves. The fear of the Lord is the beginning of wisdom, and also of morality [Psa. cxi, 10];

"fear the Lord and keep his commandments," says the Preacher [Eccles. xii, 13]; this is the fundamental idea of morality in the Old Testament [comp. Deut. x, 12, 13]. There is *one* Lawgiver and Judge who is able to save and destroy [James iv, 12]; in the unity of the lawgiver and judge lies the guarantee and holy potency of morality. Whoever believes, not merely in an All, but in the living God, and knows that all that is hidden from human eyes is known to the all-knowing One, and that all secret sins rest under the curse of Him who can kill and make alive, who can wound and heal, and out of whose hand there is none that can deliver [Deut. xxvii, 15 *sqq.*; xxxii, 39],—such a one will evidently have a very different dread of evil from that of him who regards it as a mere world-inherent necessary transition-stage to perfection.

SECTION LXXV.

God is the basis of the moral, (4), in that as holy *Lawgiver* he reveals his eternal, holy will in time. The totality of created being is, in the design of the creative will, to be in harmony with God and with itself. The idea of this harmony, as active in God under the form of will, is God's *law*. Unfree creatures have it as an inner necessity, and *must* fulfill it; free creatures have it as a *moral command*, and *should* fulfill it; for the former it exists as an unconscious instinct or impulse, for the latter it is *revealed*; as *God's* law, it is made known to rational creatures by revelation. The *moral law* is therefore the revealed will of God as to the rational creature,—namely, that the same should bring its entire life, consciously and with free will, into harmony with God's purpose.

A law which cannot be derived from God's will is not a moral law, but at best a civil one. That the moral law is based in the inner essence of the human reason is not controverted by the proposition, that it is God's will, but it is in fact confirmed. Human reason is conditioned by the same divine will which wills the good; and as, among the goods which God himself created, the highest is reason, hence the inner essence of the reason must involve also the moral,—not, however, as something conditioned independently of God, but in fact as God's will revealed to the reason, in so far as the latter has kept itself unclouded. However, this moral law, as immanent in the reason, is not to be conceived as implying that the rational *will* gives law unto itself; it is the part of the will to submit itself to the law, but not to give it; the moral law is *above* the will, *above* human reason in general; and the latter, in its consciousness of the same, recognizes it in fact as divine, and consequently as absolutely valid and beyond the scope of human determination. As little as man can give to himself reason and its dialectical laws, so little can he give to himself moral law. Freedom of will has to do only with the fulfilling, but not with the conditioning of the law. The morally cognizing reason simply *finds* revealed within itself the divine law, but does not *make* it. The Scriptures uniformly present the moral law as being essentially the will of God, without, however, thereby interfering with the idea that the same is the expression of the inner purpose of being itself. "Be ye transformed," says Paul, [Rom. xii, 2], "by the renewing of your mind, that ye may prove what is that good and acceptable and perfect will of God;" the "will" of God is here the fundamental; any thing is "good" only because it expresses the will of God which is itself good *per se;* the "acceptable" is that which is good relatively to the spirit that is contemplating it,—that excites approbation in the rational spirit, and is in harmony therewith,—in a word, that is in harmony with God and his thoughts, and with God-related spirit in general; and the "perfect," the goal-attaining, is whatever is the realization of the divine and good end. Thus the apostle expresses the essence of the good under all its phases; the good is good both as to its origin, as to the cognizing spirit, and as to its end.

SECTION LXXVI.

In treating of the moral law as the expression of the divine will, we have two points to consider, first, the communication of this law by God to man, and then its inner essence.

I. THE REVELATION OF THE DIVINE WILL TO MAN.

This revelation reveals to us not only the *contents* of the divine law, but must also reveal it as the *divine* will. This manifestation of the holy will of God is of a twofold character. In reason, which is the more especial embodiment of the divine image, and which is consequently the God-ward phase of man, man has the power of recognizing the divine will in regard to reason,—the rational life-purpose of the rational spirit. Hence, by virtue of his rationality, man has the divine law *in himself* as a personal knowledge attained to through free self-development. The divine will-revelation is therefore primarily an *inner* revelation *within* the rational spirit conditioned by the creative will itself. As, however, this knowledge cannot be a directly-given one, but must be first attained to by morally-spiritual activity, hence it cannot be for morality the sufficient antecedent condition. There is a necessity therefore, in order to the commencement of the morally-rational life of humanity, of a special *training* of the same by God unto moral knowledge,—of a direct extraordinary *objective* revelation by means of which man may have from the very beginning a definite consciousness as to the divine will, and a firm guarantee of the truth.

(*a*) The *extraordinary, positive* and *supernatural*

revelation of the divine will, in the educative guidance of man by God, precedes indeed his own reason-knowledge as arising from the inner, general, natural revelation, but in a normal development of man it then gradually retires into the back-ground in proportion as his spiritual ripening advances. Its purpose is to *awaken* rational knowledge, and to conduct the awakened spirit to its spiritual majority; and hence it involves the virtualizing of the moral freedom and of the independent personality of the rational spirit.

The seeming contradiction that lies in the facts, that rational knowledge cannot be given in an immediate and ready form, but must be first attained to through moral effort, and that, on the other hand, all moral activity presupposes already the consciousness of the moral, is reconciled solely and simply by the fact that the creating God is also an educating one,—that He reveals to man Himself and his will,—even as also the child does not ripen to reason and maturity by being abandoned to itself, but by being educated by reason and to reason,—by having the moral consciousness which as yet slumbers in it *awakened* by instruction, and, when once awakened, then strengthened by actual moral example. Without instruction and training the child never becomes a truly rational person; and when, in harmony with the Christian system, we affirm the same thing of the first man, we do not thereby state anything inconsistent with the nature of man, but in fact simply that which is implied in the very nature of rational spirit-development. If for a moment we should, with Rousseau, conceive of the first generations of man as in a condition of animal unculture, creeping on all fours, and without speech, then we are utterly unable to learn from any of the champions of this theory in what manner these human-like animals could ever attain to reason and to a moral consciousness. We have in fact, in the case of the uncivilized tribes of the race—who, low as they are, are yet not so low as the above-supposed semi-men,—positive proof that man when once sunk into the condition of a savage never again rises to a higher culture, of his own strength.

Without a consciousness of God and of his will, man is as yet, on the whole, not rational; but man was created by God after his own image, and hence unto reason and unto morality. This implies of itself that this consciousness was necessarily shared in even by the first man. Now as man knows nothing of nature save as nature communicates herself to him through sensuous impressions, so also can man know nothing of God unless God reveals himself to him; and in fact a God who should not reveal himself is utterly unconceivable. If now a consciousness of the moral, that is of God's will, is the necessary antecedent condition of all moral activity, and if, at the same time, all real rational knowledge springs from a moral using of such knowledge, then is it perfectly self-evident that the beginning of this knowledge must have been directly prompted by God himself. The fact that this first revelation is termed, in distinction from the self-wrought-out knowledge, an *extraordinary* and *supernatural* one, does not imply that it stands in contradiction or antagonism to the inner revelation in the self-developing spirit. On the contrary it is for the development of humanity in general both very natural and in harmony with general order; for, *all* life of individual objects, both in the spiritual and in the natural world, requires a first stimulation, an awakening influence from other already developed objects and beings; and this stimulating rises toward *educative* training in proportion as the perfection of the species rises; man has therefore, by virtue of his rational nature, a claim upon an educative influence from the rational spirit; and this is in fact the historical revelation. Man *is* not by his birth or creation already really a morally-rational spirit, he *becomes* so only by an educative influence from the rational spirit, and hence, in the case of the first man, from a primarily objective revelation from God. This revelation, however, does not *remain* in this objective character, but, in stimulating man to a moral consciousness and to moral activity, it brings him to the inner revelation in the rational nature of man himself—to a consciousness of his own God-likeness, and hence also to a consciousness of the divine prototype. The first man sustained to God an absolutely child-like relation, as to an educating *father;* and such is precisely the Biblical account of the primitive state. If we do not presuppose such an educative primitive revelation of the moral, then, either the moral law would have to exist, (as in irrational nature-creatures, so also in man) as a direct instinctive impulse,—in which case man would not be a moral being, but only a peculiar species of animal; or, a rational knowledge of the moral would have to be already created in him,—which would be contrary to all our notions of man's spiritual development, and surely a much greater miracle than the one which it was designed to dispense with. That which has no need of training is either not a rational being, or it is God himself. The educative revelation presupposes indeed a corresponding moral endowment in man; but this moral endowment, the unconscious germ of the moral, has need, in order to its developing itself into reality, of a spiritual training. This training does not *create* the moral consciousness, but only awakens it—gives to it primarily definite contents, which the thus stimulated morally rational consciousness then perceives as not in antagonism but as in harmony with itself, and for that very reason appropriates to itself.

In order to man's being really moral he must be conscious that in his free acting he freely subordinates himself to the will of God; but he can do this only when he recognizes the moral, not merely as such, but also as being of divine origin, and this he can do only when he distinguishes the divine will from his own; this distinguishing, however, is possible, for the first man, only when the divine will presents itself to him as other than his own, as objective to him,—when God expressly reveals himself to him. On this definite *distinguishing* of one's own personal, from the divine will, depends all morality; a merely unconscious following of propension is not moral, but immoral. Man must become conscious that he does this or that act not simply because it pleases *him*, but that it pleases him because it pleases God. In this conscious, discriminating, free choosing of the divine will as distinguished from the merely natural individual will, man is expected to discover his essential difference from nature, his belonging to the kingdom of God; he is to learn to distinguish between "can" and "should," between his ability and his obligation, and thus to become conscious of his moral destination to freedom. Were the moral consciousness or the moral impulse inborn in man, then he could not come to a consciousness of his freedom—of his ability morally to rise *above* his merely individual being, and freely to choose the divine. Herein lies the high *moral* significancy of the notion of an historical divine revelation. In the interest of *freedom*, in the interest of the training of man into a moral *personality*, we would have been forced philosophically, to presuppose such a revelation, did we not already know of it from Biblical teaching.

SECTION LXXVII.

(*b*) The *inner* revelation of the holy will of God in the rational consciousness of man is not a mere *instinctive impulse*, as this is the characteristic of irrational nature-creatures, nor is it a mere *feeling*, inasmuch as this, so far as relating to spiritual things, always presupposes a knowledge, a consciousness, but it is a real *consciousness*, which, however, is at first only obscure and indefinite, and receives more definite contents only through educative revelation, whereby it is developed into full clearness. The inner and the objective revelations, though differing from each other as to the order of their taking-place and as to their form, do not differ in their essential contents, nor indeed as to their certainty; and the objective revelation is no more rendered superfluous by the inner one, than is the latter by the former; each mutually calls for the other.

Just as the educative influencing of the child does not render superfluous its own active moral self-development, but in fact calls for the same as its end, and as the latter without the former is not possible, so is it also with the twofold revelation. If the historical revelation did not lead to a knowledge of the moral law as immanent in the reason itself, man would remain in perpetual nonage,—would not come to a consciousness of his rationality; in fact this revelation has its own withdrawal into the back-ground as its ultimate end,—as indeed since the accomplishment of redemption it has actually, in a large degree, so withdrawn.—By *inner* revelation, here, is not to be understood a real inspiration as in the case of the prophets, for this would in fact be supernatural and extraordinary; it is simply the gradual coming forward of the divine image in man,—the rational spirit's becoming-conscious of itself as such image. This becoming-conscious on the part of one's own rational nature is properly called a revelation, for the reason that this God-likeness is not conditioned by man himself but is created by God in the state of a germ, and is by the free activity of man, simply developed. The positive revelation is the light whereby this divine image, hidden in man's inner nature, becomes visible to his understanding, or more properly, it is the warming sunlight under whose influence the germ of rationality unfolds itself out of secrecy into day. The inner revelation is neither in antagonism to, nor is it identical with, the objective; it is no more in antagonism therewith than is man's own active self-development to moral maturity in antagonism with his training received from others; nor is it so nearly identical therewith as to amount to a repetition of the same thing. Their respective difference of origin continues to hold good also for the morally mature; even for the regenerated Christian, though he possesses the law of the Spirit as a living power within him, the historical revelation continues to serve as a permanent unvarying basis for the development of his moral consciousness, and as a sure criterion for testing the truth of the light within him; Christ came not to destroy the law.—As in their origin, so also in their *form*, they are different; the positive revelation bears a thoroughly *historical* character; the inner, a *psychological*. The former assumes the form of positive laws given at particular times, and through particular personal instrumentalities; the latter is continuous in every individual throughout his life.

On this inner revelation through the God-likeness of the rational spirit the Scriptures lay some stress, notwithstanding that they speak of it simply in connection with man as perverted by sin, in whom the natural consciousness of God and of his will is seriously obscured and in need of special illumination,—for which reason the natural inner, and the supernatural inner, revelations are not strictly and formally distinguished. In allusion to moral wisdom, it is said: "It is the spirit in man, the breath of the Most High, that gives him understanding" [Job xxxii, 8; comp. Prov. xx, 27]; and it is prophesied of the new Covenant: "I will put my law in their inward parts, and write it in their hearts" [Jer. xxxi, 33], —as in contrast to the Old Covenant under which the law was predominantly objective and in sharp antagonism to the sin-blinded heart. But what is true of the New Covenant is likewise true of the unfallen state. This prophecy refers, it is true, to the working of the Holy Spirit, but unfallen man was *per se* already filled with this Spirit. Paul speaks of a natural consciousness of God and of the moral, even in the heathen [Rom. i, 19 *sqq.*]; by how much more must this be true of man as unfallen. This natural God-consciousness is the general manifestation of that "life" which was the light of men [John i, 4].

It is a favorite manner with some to speak of a moral "feeling," and even of a moral instinctive "impulse," as the primitive germ which subsequently develops itself into a moral consciousness. If by such feeling or impulse so much is meant as a knowledge as yet indistinct—a presentiment rather than a comprehension,—we can readily admit it, though in any case the expressions are very inappropriate, and serve only to confusion. Understood in their proper sense, we must emphatically reject them; for feeling is simply an immediate becoming-conscious of a *state* occasioned in the subject by an impression, and is hence always of a merely subjective and strictly individual nature, whereas the moral law is *per se* necessarily objective and universal—an idea; an idea cannot be felt, but must be known, though indeed this knowledge may be primarily as yet indistinct. A direct feeling can be occasioned only by a *sensuous* impression; of spiritual things I can have a feeling properly so-called, only after they have become an object of my cognizing consciousness; every feeling presupposes either a sensuous impression or an idea, a conception. To consider feeling, in the sphere of the religiously-moral, as the fundamental antecedent condition *before* all knowledge, is simply to confound an, as yet indistinct, anticipatory consciousness with feeling proper, and poorly serves to the attainment of scientific clearness. Still less can we speak of a moral *impulse*, in the strict sense of the word, as the primitive antecedent; an impulse that does not rest on a moral *consciousness* belongs not to the sphere of the moral but to that of the merely natural, and in the exact proportion that we attribute power to some such pretended impulse, we violate the freedom of the will. If an unconscious impulse toward the good is the primitive antecedent in man, then is a choice of the evil utterly impossible. If, however, we should assume, as the primitive condition, that there were in man contradictory impulses, the one toward the good, the other toward the evil, still we would not, by this anarchical duality, safeguard the freedom of the will, if we did not assume as *above* these mutually conflicting impulses, also a higher moral consciousness,—whereby in fact the hypothesis itself would be destroyed.

SECTION LXXVIII.

The revelation of the divine will to the moral subject, as given in the rational self-consciousness, is the *conscience*. This is not an originally ready power, but, as given at first only in germ, it must be developed,—stands in need of culture, primarily by God himself, and, in all after the first generation, by the already morally-matured spirit of men; and with its further moral development it constantly becomes more definite, more clear and more rich in contents. Now, as sin separates man from God and from the knowledge of Him, and also damagingly affects the moral training received from others, it is clear that the conscience has its full purity and power only in a sinless state.—As relating to the moral life-manifestations, the conscience appears as a morally-*judging* power, and as such it is either in harmony with the particular manner of action—in which case it awakens a joyous feeling of approval,—or it is in antagonism therewith, and in this case it awakens a painful feeling of disapproval; and either feeling prompts to a corresponding course of action. As the conscience is a revelation of the moral law as the divine will, hence it never exists *without* a *God-consciousness*,—it is itself, in fact, one of the phases of this consciousness, and is *per se* of a religious character, and is inexplicable from the mere world-consciousness. In its germ it is a primitive and not a derived power, and in this sense it is already presupposed on the entrance of the positive divine revelation. The actual acceptance of this revelation is of itself already a moral act which presupposes the conscience; but the latter is excited to activity and to full development only by the positive revelation. Conscience is essentially an integral part of man's God-likeness,—is, like rationality in general, a divine life-power imparted to the creature.

The conscience is in its essence, not different from the God-consciousness, but is only the bearing of the God-consciousness upon the moral; as relating to the good, it relates also to God, for none is good but God alone [Matt. xix, 17]; and God is the criterion of all good, for the good is the God-answering; a conscience which is not a God-consciousness is a perverted, an unanchored one. As the conscience is an inner revelation of God to man, we place its discussion in this section, although it is an essential element of the moral *subject*.—The manners of conceiving of the conscience differ very widely; it is, in turn, regarded either as a cognizing consciousness, or as a feeling, or as an instinctive impulse; and consequently it is sought for in all the different spheres of the soul-life; it is indeed true that the conscience cannot be real without embracing in itself all three of these spheres; and hence the word may be used in all three significations. In the expression: "Conscience says to me," or "it approves this and rejects that," it is conceived of as a cognizing, judging consciousness; but we also speak of a joyous, or a chastising conscience; and again we say: "conscience compels me to this act or deters me from it." The question, however, is: which of the three phases is the *primitive*, the *fundamental* one? which constitutes the *essence* of the conscience? According to what we have previously said as to the relation of feeling and willing to the cognizing consciousness, it follows very plainly that the essence of the conscience is to be found in that which its name directly expresses in various languages, namely, a *being-certain*, hence a certain *knowing*, a cognizing consciousness; in the New Testament the term συνείδησις—(from σύνοιδα, *conscious sum*, strictly: "I am a fellow-knower," and in a higher sense: "I know with God," in whom all knowledge centers),—an *associate knowing* with God, in virtue of his indwelling in rational creatures, is used of the conscience, both in so far as it leads to the good (αγαθή συνείδησις, or καλή or καθαρά), and in so far as, by reproving, it punishes evil [John viii, 9]; and the same word is used also directly in the sense of religious consciousness, presenting the conscience as a consciousness of the divine will [1 Peter ii, 19; Rom. xiii, 5; Heb. ix, 9]. The conscience, as differing from the enlightening influence of the Holy Spirit [Rom. ix, 1], is a power inherent in the essence of man *per se*, see Rom. ii, 14, 15; in this passage the λογισμοί are not the conscience, but the reflections that spring from the conscience, which itself is the "work of the law written in the hearts," that is, the consciousness of the contents, of the requirements of the moral law; Paul is not speaking here of the true and perfect conscience, but of the natural conscience of sinful man; the essential features of the true conscience, however, still lurk in the disordered one; and this essential character appears here evidently as a consciousness of the moral. In the Old Testament the conscience is designated by the word heart, לֵבָב [Job xxvii, 6].

The conscience is not a mere simple knowing, it is an utterance of the *practical* reason, a direct judging of moral thoughts and actions, an approving or condemning *witness* as to the moral conduct of man [2 Cor. i, 12; v, 11; Rom. xiv, 22; Acts xxiii, 1;

xxiv, 16; 2 Tim. i, 3; 1 Peter iii, 16; Heb. xiii, 18]. Such a judging presupposes the consciousness of a moral law, according to which the decisions are made; and this consciousness is the inner essence of conscience itself. The conscience is a *judging* power, for the reason that it is *per se* a consciousness of the law as the divine will; it *utters* itself discriminating and deciding (κρινών) because it *is mindful* of the eternal ground of the holy,—because it is the inner essence of the divine image as coming to self-consciousness; this latter is the essence of the conscience, the judging is its active manifestation.—The conscience can be awakened, cultivated, and refined by human instruction, but not generated; it is a perpetual witnessing of God as to himself and his holy will in the rational spirit of man, and for this simple reason it is not within the control of man, but is a power *above* him; it may be silenced temporarily, and led astray in its particular utterance as a discriminating power, but it can never be eradicated nor definitively perverted. It is not the person, strictly speaking, who has the conscience, but it is the conscience that has the person; it dwells indeed in the individual personality, but it is not itself of subjective character, since it is of divine quality; it does not express *my* personal peculiarity, but the holy will of God in regard to me. Conscience is the fact of the divine morality in man antecedent to all human morality; it is the germ proper of man's God-likeness,—the God-likeness itself as bearing relation to free conduct, in so far as this consciousness constitutes a part of the essence of rationality. Without this divine germ of the moral in man, morality would be impossible—as impossible as is seeing without eyesight, no matter how much light there might be, or instruction without previously existing rationality as a basis. A convicting by argumentation is possible only when there is antecedently existing in the subject some certain knowledge wherewith the new truth shall agree. What axioms are in mathematics, that is the conscience in the moral sphere. He who does not recognize the axioms, and hence has, as it were, no mathematical conscience, is beyond the reach of instruction. He alone can become rational and moral, and live so, who is so already in the original structure of his being; and this deepest ground of moral rationality is in fact the conscience.

He in whom the witness of the holy God does not witness for the holy, cannot be moral; but such an abandoned one there cannot be in the entire creation of God, for to none has he "left himself without witness." A man may become ungodly, may be unconscientious, and yet not be free from the *power* of conscience; he may deprive himself of his eyes, but not of his reason, and consequently not of his conscience. For this simple reason, every sin is a fall of man from his own proper nature, an unfaithfulness toward himself. Conscience rests on the discrimination of the personal creature and its will from the personal God and his will; it finds its universal expression in the words of the Lord: "Not *my* will but *thine* be done." Whoever supposes himself to act from necessity, or merely according to his own individual will, for him the idea of the conscience is obscured; the irreligious are necessarily unconscientious. It is for the simple reason that it is not the individual ego, but the divine, that speaks in the conscience, that there can be a reproving, an evil, conscience, in which the difference of this twofold ego appears in an irreducible antithesis. But this voice of the divine ego does not first come to the consciousness of the individual ego, *from without;* rather does every external revelation presuppose already this inner one; there must echo out from within man something kindred to the outer revelation, in order to its being recognized and accepted as divine. Even as Adam at the first sight of the woman recognized at once that she was flesh of his flesh, so recognizes man immediately on the utterance of the divine will by special revelation that this is spirit of *that* spirit which dwells and speaks within him,—not, however, as *his* individual ego, but as distinct from it, and as having uncontested right to rule over it.

The first manifestation of conscience in the Scriptures appears in the words wherein Eve opposes the temptation: "We may eat of the fruit of the trees of the garden; but of the fruit of the tree which is in the midst of the garden, God hath said: ye shall not eat of it." Here Eve distinguishes the command, as the divine will, from her own will; which latter, however, she afterward carries out; but this adversely judging conscience presupposes a previous first activity of the same, namely, the recognition of the divine command as obligating. The command itself spoke in fact, primarily, only to the understanding; the recognition of it as divine, as a legitimate determining authority for the individual will, the receiving of it into the heart, and the willingness to conform the individual volitions to it,—all this is not a matter of the cognizing understanding, nor in general of the individual spirit as such, but of that divine element in man which responds to the divine command—the *conscience;* and in the very first utterance of this power, it shows itself primarily, indeed as a consciousness, but then straightway also as a feeling of love as toward the congenial, the right, and as a willingness arising from this consciousness and this love.

The cognizing activity of the conscience relates primarily and directly only to the God-pleasing, and not also to the God-repugnant; for the former is real, but not the latter, and all true and real cognition relates to something real. Hence the second phase of conscience, that where men's "eyes are opened" and they "know the good and the *evil*," does not belong to the primative and pure conscience, but is a manifestation of the conscience as already in antagonism to the moral actuality of man. As primarily relating to the Godlike, and hence as attended by a feeling of approbation, the conscience has originally nothing to do with fear of punishment, but is on the contrary an expression of *peace* with God; fear presupposes already a disturbed harmony and a knowledge of good *and evil;* hence in the Scriptures we find conscience expressly distinguished from fear. [Rom. xiii, 5.]

According to Rothe, conscience is the divine activity in its *passive* form, that is, it is the soul's self-activity as being determined by the body, or, in general, by material nature, and, in the final instance, by the divine self-activity, or, in general, by God himself,—that is, it is instinctive *impulse* as religious. In his opinion conscience lies not on the side of the self-consciousness, but on that of the self-activity, and relates not to conceptions and to the understanding, but to volitions and to actions. Conscience has essentially an individual character,—is of subjective, not of objective, nature; hence it is not correct to speak of a tribunal of conscience. "The conscience of another has not the least binding force for me, but only my own; when an appeal is made to conscience, there all further discussion is cut off, there all objective arguments become powerless; whatever is a matter of conscience to me is to me a *sanctum sanctorum* which none dare violate"—not even for objective reasons; nor does my conscience bind any one else. Conscience is essentially a religious instinct-impulse; and as being an activity of God in man under the form of an instinctive impulse, and hence also a *sensuously* perceptible one, it is attended by sensuously-somatic phases of feeling. Now every instinct-impulse is either positive or negative, hence conscience is either approbative or disapprobative; as disapprobative it is religious *aversion*,—an instinctive impulse toward the counterworking of the sin (hence stings of conscience); as approbative it is the religious *appetite*. Rothe takes occasion here to complain seriously of the hitherto prevalent confusion of phraseology on this subject,—namely, in view of the fact that conscience is treated of, sometimes as a propension, sometimes as a moral feeling, sometimes as a religious feeling, sometimes as such and such an instinct-impulse, or as such and such a sense; in this, however, he is manifestly unjustifiable; it is to no good purpose to quarrel with language which is, in fact, often profounder and truer than the boldest theoretical systems. No one has a right arbitrarily to define ideas contrarily to the general consciousness, and then to find fault with language because it does not harmonize with the definitions. In the present case we find language perfectly justifiable in making so wide a use of the term conscience, inasmuch as all the above phases are in fact embraced in it, though indeed not in equal degrees. The strange notion that conscience rests on a determination of the personal soul by the material body, so that by implication a rational spirit without a material body would not have any conscience, we pass over in silence, and make only the following observations. Should we admit that conscience relates to volition and action, it does not follow from this that it is not *per se*, and primarily, a consciousness; thought in fact may influence volition; and the necessary presupposition of every volition is a thought; but an unconscious instinct-impulse is neither religious nor moral, but irrational. The fact is, conscience lies most strictly on the side of the self-consciousness; otherwise an evil conscience could not contain a self-accusation. That the conscience is of *subjective* nature is only in so far correct as it constitutes an integral element of rational personality; but it is entirely incorrect in Rothe to reduce it to a mere *individually*-subjective phenomenon, and entirely to deprive it of *objective* character. If conscience is to be at all of a rational character, it *must* have a general, and hence also an objective significancy. That which is *merely* subjective has not the least moral significancy, rather is it the opposite of the moral; what is holy for *me* must be also holy *per se* and before God, and what is holy before God must be holy for all moral creatures. *My* conscience is true only in so far as it is an expression of the moral idea; but the moral idea is not of a merely subjective nature. For *every* Christian, it is a matter of conscience to follow Christ; this holds good in general as well as in particular, and not simply for me as such and such a particular person. The more the conscience bears a merely subjective character, the more defective it is; in a normal condition of humanity all moral consciences would necessarily be essentially concordant, inasmuch as there is only *one* God and only *one* divine will, and inasmuch as conscience is the expression of this will. Rothe comes himself into violent contradiction with his assertions, in that he makes conscience to be determined by a divine activity; for this divine activity must be objective to the subject; and, as of a holy character, it certainly does not determine each individual to a different decision; and a little farther on Rothe himself takes this position: that the conscience as an activity of God in man, has a direct and unconditional authority, and from which man cannot in any manner escape; that arguments avail nothing as against conscience,—that perfectly convincing arguments may be urged and yet the conscience remain unmoved; that consequently conscience is also infallible, that it *never* deceives and is incapable of being bribed; and that though we may blind ourselves as to its decision, yet it is itself not to be deceived. These positions, so utterly extreme and so contrary to all experience, are manifestly irreconcilable with his previous position, namely, that conscience, being entirely devoid of objective character, is a mere subjective phenomenon; for in the notion of an authority in conscience, and especially of an unconditional one, it is manifestly implied that the subject is subordinate thereto.*— According to Schenkel (*Dogmatik*, 1858, I, 135 *sqq.*) the conscience is a special faculty of the human soul, or rather that one of its organs which has to do with religious functions, whereas the reason and the will do not relate directly to God but to the world; this conscience, in which the God-consciousness is primarily and immediately given, is at the same time also the ethical central-organ. What is to be gained by this freak of fancy it is difficult to determine. When men thus arbitrarily, and contrary to prevalent usage, limit the notion of the reason and the will, it is of course an easy matter to discover new faculties of the soul and new organs of the same; but whether anything important is gained thereby, and whether the supposed epoch-making new discovery will meet with much favor, we may seriously doubt.—Trendelenburg shows much more circumspection and acumen in considering conscience as the reaction and pro-action of the *total* God-centered man against the man as partial, especially against the self-seeking part of himself (*Naturrecht*, 1860, § 39).

II.—THE ESSENCE OF THE MORAL LAW AS THE DIVINE WILL.

SECTION LXXIX.

The essence of the moral law as the divine will cannot be deduced from the nature of man alone, but essentially only from the idea of God as ruling righteously in his creation.—(*a*) As morality rests on freedom, and as freedom consists in the fact that a man chooses, by a personal independent volition, a

---

* Rothe appears to have become dissatisfied with this exposition of the conscience. In his revised edition (*Theol. Ethik*, 2 *Auf.*, 1867, § 177, *Anm.* 3) he carries his dissatisfaction with the term conscience so far as entirely to exclude it from his work. He declares the word as "*scientifically inadmissible*," inasmuch as it is devoid of "*accurately determined* logical contents;"—it is but a popular expression for the *collective moral nature* of man.—TRANSLATOR.

particular mode of action among several possible ones, hence every moral action is at the same time the leaving undone of a possible contrary action. The moral law is therefore *per se* always twofold; it is *command* and *prohibition* at the same time, and consequently there is in fact no essential difference whether the law appears in the one or in the other form; and as the moral life of man is a continuous one, hence he must at every moment of time be fulfilling a divine law; a mere non-doing would be a negation of the moral. It is in consequence of the freedom of choice, and not in consequence of sinfulness, that the divine law bears the form of a "should."

Every presentation of the moral law from the stand-point of man alone, that is, purely from the nature of man, without deriving it from God, is anti-religious, and can never include the whole truth of the moral idea. And in precise proportion as we conceive more highly of the moral nature of man from that stand-point, we render unavoidable his Pantheistic exaltation into the highest realization of God himself—the putting of man in the place of the personal God. We cannot possibly understand the moral law save as the divine purpose in regard to free creatures, and we can base it on the nature of man only in so far as we recognize in and through this nature the divine creative will, the fulfillment of which lies in the realized moral perfection of man.

The fact that any particular action is morally *good*, necessarily implies as *possible* a contrary, or non-good one; and the commanding of the former is *per se* a prohibiting of the latter; every command directly implies the prohibition of the contrary form of action. Now it might seem as if the converse did not hold good, namely, that a prohibition does not imply at the same time also a command; the laws: thou shalt not kill, thou shalt not commit adultery, seems to require simply a non-doing. This, however, would be possible only on condition that a mere non-doing were in general a moral possibility. But as life is strictly continuous in all of its stages, and as even a momentary real cessation of life is death, hence least of all can the highest form of life, the moral life, be a non-living, a simple non-doing, without thereby turning into the contrary, namely, into spiritual and moral death. As the human spirit, even in the deepest sleep as conditioned by the weariness of the body, is never idle, but keeps up an activity in remembered or unremembered dreaming, so also the highest form of spirit life, the moral life, is never interrupted by a pure inactivity. Hence a prohibition that should include in itself no contents of a positive character, no command, could not be of a moral nature. The *moral* non-doing of a morally prohibited action is in and of itself necessarily the doing of the contrary. Hence, Luther, in his elucidation of the Commandments, is strictly right in never leaving them in the form of a simple "thou shalt not," but in uniformly deducing from them a very positive "thou shalt." The law: "thou shalt not kill," though in form a simple prohibition, nevertheless directly implies the enjoining of all that man, in his intercourse with others, ought to do as contrasting with the disposition that leads to murder; we should not only not kill our neighbor, *but* we should help and succor him in all his bodily perils;—a mere non-doing in the face of such perils would be a direct violation of the law. If man is *not* to commit adultery, then must he, in the conjugal relation, not only *not* do any thing that stimulates and nurtures an adulterous disposition, but he must do the contrary thereof; that is, he must live purely and chastely in words and acts, and love and honor his own consort.

Nevertheless it is not indifferent as to which of the two forms the moral law assumes; the difference, however, lies not in the essence, but in the practical educative adaptation. As the essence, the end, of the moral life is not negative but has positive contents, the true and perfect form of the law is in fact that of the express command; "thou shalt" is higher than "thou shalt not." But for man while as yet undeveloped to moral maturity, the form of prohibition is the more obvious and simple, since, on the one hand, it brings his moral liberty of choice more clearly to his consciousness, and, with the exclusion of the immoral, opens to him the whole field of the *discretionary*, and since, on the other, it establishes protecting limits for the field within which he is to train himself up to moral maturity, to a consciousness of the good. With the child, education always begins in the prohibiting of what conflicts with its well-being; God's first law to man was a free throwing-open of the field of the discretionary in connection with a limiting prohibition [Gen. ii, 16, 17], whereas the real command appears primarily only in the general form of a *blessing*, as expressive of the goal of moral effort, the good [Gen. i, 28]. While the Mosaic Commandments bear predominately the character of prohibition, Christ sums up the moral contents of the divine law in the form of a positive command: "Thou shalt love the Lord thy God with all thy heart, and thy neighbor as thyself;" and at the same time Christ declares that this command embraces the whole ancient law. Hence, while the essence of the divine law continues ever the same, the revelation of it gradually advances from the predominantly prohibitory form to that of the positive command.

As both forms of the divine law present a *duty* to the free will of man, they both bear the expression of a command, a "should." This is the form assumed by nearly all laws, from the first one given to Adam to the perfect laws of Christ. Since the time of Schleiermacher, however, many take offense at this "should," and strive to banish it, at least, from the pure moral law. In Schleiermacher's Philosophical Ethics, this rejection of the "should" is entirely consequential; for here the moral is quite as necessarily-determined a phenomenon of the universe as is the natural, and for freedom of will there is no place whatever; consequently ethics has no other task than simply to *describe* that which takes place from necessity, but not to present laws under the form of requirements, of duty. Rothe follows this view only up to a certain point; he rejects the form of the "should" only for sinless man, as indeed also one cannot apply the idea of "should" to God; only for sinful man can the moral appear as a duty (*Eth.* 1. *Auf.*, § 817). As relating to God this is doubtless correct, inasmuch as God's freedom is not human liberty of choice, and as it absolutely excludes the possibility of sinning, and since God is absolutely his own law. But as relating to free creatures, even though they be as yet perfectly sinless, it is erroneous,—at least unless we are to regard the moral perfection of the same as a cessation of all freedom of choice and likewise of all moral duty. As long as man does not cease to propose to himself moral ends, and freely to aim to reach them, so long will duty as yet continue. This form of the law would be unsuitable for perfect man only when it should be conceived of as something uncongenial to man, as some sort of oppressive yoke, which, however, is by no means the case. The as yet unrealized state of a freely-to-be-attained goal always implies a "should." It is only from some such misconception as if the "should" implied something foreign and burdensome to man, that we can explain why even Harless limits the application of this word to the fallen state (*Christl. Ethik*, 6 *Auf.*, *p.* 80 *sqq.*). There is, however, no shadow of censure in the form "thou shouldst;" in fact, there is for the free will no other form of law conceivable than that of the "should." Without a *distinguishing* of the divine will from that of the subject, no real conscious morality is possible; and simply this distinguishing and nothing more—not an antagonism of estrangement—is contained in the idea of the "should." It is in this idea in fact that morality and piety find their unity, the moral being conceived as the divine will [Deut. x, 12; Micah vi, 8]. The child that does the good for the reason that it knows that it is the will of its parents that it *should* do so, stands morally higher than the one that does it without a consciousness of its duty; the former, but not the latter, is able to offer resistance to temptation; for temptation is overcome only by the thought of the divine will, or of duty. A command does not presuppose a contrary inclination, but only the possibility of sin, that is, it presupposes freedom of will. In denying to man while as yet in a sinless state all consciousness of the divine law, and supposing him to act simply from a direct impulse of love, we not only contradict the express declaration of the Scriptures as to a revelation of the divine will to primitive man, but we also render the fall into sin an impossibility.

SECTION LXXX.

(*b*) Whatever is morally good is God's will, and is hence also moral law; and this law has, as God's will, an *unconditional* claim,—presents itself always as a *requirement* from which there is no escape, and cannot possibly be construed into a mere *counsel* the non fulfillment of which would not be a sin, and the voluntary fulfillment of which would constitute a supererogatory merit. The moral goal of *every* human being is moral perfection, and all that conducts thereto is for every such being an absolute duty, that is, it is God's will and law concerning him. No one can do more good than is required of him; for the human will cannot be better than the divine, and God's law is not less good than God's will. That which in the Scriptures has the appearance of real moral counsel is simply a conditional law, the fulfillment of which becomes a *duty* to the individual only under certain, not universally-existing, circumstances; but wherever it does become a duty, there it is so absolutely, and hence its non-fulfillment is a violation of duty; and wherever it does not become a duty there its fulfillment has no merit.

Here, for the first time, we meet an antagonism of moral views between the different Christian churches; and it is a far-reaching one; and from this point on, in our attempt to construct a system of Christian ethics, and not simply of the ethical views of this or that church, we must seek for the essence of Christianity, not merely in those generalities which are common to all particular churches, but, wherever two views are in irreconcilable antagonism, we must necessarily decide for that one which is of a really Christian character, and cannot regard both as equally legitimate. And although the question in this connection is nearly always, as to counsels to redeemed *Christians*, still it properly belongs in this place, since in fact unfallen man would be, even much more than the redeemed, in a condition to obtain a higher merit than is strictly required.

On a superficial examination it might seem that by the dogma as to the evangelical counsels (*consilia* as distinguished from *praecepta*) the moral requirements were advanced *higher* than the generally-sufficient degrees of morality; the fact is, however, the very opposite. The notion that there is *some* good which is not also a duty, can only be obtained by lowering the moral requirement from that of the highest possible moral perfection to an inferior requirement; and a supererogatory merit becomes possible only where the idea of the good embraces *more* than the moral requirement. The Protestant church, however, holds fast the view that all real good is *absolutely* a duty, and hence that man is *obligated* to do all the good within his power,—that he should unconditionally strive for the highest possible perfection. The Protestant view as to the moral requirement stands therefore *higher* than the opposing view. The Protestant church rejects the notion of moral counsels, and of the meritoriousness of their fulfillment, for the reason that it regards their contents as not absolutely good, as not *per se* moral, but as only good under certain not universally-existing circumstances, but as absolutely *commanded* when those circumstances do exist. That which is good in a particular conjuncture is, when that case arises, an absolute duty, and not a mere discretionary and non-obligating *counsel*. The saying of Christ [Luke xvii, 10]: "When ye shall have done all those things which are commanded you, say: we are unprofitable servants,"—which is not designed to disparage the worth of true morality, but simply to lead man to humility by reminding him of his sinful state, and of his redemption by grace alone,—is, however, applied by the theologians of the Romish church to the doctrine of the evangelical counsels, in that they say that man should in fact not remain a mere unprofitable servant, but should be a child of God, as indeed also Christ was not an unprofitable servant; and even some Protestant exegetes try to escape this inference simply by referring the works here in question not to Christian morality, but merely to the Mosaic law. We regard both the inference, and this mode of escaping it as inadmissible. It is indeed true, man should not be simply an unprofitable servant but a child of God; but from this very fact it follows that that which morally conditions this filial relation to God, must also be a positive moral requirement and duty, and not a mere counsel, which we may leave unfulfilled and yet not fail in doing all that is actually required of us; man is in fact absolutely *bound* to become a child of God. Now as a limitation of these words of Christ to the Mosaic law is not justified by the context, seeing that just previously (verses 5, 6) the question had been as to the power of faith, hence their true scope is, we think, as follows: man, even though redeemed but not yet free from sin, is unable by his dutiful works to acquire merit before God in such a sense as that he could claim of God the blessedness of the children of God as a reward due, and which God would be *required* by his justice to grant, but on the contrary he can regard this blessedness only as a gracious gift conferred upon him in virtue of his faith in the compassionate love of God in Christ. To the works owed, it is not other non-owed and hence supererogatory works that are compared, but *faith*, which, though indeed also a moral requirement, yet differs essentially from works properly so called (comp. verse 19; "thy faith hath made the whole"). Christ's utterance, therefore, teaches clearly the very opposite of sanctification by works as prevailing in the Romish church.

The Romish church finds further support for its supererogatory good works,—which consist essentially in intensified self-denial, that is, in voluntary celibacy, poverty, obedience to man-devised rules, solitary life, etc.,—in those texts of the New Testament which seem to present celibacy and voluntary poverty as a higher morality not to be expected of all Christians. To the rich young man, who, as he himself affirmed, had kept all the commandments, Christ says [Matt. xix, 21]: "If thou wilt be perfect, go and sell that thou hast, and give to the poor, and then thou shalt have treasure in heaven; and come and follow me." Now, it is argued, the moral law does not in fact require of all men the giving up of their possessions, and yet this young man had fulfilled all the commands which Christ mentions to him; hence this giving-up was over and above these commands. This is a very unfortunate inference, for surely a morality which does *not* lead to the perfection of man, can hardly be pure and required by God; and in the case of this young man the giving-up of his riches was the condition of his perfection, and hence, as we hold, an unconditional *requirement*, in case he really desired to attain to the highest good. The young man in declining the requirement *failed*, as Christ says, to have part in the kingdom of heaven; all his presumed fulfillment of the law was insufficient. Now this is in plain antagonism to the Romish doctrine, according to which the fulfillment of the law, even without obedience to the counsels, is amply sufficient to a participation in the kingdom of heaven, whereas the supererogatory works simply serve to a more *speedy* attainment thereof, or to a higher degree of blessedness. Hence those who refuse to admit that certain particular actions become a duty only under particular and not universally-existing relations, but that when these do exist, then they become in fact a positive requirement, would have no other alternative left, than to regard the requirement made of the rich young man as a general duty for *all* Christians. We can distinguish universally-valid commands from conditional ones, not, however, moral commands from mere counsels. Also the conditional commands are, when the particular conjuncture arrives, of absolute obligation, and not to fulfill them is disobedience to God's command; whereas, in the Romish view, the non-fulfillment of the counsels does not incur the least moral blame.—When Paul says of himself [1 Cor. ix, 12–18] that he has denied himself many things to which he had a right, that he has labored without charge, etc., the Romanists here find a supererogatory work to which the Apostle was not obligated. Paul, however, declares expressly that he so acted in order "not to *abuse* his power [liberty] in the Gospel." Now if the taking advantage of his discretionary power, under these particular circumstances, would have been a misuse of his liberty, then the course of action adopted by the apostle was evidently simply his *duty*, and by no means a supererogatory work.—But the greatest emphasis is placed on the utterances of Christ and of St. Paul as to abstaining from marriage: "All cannot receive this saying, but they to whom it is given" [Matt. xix, 11].

Now, that those who do *not* receive the saying can be believing Christians who attain to the kingdom of God, although not to that higher stage of salvation which is conditioned on supererogatory works as Romanists understand it, is not only not said, but, to the contrary, it is said that the self-chastening in question is done "for the kingdom of heaven's sake," and hence plainly in the sense that the same is a *condition* of attaining to the kingdom of heaven. But the *opera supererogationis* of which one is found here, are *not* regarded as a condition to participation in the kingdom of heaven. When Paul [1 Cor. vii] commends to Christians to abstain from marriage, this is certainly *not* offered as a universally-applying command, but manifestly as a mere *counsel* (comp. verse 12), not, however, in such a sense as that individuals may disregard it at perfect pleasure and without moral detriment. On the contrary, the apostle expressly gives the ground of his advice: "I suppose that this is good (καλόν) for the present distress;" "such (as marry) shall have trouble in the flesh; but I spare you." From this it follows that where such a "present distress" does *not* exist, or where there is full moral power and readiness to endure the worldly trials, there the advisableness of celibacy no longer applies. In general the principle is valid: "If thou marry thou hast not sinned" (verse 28); but in every definite case the duty becomes definite also. Where there is such a pressure of "distress," and where higher duties are to be fulfilled, and there is not sufficient power to bear the worldly trials without danger to faithfulness, there to marry is not only not a mere non-sinning, and abstaining from marriage a good counsel, but the former is a positive sin, and the latter a duty. And wherever any one, in view of these particular circumstances does remain unmarried, he does not thereby acquire a higher, a supererogatory desert, but he simply fulfills his duty. Such a supererogatory desert is moreover directly excluded by the fact that the apostle proposed by freedom from marriage to preserve the Christians, in that time of distress, from temporal "trouble;" now he who renounces an otherwise legitimate privilege in order to be spared from worldly trouble, cannot possible lay claim to a special higher desert and to a special recompense for the same. In fact, we can readily conceive of cases to the contrary, where the greater desert would consist precisely in the assumption of these trials by marrying, and where therefore to marry would be a duty.

According to the Romish doctrine there is a difference between God's holy will and his moral law; the former has not an unconditional validity, but is, in relation to man in the sphere of higher moral perfection, simply a wish the fulfillment of which would indeed be pleasing to God, but with the non-fulfillment of which He will nevertheless be satisfied. Bellarmin says, apropos to Matt. xxii, 36: "He who loves God with his whole heart, is not bound to do all that God counsels, but only what He commands,"—an assertion that must appear to an evangelical conscience as a reversal of the moral consciousness. Hirscher, in his earlier writings, defended this doctrine thus: "Love is a command given to all without exception, whereas a specific *degree* of love is *not* commanded; rather is love, when once really existing, left to its own nature; it in fact presses forward of its own prompting, and it is inconsistent with its inner nature that the rude hand of a command should impose upon it that which it will always freely bring forth from its own heart; hence love is *in general* an absolute duty, not, however, a specific higher *degree* of love; the absence of the higher degree does not involve also an absence of righteousness in general, but only a certain higher range of the moral affections; so was it with the rich young man in the Gospel." Now, all this is manifest sophistry. It is true the *degree* of love cannot, for every particular case, be stated in a particular legal formula, still, however, this degree is an absolute duty; it simply depends on the spiritual and moral culture of the individual, but is in no case left to individual caprice. Whoever loves God or Christ, or father, mother, or consort *less* than his moral culture enables him to do, simply commits sin; and he who loves with all the capacity of his soul does not do any thing supererogatory, but simply his bounden duty; and it is nearer the truth to say that all will have to accuse themselves of loving too little, than that any single soul may boast of loving God more than with the "whole heart and soul and strength." (In the fifth edition of his *Moral, II, p.* 328 *sqq.*, Hirscher so tones down the above teaching that only a mere shadow of it remains.)

The Romish doctrine, in making perfection dependent on the fulfillment of the counsels, implies thereby that God's will, as expressed in the moral law, *is not* that man should be perfect, but it is on the contrary rather an individual courage transcending the mere will of God, that leads him out beyond the moral goal set for him by God himself.*

SECTION LXXXI.

(c) While, on the one hand, there is no form of action which could be to the subject, in any given moment, morally *indifferent*, that is, neither in harmony nor in disharmony with the divine will, neither good nor evil, still, on the other hand, no definitely-framed form of *law* embraces within itself the total contents of the moral life-sphere; for as every law has only contents of a general character, while the moral activity itself is always of an individual character, so that the moral actions of different men that fall under the same moral law offer a great diversity, hence the moral law does not sustain to the actions that answer to it precisely the same relation as an idea to its direct realization and manifestation; the particular moral action is not the simple, pure expression and copy of the moral law itself, but it always contains something which does not arise from the law, but from the individual peculiarity. The law as appropriated by the person is fulfilled only in such a manner as expresses also the peculiarity of the person. Every moral action contains therefore two elements: a general ideal one, the moral law, and a particular and more real one, the personal element,—

---

* See, for the Romish view, *Thom. Aqu., Summa, II,* 1, *qu.* 108, 4; *Bellarmini, De Controv. Fid. II.* 2, *De Monachis, c.* 7 *sqq.*—For the opposite view: *Joh. Gerhard, Loci Th., Loc.* 17 (*De Evang.*) *c.* 15; *M. Chemnitius, Loci, De Diser. Praecept. et Cons.*

which latter, as the expression of the personally peculiar character, has also its perfect legitimacy. God's moral will is not that men should be mere impersonal, absolutely similar expressions of the moral law, but that the latter should come to its realization only as appropriated by the particular personality. This *personally*-peculiar element that inheres in every actual moral action cannot be embraced in any general legal formula, inasmuch as in its nature it is in fact *not* general, but a pure expression of individual personality. Every real moral activity is therefore the product of a twofold freedom: of that which subordinates the individual personality to the law, and of that which does not merge the personality into a mere abstract idea, but preserves it in its legitimate peculiarity, and which is to a certain extent a law unto itself.

By this notion of the right of personality Christian Ethics differs from all non-Christian systems, not excepting those of the Greeks, notwithstanding that the latter lay such great stress on the freedom of the person; and this feature is of wide-reaching significance. The decided rejection of the notion that there may be morally-indifferent actions and conditions, and the emphasizing the rights of personal individuality, are very essential to a true understanding of the moral. By insisting disproportionately on the former, we leave too little room for the peculiarity of the moral personality, and make it necessary that for every particular action there should be also a special law; this leads inevitably to a legal bondage hostile alike to all vital individuality, and to the essence of personal freedom. This is the stand-point of Chinese and of Talmudic ethics, and to a certain extent, of the casuistics of some Romish moralists. On the other hand, if we insist too exclusively on the peculiarity of the person, we incur the danger of trespassing on the unconditional validity of the law, to the profit of the fortuitous caprice of the subject,— somewhat as recently in the period of the so-called "geniuses" and of the genius-less freethinkers who followed them, all morality was made to consist in the uncurbed development of the fortuitous peculiarity of the individual, to which peculiarity every thing was freely allowed provided only that it was "genial." The only true course is, in harmony with the general Christian consciousness, to hold fast to both of these elements.

At each and every particular point of time, the moral activity and the moral state are either good or evil, either in harmony with the moral idea or not so. Although in the same action there may be different phases which have morally different characters, and which place good and evil in close proximity, still these contrary elements never coalesce into a moral *neutrum*, into a morally-indefinite fluctuating between good and evil—a moral indifference. An individual may indeed be morally undecided, neither cold nor warm; this indecision, however, is not of a morally-indifferent character, but is itself evil. There may be different *degrees* of good or evil, but not an action that is neither good nor evil. This will become self-evident if we fix our mind on the fundamental idea of good and evil as that which answers to, or does not answer to, the divine will; between these two a third is absolutely inconceivable, just as in mathematics there is no medium between a correct and a false result, or in a clearly presented legal case no medium between yes and no. The bride who cannot answer "yes" to the question as to her willingness to the marriage, says thereby, in fact, "no;" and whoever does not at any given moment say "yes" to God's never neutral will, simply rejects it. The essentially self-contradictory assumption of a morally-indifferent middle-sphere between good and evil, is in itself anti-moral; and every immoral person is only too ready to transfer all his immorality, in so far as he cannot explain it into good, into this pretended sphere of the morally indifferent.

And yet this so widely prevalent tendency to assume that there is a morally-indifferent sphere of action, is based on an actual, though falsely interpreted, presentiment of the true relations in the case. The fact is, every feature in correct moral action is not *directly* and specifically determined by the moral law, but a very essential phase of such action, has *an-*

other source than the general law; nor is the truly moral man simply a mere expression of the moral law, but, as differing from other equally moral men, he is entitled as a person to have and retain his special peculiarity. This phase of the moral life appears at once, and very clearly, in that which lies at the basis of all moral society—wedlock-love. Love, and, more specifically, conjugal love, is a moral command; but the fact that this love fixes itself exclusively and continuously upon precisely this particular person, is a personally-peculiar shaping of the moral law; no law can prescribe what particular person shall be the object of my conjugal love; and the personal element is here so manifestly legitimate that the eliminating of it—the indulging in love, not to a particular personally-chosen person, but to the other sex in general—results in "free" love, the very quintessence of immorality and vulgarity. Wherever moral theories ignore the rights of personality, there the tendency is very strong to base marriage, not on personal choice, but on the choice of the State, as in ancient Peru. Now, what is true of conjugal love is true also, though not always in such striking consequences, of all moral activity. When two equally moral persons do the same thing, fulfill the same law, it is, after all, not the same action; nor indeed should it be; what is right and good in one person may, in that particular form, be even wrong in another, notwithstanding that the moral law is the same for all. Paul employs his moral activity in a different manner from that of Peter and James; in fact, in the living communion of Christians there is presented not only a great diversity of spiritual "gifts," but also of personally-moral idiosyncrasies; even in the purely spiritual sphere there are manifold gifts, but only *one* Lord. The normal difference of moral life-tendency as seen in the sons of Adam, and which must have occasioned as great a difference in the fulfilling of the moral commands as it did in the manner of offering worship, presents a type of the manifold moral diversities into which the moral law is shaped by peculiarities of personality.

The virtualization of the personal element is not to be understood as a something conflicting with the divine law; on the contrary, it is in fact the divine will that the peculiarity of the personality be preserved. If, at first thought, it should seem questionable to place along-side of the universally-valid law another essentially variable element, lest thereby the unconditional validity of the law be infringed upon and negatived, let it be observed, in the first place, that the personal peculiarity finds in the moral law both its limits and its moral criterion, so that consequently it can never come into antagonism with the same, but that, nevertheless, there is, within the scope of the personal spiritual life, a field into which the law, because of its general character, does not dictatingly enter. So long as the moral consciousness is not yet truly mature, there is, indeed, in the personal element of the moral, a peril for the moral life, inasmuch as the law cannot give specific directions for every special case. Hence in the Old Testament God complemented his earlier legislation by special revelations of his will through priestly and prophetic inspiration; now, however, since the Spirit of God is poured out upon all men, there is no longer any need of this extraordinary revelation of the divine will in individual cases, for now the human personality, having come into possession of the truth, has also become "free indeed,"—is so imbued with the divine law that, in loving and acting as prompted by its divinely purified heart, it fulfills the divine law in the very fact of developing its personality; and, in fulfilling the law, it preserves also at the same time its personal peculiarity,—as, for example, in a happy marriage there is no longer any antagonism between the fulfilling of the will of the one party by the other, and the acting-out by each of his own personal peculiarity, but, on the contrary, in each of the two elements the other is already implied. And the moral unripeness of individual persons, that necessarily still exists even in a normal condition of humanity, is complemented to full moral safety by the spirit of the moral community,—as in fact this thought is vitally embodied in every true Christian church-communion.

SECTION LXXXII.

The sphere of the personally-peculiar element is that of the *discretionary* or the *allowed*. That particular action which is neither commanded nor forbidden in general by any moral law is an allowed action; this circumstance does not, however, by any means make it of a morally-indifferent character; on the contrary, the morally-allowed belongs *per se* to the morally-*good* in so far as the development of personal individuality is *per se* legitimate and good. The idea of the allowed relates therefore less to the moral activity *per se* and in general, than rather to the peculiar manner in which an end that is *per se* good, that is, correspondent to the moral law, is realized in particular, by virtue of the personal peculiarity of the actor; and the same moral law may be fulfilled in many ways, the moral quality of which, however, is conditioned in each particular case by the said peculiarity. There is nothing that is allowed under all circumstances; and all that is allowed, and all so-called indifferents (*adiaphora*) are in each particular case either good or evil, but never morally neutral, notwithstanding that such actions may be *per se*, that is, generally considered, morally undetermined, and neither commanded nor forbidden. The moral quality lies not so much in the action objectively considered, as in the disposition from which it springs and by which it is attended.—The sphere of the allowed is different for every stage of the moral development and for each particular circle of life. The farther the moral development of the person has progressed, that is, the more the moral law has become identified with his personality, so much the higher will also be the rights of his personal individuality, so much the higher the morally-personal freedom, and consequently so much the wider also the sphere of the allowed; to the pure all things are pure. Free movement within the sphere of the allowed is therefore essential to a truly moral life, and conditions the all-sided development thereof; this movement is *per se* good, and it is in itself a good, the significance and compass of which increase with the moral development of the subject. Herein lies the contrast of the Christian freedom of the Gospel to the bondage of the law.

This is one of the most important and, at the same time, most difficult points in ethical science, and both for the same reason, namely, from the necessity of giving play to personal freedom, and of doing this without infringing on the unconditionally-valid moral law; and in exact proportion as a system of ethics embraces the idea of personal freedom, will it also be able to embrace the idea of the allowed. As in express laws—commands and prohibitions—God manifests himself as *holy*, so in the concession of the allowed he shows himself as *loving*. As in the fulfilling of the command and in the observing of the prohibition, man becomes *conscious* of his moral freedom, so, within the sphere of the allowed, this freedom becomes to him an *enjoyment*. Now, as freedom of will is not a mere antecedent condition of all morality, but also itself a moral good, and as every good is *per se* an enjoyment, hence free-created beings have also a moral claim upon the legitimate *enjoyment* of freedom,—not simply of freedom as subject to definite commands, but also of freedom as *entitled* to free choice in various directions,—that is, they have *discretionary power* to free activity; this constitutes in fact the divinely conceded sphere of the allowed, wherein mainly the personally-peculiar element of the moral comes to virtualization.

The very first moral direction, or rather blessing, that was given to man, contains implicitly the notion of the allowed or discretionary: "Replenish the earth and subdue it and have dominion over the fish of the sea," etc. This is really not so much a command as a blessing,—it proposes a moral goal, a good. But in this good that is to be sought after, namely, dominion over nature, there is at the same time implied a *command* to realize this supremacy of the rational spirit through moral activity. But within this command there lies also a discretionary field. The particular manner *how* man is to realize this dominion, is *not* expressed in the command, but is left to his free personal self-determination—in so far as he does not thereby come into collision with other moral commands. Thus, man *may* use animals for his own purposes, may domesticate them, train them, force them to help him, and use them for his nourishment; but as to what choice of them he shall make, and as to what kind of service he shall exact of them, this is left to his discretion,—here he may act freely, here he has the full enjoyment of his freedom. For unfallen man there was no need of narrower limits; but when depravity gained the upper hand these limits were drawn closer, and the Mosaic law gives very specific and narrower bounds within which man, as no longer morally stable, was to exercise his freedom upon nature.—The first definite command of God presents at once, along-side of the expressed command, also the allowed: "Of every tree of the garden thou *mayest* freely eat; but of the tree of the knowledge of good and evil thou *shalt not* eat;" whatever he may choose of the other trees is *per se* good; the choice he shall make is not prescribed; simply a boundary is set, beyond which begins evil. Now, we cannot say that this choosing within the given limits is of a morally-*indifferent* character; rather is such choice, as the realization of a good, itself morally *good;* and this goodness consists in the simple fact that every choice is good, and that the choice of the one is not better and not worse than the choice of the other. To infer from this that the single objects of the choice are morally indifferent, would be to overlook the fact that the moral element does not lie in the object, but in the choosing person, and that the latter exercises his morality precisely in the fact of freely choosing in accordance with the peculiarity of his personality; not to choose *at all* would be to despise the divine gift, and hence immoral.

In the state of innocence the sphere of the allowed was, notwithstanding the indispensable educative limitation, wider than it was subsequently in the state of sin, not, however, because men were then morally more contracted, but because they were morally purer. In consequence of redemption from the power of sin, the now sanctified personality becomes also freer, and the sphere of the allowed is enlarged;

herein lies one of the most essential differences between Old Testament and New Testament ethics. The moral itself receives, in contrast to the specifically and particularizingly prescribing ancient law, a more general form, and the whole law and the prophets are summed up in one short command: "Thou shalt love the Lord thy God with all thy heart, and thy neighbor as thyself." The sanctified personality acts within the limits of the law with more freedom; the boundaries of the allowed, as established for the state of sin, are thrown more into the back-ground; the laws as to the Sabbath and as to meats and other similar prescriptions, are thrown into a freer form by the personality as made free in Christ. Instead of the limiting laws regulating the use of "meats," and other material objects in general, and which were framed with reference to the sinful impurity of man, Christ gives the broad principle: "Not that which goeth into the mouth defileth a man, but that which cometh out of the mouth, this defileth a man" [Matt. xv, 11]; and Paul expresses this in a still more general form: "Every creature of God is good, and nothing to be refused, if it be received with thanksgiving" [1 Tim. iv, 4]; and elsewhere [Titus i, 15] he states the thought in its highest exaltation: "Unto the pure all things are pure;" that is, the higher the morality rises, so much the wider becomes also the sphere of the allowed, and hence of freedom; and upon him who is morally perfect, who is inwardly fully identified with the divine will, there is no longer imposed any degree whatever of outwardly-legal limitation to the employment of his freedom; for whatever he can love, that God loves also, and his sanctified personality *cannot* choose any thing that would be offensive to God,—and such a person is again invested with his original full right of dominion over nature, with his full right of free choice; and whatever he does of free choice, that he does to the glory of God [1 Cor. x, 31].

The words of Paul [1 Cor. vii, 28] may serve as a further illustration of the notion of the allowed: "If thou marry, thou hast not sinned;" whereas on this very occasion the apostle dissuaded from marriage. The Christian has a *right* to marriage; whether, however, under circumstances that would otherwise morally admit of it, he put into execution this right, does not depend on any particular legal prescription, but on his own untrammeled personal choice. Paul had discretionary "power to lead about a sister, a wife, as well as other apostles" [1 Cor. ix, 5]; but he did not do so; all have the "power to eat and to drink" [verse 4], but our choice is, within particular limits, left free. Ananias was at liberty to keep his field or not [Acts v, 4]; what he did was of his own election; it was not a moral law, but solely his personal choice that determined his conduct. [Comp. 1 Cor. vi, 12; x, 23; Rom. xiv, 1 *sqq.*; xv, 1 *sqq.*; Matt. xii, 3, 4.]

The sphere of the allowed is the more special theater of personal freedom, as distinguished from mere moral freedom. In obedience to the commanding law I am indeed free, but this freedom is nevertheless a controlled one; it is true, I *can* will and act otherwise than the law wills, but I *dare* not; and if I in fact do so, then I violate the law, then I am an enemy of God; I have the liberty but not the right so to act. Commanded duty has consequently, notwithstanding the liberty on which it rests, always still a certain constraint in it; and though in the *mere* literal fulfillment of the law, man becomes conscious of his freedom, yet he does not come to a proper and full enjoyment thereof. If God's law actually entered, prescribing and prohibiting, into all the details of individual action, without, by some concessions, allowing playground for discretionary action, then, though man would indeed have the privilege of freely obeying or disobeying at each particular moment, nevertheless he would feel the law as a burden upon him; and Paul was very apt in expression when he spoke of the preparatory law of the Old Covenant as a chastening-master. For the simple reason that the essence of man is freedom or self-determination, it is natural for him to aspire to become also fully conscious of this freedom,—to put it into exercise in so far as consistent with his moral obedience,—and hence he needs a free field wherein he may act with real freedom, without having his actions in every respect prescribed to him, without being strictly bound by the law,—where, in a word, he may say: I may choose this, but I do not need to choose it; and whether I choose this or that depends entirely on my personal self-determination, and that too without detriment to my moral duty.

The sphere of the allowed stands in the same relation to that of the express law as *play* to earnest activity. Play also is an element essential to the full development of youthful moral life. With the child, play is of high moral significancy, as it is thereby that it learns to comprehend, to exercise, and to enjoy its full personal freedom. In learning and working the child is also free; but however good and zealous of work it may be, it is nevertheless conscious at the same time of being controlled by an objective law to which it must adapt itself; the other and equally legitimate phase of its life, that of personal freedom and self-determination, is revealed to it in its purest form only in play; and the child, even the morally-good one, finds so great a delight in play, for the simple reason that it thereby comes to the enjoyment of its personal freedom; and the essence of its enjoyment lies in the simple fact that in its playful activity and feats it is free lord of its own volitions and movements; and those children become spiritually dull whose plays are strictly watched over by tutorial intermeddling. Playing is freedom, however, only in form, and is without definite contents; hence it is essentially only a transition-occupation appropriate to the age of childhood. The sphere of the allowed in general, is the wider and positive-grown extension of that play. Here belongs *recreation* after labor, as in contrast to the positive fulfilling of the law; recreation is *per se* morally good and its essence consists in freedom; that I select precisely this path for a promenade, or busy myself thus or thus, is neither prescribed to me by any law, nor is that which I do not select forbidden. It is entirely erroneous to say that man must be totally swallowed up in his calling, that he has a definite duty to fulfill at every moment; this would be a moral slavery. The sphere of personal liberty has also its own good right, and for the plain reason that man is not merely an obligated member of the whole, but also a free individuality. Recreation *per se* is therefore by no means of a morally indifferent character, but the particular mode of its realization is discretionary, and the moral law is not, at this point, of a detailed particularizing character, but it simply hovers protectingly on the outskirts, and wards against abuses,—even as a prudent educator simply exercises a protecting oversight over the child's play, but does not prescribe the details. Man is indeed moral at every moment of his existence, and should at each moment be and act morally right, but every thing that he does is nevertheless not a direct expression of some moral formula, on the contrary there is a share therein that belongs, and rightly too, to personal free choice,—just as, in regard to his clothing, a sensible man, though in the main following the prevalent mode, will nevertheless reserve the privilege of deviating therefrom whenever it better suits his personal individuality.—Even as a fish in the water, though indeed swimming according to the natural laws of gravitation and motion, yet, within the scope of these laws, disports itself at pleasure, and exhibits precisely in this free motion the traits which distinguish it from the unfree plant, so also does man, within the limits and conditions of the moral law, comport himself freely on the field of the allowed, and in so doing manifests the characteristics of the free child of God as in contrast to servitude under a chastening law.

Schleiermacher (*Werke* III, 2, 418 *sqq.*) denies the admissibility of the notion of actions that are merely allowed. We have, in his opinion, no time for that which claims to be, not duty, but simply allowed, not morally necessary, but only morally possible; every performance of such an action implies a definite willingness to act otherwise than from moral motives,—which is immoral; the idea of the allowed belongs not to ethics but to civil law. This we concede in so far as Schleiermacher speaks of such actions as are held to be neither in conformity nor in disconformity to duty, that is morally indifferent, but this is by no means the true idea of the allowed. However, we do not admit the existence of *such* a class of actions; but in morally-*good* actions there is a *phase* which is not determined by the law itself, and which constitutes the allowed.—Rothe (*Ethik*, 1 *Auf.* § 819) finds the idea of the allowed in the fact that particular forms of action cannot be referred with certainty to a particular legal formula, so that consequently their moral worth cannot be estimated thereby beyond a doubt. The reason of this may lie in the incompleteness of the law; hence the allowed has a larger scope in the minority-period and with children; but as the law becomes more definite and perfect, the sphere of the allowed grows *narrower;* the more fully man is as yet without positive law, so much the more numerous are the actions that are allowed to him; but there arrives a turning-point in the development where the relation again changes, and for the reason that, then, the law begins to retire into the background and to become progressively simpler, so that the sphere of the allowed becomes again more extensive. With this view of Rothe we cannot coincide. According to it the sphere of the allowed rests only on a lack of the law, and it would be more properly termed the sphere of the morally doubtful. Adam, however, to whom the allowed was at once presented in connection with the commanded and the prohibited, could not possibly be in doubt as to what would be moral for him; and the divine word placed before him with perfect definiteness the sphere within which he was *allowed* entire freedom of action. And it is utterly erroneous to say that in childhood the sphere of the allowed is wider than in maturer years. The fact that many a thing is allowed to the child which does not become it in later years, is not a proof that it has a wider liberty, but only that at this period the allowed lies in a different circle, and one that answers to the childish understanding; on the contrary, the fact undoubtedly is, that to the child more things by far are not allowed which are allowed to the man, than conversely; and every wider stage of development brings to the youth a consciousness of an increased freedom of self-determination, although, on the other hand, it is true that the more earnest demands that are made by the growing positiveness of the life-work, exclude much of the earlier childish liberty. But that there comes again afterward a turning-point when a contrary relation begins, cannot be substantiated, and moreover it conflicts directly with the idea of a constantly progressive development toward moral maturity.—With a similar tendency, Stahl (*Rechts-philos.* II, 1, 112) transfers the allowed beyond the sphere of the ethical proper, as being in its fulfillment morally indifferent, and into the sphere of *satisfaction,* that is, of earthly enjoyment; hence he infers consistently enough, that the sphere of the merely allowed must constantly *decrease* as morality advances, and that satisfaction is ultimately to be sought only in that which is at the same time a fulfilling of the moral law,—as, for example, in the exercise of benevolence, etc. Christian Friedrich Schmid arrives at the same conclusion (*Sittenl.*, p. 450 *sqq.*). According to this view the sphere of the allowed would amount in fact but to a sphere of the non-allowed, and would be simply a temporary concession to moral immaturity and weakness. This seems to us incorrect. For a truly rational man, there can be no other satisfaction than a moral one; whatever he does and receives, he does and receives in faith and love and with thanksgiving, and in virtue of this thankfulness every truly allowable enjoyment becomes invested with a moral character. Stahl appeals to the fact that, with the progress of moral development, many a thing that is otherwise allowed must be renounced; but this is only in appearance a greater limitation; for though it is true that mature man' no longer allows himself many of the pleasures of his unripe youth, yet he has in their stead other and wider fields of the allowed which are denied to youth. The greater freedom of the Christian as compared with the law-observer of the Old Testament, is perfectly evident. It is true, many things were allowed to the Jew, which, because of the higher morality introduced, are no longer allowed to the Christian, such as the putting away of wives, and retaliation [Matt. v, 31 *sqq.*], so that it might seem as if the sphere of the allowed, and hence of personal freedom, were really more narrowly limited in Christianity than in Judaism. However, when we reflect upon the above-cited declarations of Paul as to the contrast of Christian freedom to the yoke of the law, the matter will doubtless appear in reality very differently. Many things were not indeed morally allowed to the Jews, but only *tolerated* in them, because of their hardness of heart; the *whole* significancy of the moral law was not yet exacted of them, just as in children many a thing is tolerated and overlooked because of their more limited moral knowledge, which in riper persons would be regarded as improper and blameworthy, without implying, however, that that which is tolerated is actually admitted as allowable. The fact is, that as the moral consciousness grows in clearness, the compass of *duties* grows wider also, so that many a thing that was not previously a moral *requirement* now becomes really such. This does not, however, render the sphere of the allowed narrower, but in fact wider, inasmuch as every duty admits also of a variety of ways of fulfillment, and consequently also a diversity of ways of virtualizing our personal peculiarities. Thus, the fact that consorts may no longer discard each other, though at first sight a seeming limitation of the sphere of the allowed, yet really greatly exalts the moral personality of both parties; they have by far a higher right in each other,—*may* require more of each other, may more strongly emphasize the right of their moral personality, may each *allow* to the other, and to himself toward the other, more than would be proper were marriage merely an easily-dissolved contract,—even as the son of the house is freer and may allow himself more liberty than the servant, and for the simple reason that the former is more indissolubly united with the house than the latter;—the closer and firmer the bond, so much the greater mutual trust and confidence, so much wider also the sphere of the allowed.

Writers often admit two different species of the allowed: the one is allowed because of the meagerness of the moral knowledge, as with the child; the other, conversely, because of the advanced state of the moral maturity. This difference, however, is by no means a real one; and, when expressed in this form, the idea of the allowed has no longer any unity, but involves a direct antagonism. Rather do both of these forms of the allowed fall under the one notion of the rights of the personal peculiarity. Many things are, for the peculiar nature of the child, morally good, which are not so for a riper person, and for the simple reason that the unsuspecting child, in doing that which would be improper in those of riper years, "thinketh no evil," and because the sentiment holds good also of unconscious innocence, that "to the pure all things are pure." And the case is essentially the same with him who is morally matured; simply the form is different. When man has come, through moral growth, into a state of *conscious* innocence, then also to him, as being pure, many a thing is pure which would be impure to the sinful.

SECTION LXXXIII.

In so far as the moral law is made into a moral possession of the person, that is, a constituent element of his personally-moral nature, it becomes to him a moral *principle*, a *life-rule* or *maxim;* without moral principles there is no real morality. As in this union with the personal peculiarity the moral law itself enters into this peculiarity, hence though it is in fact the same always and for all men, still the life-rules that grow out of this law, among different persons and nations and under different conditions in life, must evidently also be relatively different. The correct shaping of the moral law into life-rules correspondent to the peculiarity of persons and circumstances, constitutes the principal work of *practical wisdom.*—A disregarding of the rights of the personal peculiarity in the moral life, and the exclusive application of general and definitely-expressed laws as direct rules of life, result in a servitude to a legal yoke (rigorism) which is incapable of producing any truly personal morality, and has no justification save as a temporary disciplinary process in a state of depravity.

The law is not of man, but solely of God; life-rules each person makes for himself, not, however, independently of the law, but as based on it, though peculiarly modified by his moral personality. The life-rule or maxim is the law as incarnated, as having become subjective; in it man has appropriated the law as a personal possession,—has merged it into his flesh and blood. My life-rule, even in so far as it is perfectly correct, is valid in this definite form only for me, and it may legitimately enough be widely different at different life-stages and under different circumstances. The manifoldness of life-rules contributes to the esthetic richness of the collective life of the race; in them the moral idea, though essentially one, yet shapes itself into a variegated diversity, just as the light of day, though in itself essentially colorless, is reflected back from flowers in a thousand varying tints. It is true, the giving scope here for freedom of will involves also a possibility of immoral self-determination; and it is also true that sin, in consequence of its essential deceptiveness, seeks almost always to hide itself under the cloak of pretendedly legitimate life-rules, and thereby attains to its seductive power, and that the free personal shaping of the moral law into life-rules is possible without danger, only as proceeding from pure and sanctified human nature, so that consequently the severe discipline of the tutorial law appears as peculiarly appropriate for the divine training of mankind before the full realization of redemption; but wherever morality is to become perfect, that is, free, there the law itself must become an inner freely-appropriated one,—must be received into the personality as its essential possession, and not as a foreign element, but as one that has coalesced with its essence; and this essence is a personally-peculiar one. Even as natural nutriment does not nourish in its natural crudeness, but only in so far as it is received and really appropriated into the natural organism and into its peculiarity, so is it also with the moral law. From the possible danger of subordinating the unconditional validity of the divine law to individual caprice, there does not follow a condemnation of the personally-peculiar molding of the law, but only the requirement that morality be based not on merely unconscious or obscure feelings or impulses, but upon a positive clear consciousness of God's will and of one's own moral condition. The non-governing of one's self, the yielding of one's self to immediate natural impulses, the giving rein to the spiritual and sensuous proclivities that already exist irrespective of a knowledge of the divine will, is *per se*, even where sin does not yet exist as a power of evil, immoral. Moral life-wisdom is not an acquisition attained to in unserious play; and slavish submission to an all-specifying, rigorous law is easier than the free, moral developing of life-rules on the basis of the more general moral law. The less ripe the moral personality, so much the more dictating must be the objective character of the law, so much the more severe must be its *discipline* [Gal. iii, 24]; and the riper the moral nature of the person becomes, so much the more freely and independently may and should he shape the law into life-rules for himself.

It creates confusion to confound the moral law with personal life-rules; it inevitably leads either to legal bondage or to moral laxity. The Scriptures contain not only moral laws, but also life-rules for particular, not generally existing life-relations, and the regarding these latter as general moral commands or counsels has sometimes led Christian ethics into error. When the apostle recommends celibacy because of the "present distress" [1 Cor. vii,] he gives simply a life-rule for particular, expressly-stated circumstances; and, in order to prevent all misunderstanding, he says, in relation to the unmarried: "I have no commandment of the Lord" [verse 25]. By this, Paul does not mean that he establishes on his own authority a new command without reference to any divine law, but only that this specific life-rule is not itself a divine law, but rather simply a rule of conduct applying the divine law to particular circumstances. The law on which it is based, however, is not: "Thou shalt not marry," but: Care for the things that belong to the Lord, and not for the things that belong to the world [see verses 32, 34]. Monasticism made of this life-rule an objective law or counsel. The instructions of Christ to the apostles, when sent out to prepare the way for himself [Matt. x, 9 *sqq.*]: "Provide neither gold nor silver nor brass in your purses," etc., are not given as a moral rule to the moral man in general, but to the apostles for this specific mission. But the mendicant orders made of this also an objective law. When Christ required of the rich young man to sell all that he had and give it to the poor, it is perfectly evident that this was simply a specific injunction for this particular person, seeing that neither Christ nor the apostles required in all cases, or in any manner, the giving up of possessions, notwithstanding their strong emphasizing of the duty of charity [Acts v, 4; 1 Tim. vi, 17 *sqq.*; 2 Cor. viii, 1 *sqq.*]. The monastic vow of poverty is a perverted application of this injunction. To the same category belong the rules of propriety for women, as given in 1 Cor. xi, 5, 10 *sqq.*, and in part evidently also the resolution of the Apostolic Council [Acts xv,

20, 29]. In all such rules either the assigned or the directly implied reference to particular, but not generally existing and permanent relations and circumstances, distinguishes them very readily from general moral laws, the characteristic of which is to be valid absolutely and always.

SECTION LXXXIV.

The moral law as (by virtue of the particular form into which it is thrown by the peculiarity of the moral person) requiring its realization in a particular case, is moral *duty;* duty is, therefore, the law as coming to actual application in moral action through the moral life-rules into which it has been shaped by appropriation into the moral person,—that is, it is the law as realizing itself under the form of life-rules, in other words, it is the law as shaping itself *in* and *for* a particular person under particular circumstances, and as becoming in him a determining and actuating power. I fulfill *the* law in that I do *my* duty. The duties that spring from the same law are *different* for different men and for different circumstances.—As, therefore, duty is the product of two elements, the moral law and the peculiarity of the person, and as the moral laws collectively, though existing under the form of a plurality, must yet of necessity constitute a concordant whole, hence, if we leave out of view the actuality of sin, a conflict of different duties with each other (*collision* of duties) is utterly impossible. The distinction of *conditional* and *unconditional* duties is not correct, and rests on a confounding of the notions of law and duty.

The moral person does not directly and strictly fulfill the law, but simply his duty. Even ordinary speech indicates the difference; we do not say, "my law," but always, "my duty." The law *per se* is general and *above* man; duty is always special and personal. No one person can do the duty of another; and what is duty for *me*, may be a violation of duty for another. The law alone is directly prescribed; to what particular form of action this law, as appropriated into my personality, determines or *obligates* me, is not directly expressed in the law, but is the result of a moral judgment in view of my special moral peculiarity and circumstances. We cannot, therefore, with propriety institute a contrast between conditional and unconditional duties. The condition is already implied in the relation of the fulfillment of the law to the fulfillment of duty; what I may not or cannot now do, is simply not my duty; at another time, however, this same form of action may become my duty. Any and every duty may, with as much propriety, be called conditional as unconditional; in its becoming a duty it is always conditional; whenever, however, it actually presents itself, there there can no longer be any question of conditionality. Whoever is in a condition to rescue a person from imminent life-peril, has the unconditional duty of doing so; whoever cannot do so, has no duty whatever in the matter; between these two positions there is no third one possible. With like propriety we may say also that the law is at the same time conditional and unconditional, but in a converse relation; in its essence it is unconditional, in the manner of its fulfillment it is always conditional. The law, "Thou shalt love thy neighbor as thyself," is in its moral contents unconditional; every human being is an object of this love, but how this love is to be *exercised*, in what manner it is actually to manifest itself in actions, that is, to what definite duties it shall lead, this depends on manifold conditions not contained in the law itself; to one's husband or wife, or to parents, one owes a very *different* love from that due to friends, and the very same sacrificing love will manifest itself very differently toward the moral and toward the immoral.

When the law is presented in the general form of command or prohibition, the manners in which the manifold relations of life make it the duty of different persons to fulfill it are so different, that there may even arise an appearance of contradiction. The fact is, however, that for a real *conflict* (collision) of duties (a subject which has from of old been a favorite and much discussed one among moralists) there is in a normal state of humanity no possible place. Moral laws *cannot* come into conflict with each other, otherwise the idea of the moral, and the moral order of the universe itself, would be undermined; and there is just as little ground for a conflict between duties, seeing that their conditionment is in fact based in part on the personal peculiarity and special circumstances of the subjects. The personal peculiarity of a *sinful* man may indeed come into conflict with the moral law; but in so far as this is the case it forms no legitimate element in the construction of the notion of duty; rather will it become our duty in many respects to counteract this element. But all legitimate personal peculiarity is itself formed in harmony with the moral idea, and hence cannot come into conflict therewith. For an irreconcilable collision of duties there is, therefore, nowhere any manner of possibility.

The idea of duty is often otherwise understood than as here presented. Duty is frequently declared to be the divine law itself. Now if by this is meant, that which God requires of us in each particular case, and that too of each individual in particular, then it would be correct,—this, however, is not expressed by the term "law;" but if it means, that duty and the divine law are identical, then it is incorrect. More definite is the statement, that duty is the manner of action which conforms to or harmonizes with the law. The Kantian school explains duty as that which, according to the law, *should* take place, or which, by virtue of a law, is practically necessary, or which answers to an obligation,—obligation being understood as the necessity of an action in consequence of a moral law. All these statements are inadequate, inasmuch as the personal peculiarity is left out of the account, so that consequently no difference whatever is made between duty and law; and as to how obligation differs from duty we are utterly unable to see. Schleiermacher in his *System* (§ 112 *sqq.*) defines duty as "the form of conduct in which the activity of the reason is at the same time special, as directed upon the particular, and also general, as directed upon the totality," or, the law of the free self-determination of the individual in relation to the common moral life-task of the race, or, the formula for the guidance of rationality in single actions in the realizing of the highest good. That these, in the main, correct statements, are still too indefinite, is shown even by their numerousness. Similarly, but more definitely, Rothe explains duty as that definite form of action which is required by the moral law as under the form impressed upon it by the individual instance.

SECTION LXXXV.

To duty on the part of the moral subject, corresponds *right* on the part of the law. My duty is to fulfill the right of the moral law, that is, the right of God to, or his claim upon, me. The substance of dutiful action is therefore justice or right, and the product of this action is the *right*, i. e., the realized claim. Hence dutiful action is *per se* right-doing. Duty and right call for each other,—are but two phases of the same thing; to every right there corresponds a duty, and conversely,—simply the subjects are different; every duty is the expression of a right; another's right in regard to me is for me a duty, and to the fulfillment of another's duty in regard to me I have a right; the two ideas are absolutely correlative and co-extensive. In virtue of duty I accomplish the moral, for the law has a right, a claim, upon me; in virtue of right the moral *is accomplished* upon *me ;* in the fulfilling of duty I keep the law; in my accomplishing of the right the law keeps *me.* The fulfilling of my duty obtains for *me* a right to, or claim upon, the moral law in so far as this law is an element of universal order, namely, the right to be a real, living, and hence free, member of the moral whole,—in other words, a moral claim on the just recompense of God. There is, morally, no other right of an individual than such as is conditioned by a corresponding fulfillment of duty on his part;

rights without duties would be a reversing of moral world-order. God has an absolutely unlimited right because he is absolutely holy, and man, as related to God, is under absolute obligations. All right has therefore its basis in God's right and in God's love. Hence in the Scriptures the notion of duty is nearly always presented as an *indebtedness*,—as the right of God to man, as what man owes to God. God's righteousness has a right to righteousness in man, and hence righteousness is man's duty; those who fulfill their duty are therefore the *righteous*.

As duty is not merely of a subjective character, a mere utterance of the individual consciousness, but the law as appropriated by the person, so also, and equally emphatically, is right also not a mere subjective something with no better basis than a merely fortuitous power of the individual. Every right of the individual is a special expression of the right of the whole, and is valid only in so far as this individual is in moral harmony with the whole. Whoever by undutiful conduct dissolves his union with the moral whole, loses thereby, in like measure, his right to or claim upon the whole. Duty and right are both an expression of the moral; the former is the moral as subjective obligation, the latter is the moral as objective requirement; both manifest the essence of the moral as an essential law of collective being. The individual has duties and rights only as in vital union with the whole. I have duties and rights, not in virtue of being a mere individual, but in virtue of the fact that the totality of being bears a moral character. From this it follows at once, that there can be true duties and rights only where the morality of the whole is based, not merely on the morality of the individual persons,—which would be a mere arguing in a circle,— but where it is based on the holiness of the personality of God. I can keep and fulfill the law only when the law keeps and fulfills me; I can do my duty only when I therein recognize a *right* or claim of the moral whole, and hence of the holy God, upon me. An impersonal whole has no right to, nor claim upon, the personal spirit; from such a servitude Christianity has definitively emancipated human thought; nor has one man, as upon his fellow, any other right or claim than such as he derives from God; that is, he has it only by the grace of God; that man has *per se* a right upon his fellow, irrespective of God, is an un-Christian view; "Be not ye the servants of men" [1 Cor. vii, 23]; this is *Christian* right and Christian freedom.

In such a moral world-order where duty and right are absolutely correlative, where right extends as far as duty, and duty as far as right, every one receives strictly *his* own right —his due. The dutiful man has a right upon the moral whole,—a right to have his personality respected,—and it is thus that the moral law, the moral world-order, realizes itself *on* man; it upholds in a just and honorable position *him* who has upheld it. He who gives honor to God, to him God gives also *his* honor. Also he who violates duty receives *his* right; every punishment is the fulfilling of the right of God and of the collective universe upon the individual; the criminal has a right to the punishment; when the criminal comes to his right mind he demands himself his own punishment, and a child that is not totally perverted finds a moral tranquillization in suffering the punishment it deserves,—it even calls for it.

The notion that the fulfillment of moral duty acquires for man a claim upon the moral order of the world, and hence upon God, is emphatically rejected by Schwarz (*Eth.* I, p. 199), who even declares such a view as blasphemous; God alone, he holds, is the absolutely-entitled One; man has, as toward God, simply duties, but no rights;.God only can have claims upon us, not we upon God. And he appeals for support to Rom. ix, 20; xi, 35 *sqq.;* Job ix, 12; Luke xvii, 10. The first two passages, however, relate to the impossibility of fathoming the eternal divine counsel, and declare any doubt as to God's holiness and righteousness as unjustifiable; moreover all of them relate exclusively to the condition of sinfulness, in which we of course concede, in harmony with Scripture, that all salvation rests exclusively on the undeserved and compassionate mercy of God. We are now speaking, however, of man as not yet under sin, of the moral life in its unclouded purity, and here the matter stands very differently. If God's righteousness is not a mere empty figure of speech, it must form the basis of a moral right; we cannot doubt that God rewards each according to his moral conduct; and when a truly moral creature receives from God a just reward [Rom. ii, 6, 7, 13], this is not a mere compassionating gift, but it is justice, and the creature has, in virtue of his righteousness, a claim upon such a reward. It is indeed a gracious gift of the Creator, that he has made the creature thus noble, that it is permitted to bear in itself God's own image; but that God regards and treats the creature that has become positively holy, in view of and in reference to that fact, is simply justice. As the sinner receives but his right when the divine punishment falls upon him, so also the sinless creature receives but his right when he is an object of the divine pleasure. To think otherwise on this point would be to overthrow our notion of a holy and just God. The Scriptures express very distinctly this thought of the *right* of the moral person upon God, even in circumstances where, because of sin, there can no longer be any question of a right strictly speaking,—so that, then, it is in fact a pure grace that God, notwithstanding this, yet concedes to man such rights. Of the justifying faith of Abraham, Paul says, "To him that worketh is the reward not reckoned of grace, but of debt" [Rom. iv, 4]; if therefore man should really and truly fulfill the law of God, then his reward would fall to him in due course of justice. The inference of the apostle, as to the worth of faith for sinful man, would not have the least basis should we presume to regard this declaration of his as *per se* meaningless and impossible; and this holds good in the fullest sense of man as untouched by sin, as also it is true of the Son of man. The true and real fulfilling of the law has in fact eternal life as its just reward [Matt. xix, 17]; the only question is, as to whether in fact any person perfectly fulfills the law as Christ did. The doctrine of grace for the redeemed is not interfered with by that of a claim of the moral man upon God, but receives in fact thereby its proper foundation. In the idea of the *Covenant* which God made with the Patriarchs, and as to which he himself says: "I have made a covenant with my chosen, I have *sworn* to David my servant: Thy seed will I establish forever," etc., there is contained also the idea of a *right* upon God as graciously conceded even to sinful man, provided he should obey the voice of God and keep his commandments [Psa. lxxxix, 4; Exod. ii, 24; xix, 5; Deut. vii, 8, 9, 12; ix, 5]. That God should make such a covenant, is pure grace; but now that He, the truthful One, has made it, it follows that those who keep it acquire thereby a right to its fulfillment on the part of God; and hence the pious of the Old Covenant make appeal in their petitions to the promises of God [Gen. xxxii, 12; Exod. xxxii, 13; Deut. ix, 26 *sqq.*]. The great emphasis which the Scriptures place upon the thought of the covenant of God with man, which is, in fact, more than a promise, implies very clearly that here the moral character of God, as well as that of man, is essentially involved. We need only separate from the idea of a right all that the sinful heart has associated therewith, all that is presumptuous and self-seeking, and it will no longer have the least feature that could give offense to the most reverential mind. The Scriptures present the thought of duty as intimately connected with the idea of right; and this involves, in fact, the profoundest conception of the moral. Here, all dutiful living, on the part of man, is a right of God upon him (מִשְׁפָּט), a paying of his debt to God,—it is ὀφειλή,—and man is debtor to God and to the brethren [Rom. i, 14; viii, 12; Luke xvii, 10; comp. 1 Cor. vii, 22]; and God's laws are an expression of the rights of God [Lev. xviii, 4, 5; xix, 37; xxv, 18; Deut. vii, 12; xxxiii, 10; Psa. xix, 10; 1, 16; cv, 45; cxix, 5 *sqq.;* Isa. xxvi, 9; and others]. By virtue of his moral nature, of the likeness of God that was impressed upon him, man becomes in turn a *debtor*, —is under obligation to bring this nature into realization, to fulfill the claim or right of God upon him; and he who fulfills this right is consequently just or righteous: "He hath showed thee, O man, what is good (the moral law); and what doth the Lord require of thee (as duty) but to do justly (the right) and to love mercy?" [Micah vi, 8; comp. Deut. x, 12, 13]. Thus, as it appears, the Scriptures present rather the objective phase of the moral, the right of God and of the divine law upon man; whereas the moralists of recent times, especially since Kant, devote their attention rather to its subjective phase, as duty.

In the manner of viewing the relations between right and

duty there often prevails some confusion; right is often confounded with discretionary power, whereas, in fact, the former is more than the latter, and contains an actual requirement; or, right is regarded as the mere possibility or liberty to act. Furthermore a great difference is frequently made between *right* and *the right*, the two being taken as capable of excluding each other, so that I may have a right and yet its execution be not right. This, in so far as the question is as to *moral* right, is manifestly absurd. It is true, according to civil law, I may have a so-called right in the exercising of which I shall do wrong; but of such civil right we are not here speaking; in the sphere of morality I can never have a right to what is wrong, and I can never exercise a right without doing the right. I have *a right* only in so far as the moral law takes me under the protection of the moral order of the universe; I have a right upon another in so far as he has a moral duty to fulfill toward me; I have right conduct in so far as I myself realize the moral law; and this I do in fact when I do not throw away my own moral right, but maintain it intact. Whenever I have a moral right, then is it also right to realize it.

CHAPTER III.

THE OBJECT OF THE MORAL ACTIVITY.

SECTION LXXXVI

As the moral is the free realizing of the good, and as the good itself is the inner law and nature of the divinely-created All, hence, in every moral activity, man comes into relation to this All, and this All—as well as also God himself—becomes in its entire existence, so far as within the scope of man, an *object* of the moral activity, namely, either in that as a good it is brought into unity with the moral person, or appropriated by the same,—or in that, as material capable of being modified, it is formed by the moral activity.

I. The moral life relates primarily always to *God*. God can be an object of the morally-pious activity only in so far as he is conceived of as a personal spirit; to an impersonal God there can be no moral relation. This moral activity is not a mere receiving, but it is a real acting, namely, in that man not only turns himself toward God, but in that he also turns God toward himself; the good that is realized by this activity becomes actual, however, not in God, but in *us*, in that it brings us into communion with God, so that consequently all pious activity is at the same time a moral producing for ourselves.— As God upholds, and rules in, all creatures, hence all moral activity without exception stands in relation to God, and all realizing of the good works communion with God. All that is moral is also pious, and all that is pious is also moral. Hence all duties are also duties to God, and religious duties do not stand *along-side* of other duties, but they include them in themselves.

Every view is defective which excludes from the moral life any thing whatever that comes into the life-sphere of man. This is precisely that which distinguishes rational creatures from the irrational, namely, that the latter have always simply a quite definite and restricted scope for their life-manifestation, while every thing else is indifferent to them, and as good as not existing, whereas rational creatures have an interest in all that exists, and bring it into some manner of relation to themselves. Perfect indifference to the world is Indian, but not Christian, wisdom; God is indifferent to nothing, and for this reason moral man, the image of God, is so also. The collective All and God himself constitute the life-sphere of the moral. Because of the inner unity of all things, every moral act not only reverberates in the whole universe, and there is joy among the angels in heaven over one sinner that repents, but this act itself acts upon the All, for all that is good and all that is capable of good belong together in one great unity. The declaration: "Whether life, or death, or things present or things to come—all are yours" [1 Cor. iii, 22], holds good in its fullest sense of the moral life, although indeed our moral bearing toward the different forms of existence is correspondingly different; to nature the moral spirit is related as dominating, to God as obeying.

The conceiving of God himself as an object of the moral activity is a fundamental point in Christian ethics. It is true the heathen also required reverence toward the gods, but this exercise of piety did not rise to a dominating power over the entire moral life. In recent times it has become a favorite view to regard the moral as not relating to God at all, but only to man, or indeed also to nature; it is even said that God cannot be an object of the moral activity, seeing that because of his unapproachable sublimity he must be inaccessible to all human influence. Evidently, with this view of the matter, prayer is narrowed down to a mere pious exercise without any other possible efficacy than to benefit the person so exercising; it would be more consequential, however, for those who think thus to follow Kant, and discard prayer altogether as empty and meaningless. It does not come within our scope to answer here the question, how the answering of prayer is reconcilable with the eternally-immutable nature of God, but we simply accept from dogmatics the unquestionably Scriptural principle, that God actually does hear and answer prayer, that prayer and its answering are not a delusion, but that proper prayer really and truly conditions the answering of the petitions, and that consequently it has a positive influence on the bearing of God toward man. True prayer is impossible so soon as I entertain the opinion that it has no effect, that the gracious turning of God toward me is not in some way conditioned thereby. This does not imply that God comes into any manner of dependence on man; whatever he does is eternally self-determined, but it is determined in view of the moral bearing of man as divinely gifted with rational freedom. In this sense, prayer is really a moral activity in relation to God, and God is a real object of the same. Prayer is the beginning and the end of all moral activity. The sentiment: "Pray and work," holds good of all and every moral life; the two do not stand *beside* each other, but consist only in and with each other.

God, as living and personal, cannot sustain a relation of indifference to human conduct. If we can speak in any proper sense of a displeasure of God at sin, of a wrath of God against sin, then must also, conversely, the pleasure of God in the moral conduct of man be of a real character, and hence, in some manner, conditioned by said conduct. The moral activity as relating to God is *per se* necessarily *pious;* but to presume, for this reason, to exclude it from the sphere of the moral, would be very inconsistent; for in fact it takes place with freedom, and with moral consciousness and with moral purpose, and it is frequently, in the Scriptures, expressly required as a duty; and all duties are moral. But, on the other hand, all duties are also pious, inasmuch as morality is always in very close association with piety (§ 55), and no duty can in fact be truly fulfilled without being regarded as an expression of the divine will, and hence without pious submission to that will. We therefore must reject the view that there are no moral duties toward God, and no moral influencing of God; if there are sins against God, as, for example, blasphemy, then there must also be duties toward Him,—and we must, further, reject the view that the duties toward God constitute a special group entirely distinct from the others, so that in fact the duties toward man might be fulfilled without at the same time also fulfilling those toward God.

The distribution of the subject-matter of ethics into duties toward God, duties toward one's self and duties toward other men, was formerly very usual; it was, however, only partially correct. God fills, in fact, heaven and earth, and the statement of Christ that whatever "ye have done unto one of the least of these my brethren, ye have done it unto me" [Matt. xxv, 40], is of course true also in relation to God. It might, however, be said that, while it is true that all other duties imply in themselves also a fulfillment of duty toward God, yet that the converse is not true, so that consequently the duties of piety might be considered by themselves, seeing that in fact in the duty of worshiping God no other duty is directly implied. This is, however, only seemingly so; for in every duty toward God, I fulfill also directly at the same time a duty toward myself: I cannot possibly love and honor God without exalting myself into communion with Him; whatever man does to the honor of God is at the same time a self-transfiguration; he cannot praise God as his Father without confirming himself as the child of God. Moreover he can do this only in so far as he, at the same time, divests himself of illegitimate self-love; and only that one can be in communion with God, who likewise enters into communion with the God-fearing. The fulfilling of our moral duties toward God implies consequently in itself, really and directly at the same time also, the fulfilling of our duties toward those who are beloved of God. Hence, the moral relation to God is the central spring of all other moral life, and our duties toward God do not stand co-ordinate with and apart from our other duties.

SECTION LXXXVII.

11. The moral activity as strengthened by its moral relation to God, that is, by communion with Him, comes now, and only in consequence of this strengthening, into a truly moral relation to the *created*,—comprehending both the moral person himself and also the, to him, objective world.

(1) The moral *person* is his own *object*. Man is morally to form, to cultivate himself—to make his personal peculiar reality a product of his moral activity. Man is what he is as a person solely in virtue of moral activity; without this activity he remains in spiritual unculture, and is essentially impersonal. Hence man is, in so far, an object of his own moral activity, as he has not yet attained to his ultimate perfection,— in so far as he is a cultivable and, as yet, relatively incompleted being, that is, in so far as there is yet a difference between his ideal and his reality. Man is to form himself into a *good* entity, that is, into a personal reality that is in full harmony with God, with itself and with the All, in so far as this is good.

The possibility of man's bearing a moral relation to himself rests on the nature of rational self-consciousness, wherein man becomes in fact an object to himself. If man were from the very start absolutely perfect and complete, he would still be, even then, an object of his own moral activity, only however under its conserving, but not under its formative, phase. Progressive development is implied in the very nature of the created spirit, and there is no stage of temporal life conceivable where man would not have a still higher perfection to attain to, and further moral culture to work out.— All self-forming, unless kept in harmony with God, becomes necessarily anti-moral. Man can, it is true, develop himself in harmony with himself *without* being in harmony with God,

—this is, however, a culture of self into the diabolical; and if he forms himself merely in harmony with the world, he becomes an immoral worldling, and if in this worldliness he leaves self-harmony out of the question, then he becomes simply characterless.

(*a*) The *spirit* is an object of the moral activity in virtue of its being *per se* merely the possibility of its real development into a rational spirit,—the germ of itself,—and because it does not develop itself into its full reality by inner nature-necessity, but by freedom. Man has, in virtue of his very constitution, the task of forming himself into the full reality and truth of spiritual being, namely, in respect both to his knowing, to his feeling, and to his willing,—that is, into the perfect image of God. The soul-life of brutes shapes itself by inner nature-necessity; brutes have no need of education; man, however, without education and without moral self-culture would sink below the brute, and for the evident reason that he would thus fall into complete self-antagonism; his freedom would become unbridled barbarity. Spirit lives only by continuous development; where it is not morally trained, it pines away and degenerates. What Christ says of the received talents [Matt. xxv, 14 *sqq.*] is especially true also of the moral culture of the spirit.

(*b*) The *body* is an object of the moral activity in so far as it is the necessary organ of the spirit in its relation to the world. It is not from the very start an absolutely subserving and perfectly spirit-imbued organ (§ 65, 66), nor does it become such by purely natural development, but it is trained into such only by the rightful dominating of the rational spirit over it. The merely natural development of the spirit forms not as yet a spirit's-body, but only an unspiritual animal body. Even as in the features of the countenance, spiritual unculture and spiritual refinement are almost always visibly expressed, so is also the body in its entire being subject to the refining influence of the moral spirit; and this influence ought not to be of a merely mediate and unintended character, as resulting from the unconsciously-ruling potency of the spiritual life in the body, but in fact also of an immediate character. The good that inheres in the body is to be faithfully preserved,—the germs of higher perfection to be developed.

Whatever is originally given in the body, whether as actuality or as capacity, is a legitimate possession of the spirit and should not be lightly esteemed. To despise the body is to dishonor the Creator. It should not be honored, however, as *merely* corporeal, but as subserving the spirit in its rational life-work,—not as an end in itself, but as an end for the spirit. "Glorify God in your body;" this moral precept, the apostle bases on the fact that this body is "a temple of the Holy Ghost which is in you, which ye have of God, and ye are not your own" [1 Cor. vi, 19, 20]. The body is not a mere nature-object, but a holy temple of a sanctified spirit,—bears the consecration of a sacred destination; man has not discretionary power over it, as over a mere nature-object,—not merely as over an unconditional possession, but as over a good intrusted to him by God, and belonging to God, and for which he must give account to God.

SECTION LXXXVIII.

(2) The *external* world as an object of the moral activity,—the widest and almost endlessly diversified field of this activity,—is—(a) the world of *rational* beings,—primarily and chiefly the *world of humanity*. To the moral person other persons stand, on the one hand, in the relation of *similarity*, in virtue of the common possession of a rational nature, and, on the other, in the relation of *difference*, in so far as each individual is an independent moral person with a special peculiarity; and it is the part of the moral activity at once to respect, to acknowledge, to preserve, and to promote both these features, and to bring them into reciprocal harmony. A human being never becomes, for the person acting upon it, a merely dependent rightless object, but in all cases continues to be a personality that is to be respected in its legitimate peculiarity, and hence it should never become an unfree and as it were impersonal

creation of another, but it is an object for the moral activity only so far as it is itself at the same time recognized and treated as a moral *subject*. The moral bearing of man to his fellows rests essentially on the thought of the inner, and not merely conceived, but also real, *unity* of the human race, which finds its whole truth only in the thought of the common origin of all men from a first-created primitive individual.

Here also Christian morality comes into striking antagonism to all non-Christian morality. The thought of mankind as a homogeneous whole of which each individual is a legitimate rightful member, is peculiar to Christianity; the heathen know only nations and compatriots but not humanity and man; even the free Greek and the Roman make the distinction both in fact and in law between persons and slaves; the slave is only a thing, not a moral personality. All acting upon others which aims *simply* to exert an influence upon them without also receiving an influence from them, is immoral. Even the immature child necessarily exerts some influence upon its educator; and when Christ presented a child to his disciples as a moral pattern [Matt. xviii, 3, 4], this is not to be regarded as holding good simply in a loose sense and for the morally immature, on the contrary it is the moral *essence* of the child, its God-likeness, that is, in fact, a true mirror of the moral even for the relatively mature educator, and that has a right to his respect. That person is a pernicious educator who has never experienced a real moral influence upon himself from the child,—who has never recognized in the soul of the child the features of the image of God, nor been impressed with respect for child-*naïveté;* and it is the acme of meanness not to respect and sacredly to protect child-innocence.

The moral conceiving of man as an object of the moral activity, presupposes that we have in fact to do with real true men, men who are not only similar to us, but who are bound to us as members of *one* body. To creatures which, while belonging to the zoological order *bimana*, and while differing from the ape by the formation of the skull and of the feet and by an erect walk, yet should have been from of old distinguished, both in their origin and also in their spiritually-inferior nature, from the so-called "nobler" race of the whites, we could not come into the same moral relation as to those who are our brethren. The question as to the origin of the different races of men has a deep moral significancy, and is of fundamental importance for ethics. The natural science of the present day, which has become largely infected with a spirit-denying materialism, is well known to have until quite recently declared it as a fully-established fact that the various physically-differing races of men are of different origin, and cannot have descended from a single primitive race; and there are not a few persons, in other respects favorable to the Christian faith, who recognize these pretended "results of modern science" as really such, and regard them as beyond question. It is not here the place to examine the scientific worth of these so-esteemed results; we have to do with the question here only in its moral significancy. We merely remark in passing, that we must absolutely deny to an experimental science—and this is the pretended source of said results—the right to decide upon matters that lie beyond all experience. Such science can simply affirm what *is*, or is *not*, but it cannot decide what *cannot possibly* be. "Empirical" natural science may be justifiable in saying, that so far as experience goes, a white person is never born of a negro, nor a negro of a white person, though even this is not uncontested, but it has no scientific ground for inferring, that, consequently, it can also *never* have been otherwise. Inferences of this kind, illegitimate even according to the simplest rules of logic, are overturned almost daily by the mere progress of science. Moreover, it is not unworthy of remark that the position: "as it is in the life of nature now, so must it always have been," is applied to the question before us by the very same persons who cannot admit that the human race could have otherwise originated than through some extraordinarily potent nature-process—through human germs, forsooth, that were cast from the sea upon the shore,—and who in reply to the question: why then this interesting nature-process has not repeated itself also in our own day, or at least during the historical period in general? immediately exclaim, that nature has declined in her generative power. On the whole, therefore, and in view of the fact that the latest "progress" of this particular wing of natural science takes ground in direct antagonism to the above pretended unassailable "results," namely, in regarding man as an advanced development of the ape (Darwin), we may without the least anxiety spare ourselves the trouble of refuting the above-mentioned earlier view, and abandon this "modern" science to its own further self-dissolution.

Christianity has from the beginning had a clear consciousness of the *moral* significancy of the original unity of the human race. Though God had undoubtedly the power to create thousands of men in the different parts of the earth, instead of one, as he did in fact do in the case of plants and animals, nevertheless it must be for good reasons that in the Scriptures the whole human race is assumed to have sprung from a single stock [Gen. i, 27, 28; ii, 18; iii, 20]. There is involved here an antagonism of the natural and the spiritual stand-points, and that too in a moral respect. According to naturalism the unity of the world is a merely conceived something,—in reality it is a product of a presupposed multiplicity of single existences; and also the good, which in its nature is a manifestation-form of unity, is not an element fundamental and presupposed in every single existence, but it is simply a consequence—a product of the active individual; the good is ever *to be* without ever and truly *being*. According to the Christian system, however, the real unity and the real good are every-where the first, the fundamental, while multiplicity is only of a derived character. Here the moral is simply and solely the following of God as the absolutely good One, a free manifestation of a unity with God which in fact, however, originally existed,—which had not first to be realized, but only revealed, witnessed, and freely virtualized. Man *is able* to be moral only *because*, in his nature, he is already at one with God. So is it also in his moral relation to mankind; the unity of the total sum of individual men is not first to be created out of an original multiplicity, and to be constituted as an entirely new something, but it is simply (and this is the origin and the reason of this plurality) to be freely and morally witnessed and confirmed. Humanity is to become morally one, for the reason that in their origin they are already one; love to mankind is simply *fidelity* to the nature of man as existing from the beginning. This view is in diametrical antagonism to naturalistic ethics; and hence Paul presented it very prominently, at Athens, as the peculiarly-Christian view in contrast to heathenism [Acts xvii, 26; comp. Rom. v, 12, *sqq.*]; the latter estranges humanity into an original diversity; the former attributes all hostile antagonisms to the workings of sin.

The very natural and in fact morally legitimate feeling, that blood-relatives stand to us in a closer relation of duty than entire strangers, contains a profound truth. It calls forth really a very different and morally more potent feeling, when we know that even the degenerated negro is of our own blood, our brother, sprang from *one* father, than if we should assume that he is originally, and by nature, of a spiritually and corporeally inferior species [August., *De Civ. Dei.*, xii, 21]. That which forms no unessential part of the world-historical honor of Christianity, namely, that it has made slavery *morally* impossible, has been again absolutely put into question by the teachings of naturalism; and it is scientifically as well as morally a signal indication of inconsideration, and especially so on the part of theologians, to declare the decision of the question as to the original unity of the human race as a mere non-essential matter. By the assumption that there were originally different races, the slavery-system is not only excused, but it is directly justified. In fact man has not only *not* the duty, but he has not the right to break down the original and naturally-constituted differences of spiritual existence. But the moral influencing of the degenerate races consists essentially in *raising* the actually lower-standing individuals of the colored races to the height of the whites,—in placing them both, in spiritually-moral respects, on an equal footing, in making of the colored races our true and proper brothers, in doing away, in fact, with whatever places them actually below the whites. But the effort to do this would be, in the eyes of the above-mentioned teaching, a simple presumption, a transgression of the limits prescribed to us by nature herself; according to it, the negro is destined by his primitive and manifestly inferior peculiarity, to service under the higher race, and it would be a criminal interference with the ordinances of nature to wish to change this. That which has hitherto passed for the greatest stain upon a perverted Christian civilization, the re-establishment of slavery, can find no more desirable an apology than these results of a perverted science; and it is a standing and entirely consequential opinion among even the most liberal-thinking champions of this tendency, that negroes are in fact but *half*-men and should remain such.

SECTION LXXXIX.

(*b*) *External nature* as an object of the moral activity is such not merely in its single manifestations, but also in its totality. On the one hand, nature exists not for itself but for the rational spirit for man; on the other, it is, as a work of divine creation, a good thing, and hence has rights in and of itself.—(1) Nature is by origin and essence destined to be dominated by the rational spirit as God's image,—to be formed by the spirit into its organ and for its service. As nature is not *per se* moral, hence man's moral relation to it does not consist in his receiving from it a direct moral influence, though indeed he does receive from it a mediate moral influence through the contemplation of the image of God as manifesting itself therein, but in his acting morally upon it. For the single individual, this action is always limited to a narrow theater, but for humanity it extends to all terrestrial nature. As the body is related to the individual spirit, so is nature related to humanity in general; nature's destination is to be perfectly subservient to man and to be exalted in the service of his rational destination.—(2) But this dominating of nature is essentially conditioned on the truly moral and hence rational self-culture of man, in virtue of which nature is not to be subjected to the whims of irrational caprice; for, as God's work, nature has claims upon man; it is legitimately an object for human activity only in so far as man subordinates himself to the divine will, whose peculiarity it is not to destroy but to preserve.

The relation of nature to the rational spirit is neither that of an object absolutely different from and foreign to it, seeing that both are the work of one creative spirit, nor that of a power entitled to dominate *over* the same; this would be a reversing of the moral order of the world; for that which is *per se* higher and rational should not be enslaved under that which is inferior and irrational. If, therefore, nature and spirit exist *for* each other, and if they are to constitute an intimate unity, then the only relation possible is, that the spirit shall be the dominating power over nature,—the power that forms and molds it. And if in reality the relation is in many respects now actually otherwise, still this should not lead us astray in conceiving of the true relation between them in a sinless state. The rational consciousness of all nations has at least some presentiment of the proper relation. Even as in all forms of superstition a more or less clear expression is given to a presentiment, though indeed misapplied, of a corresponding deeper truth that lies beyond the grasp of the superficial understanding, so also has the notion of *magic*, so widely prevalent throughout heathendom, its roots in a presentiment of the true relation of reason to nature.* It is but the childishly perverted thought, that the spirit should not be enslaved under unspiritual nature,—that its true destination is to cause nature to subserve it in its own purposes. When Christ, in his character of Son of man, exerts his mastery over nature, and by his miraculous deeds counterworks the sufferings that have sprung from the enslavement of sinful humanity under nature, and when he promises like power also to his disciples on condition of faith [Matt. xvii, 20; Mark xvi, 17, 18; Luke x, 19; xvii, 6; John xiv, 12], he simply indicates, though primarily only in a typical manner, the true goal of human development

---

* See the author's *Gesch. des Heidentums*, i, 141, and his *Deutscher Volksaberglaube*, 1860.

in its relation to nature. The miracle does not play feats with nature, it simply dominates it,—subjects it not to the irrational caprice of the individual will, but to the rational will of man as in union with God; and it is a rational demand of the rational will, to be free from all fetters that lie outside of the rational will,—to be untrammeled in its activities by sufferings that spring from bondage to spirit-hostile nature.

Nevertheless nature is not to be considered as mere material for the active spirit, and absolutely without rights of its own; it has a right to be respected, because of the rationality that is impressed upon it. From the face of nature the Spirit of the Creator beams forth upon us with striking evidence; here also there is holy ground which man should not tread with unwashed feet. That is not a moral bearing toward nature which forgets the image of God that is stamped upon it, and which, in the zeal of shaping and enjoying it, perceives not that also natural objects, even while as yet untouched by the plastic hand of man, proclaim the glory of God. The Hindoo's dread-reverencing of natural objects, though indeed oblivious of the Creator, has yet a positive presentiment of the divine in the works of the, to him, unknown God.

CHAPTER IV.

THE MORAL MOTIVE.

SECTION XC.

EVERY motive to action is primarily a *feeling;* but feeling springs from a consciousness. And feeling is such motive under both of its forms of manifestation, as feeling of *satisfaction* or of *dissatisfaction,* and hence of *pleasure* or of *displeasure.* The feeling of displeasure is to be assumed as existing to a certain degree also in a state of strictly normal life-development, namely, in so far as man, before reaching his last stage of perfection, has always a consciousness, that as yet something is *lacking* to him to which he is yet to attain. This is not pain, but yet it is a feeling of want.

Any view is contrary to the nature of the soul-life which assumes any other soul activity, as, for example, cognition, as the most immediate motive of the moral. Thought *per se* contains nothing that moves the will; but thought is in fact never absolutely alone, is never a merely inert possession, but it excites at once and necessarily a feeling, and then, through this feeling, the *will.* I *feel* myself in some way affected by the perceived or conceived, more or less agreeably or disagreeably, according as it is in harmony with, or in contradiction to, my present state. An entire indifference is here impossible, though indeed the shades of the feeling of pleasure or displeasure may be very different,—impossible for the reason that that which I receive into myself sensuously or spiritually, must necessarily come into some sort of relation to my present corporeal or spiritual reality, and for the reason that this relation must always be either one of harmony or disharmony. It is true indeed that the different phases of a received impression may have different bearings, and hence the feeling that arises from them may be of a complex character; nevertheless in this complexity the elements of the pleasant and the unpleasant remain always distinct,—do not coalesce together into a feeling of total indifference, just as every object that is taken for nutriment is either strengthening or weakening to the body, but cannot be absolutely indifferent. Now, every feeling stirs up also straightway the will, and hence activity in general; in case it is a pleasant feeling we desire to *possess* its object, either by preserving it or by appropriating it; in case the feeling is unpleasant we seek to *get rid* of it. In this double-movement all action is embraced, and hence also all that is moral; and this movement itself rests absolutely on an antecedent feeling. Thought, it is true, is the *foundation* of the moral, but it is only the feeling excited thereby that is the motive proper of action. Only he can will the good who has *pleasure* in the law of the Lord [Rom. vii, 22; Psa. i, 2; cxii, 1]. —When the thought of something not yet existing, but which may be realized by my action, awakens in me a feeling of pleasure, this is in fact the thought of a *good*, which, by virtue of this feeling, becomes an *intention*, which differs from a *resolution* in the fact that the latter relates not to the good itself but to the means of realizing it. While, however, an intention refers to *a* good, a *purpose* refers to *the* good. I purpose to become a perfect man; I have an intention of mastering a science; I form a resolution or determination to study. But a thought becomes to me a purpose only by the accession thereto of the feeling of love; in a resolution the will stands forth a little more actively.

It might, now, seem that while in the condition of the primitive sinless goodness of human nature, there would be place for feelings of pleasure, that is, of happiness, yet there would not be occasion for the feeling of displeasure. This would be only then correct when man's original perfection should be conceived of, contrary to the very idea of life in general, as a state of completion. But all capability of development implies a certain lack, though not a fault, nor a non-good; and every consciousness of a lack awakens the feeling of a want, which, though it is not a pain, and does not destroy inward happiness, is yet also not the pleasurable feeling of complete satisfaction. That even he who is perfectly constituted, and who remains in this perfection, should still have bodily and spiritual wants, which are *per se* necessarily attended with a certain, though indeed only momentary, feeling of displeasure, is implied in the very nature of the creature and of its development.

SECTION XCI.

Feeling as relating to the object that excites it, is, as a feeling of pleasure, *love*, and, as a feeling of displeasure, *hatred*. Between these two there is no third, although both may exist in different degrees and even in association with each other. Hence love is the feeling of pleasure which springs from the consciousness of the harmony of a real or conceived object with the actual state of the subject, together with a *desire* to preserve and to perfect this harmony, and hence also to preserve the being and essence of this object. *Hatred* is the feeling of displeasure which springs from the consciousness of an irreconcilable antagonism between the object and the subject, together with a desire to destroy this antagonism in the object, even should this involve the destruction itself of that object. In a normal moral condition of things where all that exists is *good*, love alone has a real object, while hatred has only a possible one.— Love is essentially of a *preserving* character, hatred is essentially of a *negating, destroying* character; as, however, all moral action aims to create a reality by continuous development, hence preserving love is necessarily at the same time also *promotive* of the being and nature of the beloved object, and negating hatred is at the same time a confirming of the opposite of the hated object. Hence love works in order to be able to love always; hatred works in order to destroy itself; love lives in order to be eternal; hatred lives in order to come to an end; only *that* hatred can be endless whose object is eternal—namely, Satanic hatred. As moral hatred is necessarily an effort to destroy the antagonism of existence, that is, to re-establish its harmony, hence it is in essence the same thing as love. Hatred is *per se* as moral as love,—is but its necessary reverse phase. There is no moral love without hatred, and no moral hatred without love; pure hatred without love would be simply Satanic hatred. As moral hatred is in its essence love, hence the actual motive of *all* moral activity is *love*.

"Love is the fulfilling of the law" [$\pi\lambda\acute{\eta}\rho\omega\mu\alpha$, Rom. xiii, 10]; in this formula the Christian idea of the moral motive is very definitely expressed; love leads to the fulfillment of the law; it is the rich fullness in which all law is included. Without love there is no morality; and where love is, there morality is truly free, for love develops itself into all forms of the moral. Hence Christ, after the example of the Old Testament [Deut. vi, 5; x, 12; xi, 13], sums up the whole law in the one precept of love to God and to our neighbor [Matt. xxii, 37; Luke x, 27]; "This is the love of God, that we keep his commandments" [1 John v, 3]; love is not and cannot be a mere inert feeling, but it is by its very nature active, it produces that which its subject loves,—brings about the full and free harmony of the person and his life with God. Whoever assigns any other motive for morality than love, knows nothing of the moral. But love tends by its essential nature to a unity of the diverse, —seeks not its own mere isolated being. Mere self-love to the exclusion of love to others is not love at all, but only immoral self-seeking; it is indeed a motive to action, but to anti-moral action. Even that which appears in the animal world as an unconscious symbol of moral virtue, is based on love, and is an expression thereof. There is no form of moral activity conceivable which would not be an expression of love

[1 Cor. xvi, 14].—The moral love of the divine is, *per se* and necessarily, also hatred against that which is ungodly. But as the ungodly is primarily not real but only conceivable, and as this thought itself becomes really vital only through the reality of sin, it does not come here properly within our scope.

Love is taken here primarily as not yet a virtue or a disposition, but as a simple feeling occasioned by a consciousness of harmony or of disharmony. The love that is *required* as the fulfilling of the law is more than mere feeling, though indeed it has feeling as its basis and essence. And yet the love here in question is not a mere feeling of pleasure, not a mere impressed state of the heart, but it contains in itself at the same time a power prompting to an active relation to the beloved object. All love has for its object a something that is good, and hence, as relating to the subject, a good (§ 51), and it evidences the existence of this good by the outgoing and recognizing life-movement of the subject toward it,—by the effort of the subject toward the object in order to preserve or intensify its unity, its harmony therewith. Now as all existences are created for each other and destined to a self-harmonious life, hence love is the primitive feeling of all rational creatures,—the direct witness of the goodness of existence, an echo of that first witness of the Creator as to his created work, and hence also the innermost vitality of the moral life, the purpose and essence of which is in fact harmony, or the good. Directed toward the good, and hence the divine, love has for itself the pledge of eternity; whereas moral hatred, as directed against all non-good, that is, antidivine, has, in virtue of its negating nature, for its purpose, the destroying of its object and of itself with it. *Peace* is the goal of love and also of hatred,—is an essential phase of the highest good itself.

SECTION XCII.

If love is the motive to all moral action, and consequently also the necessary presupposition thereof, hence there must also be an *ante-moral* love, one that is *per se* not yet moral but which simply leads to the moral. In man's originally-possessed, though not as yet developed, God-likeness, there is in fact implied an original love antecedent to all moral volition,—an immediate love of the created spirit for the Creator as revealing himself to it, and for the surrounding universe as proclaiming the Creator's love. This direct and not morally-acquired love is, however, not an unfreely-operating, compelling instinctive impulse, but receives the character of moral freedom through the simultaneously awakening consciousness of personal independence and of the therein-contained love of the person to himself, so that in virtue of this twofold primitive love, which offers the possibility of an antagonism as well as of a harmony, man is invited to a free self-determination.

If the feeling of love is a directly excited one, and, as such, the presupposition of the moral activity to which it leads, it would seem as if moral freedom were actually precluded. For this feeling is as yet involuntary and unfree; and love and hatred produce, directly, a desire or a rejection. On the other hand, we cannot possibly exclude love from the sphere of the moral, and make of it a mere antecedent condition of the same; for according to the Christian consciousness at least, man is morally responsible for his love and his hatred; love is an object of duty, and *is required* by Christ as the essence of all fulfillment of the law. This seems like an irreconcilable contradiction.

In the first place, it is unavoidably necessary to admit that there is an *ante-moral* love. Brutes even have love, and are thereby impelled to activity; also the child at its mother's breast feels and manifests love. This is not a love springing from free conscious volition,—not a moral love,—but a purely natural love, which forms, however, the necessary antecedent condition of all development to morality. Primitive man must also have had such a love, inasmuch as without this a life of God's image is not conceivable. Created in harmony with God and with the All, he must have had also a direct *feeling* of this harmony, must have felt happy in his existence and in his Paradise-world; and in this feeling of happiness he must also have loved that whereby it was produced in him; there met him on every hand the image of divine love, of the harmony of the universe, and he must have felt and loved it; and when God revealed himself to him as the loving Father, then must man have experienced also toward Him a feeling of harmony and love. But all this love is as yet simply a directly-excited one,—is not freely produced by moral activity, and is consequently not yet a moral love, though it indeed conducts to moral activity and thereby to a transformation of itself into moral love. If now this first ante-moral love of man for God and his work were the sole love really existing in man, then evidently the action answering to it, and hence also to the will of God, would flow out of it so immediately and necessarily that the possibility of a contrary self-determination would be scarcely conceivable, so that though indeed moral freedom in general would not be thereby destroyed, yet liberty of choice would actually and essentially be precluded. Man would not stand in free self-determination between the choice of the good and the evil, but he would be overpoweringly driven by an inner potent impulse to a choice of the good. Now, though this would in fact render conceivable an absolutely sinless development, still it would render all the more inconceivable the possibility of a determination to the sinful.

But the matter assumes a very different aspect when we take into account the equally natural and immediate ante-moral impulse of *self-love*. This must, in fact, also be regarded as ante-moral, for the reason that it is the involuntary natural expression of soul-life in general, and hence exists also unconsciously among brutes. The fact that with man it is conscious, and constitutes a phase of rational self-consciousness, does not make it *per se* moral, but simply renders it capable of being formed into a moral quality. While now in the case of the brute the unconscious self-love can never become really evil, the self-love of man is, by virtue of the higher independence of the free spirit, only in a *possible* harmony with the love to God and the universe, but *should* come into *real* harmony therewith. Self-love is *per se* good,—is by no means the same as self-seeking or selfishness; Christ himself represents self-love as morally right, and as the measure for our love to our neighbor [Matt. xxii, 39; Luke x, 27; comp. Rom. xiii, 9; Gal. v, 14; James ii, 8; Eph. v, 28, 29, 33; 1 Sam. xviii, 1, 3]; but the goodness of this love consists not in an antecedently-established harmony with the love to God and the world, but simply in its liberty to confirm this harmony spontaneously. The love of God and the love of self are both equally primitive, and are *per se* not in antagonism with each other in the least, but yet they are different from each other and relatively *independent* of each other. In this mutual independence of these two forms of love there is afforded opportunity for the freedom of human choice. Man is *called* freely to confirm the harmony of his self-love and his divine love, and that too not by suppressing the one or the other, nor by making his love of God dependent on his self-love, but in fact by making his self-love dependent on his love of God,—by freely *subordinating* it thereto. As soon as the divine command was given to him, man was at once conscious that there was a difference between his self-love and his love to God, but also, at the same time, that it was his duty to develop this difference, not into antagonism but into harmony. The one (logically) possible mis-choice, of suppressing the *per se* legitimate self-love by disproportionate exaltation of the love to God, was impossible in fact, inasmuch as the love to God necessarily involves in itself all possible good, and hence also the proper love of self, for God preserves that which He himself has willed; so that consequently there remained possible only the other mis-choice (which was therefore morally forbidden), namely, of subordinating the love of God to self-love, instead of preserving the latter in its true character through its proper subordination to the former. If *simply* the love of God had been primitive in man, then a choice of the ungodly would have been impossible; if *simply* self-love had been primitive in him, then a choice of the good, of submission to the divine will, would have been equally impossible, and man would have been in the one case irresponsible for the good, and in the other for the evil—without desert and without guilt. But by virtue of the fact that the love to God and the love of self are alike primitive, as the ante-moral germ of the moral, it follows that man is fully responsible for the confirmation or the disturbance of the harmony of this twofold love; for this determination was not already involved in the constitution of man, but was proposed as a moral task to his free will. The mere love to God would have made man good but not free, the mere self-love would have made him seemingly free but not good; the twofold love made him free for choosing the good, but also free for the possible choice of the evil,—which, under these circumstances, assumed, in consequence of the equally real original love to God, the form of infidelity to God, of a punishable *sin*. The case is quite similar with the moral culture of the child. The child, as soon as self-conscious, has love for its mother, and also a *per se* strictly legitimate love for play; when the will of the mother calls the child from its play, it becomes conscious of the difference of the two forms of love; it knows also that it can prefer its love for play, and leave the will of the mother unheeded. It must by a morally-free choice, make a decision,— must subordinate the one love to the other; if it chooses obedience, then in thus choosing, and thus only, it feels itself truly free. If there had been no difference of a twofold love, the child would have had no choice; it would have just as unfreely, and without a consciousness of the good or a right to praise, followed its mother, as, on the other supposition, it would have unfreely and without a consciousness of the evil or a desert of blame, preferred its play. It is only such cases of choice, of moral self-determination, that bring the child's morality to development and to maturity.—It would be very erroneous to consider self-love as *per se* evil, and as a natural germ of the evil; the fact is, it simply offers—not *per se*, however, but in its normal difference from the love to God—the *possibility* of evil, but equally so also the possibility of *moral* good in general. It is only in the consciously-wrought free subordination of self-love to the divine love, that the latter as well as the former becomes *moral*. There can be no question of a "*must*" in the determination, whether in the one direction or in the other, but only of a "*should*" and a "*should not*."

SECTION XCIII.

The primitive love of man to God and his works becomes *moral* only, when, with consciousness and free recognition, it is confirmed by the self-loving spirit, and when the love to God is made to control the love of self, that is, when this twofold love becomes a *striving* of the self-love to put itself into harmony with all love, through free self-subordination to the love for God. Love as moral, and as consciously striving toward its object, becomes *disposition*. Hence for all further development of the moral life, a moral disposition is the necessary antecedent condition; and it is such in its twofold form, as the affirming disposition of love, and, with reference to evil, as the negating disposition of hatred. It is only as disposition, but not as ante-moral natural love, that love is an object of the divine law, a moral requirement, whereas the ante-moral love is simply an element of the good that is conferred in creation itself. Hence, as moral motive, love is also the *basis* of the moral in the fullest sense of the word, the life-inspiring germ of all other moral activity.

By the fact that love becomes a moral duty, it does not cease to be a moral motive. Man, as awakened to moral consciousness, is to have no other motive of his moral activity than one which he has himself morally constituted,—not a merely natural ante-moral love, but love as a disposition. Many are led to deny that love is at all an object of the divine law, from the simple fact that they reduce it to a mere involuntary feeling. Also Rothe affirms that we cannot command to love, but only *to learn* to love. This is very nearly a distinction without a difference; for if we can command to learn, and this learning has a necessary result, then evidently in commanding the learning we also command the result. The notion that man is *per se*, and irrespective of his moral depravity, not master of his own heart,—that he cannot dominate his proclivities, his love or his repugnance,—simply destroys his moral responsibility. If man cannot control his love and his hatred, and bring about in himself moral love, but must allow himself to be ruled by blind inclinations, then is he no longer a moral creature, but simply a dangerous sort of animal. If marriages are contracted only from "irresistible inclination" and dissolved because of "irresistible aversion," then they lie outside of the sphere of morality. Christian morality does not indeed require that marriages shall continue to exist despite the pretended "irresistible aversion;" on the contrary, it denies fundamentally that the notion of such an ungovernable aversion is to be admitted, inasmuch as it makes man morally responsible for his love and his hatred. It would not only be a monstrous but also an absurd theory of morals which should admit, on the one hand, that we are not at all master of our love and our aversion,—that love cannot be commanded as a duty,—and yet, on the other hand, should require that man should not *act* according to his love or aversion, but according to requirements of the moral law that have no connection therewith; he who has not love cannot practice love without hypocrisy; but that he has it not is his own fault. Christian ethics requires not to proclaim love in our deeds where there is no love, for it cannot require falseness; but it requires us to *have* love for all, and, *for that reason* also to practice it. The Scriptures declare unequivocally that love, the motive of all moral action, is also a *duty* commanded by the moral law; the law "Thou shalt love thy neighbor as thyself" [Lev. xix, 18; Matt. xxii, 39; Mark xii, 31] is called a "royal law," that is, a law that dominates all others [James ii, 8; comp. Gal. v, 14; Col. iii, 14; 1 Tim. i, 5; 1 John iii, 11 *sqq.;* iv, 7 *sqq.*].

SECTION XCIV.

As morality is the free fulfilling of the divine will, hence moral love is primarily always *love to God*, and the love to created things is moral only in so far as it springs from the love to God,—considers created things as the work of God, and loves them in him.

The God-consciousness, as developed into a moral love of God, is *piety* (εὐσέβεια); hence all morality rests on piety. All non-pious love is immoral, and hence also all love to the creature as such, taken in itself without connection and interpenetration with the divine love. But all love to God rests on our consciousness of God's love to us; love is produced only by love; all moral love is, in its essence, reciprocal love; a non-loving creature can be loved only in so far as God's love is reflected to us from it; and for this very reason moral love to persons *seeks* indeed their love in return, but does not *need* it.

As rational thought finds the unity of its thought-world only in the thought of God, so also moral love finds its rest and its unity only in love to God; it is not content with the semblance thereof but only with the truth; and all things have their truth only in their relation to God. As that love is higher, truer, and mightier which loves, in a person, not merely the earthly but also the soul, so is that love higher, truer, and mightier which loves in man, not merely the creature but also the image of God, and, through it, God himself. Love is the more genuine the higher its object; he who sees in creatures the trace of God, and loves God in them, he alone loves with the whole might of love. The proper love to the creature rests on the consciousness that "the earth is the Lord's and the fullness thereof" [1 Cor. x, 26]; this does not lower the creature in the eyes of the love, but elevates both its worth and the love for it. Thus also Christ presents the precept of love to God as "the first and great commandment;" and "the second is like unto it," that is, it is already implied in it, though it does not absolutely coincide with it,— it is in fact the reflection of our love to God back upon our neighbor; our love for our neighbor is erroneous, when it does not rest upon love to God. Hence Christ says: "He that loveth father or mother more than me, is not worthy of me" [Matt. x, 37]. To the natural man this sounds hard and severe; but from a Christian stand-point, nay, even from a religious stand-point in general, no other view is possible than in fact, that a love for the creature without the higher divine love, or with one that prevails over the latter, is sinful. By this relation of all love to the love of God, this love is preserved also from one-sided narrowness,—clings not, in irrational caprice, to isolated objects,—but extends itself to all that is created, though indeed different degrees of such love are possible, from the fact of the differing peculiarity of the object and of the loving person.

This true mutual relation of our love to the creature and our love to God, appears still more striking when we attentively consider the relation of human love to the divine love. As human thinking is only a reflection of the divine thought, so also is human love only a reflection of the divine love. All that is true and good in the copy is enkindled by the true and the good of the prototype; "He that loveth not knoweth not God, for God is love" [1 John iv, 8]. Man could not love God, and hence could not love morally at all, were he not loved of God. God's love is a love of grace; man's love is a love of gratitude,—the answering love of a child. Love cannot love any thing else but love [Psa. ciii, 1 *sqq.;* Col. iii, 17; 1 Thess. v, 18; 1 John iv, 11, 19]. For this reason there is no pain so great as where love remains unrequited. But to the pious heart it is not unrequited; such a heart finds the love which it seeks; Christ says: whatsoever "ye have done unto one of the least of these my brethren, ye have done it unto *me;*" and where, against the loving one, the heart of man coldly closes itself, there the love of God comes in its place.

SECTION XCV.

While our love to created things is either simply a love to the inferior, or to the equal, or to the merely relatively higher, and hence always meets its object with a consciousness of its own independent power and of an individual personal right, our love to God is, as directed to One that is absolutely superior to all that is human, always associated with a consciousness of our own impotency as in contrast to the infinite holy power of the Beloved, and hence is a love of *fear*. Love to God is essentially *God-fearing;* there is, however, no moral fear of God without also love to God. Mere fear alone is not a moral motive, for only love is this.

In all love to a created object our moral action is complementive and promotive of the being and life of the same; we render to it in our love a real service, and obtain for ourselves a claim upon its grateful, answering love. But God's being and life cannot be complemented and heightened by our love; we cannot render to him a real service for which he would be under obligation to us [Job xli, 2; Rom. xi, 35]. Our love to God consists only with the consciousness that we receive every thing from God, and God nothing from us,—that our entire being and life stand absolutely in his power. Such a consciousness includes necessarily the feeling of fear—not fear of a mere power operating without reference to moral action, but of a righteous God who opposes all that is unholy; and in this sense Christ himself makes a regard for the penal judgments of God a motive for moral action [Matt. v, 22, 25 *sqq.;* xxv, 45, 46]. Fear of God in the absence of love is, in fact, by no means irrational; rather is it, wherever such love is lacking, the natural expression of the antagonism between the unholy nature of the person and the holy God, but such fear is not a *moral* motive. It presupposes the antagonism which the moral denies; and it cannot do away with it, for it is love alone that harmonizes. That nevertheless this slavish fear is of moral significancy for the state of sinfulness, we shall subsequently see. For the unfallen state, mere fear has neither reason nor possibility, for mere fear is, in its essence, *hatred,*—hatred against the more powerful being with whom we are not united by love.

Mere love, however, without fear, as toward God, is not truthful, for that would be only a love of familiarity as with our equal. He who is conscious of his moral freedom, must also be conscious, as often as he makes use of this moral freedom, that God opposes his holy power to its misuse. The feeling which springs out of such a consciousness is not contrary to love, nor is it yet love itself, but it is genuine moral fear. Hence this moral *awe* of God, the true *reverence* for God, is the beginning of all wisdom and the condition of all morality [Deut. v, 29; vi, 2; x, 20; Prov. i, 7; viii, 13; ix, 10; xv, 33; xvi, 6; Psa. cxi, 10; cxii, 7; Job xxviii, 28; 2 Cor. vii, 1]. Only those who fear the Lord trust in the Lord [Psa. cxv, 11]; for only the holy God gives surety for his love and truthfulness; not to fear God involves being godless [Prov. i, 29; Rom. iii, 18], and piety is synonymous with the fear of God (φόβος θεοῦ) [Acts ix, 13; Eph. v, 21; 2 Cor. vii, 1]. The reference is not to this pious dread of the holy God, but to that mere servile fear which is at bottom hatred, when St. John says: "There is no fear in love, but perfect love casteth out fear; because fear hath torment (κόλασιν ἔχει, is a feeling of estrangement from God, of unblessedness); he that feareth is not made perfect in love" [1 John iv, 18]. The true fear of God is closely allied to the love of God [Deut. x, 12].

SECTION XCVI.

Where the love to God is true God-fearing, there it is also a firm *trusting in God*. Trusting is the reverse side of this fearing. Man-fearing is devoid of trust; God-fearing is *per se* also God-trusting. In relation to all that is evil, I *fear* God, who will bring it to naught and me with it; in relation to all that is good, I *trust* God, who will not permit me to come to naught, but will gloriously accomplish that which I begin in his name. God-fearing love is full of *confidence* in the results of its moral strivings; because it fears God, it has no reason to fear any power that is hostile to God. Certain of its victory, and certain that it works in God and for God, and hence that it accomplishes divine and imperishable work, it becomes *enthusiasm*, which is the highest and truest moral motive, and the only sufficient power where there is involved a moral working for general interests that transcend all temporal individual interests,—where the temporal happiness of the person must be sacrificed to a moral principle,—which, however, is conceivable only where sin is dominant.

Trusting in God is faith, love, and hope at the same time; primarily, however, it is not a result of moral self-culture, but it is simply the germ of that threefold life that is antecedent to all actual moral life. As the awakening consciousness of the child expresses itself in an, as yet, obscure trust to its mother, so is it with man's first life-relation to God. Man attains a trust not simply *through* faith and *through* love, but faith and love are *per se*, and of necessity, trust already; and hence trust is a necessary antecedent condition of all moral life. Trust relates to the idea of an end; the mere desire of an end is not a sufficient motive to inspire moral effort toward it; it may be a hopeless, and hence an inactive, desire; doubting Peter sinks in the waves; it is only an unshaken trust that confirms courage and awakens strength [Psa. xviii, 31 *sqq.*; xxvii, 14; xxxiv, 9; xxxvii, 3 *sqq.*; lxii, 6 *sqq.*; lxxxiv, 13; Prov. xvi, 20, and elsewhere].—There is no enthusiasm for evil,—at furthest only a Satanic pleasure in evil, but this pleasure is attended with fear and malice, but not enthusiasm. Man as sinful may err as to what is good or evil, and he may therefore have enthusiasm for a folly, but only from the fact that he takes it for something good and noble. Nor can the merely individual and temporal awaken enthusiasm; nothing but the ideal can do this,—that which is, or is conceived of as, absolutely valid, as eternal truth, and hence of divine significancy, in a word that in the victory and permanent endurance of which the person has entire confidence. For that which is merely individual or useful I may indeed have energy or passion, but not enthusiasm. Only the absolutely good, the divine, is free from all doubt. Doubt is death to enthusiasm; without faith it is not possible morally to battle for the divine. Without enthusiasm there can be but a cold, calculating working for temporal ends, but no effort for the divine and eternal; hence whatever is not of faith is sin, for it is non-moral, whereas man ought constantly to be moral. The apostles had indeed, during Christ's earthly life, a warm love for their Master, so that they were ready even to die with him [John xi, 16], but they had enthusiasm only after the pouring out of the Holy Ghost.

SECTION XCVII.

As love springs from the consciousness of the harmony of the person with his object, and as the feeling of such a harmony is the feeling of *happiness*, hence all love is *per se* also happiness, and its striving is necessarily a striving for happiness. As, however, love does not seek its own, but finds its bliss alone in that of the beloved, it is clear that this striving for happiness, as based on moral love, is in nowise self-seeking and narrow-hearted, but, on the contrary, a proper motive of moral activity,—only, however, *in so far* as it is in unison with the right love, and does not appear as something different from it,—not as the first and fundamental element, but only as a derived one; but it becomes an immoral motive in so far as it is an expression of mere self-love (Eudemonism).—The tendency to the good, which is produced by moral activity, becomes in turn itself a higher motive to the moral.

The question as to the morality of happiness-seeking as a moral motive, cannot be answered without a more definite characterization. The "eudemonistic" view proper, that of the Epicureans, is evidently immoral, as it rests on mere self-love. Heathen ethics could oppose to this self-seeking happiness-principle nothing other than the notion that virtue should be sought after for its own sake. If there was here a seeming subordinating of the person to a general moral idea, still, because of the inner untruthfulness of the position, it could not possibly be otherwise than that in fact, even in the strictest Stoicism, the mere proud self-consciousness of the individual should be, after all, the influencing motive proper. The thought of *love* as the true moral motive was entirely wanting to heathen ethics,—is peculiar to Christianity. The Christian idea of love harmonizes the legitimate self-love with submission to the moral law. In loving God, man loves also himself as a child of God, and in fulfilling his duty he at the same time realizes his happiness. The love to God and to His creatures is, on the one hand, a feeling of happiness, and, on the other, a motive to moral activity. The old controversy about the happiness-principle, which has in recent times been revived, especially by the school of Kant, receives its proper solution only in the Christian view, namely, in that, while Christianity recognizes in the proper seeking for happiness a strictly moral motive, it also exalts the character of this seeking by the love in which alone it bases it. It is therefore a very one-sided illiberality in Rationalists to reproach Old Testament ethics with "Eudemonism." It is true, the Old Testament recognizes the seeking after happiness as a proper motive in the fulfilling of the law: "That it may go well with thee and with thy children after thee, and that thou mayest prolong thy days upon the earth [Deut. iv, 40; Exod. xx, 12; Deut. v, 16; xxix, 33; Psa. xxxvii, 37; cxxii, 6, etc.]; the formula "Blessed is he that," etc., [Psa. i, 1; ii, 12; xxxiv, 8; xl, 4, etc.] and other similar ones, are very frequently given as an encouragement to moral obedience; but also Christ himself and the apostles expressly present such a motive: "Do this and thou shalt live" [Luke x, 28; comp. Matt. xix, 16, 17, 28, 29; vi, 19, 20; Mark x, 21; Luke xii, 33; John iii, 36; Eph. vi, 3; Rom. ii, 7; 1 Tim. iv, 8;'vi, 19]; the "crown" of life is promised as a reward to fidelity [1 Cor. ix, 25; 2 Tim. iv, 8; 1 Peter v, 4; James i, 12; Rev. ii, 10]; but neither the Old nor the New Testament separate this striving for happiness from the love to God and our neighbor in which, in fact, both Covenants find the true motive to moral action. There is, in reality, no essential antagonism between love and the striving after happiness; but the latter is directly implied in the former, and is, in the nature of the case, inseparable from it. Christianity knows no other happiness than love to God in the consciousness of being loved by him.

All moral activity has necessarily a permanent result in the person himself; it makes the moral his possession and property,—forms more and more his moral character, and hence creates a *tendency* to, and a *readiness* in, moral acting. This moral possession, as a result of moral activity—*virtue*—becomes in turn itself, as an active power, a motive force to moral life, so that by his moral activity man constantly increases the actuating power of the same. Of this readiness or skill in moral acting we will have occasion to speak hereafter; we merely remark here, that by virtue of acting morally the originally as yet undetermined freedom of choice receives a determined character,—takes up into itself the morally good as such. The moral develops itself into a constantly increasing power,—renews itself on a progressively larger scale in the organic circulation of life. The good becomes to the moral man, as it were, a second nature, which, in turn, works out of itself by virtue of its own power; it is no longer simply something objective to him, nor merely a natural quality conferred *upon* him, but it is a vital possession, and hence an actuating power *within* him.

CHAPTER V.

THE MORAL ACTIVITY.

SECTION XCVIII.

Love works the accomplishment of the lovingly-willed end; the moral motive and the accomplishing of the end belong, therefore, morally, inseparably together. The moral element lies neither exclusively in the motive, nor exclusively in the action; neither exclusively in the intention or end, nor exclusively in the means to the end, but in the unity of both. A good end does not sanctify the means, nor do good means sanctify the end, but a good end is accomplished morally only by good means; an end which actually *can* be realized by immoral means, is itself immoral.

As the moral is a free realizing of a rational end, the question naturally rises, wherein the moral element properly lies, namely, whether in the end and in the motive? or in the means to the end, that is, in the acts that lead to the realization of the end? or whether in both at the same time,—that is, whether we are to judge of an act exclusively from the intention, or exclusively from the action itself, or in fact from both together? The first of these queries has been answered affirmatively by the Jesuits—though this is not peculiar to them, but is involved more or less in all perverted moralizing, especially in that of worldly society at large; outside of the sphere of Christian earnestness there prevails every-where in fact a tendency to distinguish between the morality of the end and that of the means.

From the very idea of the moral it follows necessarily that the conscious end, and hence the intention, occupies with good right the chief place in determining the moral judgment, and that consequently only that action can be good which aims at a good end—one in harmony with the moral order of the world. Whatever accomplishes such an end *must* consequently be in harmony with the moral order of the world, and hence be itself good; when therefore the axiom: "The end sanctifies the means" is understood to mean "that the means which answer to a really good end are necessarily also good," then it is entirely unobjectionable; it becomes false only when either the end is only seemingly good, or the means only seemingly appropriate, or where it is assumed that the means, that is, the actions, are *per se* morally indifferent, and receive a moral character only *from* the intention. As, however, all free action falls within the sphere of the moral order of the world, and as the reality that is produced by this action is either in harmony or in disharmony with this order, hence also the action, *per se* and irrespectively of its end, is either good or bad,—though indeed, in order to its *full* moral appreciation, its end also must be taken into the account. He who sets a house on fire from negligence may have had no evil intention, but he is punished nevertheless, and justly so, for his action was *per se* evil, and might have been avoided by him. If we suppose instead of an absolutely good end, that is, such a one as is a part of the highest good, simply particular ends, the goodness of which consists only in their subordination to the order of the whole, then the axiom: "The end sanctifies the means," is false, in so far as the end or means do not consist with the order of the whole. He who burns down a house in order to drive the rats out of it attains indeed his end, but at the same time he destroys the super-ordinate end of the house. The question becomes difficult only when bearing upon moral action in a *sinful* world, in which *evil*, and hence the infliction of evils for punishment, for discipline and defense, has a legitimate place. But of this we can only speak further on.

Moral action, as flowing from love, may be considered from two points of view: first, *in itself*, according to its inner differences, that is, moral action as such; secondly, in relation to the different moral *objects* in virtue of the differences of which the moral action itself assumes a different form.

Subdivision First.

THE MORAL ACTIVITY *PER SE* IN ITS INNER DIFFERENCES.

SECTION XCIX.

As moral action always seeks to effect a harmony between the acting person and the moral object, hence it stands in relation, on the one hand, to the former as its starting-point, and, on the other, to the latter as the goal aimed at by the life-movement. This harmony can consequently be effected in a twofold manner,—either in that the object becomes for the subject, or the subject for the object, that is, either by *appropriation* or by *formation*. As, however, every entity, in so far as it is good, has a right in and of itself, hence it has such a right also as bearing upon the morally active person, so that neither the appropriating nor the forming is without some degree of limitation, but both must respect this right of the object. The two forms of moral action have therefore, as a necessary limit, a third form of moral bearing, namely, a bearing by which the moral object is *preserved* in its rights,—moral *sparing*.

This third form of the moral bearing, which, as an activity of the will, has of course a moral character, has been very largely ignored in ethics, or at least left in the back-ground, and it is even severely criticised in its defenders, and yet it is a sphere of very essential duties, duties which can be classed into other spheres only by manifest violence, and which yet consist, in fact, neither in appropriation nor in formation.

When I check my foot in order not wantonly to crush an ant that is crossing my path, this is in fact a moral self-limitation, but it cannot be properly classed as moral forming, seeing that the end of this action is very evidently the to-be-spared animal, and not the acting person. But every moral action without exception is also a moral self-forming, a self-cultivating, without, however, that this self-culture should always appear as the end proper. Without the proper respecting of the duty of sparing, appropriation and formation would become violence. But the moral motive of all right action, namely, love, implies in its very nature also the exercising of preservative sparing; man cannot love an object, and yet not seek to preserve it in the beloved peculiarity of its being. Sparing is not of a mere negative character, a mere limiting of another action, but it is essentially different from all other action; it is of a negative character only in form but not in contents. When I do not severely reproach a person who is inwardly and deeply ashamed and humiliated because of his sin, but tenderly spare him, this is not a mere non-doing of that which I might do, not a mere limiting of my punitive activity, but it is the very opposite of this. There results here from the moral motive, that is, love, not a positive acting upon the other, but a restraining of such action; and if I thereby heap coals of fire upon the head of an enemy, and thus profit him morally, still this is not a real influential forming on my part, but a giving place for the moral self-forming of the other; my sparing procedure here is indeed mediately a forming, as, on the other hand, it is also a self-mastering; *per se* however, it is an action different from both. When, in the sphere of the freedom of rational creatures, God restrains his immediate action in order to preserve them in their freedom,—when God spared Cain, and, after the flood, promised henceforth to spare living creatures as a whole [Gen. iv, 15; viii, 21; ix, 11 *sqq.*],—this is simply a divine example of moral sparing. To spare is often more difficult morally than to appropriate or to influence, for in the latter cases the person has a lively consciousness of self, and stands forth prominently with his own rights and his enjoyment of activity; but, in sparing, it is the right of the object that stands in the foreground, and the actor must recognize and respect this right, and must morally overcome his personal will and his pleasure in self-assertion. Sparing is the preservative, the "conservative," phase of the moral life, and its carrying-out presupposes greater moral maturity than the exercise of the appropriating or forming activities; for the youthful zeal of the morally immature spirit, its practice is exceedingly difficult; not to crush the bruised reed, nor to quench the smoking wick [Matt. xii, 20], is more difficult, and involves a higher moral wisdom, than to destroy or to create anew.—As the sparing procedure is logically the most immediate course of conduct, and rather a withholding than an express acting, hence it is more appropriate to treat of it first.

I. MORAL SPARING.

SECTION C.

Moral sparing is a self-limiting of personal action in the interest of the *rights of the object;* the latter is neither appropriated nor formed by the person, but simply *let alone* in its peculiar being and nature. The duty of sparing rests upon the right of every natural or spiritual and historical entity to its existence and its peculiarity, in so far as these are good, and hence upon *love* to the object as being good,—consequently, in the final instance, upon a *pious* world theory, upon love to God. The entity is spared because it bears in itself the impress of the Eternal,—is an expression of the will of God; hence sparing is moral only in so far as it relates to the good and the divine in existence, and not to that which by virtue of its ungodly nature should be an object of moral *hatred*.—The higher the perfection of an object, so much the higher is also its right to moral sparing; the less the perfection, the more the object falls within the sphere of appropriation and formation. The highest object of moral sparing among created things is man, and whatever exists through and for him; but, above all, his moral personality itself, and hence also his *honor*. God himself cannot indeed be an object of moral sparing in the strict sense of the word, but he is such, however, in the *forms* of his *revelation* in time, and in all that symbolically represents him.

An indiscriminate sparing would be simply spiritual and moral sloth or indifference, and hence immoral. The sparing of the anti-godly is a sinning against God, is the withholding of moral love. An evil existence has indeed also, in so far as any good still inheres in it, a right to be spared,—only, however, in that which it has of good. The right to be spared is not, of course, in the case of finite existences, of an unlimited and unconditional character, and in the case of nature-objects it is much more limited than with personal beings, though indeed it never sinks entirely to zero. It is true, nature is destined to service under the dominion of the rational spirit, and, in so far as it reaches this destination, man has in fact a right to pass beyond the limits of mere sparing restraint, and actively to lay hold on the very existence of nature, transforming and appropriating it. Where the right of the personal spirit is not recognized, where God is conceived of as a mere nature-entity, there pious morality manifests itself in a wide-reaching sparing of natural objects, far beyond the measure of what is required of us; so is it with the Brahmins and the Buddhists; and, especially in the case of the former, this over-delicate sparing of natural objects is associated with a cruel *un*-sparingness toward themselves.

As the duty of sparing rests on the right of each particular being to its own peculiarity, hence this duty as well as this right rise in scope in proportion to the degree of the individual perfection. That which is absolutely perfect bears the character of eternity and unchangeableness, and though it may indeed be spiritually appropriated, yet it cannot in any respect be formed or changed. In the process of education, the dictating influence upon the child falls into the back-ground in proportion as the child grows toward moral maturity. Lifeless matter has no claim to sparing. When the Brahmin does not allow himself causelessly to crush the least earth-clod, this is simply because he regards it as the sacred body of Brahma. Plants have a better claim to be spared than inorganic objects, and the more so the higher their organization, and especially as they stand in a closer relation to man; to injure fruit-trees and other edible vegetation, without cause, is regarded as sinful even by uncultured tribes. The more an object enters into the sphere of man's spiritual life, the more it bears the impress of the spirit, constituting, as it were, a sort of larger corporeality for man, so much the higher is its claim upon sparing. This is especially the case with the human body itself, as the organ of the spirit, as a "temple of the Holy Ghost;" in the next rank stand all such natural objects as hold a relation to the spiritual life, and which are mementos of important events and of spiritual effort in general,—every thing, in fine, that has been actually produced by the human spirit, and the more so in proportion as it is of a spiritualized character,—and hence, especially, all products of industry and art. But the highest right to sparing is possessed by the personal spirit itself in its personal peculiarity; to assail the honor of another is to wound his moral being; the higher the moral culture and maturity of a person, the higher is also his right to moral sparing; by sin this right is necessarily largely forfeited.

While the heathen idol falls, of course, within the sphere of human sparing, the eternal and almighty God stands beyond the scope of this activity. Nevertheless there are sacred duties which express, in a certain sense, a sparing of the divine; the name of God and his honor are to be held sacred; and whatever is a symbol of the divine, or is a reminder of God's presence, has an especial claim to moral sparing; even uncultured tribes practice a reverential sparing in regard to all that is sacred or stands in relation to the divine in contradistinction to the worldly and the profane. From the simple fact of the sparing of whatever stands in real, or even in symbolical, relation to God, it is very evident, of how great significancy is piety for morality. The pious mind finds God's being and providence in all things and in all life, and whatever is not hostile to God is, for it, sacred and an object of pious sparing. The higher the piety of the person, so much the higher becomes the worth, and hence also the right, of all existence, in so far as this existence is good. He who is impious has no reverence for created things,—no tenderness toward them. Not to spare that which has a right to sparing, is moral *rudeness*. The immoral and the impious are uniformly rude and coarse; they have indeed fear but no awe.

Sparing is, as a non-doing, only then moral when it is a conscious and freely-willed withholding of a real out-going action, that is, when it is an *inner* activity, a moral self-controlling out of respect for another's right, and when it is in real harmony with moral forming and appropriating, so as not in any manner to interfere therewith,—that is, when it is the virtualizing of the real *rights* of the moral object. The formable or cultivable object has, however, just as good a right to be formed as it has to be spared. In so far as sparing is a mere non-influencing of the objective entity, it is not yet moral, and may even also be evil. The spiritually indolent declines even this form of activity, not, however, from love to the object, but from mere selfishness. Only that sparing is morally good which rests on *love* to the object, and which therefore implies a conscious self-limitation and self-controlling, and which is, consequently, only in outer form, but not in inner essence, a mere non-doing; mere non-doing would be *per se* sinful, inasmuch as the moral life must always be active, and it is only the seeming non-doing which, however, is an inner-doing, that can be moral. True moral sparing is, in relation to beings that are formable and in need of formation, uniformly also a formative influence, namely, in that it gives proper play for legitimate self-forming on the part of the object. A tyrannical education that extends its tutorial dictation into all the minute details, produces not a moral character but only servile-mindedness. All right education must also practice, in the interest of the training of moral freedom, a wise sparing,—must allow the child the possibility of determining itself independently, and of thereby maturing itself toward moral freedom. As the sparing of a growing plant is at the same time also a furthering of it, so also, and even in a higher degree, is this true of sparing as exercised toward rational beings; the pardoning of an offense exercises frequently a very fruitful influence on the moral development of him who is pardoned.

II. MORAL APPROPRIATING.

SECTION CI.

In the appropriating activity man effects his unity with the objective entity, by taking it up into himself,—by uniting it with himself, by making it an element of his own nature. This moral activity differs both in regard to *what* element of the object is appropriated by the actor, and in regard to *how* this takes place.

(*a*) According to *what* element of the object is appropriated, the appropriating is either *natural* or *spiritual;* the latter is the more comprehensive, and extends itself to all objective existence,—also to God.—*Natural* appropriation relates as well to the existence and preservation of the *individual* person as to the existence and preservation of the *species*, and is the necessary condition of both. In both respects, therefore, man is bound to nature and stimulated by natural instinct, and although in this respect he is freer than the brute, and all the freer the higher his personality is developed, nevertheless in respect to the preservation of the existence of the subject, this freedom is still always of a limited character, and the law of nature is, in many respects, stronger than the will, though, however, not so potent as to force the will to the immoral.

All natural existence is at the same time also of spiritual significance,—is a realized thought, the expression of an idea. But as, on the other hand, not every spiritual entity is connected with a natural one, hence spiritual appropriating is of greater compass and higher significancy than the merely natural. The higher moral worth of the former appears also from this, that it preserves the objective existence in its reality, whereas natural appropriation more or less destroys it. With the increase of moral and spiritual growth, natural appropriation constantly gives place more and more to the spiritual; with the child the former predominates; but what is normal in the child becomes immoral in mature age.

In natural appropriation there is manifested a real and normal limitation of free self-determination. When hunger predominates, the spiritual forces subside, and at last it becomes even mightier than the free determinations of the will. Nevertheless this power of nature over the will is neither unlimited nor absolutely definitive, but the moral will is capable of asserting its autonomy against it. It may indeed enfeeble the bodily force and therewith also the spiritual, but it cannot absolutely determine the will. Christ cried out indeed on the cross: "I thirst;" but when hungering in the desert he resisted the temptation. The fact that from grief or despair persons have starved themselves to death, proves at least that the will is capable of being stronger than nature, even under its most overpowering phases. He who in the last desperation of famine lays hold on human life to satiate his hunger [Lev. xxvi, 29] commits a crime even in the eyes of human law, and the violence of hunger forms no excuse. That also in this respect a great difference is to be made between man as unfallen and man as enslaved to sin, we have already observed.

SECTION CII.

Natural appropriating *per se* is not yet a moral activity, but it is extra-moral, and therefore when it appears in and of itself as the substance and chief-end of life, it is immoral. It becomes morally good only when it is the expression of an under-lying *spiritual* appropriating, that is, when it does not rest on mere sensuous impulse, but on conscious love, not so much to the sensuous object *per se* as rather to God who lovingly gives it to us. This implies further that, with a moral person, the natural appropriating should never predominate over the spiritual,—that not the attendant sensuous enjoyment *per se* should be regarded as the essential and proper object of effort, but rather the rational God-willed end of the sensuous, so that consequently the sensuous enjoyment should be aimed at only in so far as the moral purpose admits of it.

There is *per se* forbidden to man, irrespective of his sinfulness, no natural temperate sensuous appropriating; this is plainly seen in the account of Paradise and in the example and deed of Christ at the wedding of Cana. Thankfulness to God sanctifies even the sensuous appropriation of his gifts [1 Tim. iv, 3–5]. The Christian custom of *saying grace* at meals, after the example of Christ [Matt. xiv, 19; xv, 36], which prevailed also generally in the ancient church [Acts xxvii, 35; *Tert. Apol.*, 39], has a high moral significancy; it rescues the natural enjoyment from the stage of mere sensuousness,—elevates it into the sphere of the moral. As even in the opinion of worldly society the significancy of social repasts consists not in the sensuous enjoyment, but in the intellectual entertainment and interchange of sentiment, so according to Christian morals the significancy of all sensuous appropriation consists in its relation to God,—in the appropriating of the divine in and through the bread and wine of daily food. "Whether therefore ye eat or drink, or whatsoever ye do, do all to the glory of God" [1 Cor. x, 30, 31]. But man does not give God the glory when he forgets Him and finds pleasure merely in the sensuous. God neither forbids nor begrudges to man the enjoyment of the sensuous, but he forbids a beastly merging of one's self into it. He who forgets the Giver in the gift sinks below the sphere of the moral and even of the human. The world at large is not fond of grace-saying, and yet even the heathen made his libations to the gods at his repasts. Even Schleiermacher (*Christl. Sitte, Beil.*, p. 33) found in the just-cited words of Paul simply an assumption of the animal element—food-taking—"into the sphere of social pleasure," "in order to chasten mere sensuous desire," and he is unable to discover any significancy in the saying of grace.

The *observing of moderation* in natural appropriation, the regarding it as a mere means to the rational end of preserving the individual as well as the species, is not merely a moral preserving of the person but also of the object,—is a doing of justice toward the object. He who is temperate simply, *e. g.*, in order not to injure his health, is not yet moral, but only self-seeking. Appropriation finds its measure in the moral duty of sparing. All natural appropriating is more or less a destroying of the objective entity; and, as the latter has *per se* a right to sparing, it follows that the limit of appropriation is not a merely subjective one. The nightingale-tongue pies of the Roman epicures are not mentioned with detestation simply because they are a mere immoderation, but because they involved an injustice against the right of nature to be spared. And many modern table-luxuries are not of a much more innocent character.

In *sexual* appropriation the moral is conditioned not merely, as in the use of natural objects, on thankful love to God as the giver, but—inasmuch as the object appropriated is itself a moral personality—also on personal love to the same. Without this love the person of the object would be treated as a mere impersonality, as a mere nature-object, and its validity as a personal moral spirit ignored. Upon this moral recognition of the personality Scripture lays great emphasis. "Adam *knew* Eve, his wife;" the same expression (יָדַע) is very frequently used of wedlock communion, also on the part of the woman [Gen. xix, 8; Num. xxxi, 17]. This is usually explained as a mere euphemism, but it is in fact the appropriate expression to the essence of the matter. The persons mutually recognize each other as personalities bound to each other in full reciprocal possession,—recognize, each, himself in the other and the other in himself—recognize the complete belonging of each to the other in virtue of a mutual love which precludes every thing that is strange or disuniting, so that consequently the two constitute truly *one* soul and *one* flesh. The expression to "know," to recognize, refers therefore primarily solely to legitimate wedlock cohabitation, and was applied only subsequently and improperly also to sinful.

Sexual appropriation also is in part a destruction, a despoiling of the person, which finds a compensation only in the fact that the one person belongs to the other as an inalienable possession—that both persons are united to an indissoluble life in common. Hence the commerce of the sexes without marriage is self-profanation; and virginity is esteemed among all, not absolutely barbarous nations as an inviolable treasure to which only that one has a right who is united in his whole personality to the person of the virgin. And even within the limits of marriage each party has a right to sparing, and should not be degraded into a mere object of sensuous pleasure; also here there is a measure that is conditioned on the end, and the transgressing of which is a dishonoring, a degrading, of the consort.

SECTION CIII.

2.—*Spiritual* appropriation relates to all objective existence, nature included, and takes up the spiritual contents thereof into the being of the self-conscious subject,—makes it its personal possession. The moral subject enlarges thus its own spiritual being,—receives the universe as well as God into itself,—forms for itself an inner world which, as a copy of the real world, realizes under its subjective phase the moral end, namely, the effecting of the harmony of existence.

In spiritual appropriation, as the far richer field of this activity, the appropriated object is in no wise destroyed, but on the contrary preserved, nay, brought to its higher truth, namely, in that its spiritual contents not only exist *per se*, but also exist *for* the spirit, and have now in the spirit a continued existence even after the object itself outwardly perishes. That which has become a part of history and science has thereby attained to imperishableness. That which externally perishes, the natural existence, is the inferior, the less essential; that which is capable of becoming a possession of the immortal spirit is, in fact, the higher,—the essence, the idea, the spiritual contents of existence. In virtue of their spiritual contents even natural objects receive a sort of immortality by being appropriated by the rational spirit; in a still higher degree is this true of the facts of history. Spiritual appropriation is related to natural appropriation as the spirit to the body; the latter must therefore always be subordinate to the former,—must absolutely serve it.—As all nature is created not only *by* spirit but also *for* spirit, and as whatever is spiritually created is likewise for the spirit, hence it is but justice to both natural and historical existence,—but a simple right of the same upon the rational spirit,—that it be appropriated by the latter, and it is a perfectly moral requirement that spiritual appropriating be made an essential part of the moral activity. Only savages know nothing of history, of the permanent preservation of the transitory. The preservation of that which belongs to the spirit, that which has been appropriated by it, is the earliest evidence of the spiritual, the historical character of a people,—of human culture. The most ancient historical nations of heathendom, the Chinese and the Egyptians, place their chief interest in the preserving of transpired events; the Egyptians sought to rescue from perishing even the bodies of men, as the tabernacles of the spirit,—sought to appropriate them to history. The art of *writing* has as its original purpose, not mutual personal intercourse, but history,—was committed not to perishable leaves but to the rock; and also the most ancient products of architectural skill were consecrated, not to purposes of dwellings, but to purposes of history.

SECTION CIV.

(*b*) The difference of spiritual appropriation in respect to *how* it takes place, appears, on the one hand, in this, that the appropriating person is active as a rational spirit in general,—as at one with all other rational spirits, and hence in such a manner as that the appropriation might be made in like manner by any other spirit,—*general* appropriation; and, on the other, in this, that the person is active as a single personality for himself,—appropriates the object to *himself* as an individual, makes it his exclusive possession,—*particular* appropriation.—(1) *General* (universal) appropriation is *cognizing* or learning. The object is indeed received *by* the individual spirit and *into* it, not, however, as its exclusive possession; on the contrary, in this receiving, the person divests himself at the same time of his isolated character,— has the appropriated not as a mere particular possession for himself, but as a possession of the rational spirit in general,—as universally-valid. The so appropriated spiritual possession is *truth;* now truth has the destination and tendency to become a common possession. Learning or cognizing is therefore moral: (*a*) in that it seeks to appropriate to itself the real spiritual contents of existence, that is, seeks after truth; (*b*) in that it makes of truth, not a personal isolated enjoyment, but strives to communicate it to others.

All learning is spiritual appropriating, but not all spiritual appropriating is general; we here consider spiritual appropriation under another phase than in the preceding section. Where the love of sensuous enjoyment prevails to a sinful extent, there the love of truth declines. The desire of knowledge is a characteristic of the moral spirit. Man, as called to dominion over nature, is also called to the spiritual appropriating of the same, and of all existence. The striving after truth is a seal of man's God-likeness. Even as to God every thing is open, and all truth is known, so also is man only then truly a spirit when he strives after truth and seeks cognoscitively to appropriate to himself *all* things. This is a legitimate striving after possession,—after the possession of an inner world, a true copy of the real one; and it is among the most essential sources of the bliss of the perfected, that they know the truth and constantly appropriate to themselves cognoscitively more of it. The acquiring of the truth is a becoming free from the limits of a merely individual existence,—a divesting ourselves of the mere state of nature, an assuming of a more general character, an entering into the life and essence of the self-concordant All, an appropriating of the objective outgoings of spirit in general. "Ye shall know the truth and the truth shall make you free," says Christ to such as shall continue in his word [John viii, 32]. Even as light breaks down the isolation of individual being, and throws up a bridge to that which is outwardly separated from it, thus causing all separate objects to exist in some sort for each other, so the knowledge of truth frees man from the bonds of a merely isolated being, opens for him the totality of existence as his life-sphere,—throws a unifying bond around deity and the totality of his creatures. As no life of the earth is without light, so also is there no life of the spirit without the knowledge of truth; and it is not this or that truth that makes man free, rational, and blessed, but *the* truth; and the Spirit of the Lord strives to lead his disciples into *all* truth. Whoever seeks to set limits to the moral thirst for truth, whoever declares any truth as indifferent or unworthy of effort, he resists the outgoings of the spirit of truth. Moreover, there is no particular truth which stands isolated and for itself, and does not first receive its validity from *the* truth which springs from the eternal Spirit of God; and he who thinks to satisfy the thirst of the soul for truth with certain separate morsels of truths from the sphere of the finite and transitory, knows not the truth but only falsehood.

All true knowing is of such a nature that every other rational spirit can and must know in precisely the same manner, and hence has a significance beyond the possession of the individual,—is general appropriation. Hence, as moral, it is also directly connected with a tendency to make that which is appropriated by the individual person a *general* possession of all rational beings. The moral man cannot wish to retain the truth for himself alone, but the truth which has become his possession impels him, by virtue of its general character, freely to communicate it to others [Luke ii, 17; 1 John i, 1 *sqq.*]. The duty of secret-keeping has a validity and significancy only on the supposition of predominant sinfulness,—is inconceivable save on the presupposition of sin; and the weakness of being unable to keep a secret springs, in some sort at least, from a correct feeling of that which ought to be. Good-hearted persons are usually poor secret-keepers; and for innocence there is no secret. The truth, like light, cannot hide itself; it is only with designing effort that either can be concealed. Truth, morally considered, belongs not to the mere understanding but to the heart; and with that of which the heart is full, the mouth overflows [Luke vi. 45]. He to whom the truth belongs, belongs also himself to the truth,—must also *bear witness* of the truth. "We cannot but speak the things which we have seen and heard," said Peter and John in the presence of the chief council [Acts iv. 20], and they only express the inner moral necessity of such a witnessing of obtained truth. Whoever feels nothing of such an inner impulsion to witnessing either possesses not the truth, or the truth possesses not him. With the witnessing of the truth it is in some sense as it is with the first ante-moral love; the person may indeed resist the inner impulse, but if he does not do so then his immediate love of the truth will spontaneously induce him to witness for it without any need of a special effort of the will. "Ye also *will* bear witness (as well as the Holy Ghost), *because* ye have been with me from the beginning," says the Lord to his disciples [John xv. 27]; this is not an injunction but a promise; they will not be able to do otherwise; the truth is stronger than the command. Hence he who is of the truth needs no longer the law; for the truth impels him to bear witness of itself through his *life*.

SECTION CV.

(2). *Particular* (individual) appropriating is *enjoying*. Here the object exists solely for me in so far as I am an individual being,—becomes my special possession. In enjoyment I do not, as in cognizing, have the object purely as such, but I have it as it stands in accord with my peculiarity, as it has become an element of my own being. In enjoyment I have, therefore, always also *myself* as in some way affected by the object; hence the sphere of enjoyment is essentially *feeling*, namely, the feeling of pleasure. Enjoyment is either sensuous or spiritual; the former is never moral *per se*, but only with and in the latter. —As the personal spirit has an independent right in and of itself, and as true enjoyment rests on *love* to the object, and consequently is a virtualization of this love, hence enjoyment is also a moral right, and therefore also relatively a duty. The morality of enjoyment consists primarily in a conscious and complete subordinating of merely sensuous enjoyment to spiritual; and furthermore in the fact that it be always a pure expression of moral love, and hence also of thankfulness, and that it rest on joy in God,—that it stand in proper harmony with the formative activity; and also in the fact that, by virtue of the agreeable feeling manifested in it, it awake also communicative love, namely, the tendency to extend the enjoyment to others.—The highest enjoyment consists in the consciousness of the filial relation to God, that is, in the perfect appropriation of life-communion with God; and in fact to the child of God, only that is a real enjoyment, in which also God has pleasure. In association with this enjoyment of the filial relation to God, every other enjoyment is sanctified.

In learning, or cognizing, I throw into the back-ground my isolated individuality,—let the truth, as general, rule over me; my mere isolated being has no validity; in enjoying, on the contrary, I come with my separate individuality into the fore-ground; the object *per se* has no validity; in learning I have myself only as a member of the whole, but in enjoying I have myself as an individuality distinct from the whole. Hence enjoyment, as of such and such a form, is not communicable; *de gustibus non est disputandum*. Whatever one rational person cognizes as true, that must be cognized by all as true; but that which is an enjoyment for one is not necessarily such for another. All enjoyment is love, and the highest earthly love is conjugal and maternal love; but this love which is at the same time the highest earthly enjoyment, belongs to this or that particular person,—is by no means personally-communicable; a child can be loved by no one else as it is by its mother. As knowledge naturally impels to communication, so enjoyment, on the contrary, impels rather to isolation; the pleasure-seeker would fain have every thing for himself; if he seeks society, it is only in so far as society becomes to him an object of enjoyment. Enjoyment readily gives rise to jealousy, whereas knowledge tends to a liberal imparting of the acquired truth; even maternal love knows jealousy.

Christian morality begrudges not enjoyment to man, not even the sensuous, for "the earth is the Lord's and the fullness thereof" [1 Cor. x, 6; Psa. xxiv, 1; comp. Gen. ii, 9]. The pious reference of all enjoyment to God as the Giver of all good, and thankful love to him, render even sensuous enjoyment moral, in so far as it is sought in the divinely-ordained manner,—spiritualize it, in fact, by the heart-disposition of the subject, and place the joy proper in the spiritual associations of the sensuous. So soon as sensuous enjoyment is sought purely for itself, apart from the spiritual and from love to God, it becomes at once immoral, seeing that it then interrupts (§ 102) the spiritual life, which by its very nature is continuous; of the relation of enjoyment to forming, we will speak hereafter.

The communication of enjoyment,—a constituent element of its morality,—springs not from the essence of the same, but from love to man in general. It can only take place in so far as thereby the essence of the enjoyment is not affected; the enjoyment that lies in the family-life can never be made a common possession; and the fact that in the case of a few rude tribes, hospitality is extended to a communicating even of marital rights,* is evidence simply of a perversion of the moral. Manifestly, however, wedlock-happiness and that of the family in general require, in order to their being moral, that they be communicated to others, not, however, as a direct enjoyment, but through *hospitality*,—through the throwing open of the family to friendly intercourse, through the per-

---

* Tertull.: *Apolog.*, c. 39; Wuttke: *Gesch. d. Heident.*, i, p. 177.

mitting of others to share in the inner peace of the domestic life. Hence there is not lacking a moral back-ground for the custom of reserving the higher sensuous enjoyment of repasts for hospitable occasions, in which the spiritual intercourse, and hence spiritual enjoyment, occupies the fore-ground, while the sensuous enjoyment appears only as an attendant in the back-ground. The idea of Paradise is the epitome of the entire circle of true enjoyments,—it is not a mere crude or childish fancy-creation, but the very truth itself. Christian morality is not averse to enjoyment; it favors man's taking delight in this world of reality. But Paradise exists only where man is in filial communion with the divine Father,— where love to God sanctifies all earthly enjoyment. "The kingdom of God is not meat and drink, but righteousness, and peace, and joy, in the Holy Ghost" [Rom. xiv, 17]. Christianity knows no other joy than joy in the Lord; "Rejoice in the Lord always, and again I say, Rejoice" [Phil. iv, 4]. He who rejoices in the Lord, takes true delight in all that comes from the Lord [Deut. xxvi, 11]. To man as sinful many enjoyments are forbidden, because he is able to enjoy them only sinfully; to the pure the sphere of morally-pure enjoyment is much wider and richer [Titus i, 15]. The child of God has enjoyment in *every thing*, and every thing is to him a *moral* enjoyment, save alone the violation of God's law; to him the world is a paradise, for it is God's, as is also himself; and he loves not the world without God, but only in God and with God. The blessedness of the children of God, the unspeakable enjoyment of true heart-devotion in fervent prayer, in which man knows himself at one with his God, and rests in the peace of God, is not a subject for scientific synthesis and analytical description; it belongs to the sphere of the inner life, and needs to be experienced rather than described; the world knows nothing thereof.

III. MORAL FORMING.

SECTION CVI.

Moral forming works the harmony of existence, in that thereby man impresses upon objective existence the peculiarity of his own spirit,—makes it an expression thereof, that is, spiritually shapes it. The object is destroyed not in its existence, but only in its isolation and peculiarity,—receives the peculiarity of the acting spirit, is imbued with, and thus bound to, it. Forming is morally good not when it is an impressing of the merely individual and as yet not morally-rational spirit upon the object (for this would be injustice to the object, a non-sparing of its legitimate being), but when it is an impressing of the spirit as moral, as rational and as in harmony with God, that is, when the object itself is formed toward a complete harmony with the morally-rational collective spirit. Moral forming must therefore always be associated with moral sparing, and all the more so the higher the spiritual significance and worth of the object that is to be formed. As related to the moral spirit, therefore, all moral forming is an *educating*, which latter is never an absolutely all-determining forming, but a forming that respects the rights of the personality that is to be formed.

The outward-going formative activity can neither be arbitrary and purposeless, nor a mere destroying of that which exists, but must have a rational end and a right of its own. In view of the wants of the moral activity, therefore, created existence *cannot* be, primarily, at once and definitively completed and perfected, though indeed it is good, but it stands in the presence of the activity of the rational spirit as formable material to which man, as active, has a right, and the final completion of which is an end for human activity. It is only through forming that man makes the objective world *his own*, namely, in that he impresses upon it *his* stamp, and makes it by moral activity into a likeness of himself, and therefore into his own possession. "Do your own business (πράσσειν τὰ ἴδια) and work with your own hands" [1 Thess. iv, 11]; man really possesses nothing as his own but that which he has produced by working and forming; and it is not a curse but an original moral law of the universe, that the true existence of man, bodily as well as spiritually-moral, is conditioned on formative working, on labor. Even the first man was not placed in Paradise simply to enjoy its delights, simply to appropriate to himself, naturally and spiritually, that which already existed, but he was to *cultivate* the garden [Gen. ii, 15]. Man is called to dominion over nature, to be a creator of a spiritual world; this is both a wide and also a privileging and obligating field for the moral. The play of the child is a forming; that of the brute has no objective significancy; and wherever by virtue of an instinct, the brute exercises a formative activity, there we are simply presented with a natural symbol of the moral, as in the case of the bee, the ant, etc.

Forming, as compared to sparing and appropriating, appears at once as the higher, and generally more difficult, form of activity; sparing is a mere checking of the outward-going activity; appropriating, according to its kind, either annihilates the objective existence, or leaves its substance untouched; but forming interferes positively with the existence and peculiarity of the object. There is need here, on the one hand, of a considerate respecting of the *right* of the object to its own peculiarity, so that the forming may not become an unjust perverting and destroying, and, on the other hand, of a proper and clear consciousness of the rational purpose of the transforming. Appropriating begins earlier in the spiritual development of man than forming; the latter always presupposes some degree of moral maturity; forming as exercised by an immature spirit is a destroying. The formative activity of the child appears as a rending-asunder of whatever falls into its hand; the historical activity of savage or half-civilized tribes, bears also this childish character. Unripe youth have also, as relating to society and the state and to historical reality in general, great pleasure in destruction; and the revolutionary spirit of boisterous young men is only a higher degree of the destructive proclivity of the child; but on the supposition of the attainment of higher spiritual maturity, that which is innocent in the child becomes a culpable lack of judgment. Moral forming must necessarily always have also a preserving phase, inasmuch as in all that which is to be formed there is also something that has a right to existence, and hence a claim upon sparing; and an education which ignores this right in the pupil, is violent and therefore immoral.

SECTION CVII.

Moral forming differs likewise in two respects. (a) According to *that which* is formed in the object, it is either a sensuously-natural or a spiritual forming.—1. *Natural* forming is a shaping of nature-material for the human spirit by virtue of the mastery of the spirit over nature, to the end either of practical utility or of a manifesting of spirit in art-work. Nature, as created, is indeed *per se* good and perfect, but it becomes a true home for, a true organ of, the spirit and of history, only by becoming imbued with spirit. Natural forming is moral and rational only in so far as it is the sensuous expressing of a spiritual forming.

All dominating is necessarily a forming, inasmuch as the dominated is more or less an expression of the will of the dominating power. A natural entity can bear this expression only in virtue of being shaped by man and at the same time for man. In natural forming the difference between man, as a moral creature, and the brute, becomes at once plainly visible. The activity of the brute is predominantly a sensuous appropriating; that of man is predominantly a forming, and indeed primarily a sensuously-natural forming. The appropriating of nature is primarily *permitted* by God to man, and is limited by a prohibition only in one respect; the forming of nature is *enjoined* upon him [Gen. i, 28; ii, 15]. The mere letting alone of even a Paradisaical nature in its given condition, is for man *per se* immoral; he is *called* to form it into a home for himself by his personal activity.—But man cannot morally accomplish a natural forming save on the condition that there exists already in him an antecedent moral forming. The artist cannot create a work of art unless it has already been spiritually formed in his soul; and each and every object that is shaped, is to be, in its entire purpose, not a mere solitary something existing for itself, but rather one of the stones of a greater and essentially-spiritual structure,—the structure of history. Man shapes nature not for its own sake but for humanity, namely, into a home for man's spiritual life, into an expression of historical reality,—which is essentially the product of spiritual forming. Hence natural forming has always the purpose simply of serving the spiritual, even as the nourishment and development of the body take place not in the interest of the body, but of the spirit.

SECTION CVIII.

Spiritual forming relates to the spiritual essence of the object, and hence predominantly to the conscious spirit; it is a communicating of the spiritual possession of the subject to the object, a shaping of the object according to the rational idea of the subject, a putting of the former into harmony with the moral person of the latter. Each man has the duty of helping spiritually to form every other one who comes into spiritual relation with him, that is, of communicating to him his own moral nature, of *revealing* himself to him; this holds good even of the as yet morally immature in relation to the morally mature. All morally-spiritual *communicating* is a forming, and all spiritual forming is a communicating. Communicating is, however, only then a *moral* forming, when the communicating spirit itself stands in harmony with God, is itself morally good, and when its motive is *love*.

Also spiritual forming extends in a certain sense to nature-objects, in so far as these are not a mere sensuous existence, but have also spiritual contents. The training and ennobling of domestic animals is not a sensuous but a relatively-spiritual forming, inasmuch as their inner nature is raised to a higher plane. The chief sphere of spiritual forming is, however, the personal spirit. Man has neither the right nor the liberty to develop himself as a mere isolated individual,—he cannot develop himself morally save when in spiritual life-relation with the moral community; and each stands with every other in such a moral relation. And this relation is a mutual forming and appropriating, at the same time. Man is formed only by appropriating to himself spiritual elements, that is, in that another spirit reveals itself to him. Forming cannot take place morally by the imbuing of thoughts and sentiments that are foreign to the subject himself into the spirit that is to be educated, for this would be deception, and would not establish a spiritual communion; it can be done only by a self-revelation of the moral spirit. Only the morally-formed spirit can itself form; the immoral spirit can only pervert, and can do this successfully only when it affects morality. However, it is not necessary that the formative spirit should be already mature; also the child exerts a formative influence upon its elders.—In the condition of sinlessness the formative activity has no need of art or of a calculated plan; mere self-manifestation exercises a formative influence directly and of itself. All artfully-planned manners of influencing are evidence of lost purity, and cannot, however cunningly contrived, exert the power of the moral reality. The moral spirit lets its light shine before men that they may see its good works, and this light directly illumines and enlightens the spirit of others. This self-revelation, however, would be immoral, that is, hollow and empty, were it to spring from self-complacency instead of from love to others. It is love alone that divests this letting one's light shine of an appearance of parade. Loving souls hide themselves not from each other; true love impels to a full and genuine self-communication; and moral love has nothing that it would gladly or necessarily conceal.

SECTION CIX.

(*b*) According to the manner *in which* the objective entity is formatively influenced, we have to distinguish between particular and general forming.

1. *Particular forming* forms single objects for the service of the earthly wants of single or several persons, that is, for *use* for temporal ends. It is therefore *labor*, in the proper and narrower sense of the word. Labor relates not merely to natural matter, but also to the individual spirit, in so far as the latter is to be formed for the temporal earthly life, and hence is spiritual as well as natural forming.

All utility relates to the particular; that which is for the common utility is simply that which is useful for *many* particular persons. When the Rationalistic school spoke of the "common utility" of religion, it manifested simply very bad taste; religion is thus placed on a par, *e. g.*, with a public fountain or an advertising sheet. Labor concerns the individual; works for the common utility, such as roads or canals, look not to the good of humanity as a whole, as a unity, but to the many individual persons whom they are to benefit; for him who does not use them, they have no significancy and are perhaps even offensive. Their utility and enjoyment fall to the individual as such, but not in virtue of his being a man, a rational spirit. In a work of art, however, one has pleasure precisely in his character of rational spirituality; although from another stand-point this work is of no "use" to him whatever. That which is to exalt the *heart* must be more than labor. Products of labor may indeed excite a general and rational interest, as, for example, a machine or other superior fruits of skill; here, however, it is not the *work* itself that is admired, but the *art* to which the handicraft has been exalted,—the spiritual power of invention, that is, the power of spirit,—not the utility, but the beauty or ingenuity, —not the merely individual element, but the spiritual, which, as such, bears upon itself the stamp of general significancy and validity. The actual work on a machine is performed not by the ingenious inventor, the master, but by the manual laborer; and in that which this laborer executes there is little else to admire than the industry, but nothing of a general interest. The end of a work of art is not, to be used by the individual, but to be enjoyed and admired universally; and it is properly regarded as a sign of spiritual unculture when a particular age takes delight only in the *merely* useful, in *mere* labor, and not also in that which transcends labor, namely, in art,—when the age does not also exalt labor into art. In the time of Rationalistic illuminism many "useless" art-structures of the Middle Ages, magnificent castles and churches, were converted into magazines and factories,—art was turned into a hand-maid of labor; this was certainly very "useful," but it was at the same time also an evidence of shameful unculture. The spirit of mere utility is but little removed from barbarism.

Labor is not mere manual toil. Common usage is perfectly right when it speaks also, and not merely in the stricter sense of the word, of *spiritual*, intellectual, labor, and of intellectual laborers, in distinction from a higher spiritual and intellectual activity. The highest results to which the spirit can attain are *not* effected by labor; the delicate, etherial image which delights our astonished gaze was not painfully wrought out by the sweat of the multitude, but sprang forth at once from the brain of genius; but, as distinguished from this ideal activity of the spirit, there is another which is entitled to be called work in the strict sense of the word, and which consists in a strictly-particular forming. All spiritual activity which looks to the mere benefit of individuals is labor; thus, we speak of the labor of pupils, of official labors, etc. The pupil labors in order, by the appropriation of particular scientific material, to form himself as an individual for a calling in life; the teacher labors upon the pupil for the same end. All spiritual forming which looks to success in the world, to obtaining a position in it, is labor; hence also we may speak of a scientific industry; there is an immense difference between science as manual labor, and science as an art. When the learner, however, elevates himself to a more ideal activity,—when, inspired with enthusiasm for the true and the good, he soars above the merely particular, or when the teacher seeks to awaken an enthusiasm of this character in him, then the activity ceases to be labor and becomes a higher kind of forming. It is true, we sometimes speak, though in a less strict sense, of a laboring in the sphere of purely spiritual things, as, for example, in that of religion and of active love [Rom. xvi, 6, 12; 1 Thess. i, 3; Heb. vi, 10; 1 Cor. xv, 58; 2 Cor. vi, 5; xi, 27; Rev. ii, 2, 3; xiv, 13]; Paul says, "I labored more abundantly than they all" [1 Cor. xv, 10], and the pastor and the messenger of the Word may speak of their labor on souls [1 Cor. xvi, 16; 2 Cor. x, 15; xi, 23; 1 Thess. iii, 5; v, 12; 1 Tim. v, 17]; however, in this essentially figuratively-used expression [see John iv, 38; 1 Cor. iii, 8] reference is had not to the activity *per se*, but to the trouble in overcoming obstacles (hence the words κόπος and κοπιάω) which lie not in the matter itself, but in other circumstances, such as the enmity of sinful men, the feebleness of the actor himself, etc.

SECTION CX.

2. *General* forming forms the object for a general, that is, a rational end,—not merely for a particular need, for temporal utility, but for the rational and moral spirit in general,—forms it for rational enjoyment, for moral approbation, *i. e.* into a *beautiful* and *good* product,—is *artistic* forming, in the largest sense of the word. It may be a sensuous as well as a spiritual forming. The natural entity receives a spiritual form,—becomes an expression, an image, of the rational spirit, an expression of harmony in general, —a work of art. The spiritual entity is formed into an essentially God-answering, truly rational character, into a *beautiful soul*, into a child of God. Religious and ideal culture in general differs essentially from education for a worldly calling,—aims not to make man into a "useful" and serviceable being, but into one in whom both God and men have pleasure,

and who has himself pleasure in God and in all that is divine and beautiful,—seeks not to mold him into a merely isolated being, a mere citizen, a mere professional man, but seeks to bring to development that which is purely and truly *human* in him,—seeks to make the merely natural person into an image of the moral spirit, into a true image of God, into an expression of the truth. All that which is created by general forming is art-work; and when this forming, as distinguished from professional working, creates a science, then this science becomes itself a work of art. Hence, no general forming is possible without moral *enthusiasm*, that is, without being imbued with and prompted by a universal spirit which divests itself of all individual narrowness, and of all selfishness, and aspires to a universal divine ideal (§ 96).—A special phase of general forming constitutes the typical or *symbolical* activity, under which falls also the morally *becoming*.

The fruit which is aimed at in mere work is only for the benefit of the individual; works of art, and the beautiful and good in general, are for the spiritual enjoyment of rational man as such. Also the angels must rejoice in heaven, not only over a sinner who repents, but also over all that is truly beautiful. Man forms himself into a useful, a skillful, a learned member of society by labor and pains-taking, but into a beautiful soul only by enthusiasm; this is indeed not the beautiful soul as improvised by sentimental novelists, but the soul that is beautiful in the eyes of God and of all of God's children,—the child-soul of a child of God, full of love and enthusiasm,—the soul of him who is pure of heart, and which inwardly beholds God, because God looks upon it with pleasure. Hence the Scriptures look upon the higher artistic endowment as a special gift from God [Exod. xxxi, 3, 6; xxxvi, 1, 2].

Art in its deepest ground and essence is *religious*, as in fact historically it is a birth of religion; this holds good without exception of all nations. No religion is without art, without an ideal embodying of the highest ideas. Architecture, plastic art and song, among all nations, have sprung from religion, and are the subservient attendants of religion [Exod. xxxi, 2 *sqq.;* xxxv, 1 *sqq.*]; and it required all the ungenial one-sidedness and bald reflective tendency of Zwingli to banish art from the Church,—a wrong against Christian humanity which has, at least in some degree, been disavowed in most of the branches of the Reformed Church. Even *worldly* art, in so far as it has not, untrue to its essential nature, entered into the service of sin, is closely related to religion. It also elevates man above the merely individual and sensuously-natural; and, itself a birth of enthusiasm, it awakens also in man enthusiasm for the beautiful and the noble,—for that which raises him out of his isolation and self-seeking, and up to that which finds response in all moral souls. Love to art banishes rudeness,—makes the heart receptive also for the morally beautiful and divine. Hence the culture of art is so important an element in education and in the life of nations. But for this reason also art becomes such a demon-power, when, forgetting its nobility, it stoops to the role of pandering to corrupt pleasure, and when, instead of inspiring enthusiasm for the truly beautiful, it only aims to intoxicate and seduce by lustful appeals to the senses. Wherever there is a healthful religious life, there art and religion stand in intimate and mutual relations. Where faith is alive in the heart, there it utters itself in "psalms and spiritual songs," there it celebrates the glory of its God in a becoming ornamentation of his altars and courts [Exod. xxxv, 21 *sqq.*], and wherever true art prevails there it consecrates the most beautiful of its products to the honor of God. Religion created for the Greeks poets and artists, and the poets and artists created for the Greeks their gods; and however much there may have been of heathen error in these creations, still this much at least is here exemplified, namely, that the divine makes its nearest approaches to man in the words, the songs and the works of artistic inspiration. The prophets of the Ancient Covenant were also unable to bring down to the plane of mere simple prose, the visions which they had spiritually beholden; and also the Prophet of the New Covenant publishes his visions under the drapery of boldly-constructed symbols. He who finds fault with this knows neither art nor religion.

General moral forming does not necessarily take place directly and immediately; as relating to the free spirit, it consists essentially in the fact that, by the moral activity of the subject, the object is so *incited* and *inspired* as to bring about self-development through his own spontaneity and strength. In this consists the true art of education and governing, namely, in that the guiding power hides itself in some respect from the spirit that is to be molded,—does not permit its influence upon it to appear as a limiting, overpowering force, but rather simply gives scope for free and independent self-development. This does not take place, however, by a simple "letting alone" of the one who is to be guided, but by the fact that the moral and rational consciousness is quickened and strengthened in him,—that he is brought to feel and know himself, not as a mere non-obligated individual, but as a personality inspired by a holy and moral spirit,—that a moral disposition and an ideal enthusiasm become in him an actuating power, which in turn itself forms him to a higher development and perfection.

There is an important sphere of moral activity, namely, *symbolical* forming—to which belongs also the practicing of the *becoming*,—which can be understood only from the stand-point of general artistic forming;—a sphere of stumbling and offense to all champions of the merely prosaically useful. The morally-good, is not simply to become real, but the real is also to be an *expression*, a manifestation of the morally-good,—is to bear witness in its entire outward appearance to an inner ideal quality, and every single good is to show itself not merely as *per se* good, but is also to point to a higher good beyond itself. Even as in nature, the good, as a regulated means to an end, is associated with a beauty more significant than the mere fitness for an end,—even as the flower not merely possesses the fructifying organs and the delicate tissues that protect them, but also, in its graceful form, its hues and its fragrance, delights man, and, as a symbol of the eternally beautiful, reminds him of divine love and of the glory of God,

—even as the birds of song not only nourish themselves and propagate their race, but also praise the goodness of the Creator in strains that touch the heart,—even as God not only causes the sun to shine and to awaken life, and the clouds to drop rain, but also paints on the skies the color-resplendent bow as a pledge of his faithfulness and grace,—in a word, as God himself decks his creation with such grandeur that the heavens proclaim his glory, and with such beauty that the understanding is incapable adequately to comprehend it, but only the adoring heart to feel and love it,—so also man, as God-like, not only forms that which is *useful* for the temporal life, but also that which, as a significant sign, points to a higher good,—forms reality into a *type* of the true and good, —creates the *poetry* of reality. Every artistic product is such a sign or symbol, but all symbolical forming is not properly artistic in the stricter sense, though it is indeed poetical. The clothing of man is not simply for a protection against the weather, but also largely a suggestive expression of the inner life; all adornment as well as cleanliness has a spiritual suggestiveness. For him who knows not this symbolical, poetical phase of the moral, a very important and essential part of morality remains incomprehensible. A large portion of the moral precepts of the Scriptures look not to a direct and simple realization of a good, but to the expressive suggesting of a moral element not directly contained in the matter itself,—have a symbolical character; and lightly to esteem this phase of things is an indication of moral obtuseness. Doubtless it was not very "useful" when Mary, the sister of Lazarus, took a pound of pure and costly ointment and anointed the Lord's feet; and the harsh reproof of Judas was perfectly well-grounded from the stand-point of mere utilitarianism, but the Lord judged very differently from Judas [John xii, 3 *sqq.*; comp. Mark xiv, 3 *sqq.*]. To this category belong almost all the precepts of the Old Testament in regard to the clean and the unclean, to food and clothing,—in which case the object of the forming is man himself,—and also in regard to the form of worship and whatever is therewith connected, such as circumcision, etc., as well as in regard to agriculture [Lev. xix, 19; Deut. xxii, 9, 10] and to the treatment of animals [Exod. xxi, 28, 29, 32; xxiii, 19; Lev. xx, 15, 16].

The *becoming* is the outward, beautiful or symbolical form of the moral,—in a certain sense its esthetic phase. To celebrate the Lord's day in the spiritual-exalting of the heart to God, is a moral duty; to give expression to the celebration by sacred art and by a worthy outward appearance, is becoming. The ungodly world is prone to substitute in the place of the moral substance an outwardly and externally gracious form—the becoming; the suggestion: "That is not becoming," is with the irreligious world of much more weight than: "It is sinful." The outward form may indeed be hypocritically assumed in the absence of the substance, but he who holds fast to the moral substance, must observe also the form; he only is morally-*cultured* who not only observes the substance of the general precepts, but also aims at the morally-becoming; and this is in fact a general and artistic forming on the part of the moral activity. The becoming stands not along-side of the moral precept, but is essentially contained in it, as, in fact, without it man remains coarse and rude. Almost all of the above-mentioned precepts of the Old Testament are precepts of the becoming, and the New Testament also lays great stress on the becoming [1 Cor. xi, 4 *sqq.;* 1 Tim. ii, 9, and others].

SECTION CXI.

Appropriating and forming are, in a right moral development, ever in association with each other, and that too all the closer the higher their character. No spiritual appropriating is without spiritual self-forming, and no forming of an objective entity is without a spiritual appropriating of the thing formed; and in fact the forming of one's own spirit is *per se* necessarily an appropriating. The measure of appropriating and especially of enjoying stands in all right development, always in strict relation to the measure of the forming; and the two modes of forming are associated not only with each other, but also with the two modes of appropriating, as are in turn the latter with each other.

The fruit of labor and still more the work of art, are the property of the laborer and the artist; they call it *their own;* they have appropriated it to themselves in the very process of producing it. The outward-directed activity turns thus about and flows back into the acting person. In forming an objective entity, man forms his own self; he has the work not merely as his own, as a copy of his thought, but he is also himself spiritually and morally promoted both by the working and by the work. All forming is self-forming; and inasmuch as man stands to his fellows in a spiritual relation,—reveals himself to them through his culture,—hence all self-forming is directly also in turn a forming of others.—All particular forming, all work, should as moral include in itself also at the same time an element of general forming; without this the laborer falls into spiritual and moral deterioration. When the laborer unites the useful with the beautiful,—gives to his work a graceful form,—when song accompanies the work, when the heart mounts up from the work that serves a temporal end, toward the Eternal One, and thus puts into earnest practice the precept: "Pray and labor," then the particular forming is exalted and transfigured by the general. The more isolated, the more limited, the work is, so much the more preponderates the merely useful phase of it; hence no work is so dangerous, nay, so detrimental, to the harmoniously-moral culture of man as the spiritless mechanism of factory-work; and white slavery works here often much more ruinously than the black. The uninterrupted monotony of the narrow routine of the work paralyzes the spirit and subverts morality.

Furthermore, all forming is not only a general appropriating, formative of the subject himself, in that he recognizes the product of his influence, but also a particular appropriating, in that he *enjoys* it. The divine prototype of this is seen in the account of creation, where we read that God looked upon all that he had made, and found that it was very good. All moral work, and still more, all general forming, are, in and of themselves, also enjoyment, and that too the highest and purest enjoyment, even as in the above utterance of the Creator his own bliss was implicitly expressed also. But also the *sensuous* enjoyment that is not directly included in the formative activity itself, is nevertheless, in virtue of the moral order of the world, associated with it. Adam was first to dress and care for the garden, and thereafter to eat of its fruits [Gen. ii, 15, 16]. "If any one will not work, neither should he eat" [2 Thess. iii, 10]; this is a morally unassailable principle; and where the practice is otherwise, there the social relations are corrupt; and the grudge of the suffering laborer against the luxurious idler has a very just foundation. In proportion to the degree of productive activity, rises or falls the moral right to enjoyment in general, and to personal position in society. Hence the admonition: Let each labor to produce with his own hands something good [Eph. iv, 28; comp. Acts xx, 34, 35; 1 Thess. iv, 11; ii, 9].

SECTION CXII.

Inasmuch as man becomes perfect only through the perfect all-sided development of all his life-phases, and as any exclusive realization and culture of one, or simply some, of them works a disturbance of the inner harmony, hence every person should, in so far as his circumstances admit of it, realize every form of moral appropriation and moral culture. He who allows his life to be devoted exclusively to particular forming and appropriating,—to toil and enjoyment, has fallen out of moral harmony, and is consequently immoral. General, and hence, essentially, religious, forming must attend the work hand in hand; and the ordination of the *Sabbath* along-side of the days of labor has not simply a religious, but essentially also a moral significancy. *Moral* resting from labor is a rising to ideal self-culture, an exalting of the temporally-particular into the eternal, the holy, the general, the divine; the celebrating of the Sabbath is the higher and moral transfiguring of the temporal prosaic individual life by the poesy of the ideal and the infinite.

In particular forming man merges himself into objective existence; primarily he has not the object in his own possession, but the object possesses him; hence the danger, especially in a state of sinfulness, that the person lose himself in his labor,—that, as in sensuous enjoyment, he passively surrender himself to the creature [Eccles. vi, 7, in the Hebrew text]. Man should, however, hold fast to himself and to his Creator,—should withdraw himself from his absorption in finite things, collect himself in spiritual repose,—should obtain fresh moral strength for the particular forming of industry, in the general forming which springs of enthusiasm. Even as God, though merging himself into the world while creating it, yet did not lose and forget himself in it, but returned to himself and to his infinite self-sufficiency, and ever retains himself in eternal unchangeable majesty above all that is created, so also is it a moral requirement that man, in his creating of the finite and particular, should not forget himself as a personality gifted with eternal destinies; it is for man's sake that the Sabbath was made [Mark ii, 27]. It is very suggestive that in the Scriptures the repose of God after creation is made the prototype and basis for the celebration of the Sabbath [Gen. ii, 3; Exod. xx, 8 *sqq.*]. It is thereby implied that it is our innermost God-likeness that calls for the rest of the Sabbath,—the truly rational, religiously-moral essence of man, and not the mere natural need of repose and enjoyment. That which is with God only two phases of his eternal life itself, and not an alternation in time, namely, creative action and self-possession, this falls, in the case of the finite spirit, at least partially, into such an alternation,—into labor and Sabbath-rest. God blessed the Sabbath day; there rests upon its observance an especial, an extraordinary benediction, an impartation of heavenly goods, even as the blessing upon labor is primarily only an importation of temporal goods. The Sabbath has not merely a negative significancy, is not a mere interruption of labor, but it has a very rich positive significancy,—it is the giving free scope to the higher, time-transcending nature of the rational God-like spirit, the re-attaching of the spirit that had been immersed by labor into the temporal, to the imperishable and to the divine. Where God is conceived of as swallowed up in nature, as with the Chinese and in the unbelief of our own day, there there exists no Sabbath; there there is to be found only a discretionary alternation of labor and sensuous enjoyment. The celebration of the Sabbath belongs to morality *per se*, and does not depend on the fact of the state of redemption from sinfulness; but where sin is as yet a dominant power there its observance is necessarily less free, legally more strict, than where the freedom of the children of God prevails.

From the fact that *all* moral working is attended also with a general forming, it follows manifestly that, for him who is truly morally free, the antithesis of Sabbath-rest and labor is not of an absolute character,—that every day and all labor have also their Sabbath consecration, and that, on the other hand, also the Sabbath does not absolutely exclude all work. It is perfectly clear, however, that, in general, only such works consist with the observance of the Sabbath as express a general formative activity,—as bear an artistic character in the noblest sense of the word. In this category belong those healings of the sick by which the Lord incurred the reproach of Sabbath-breaking. Such works are not labor, but, as a restoring of the disturbed order of the universe, are of general and spiritual significancy.

Subdivision Second.

THE MORAL ACTIVITY IN ITS DIFFERENCES AS RELATING TO ITS DIFFERENT OBJECTS.—I. IN RELATION TO GOD.

SECTION CXIII.

As God sustains to man an essentially active and creative, but not a receptive, relation, hence in the strict sense of the word he is an object only of moral appropriating.

(*a*) The moral *appropriating* of God is directly at the same time also the highest moral self-forming of the moral person, and contains two necessarily associated elements: first, that God becomes *for us*, and secondly, that we become *for God;* that is, that, on the one hand, we take up into our moral consciousness the ever present divine, and that, on the other, we elevate our moral consciousness to God,—form it into the divine life; the former is *faith*, the latter is *worship;* neither can exist without the other. Believing is the lovingly-willed and lovingly-willing, that is, the pious recognizing of God as lovingly revealing himself to us as *our* Lord and *our* Father, and to whom we are obligated to unconditional obedience and submissive love,—it is the self-consciousness of man as having come to its rational truth, namely, in that man regards himself no more as a mere isolated individual, but thinks of himself constantly and strictly in his relations to God.

As believing is essentially the particular appropriating of God, so the knowing, the *cognizing* of Him is the general appropriating; and hence the striving for this knowledge is a high moral duty; this duty is fulfilled not without believing, but only through and in virtue of the same,—is a spiritual receiving and a true appropriating of the divine revelation imparted to us through the channel of faith, in regard to the nature, power, and will of God. The correct knowledge of God is not the antecedent condition, but the goal of the moral striving, and hence without it there can be no perfection of morality.

God is indeed *per se* already present in every creature; but in order that he shall be truly present *for* man, that is, in a manner called for by his rational nature, it is necessary that man shall freely appropriate to himself this presence of God. I possess rationally only that which I rationally and morally appropriate. All appropriating, and hence all faith, pre-supposes a difference, and at the same time a mutual life-relation between its subject and its object; what I already am, in and of myself, that I cannot appropriate to myself. That the appropriating of God is a moral act, arises from the fact that man may fully admit his difference from, and yet not heartily recognize his life-relation to, God,—may cling to himself as independent of God, may sinfully aspire even to become like God. It is a moral activity when man raises his self-consciousness, which is primarily merely individual, into a truly rational one, and conceives of himself not merely as an isolated being, but as conditioned by God, that is, as created by and obligated to God; it is only this religious self-consciousness that is moral, and this is in fact faith. Faith is not a mere regarding as true, not a mere religious knowledge, or a mere objective consciousness, but it is a *morally*-conditioned believing, a *willing*, and hence a *loving*, recognition; in faith we *will* to have God and a consciousness of him in us, and we desire this consciousness as divine, that is, as a full and true life-force, and hence as operative, as realizing the divine. The notion of faith combines, therefore, loving and willing with knowing,—is not identical with one of the three, but is the unity of them,—is not an affair of the mere understanding but of the heart (§ 53). Faith is the thankful reflection of the divine love; he who is loved by God, turns himself lovingly toward the loving One. Without the love of God to man there would be no love of man to God; man believes because he becomes conscious of the divine love; he who would only recognize received love, but not reciprocated it with his heart, is immoral; a mere recognition of God without heart-faith is sinful.

"Faith is the substance (the sure confidence) of things hoped for, the evidence of things not seen" [Heb. xi, 1]; it is not a confidence of that which falls within the immediate scope of experience, but of that which lies beyond it, not of that which already exists in realization but of that which is yet, in virtue of faith, to be realized into fact, though indeed it already exists in germ. The really complete life-communion with God, the full appropriating of the divine, is at first only an object of hope,—can be really brought about only through faith; and faith lays hold, in full confidence of success, upon the divine as lovingly revealing itself to it. Faith stands, therefore, not *by the side of* knowledge, as if not including this within itself, nor yet *below* it, as if it were but a lower degree thereof, and would cease with the increase of knowledge, but in fact *above* it, inasmuch as it is a loving knowing, a lovingly-willed and lovingly-willing knowing of God, so that consequently it includes within itself both feeling and willing as essential constituent elements. Believing leads to knowing, but also precedes actual knowing, and hence is not conditioned thereon.

As particular appropriating, believing or faith is, so to speak, an enjoying of the divine,—belongs essentially to the personality itself, and is therefore not communicable, whereas knowing may, on the presupposition of faith, be communicated by instruction. In the entire sphere of the religious life, believing precedes knowing, for without faith God would no more exist for us than would sensuous objects without our senses; believing includes, it is true, some degree of knowing, but is not *per se* complete knowing. And for the simple reason that believing includes knowing as an essential element, it is a moral requirement to bring our knowing to its highest possible perfection, and thereby also to heighten and strengthen faith. The divine revelation as received by faith becomes real knowledge by a proper spiritual merging of ourselves into it, by a full appropriating of its contents into our entire spiritually-transformed being, so that the knowing becomes thus a powerful moral motive to the loving of God and to obedience to his will [Psa. lxiii, 7 *sqq.*; Jer. xxix, 13, 14; John viii, 32; Acts xvii, 27; Col. i, 11; Eph. i, 17, 18]. The knowledge of God consists not merely in the, as yet, only imperfectly attainable [1 Cor. xiii, 9, 10; 2 Cor. v, 7; Isa. lv, 8, 9] knowledge of God's being [Rom. i, 19, 20], but also of the divine will as to us [Col. i, 9, 10; Eph. v, 15–17] and of the divine providential activity in nature and in human life, and of the holy purpose of his world-government. Though indeed a proper and ripe knowledge of God leads to a higher perfection of the moral life, still knowledge is not, as faith, the antecedent condition of the moral in general; for only he can know the truth of God who is pure of heart [Matt. v, 8].

SECTION CXIV.

The second phase of the moral appropriating of God is, that man becomes *for God*,—that he exalts himself toward God by a moral act in order to unite God actually, and not simply in inner recognition, with himself,—in order to permit the divine activity to be influential upon him; this is in fact the *worshiping of God*, which is at once a religious and a moral, and hence a holy, activity. The worship of God is either purely spiritual and at the same time affirmative, namely, in that man puts himself spiritually into direct relation with God,—rises to God in pious *devotion*, which is *prayer*,—or it is of a rather virtual and at the same time more negative character, namely, a free moral turning away from the ungodly and the unholy,—*sacrifice*. These two phases of the worshiping of God belong inseparably together; there is no prayer without sacrifice, and no sacrifice without prayer.

Faith is the purely inward phase of the moral appropriating of the divine,—the woman-like self-opening of the soul for the in-shining of the divine light; in this receiving, the person remains strictly in and with himself. Worshiping is more objective; the person goes forth out of himself,—lets his own light beam forth toward the divine original light, even as the flame of the sacrifice, when once kindled by the heavenly fire, mounts up toward heaven again. All worshiping of God presupposes faith, though it is itself more than faith. When man has by faith received the divine into himself, and imbued himself therewith; he still yet distinguishes himself as a creature from God,—puts himself into moral relation to God, raises himself by a moral action to God as to one different from himself; and this is the worshiping of God. To the pure mystic all worship falls away, for he loses sight of the distinction between the Infinite and the finite.

Worship is the immediate actual outgoing of faith; it is a religious activity which aims at making the already naturally-existing communion of God with us into a consciously-willed communion of ourselves with God; it is a sacred activity as distinguished from the worldly or profane,—from that which deals only with temporal things. In a normal moral condition of humanity, all activity whatever would bear a sacred character, and the distinction between the sacred and the "profane" could only assume the form of a conditional outward difference of a temporally-alternating occupation with earthly things, on the one hand, and with eternal interests on the other; with labor and with the Sabbath-rest of the soul during the continuance of the earthly life, and that, too, only in so far as consistent with the fact that all earthly occupation is constantly exalted and sanctified by a positive and conscious relation to the eternal. Our sacred activity relates either immediately to God,—is a purely affirmative uniting of the human to the divine; or it relates only mediately to God, but immediately to the ungodly, namely, in that by refusing the ungodly, it sets up a barrier against it,—turns the heart away from the evil, and toward God. These two features can never be separated; prayer without sacrifice, without a rejecting of the ungodly both within and without us, is morally impossible; in exalting ourselves to God in prayer we at the same time distinguish the divine from the anti-divine, and withdraw ourselves from the latter; we cannot truly pray without at the same time renouncing the worldly,—without giving up, without sacrificing, the pretentious emptiness of finite things.

SECTION CXV.

1. *Prayer*, as resting on faith in the personal God, is the free moral uniting of the believing heart with God, in such a manner that the moral personality is in fact not lost, but, on the contrary, exalted in and by God; it is the free and conscious recognizing that God knows all our thoughts, and the joyful wish that such be the case; it exalts our natural communion with God into a spiritual and moral one, the being

of God in man into a being of man in God. As it is alone in this being at one with God that the true life of the rational spirit consists, hence in the moral man, at least a prayerful disposition, if not express praying in words, must be strictly unceasing. Prayer has only then moral worth when it really springs of a praying heart, and hence, when it is offered with *devotion;* and as it unites the person with the Father of all men, hence it leads to a communion of prayer, and the higher form of prayer is therefore *social* prayer.

In prayer man enters into personal communion with God, and in loving confidence expressly communicates to him as the All-knowing One, his pious thinking, feeling, and willing; only that which is pious can be communicated to God; a consciously unpious prayer is blasphemy. Prayer is absolutely conditioned on a believing recognition of the divine omniscience; it is not, therefore, so much a means of making our thoughts known to God,—for God knows our thoughts from afar, and of what we have need before we ask therefor,—as rather an expression of our belief that God knows, and our joyful willingness that he should know thereof. A prayer that should spring from the thought that God himself needed it in order to know our inward state, would be *per se* impious and in self-contradiction; but every thought and every act that we are not willing that God should know, and that we would hide from him, is impious, and the degree of our piety is measured by the degree in which we have the desire that all our acts and thoughts should be known of God. The intermission of prayer does not shut out our inner life from the divine knowledge, it simply shuts out the divine blessing from *us.* Prayer reveals not our being to the divine knowledge, but it reveals the divine all-knowing presence to us,—brings not God down to us, but elevates us to God; it is for *us* the means of uniting ourselves truly with God, inasmuch as thereby not only is God, as the Omnipresent One, with *us,* but also we, by a religiously-moral act of will, are with God; and only when God is himself with us, not merely naturally and without our desire, but upon our express prayer and seeking therefor, are we in real saving life-communion with him. Without prayer there can be only a natural, but not a moral and spiritual communion with God; and this merely natural communion is, on the supposition that it rises no higher, in antagonism to the essence of a moral creature, and hence leads to the casting off of man by God. For him who cannot pray, God's presence is judicial and condemnatory. As in prayer man exalts himself to the highest object of the moral activity, so is prayer also the highest moral act; and all other moral action receives its moral worth solely from its relation to this, —solely as morally consecrated by prayer.

In prayer, man gives utterance to his highest moral privileges and to his free personality, inasmuch as thereby, with full and joyful freedom, he wills, recognizes and heightens that which already existed without prayer, though indeed only in an immediate, natural ante-moral manner, but which could not so remain without turning into antagonism and unblessedness, namely, the divine omnipresent domination. Only to those who desire it is God's presence a blessing, and only by those who love is the loving communion of God experienced; "draw nigh to God, and he will draw nigh to you" [James iv, 8; comp. Psa. cxlv, 18, 19]. It is the sublime significancy of prayer that it brings into prominence man's great and high destination, that it brings to expression his free personal relation to God, that it heightens man's consciousness of his true moral nature in relation to God; and as all morality depends on our relation to God, prayer is, in fact, the very life-blood of morality. The true freedom, and hence also the true morality of man, manifests itself not in his arbitrarily choosing that which is fleeting or baseless, but in the fact that with conscious free-will and glad assent he recognizes and confirms that which lies in the holy constitution of the world itself. To the limited natural understanding, prayer seems useless and therefore irrational; for this understanding is not capable of comprehending the spiritual. It is true, God causes his sun to rise upon the good and the evil, gives rain to the just and the unjust, furnishes food to man and beast,—in a word, He " gives to all men their daily bread" even without prayer; but the significancy of such prayer is the fact of our recognizing Him as the Giver of all, of our receiving his gifts with thankfulness. That God's presence and gifts be not only about us but also *for* us, that they become a blessing to us, a bond of love between God and us, a living fountain of godly-mindedness,—that they be not foreign to us, not in antagonism to us, but in fact our own and in harmony with us,—that God's being in us be also our being in God,—all this is the fruit of prayer.

Prayer is so intimately connected with the morally-religious life that it appears, under some form, even among those nations where, because of the relative ignoring of the personality of God, it has almost lost all shadow of meaning, as, for example, in India. Greek and Roman philosophers often introduce their disquisitions with prayers (Socrates, Plato); the Romans prayed on occasion of all important state-events, on the election of magistrates, the enactment of laws, etc. Of course in heathen prayer there could never exist the proper earnestness, inasmuch as the idea of God was always imperfect; no heathen could ever pray as could a pious Israelite. The first real opposing of prayer, if we except the frivolous Epicureans, was on the part of Maximus of Tyre, a Platonist of the second century after Christ; it was also opposed by Rousseau, though for very superficial reasons (because the order of the universe could not be changed by individual wishes), and, with astonishing lack of insight by *Kant*, who even finds in the Lord's Prayer, as given by Christ, a very clear suggestion to substitute in the place of all prayer simply a determination to lead a good life (*Relig. innerh.*, etc., 1794, p. 302). In Pantheism the rejection of prayer as absurd, is a matter of course.—The Scriptures present prayer as one of the most essential moral requirements [Psa. cxlv, 18, 19; Matt. vii, 7; Mark xi, 24; James i, 5 *sqq.*; 1 Tim. ii, 1–3; Eph. vi, 18]. The injunction to pray without ceasing [Luke xviii, 1–7; 1 Thess. v, 17; Rom. xii, 12; Col. iv, 2; 1 Tim. ii, 8; comp. Psa. lxiii, 7] implies the constant aspiring of our heart to God as to Him whose will alone is our law, and who gives his blessing to whatever is done in his name.—Where sin is not yet dominant, any other than a *devotional* prayer is inconceivable. Devotion in prayer is not merely the absence of distraction, but it is the praying out of a true, earnest and upright heart-disposition. Devotion cannot be required as a special duty, for it is necessarily included in the very idea of prayer; the Scriptures simply allude to the earnestness of prayer, and to the liability of self-deception in well-meant prayer [Isa. xxix, 13; Psa. cxlv, 18; Matt. xv, 8; vi, 5–7; James v, 16].

It is not as a merely moral, but as a religious, activity that prayer leads to *communion*, for religion is essentially socializing, not directly, however, but in virtue of the communion which it establishes with God. Mere individual prayer has its proper justification as bearing on the personal relation to God; it is in fact the primary and most obvious form [Matt. vi, 6]; but prayer attains to its highest, though never exclusive, character as the single-hearted prayer of the believing *communion* or church-society. And this not simply because such prayer hightens the feeling of the unitedness of the faithful, but because, in virtue of the throwing off of personal isolation and of its flowing out of the holy spirit which pervades the society, it has a guarantee of greater purity, and consequently the promise of special blessing [Matt. xviii, 20; Acts ii, 42; Eph. v, 19; Col. iii, 16].—*Christ* himself gives the moral pattern of prayer; he prayed out of the full consciousness of life-communion with God, and consequently with full confidence of being answered [Heb. v, 7]; he prayed often in solitude [Matt. xiv, 23; xxvi, 36, 42; Mark vi, 32; Luke vi, 12; ix, 28], and often in the presence of others [Matt. xxvi, 39; John xi, 41 *sqq.*], and in communion with his disciples [John xvii, 1 *sqq.*].

SECTION CXVI.

All prayer is primarily, either expressly or in virtue of its necessary presuppositions, a *confession*, a recognition of God as the unconditional Lord, and as the all-knowing, all powerful and all-loving Father. In as far as in it we are always conscious of ourselves as loved by God, prayer is at the same time also *thanksgiving*. In so far as in prayer we have respect not only to the past and present, but also to the goal of moral effort, the realization of which we regard as not in our own power independently of God, nor yet in an unfree nature-necessity, but in the will of God as co-operating with us, prayer becomes *petition*—the climax of the inner religiously-moral life, wherein the true filial relation of man to God finds its expression; and as the moral end is of a rational, and hence not merely individual, character, consequently the petition is essentially also *intercession*—the highest religious expression of our love to man. As only the all-embracing wisdom of God is capable of fully seeing the appropriateness of earthly things and relations to the attainment of the highest good, hence the petition for earthly goods, though *per se* entirely legitimate, can never be more than of a humbly conditional character; and there is no petition other than that for the *per se* unquestionably eternal good, that has no other condition than the willing, believing obedience of the subject. The promise of answering is based on the condition of believing and of humble confidence.

Prayer is *per se* a recognition of God,—it is adoration and confession both *to* God as the all-ruling One, and also *before* God as the all-knowing and holy One. In this recognizing confession itself, there is involved a thanksgiving, which consequently is included, though it may be but implicitly, in every prayer; in the Lord's Prayer it lies in the very address. All thanksgiving [1 Sam. ii; Psa. cvi, 1; Rom. xv, 6; 1 Tim. iv, 4, 5; Phil. iv, 6; Col. iii, 17; iv, 2] is at the same time a petition for the bestowal of the good for which it is offered; and the petition is, in virtue of the soul-uniting filial relation to God, necessarily also intercession for others and for the whole kingdom of God [Matt. vi, 10; John xvii, 9 *sqq.*; Eph i, 16; vi, 18; 1 Tim. ii, 1–3; Col. i, 9;

iv, 3; Phil. i, 4; James v, 16; Heb. xiii, 18]. So long as prayer remains of a merely individual character, it comes short of true prayer,—rests not yet on a consciousness of the filial relation to God, for this consciousness is inconsistent with self-seeking exclusiveness; the children of God have their home only in the kingdom of God.

Prayer as petition is the profoundest enigma for the merely wordly finitely-occupied understanding; for the religious heart, however, it is the beginning and the center of the spiritual life. He who cannot offer petitions to God is not of God. All intellectual doubts as to the nature and efficacy of petitioning prayer, have as their back-ground a doubt of the personality of God, although they may assume to be a vindication of the eternal order of the world. A God who cannot answer petitions is not a personal spirit, but only an unconscious nature-force. In the believing petition the Scriptures promise *answers* [Psa. l, 15; x, 17; xxii, 4, 5; xxxiv, 15; lxii, 1 *sqq.;* lxv, 2; xciv, 9; cii, 17; cxlv, 18, 19; Prov. xv, 8; Isa. lxv, 24; Matt. vii, 7; xviii, 19; xxi, 22; John ix, 31; xvi, 23, 24; 1 John iii, 22; v, 14; James i, 5; iv, 8; v, 13–18; 1 Pet. iii, 12]; to the impious and foolish petition they refuse it [Job xxvii, 9; xxxv, 13; Psa. lxvi, 18; Prov. xv, 8, 29; xxviii, 9; Isa. i, 15; John ix, 31; James iv, 3, and others]; and confident faith in an answer is itself the condition of the answer [Mark xi, 24; James i, 6, 7]. As the fuller development of the subject belongs to dogmatics, we here subjoin but a few general observations. The answering of prayer is not unconditional; it is conditioned, on the one hand, on the loving wisdom of God, which is higher than that of man [Eph. iii, 20], and, on the other, on the prayer-spirit of him who prays. And the answer is not a merely seeming one, so that prayer would be superfluous, but the answer is given on the basis and in virtue of the prayer [Luke xi, 5–13; xviii, 1 *sqq.,*—the lesson of which is, that if earnest prayer is effectual even with unloving men, how much more is it so with the all-loving One who gladly hears such petitions; Gen. xviii, 23 *sqq.;* Exod. xxxii, 9 *sqq.;* Num. xiv, 13 *sqq.*, 20; xvi, 20 *sqq.;* Isa. xxxviii]. Prayer does not change the eternal counsel of God; this counsel is itself not unconditional, but it is determined by the all-knowing One in view of the free conduct of his creatures; and, consequently, one element of it is, that prayer is eternally destined to be answered. *Every* pious prayer is answered, although only in the manner most wholesome to him who offers it, and hence not always in the special manner in which the answer is expected [2 Cor. xii, 8, 9.] If man deceives himself as to the sought good, still he receives the good,—not, however, the false one which he had in mind, but the true one which he had in heart. Hence no believing prayer, in so far as it relates to earthly goods, can be or should be more than a *conditional* petition, and the manner of the fulfillment must be submitted to the wisdom of God. If even Christ prays in this conditional manner to the Father [Matt. xxvi, 39, 42; Luke xxii, 42], by how much more should man so pray, whose knowledge is so limited; true faith is in fact a confidence that God knows best what serves for our peace, and brings it about; childlikeness and humble confidence give power and truth to prayer [Rom. viii, 15; Gal. iv, 6]. Under this condition, prayer for particular earthly goods is not only allowed to man, but is also willed by God and with promise of answering [Matt. vi, 11; vii, 7 *sqq.*; Phil. iv, 5, 6; Eph. vi, 18; James v, 14 *sqq.*]; and the confidence of obtaining the object sought, even in such special petitions rises to confident assurance wherever the prayer goes forth from a complete life-communion with God, and in the power of the Holy Ghost,—wherever it is prayer "in spirit and in truth" [John iv, 24; Rom. viii, 26, 27: Gal. iv, 6; Eph. vi, 18; comp. John xiv, 13; xvi, 23]; for, the more complete the union of the pious heart with God, so much the more does it partake of the illuminating power of God, and God's knowledge of the future begets in him who partakes of God's Spirit a *presentiment* of the divine counsel in regard to him; and the presentiment rises to a prayerful longing, an unshaken faith; and the true petition to a *prophecy*. The fulfillment of the petition is felt by anticipation in the prayer itself; he who truly prays is a prophet; and God is the fulfiller of the prophecy, because he is the author of the counsel. Here also Christ himself furnishes the pattern: "Father, I thank thee that thou hast heard me," etc. [John xi, 41]; his prayer related to what he had already prophetically beholden and predicted [verses 11, 23]. The primary and most essential element of true prayer is, of course, the petition for the filial relation to God and for the coming of the kingdom of God [Matt. vi, 10, 12; John xvii, 15; Luke xi, 13]. Man should beware, however, of sinning in prayer itself; but by self-seeking narrowness he does this; to pray in the spirit of God, is to pray for the kingdom of God. Model prayers are the Lord's Prayer and the high-priestly prayer of Christ.

As God's eternal decree to answer prayer is conditioned on the actuality of the prayer, hence prayer is not simply moral appropriation, but also, though not in a direct and strict sense, moral forming, seeing that, though indeed not God himself, yet in fact the particular temporal manifestation of his world-government, is conditioned on prayer. God's essence is indeed not subject to change; his doing and acting in the world, however, are, in virtue of his righteous love, conditioned on the free conduct of his rational creatures, and hence also on prayer. The real forming, however, which is directly connected with prayer relates to the personal religiously-moral being of the subject. The blessing efficacy of prayer beams back from God upon the offerer, namely, in that in virtue of the prayer not only his being in God comes more vividly to his consciousness, and has a more efficacious influence, but also God's being in him comes to a higher reality. Faith in prayer and in the answering of prayer, heighten the divine life of the children of God.

SECTION CXVII.

2. The negating and rather virtual phase of the service of God, is the actual or symbolical manifesting of the real or conditional vanity of earthly things and relations, as contrasted with God or with the God-loving, pious state of the heart, namely, in *sacrifice*, the essence of which is self-denial or renunciation. In the unfallen state of man sacrifice consists essentially simply in a free giving-up of that which is naturally pleasurable, out of regard to the divine will and for the sake of the higher good, the moral end;

hence it consists in the subordinating and giving up of earthly desire. The appropriating of the divine requires the rejection of all that is ungodly, and therein the person accomplishes, at the same time, a high moral culture of himself.

As contrasted with the highest good and with God, every thing finite appears as relatively empty and void; the actual manifesting of this nullity, out of love to the divine, is sacrifice,—a notion that is fundamental to all religions, and that constitutes the focal point of all religious life, and which is still recognizable even in the most utter perversions of the truth.* There is no love without sacrifice; the higher the love, so much the higher the readiness to sacrifice for the sake of the beloved; sacrifice is the test of love; maternal love sacrifices repose and enjoyment for the sake of the child; this is not figurative language,—the sacrifice is real and true. As God's highest love expresses itself in the giving up of his Son, so man's love to God is manifested in the sacrificing of that to the enjoyment of which man has in general a right. As, however, in the sinless state of humanity, there would exist no really untrue and vain object from which man would have actually to turn away in moral abhorrence, but only a merely relatively such, namely, the merely natural and transitory as in contradistinction to the spiritual, hence in this case sacrifice would not consist in the destruction of an entity, but in the *renunciation* of an enjoyment, an abstaining from the merely worldly. In the interest of his spiritual freedom, of his moral growth, man is not to give himself over to nature, but must by obedience renounce *some degree* of the enjoyment of nature and of his personal discretion. He is to sacrifice whatever tempts him from God, whatever binds him to the merely natural or to the non-divine; also of unfallen man it was required that he should realize his spiritual freedom by the free renunciation of a merely natural enjoyment. Christ's fasting in the wilderness was not a part of his atoning self-sacrifice, and yet it was a sacrifice on the part of the Son of

---

* See Wuttke's *Gesch. des Heident. I*, pp. 127 *sqq.*, 268 *sqq.*, 311; *II*, pp. 64, 343 *sqq*, 547 *sqq.*

man, even as was also required of unfallen man. In yielding himself to enjoyment without moral discrimination, man loses hold on the spiritual; he must renounce in order to be free. In the unfallen state sacrifice has essentially an educative end and a symbolical form. God certainly did not forbid man to eat of the designated tree because it was a bad tree, for to sinless beings there could be nothing evil in the entire circle of God-made nature; but in his educative wisdom, God required of man a sacrifice, for the simple reason that no moral life is possible without self-restraint, no religious life without sacrifice. Man stands in the presence of nature and God, both are good; but nature is a created object and may not be placed on an equal footing with God. When man enjoys nature for its own sake and without reference to God, he sins; for he ought to belong, not to nature, but to God. Hence he should recognize, and manifest in moral acts, the truth that nature *per se* is *not* the true being and the true goal of moral aspiration, namely, the highest good, but only a means to this end. Hence his moral relation to nature and to the sensuous, is, as in contrast to his relation to God, of a negative character. This "no" in regard to nature, man pronounces morally when he subordinates his relation to nature to his higher relation to God, when he says to sensuous desire: "Thou mayest *not*, shalt not absorb and dominate my thinking and willing;" he must freely hold in, check the merely sensuous, for the sake of the spiritual,—must restrain himself from the former in order that he may possess and perfect himself as a moral spirit, and that he may rise to spiritual-mindedness.

It is the antagonism of the spirit to the flesh that lies at the basis of sacrifice; in the interest of the spiritual, the spirit sacrifices the fleshly. Also man as normal and not yet sinful, had to crucify his flesh with the affections and lusts thereof [Gal. v, 24], although this flesh and its desires were not yet immoral; but to have sought the flesh as an end, as a good, would have been sinful; and God put upon him a requirement of abnegation in order that he might recognize and actually learn this fact,—that he might break away from the merely sensuous, and develop in himself the image of God. Simple obedience to this requirement, without a why or wherefore, was the purest and best of sacrifices. This Paradisaical germ of all sacrifice is, therefore, self-denial in obedience to God, a renouncing not a destroying, a giving up, out of love to the spirit, of that which is dear to the flesh; and this idea pervades all forms of sacrifice, even the emphatic sin-offering; only that which is dear to man can be to him a sacrifice; and because of the simple fact that the first man would not bring the light sacrifice required of him, it became necessary for him afterward to make severer ones; and from the hour of the fall and thenceforth the morally-religious consciousness of humanity finds satisfaction only in a series of progressively more violent and more terrible sacrifices, culminating in the offering of human victims, and that too not merely among the rude, but even among the most civilized of gentile nations.

In the idea of sacrifice it is always implied that that which the person gives up is *per se* good and right, that primarily he has a right to its enjoyment, but that he gives it up for the sake of a higher end; to give up that which is *per se* bad, is not to sacrifice; the offering that was presented to Jehovah had to be pure and spotless; and the worth of the sacrifice rises with the worth of the object offered. Thus, sensuous enjoyment is *per se* good, but it must be restrained and limited, and often refused, in order that not it but the rational spirit may be the master. But man has also to bring, in the interest of the moral, purely spiritual sacrifices. It was not the sensuous *per se* that was the temptation to Eve, but the representation made to her that the tree would render her "wise;" it was her duty, as it is the duty of man in general, to renounce the desire of obtaining from the *creature* that wisdom which only God can impart—which can be learned only in believing obedience to God.

The sacrifice that was required of unfallen man implied in its renunciation at the same time, a confession, namely, to God as the highest good and the highest love, and this again implied thankfulness for the love received in communion with God. Inasmuch as every good gift is from God hence the *thank-offering* of the believer can only be symbolical, expressive of his readiness to give up in the interest of the eternal even that which is dearest of all to him, in the consciousness that in the communion with God for whom it is given up, the real and true life is in fact preserved; in the presence of God none is to appear empty [Exod. xxiii, 15; xxxiv, 20].

Sacrifice appears in the Old Testament in its more definite form as early as in the case of Cain and Abel; we find no indication of its express institution by God; and we might therefore regard it as an immediate and natural expression of the religious consciousness; however, a positive divine prescription is the more probable. It is certainly not probable that sacrifice was first made from a consciousness of guilt; the offerings of Cain and Abel, consisting of the products of the field and of the flock, seem rather to be thank-offerings than sin-offerings; Abel's bloody offering is expressly designated [Gen. iv, 4] by the word *minchah* (present, gift) by which are subsequently designated the bloodless thank-offerings in contradistinction to the bloody, and, for the most part, atoning offerings, namely, the *sebachim;* the offering of Noah appears expressly as a thank-offering [viii, 20] The burning up of the material of the sacrifice signifies the renunciation and the eradication of the earthly desires of him who sacrifices; the pure heavenward-mounting sacrificial flame symbolizes the exaltation of the heart from the earthly to the heavenly,— the union with God. Thus sacrifice becomes a symbol of the alliance of man with God; and in the case of Noah and the patriarchs, a sign of the Covenant, and hence also a sign of the union of the Israelites who escaped from Egypt, into *one* people [Exod. iii, 12]. And, therefore, subsequently in the fully-developed sacrificial service of a sinful people, the essence of the sacrifice was in fact not placed in the outward rite, but in the submission of the heart, in the renunciation of an earthly self-seeking mind, in the complete giving up of all earthly love for God's sake [Gen. xxii, 16]; obedience is better than [outward] sacrifice; God-pleasing sacrifices are a broken spirit and a contrite heart, and "to do justice and judgment is more acceptable to the Lord than sacrifice" [1 Sam. xv, 22; Psa. xl, 6; l, 8–15; li, 16, 17, 18; Hos. vi, 6; Eccl. iv, 17; Prov. xxi, 3, 27; Isa. i, 11; Jer. vi, 20; comp. Matt. ix, 13; xii, 7; Mark xii, 33]. In the case of the very first sacrifices God warns man against the error of supposing that the essence of the sacrifice lies in the outward act; Abel's offering He graciously accepts, that of Cain He disregards. Sacrifice is an appropriating of the divine, inasmuch as in the turning away from the non-divine there is necessarily implied a turning to the divine.

SECTION CXVIII.

The moral sparing of the divine, has direct reference not to God himself, but to the forms under which He is revealed. Every thing whereby God becomes *for us* is *sacred* as distinguished from merely created objects *per se*. In the unfallen state of humanity all created objects are at the same time also sacred, namely, in so far as they are considered an expression of the divine will; and whatever is sacred is in the highest degree an object of moral sparing,—should be treated as sacred. This sparing springs from moral humility,—is an express respecting of the sacred in virtue of a holy awe, springing from a lively consciousness, on the one hand, of the divine glory even in the humbler forms of its manifestation, and, on the other, of our own existence as a limited one and as resting solely on divine grace. The objects of this sacred awe, and hence of moral sparing, are both the immediate, full and actual self-revelations of God, and also all mediating instrumentalities of His revelation and communication, as well as also every thing that relates to the reverencing of God on the part of man.

The distinction between the sacred and the non-sacred is, for the unfallen state, of a merely conditional character; it is in fact, simply the same thing considered under two phases; in all things we can behold both the created and the Creator. He who is truly pious sees himself every-where surrounded by the sacred,—he prays to God not merely in the temple of Jerusalem, or on Mount Gerizim, but every-where in spirit and in truth. Now, in so far as objects that are imbued with the divine are temporal and finite, they are capable of being abused and desecrated,—hence the moral duty of sparing. The direction of God to Moses on occasion of the revelation in the burning bush [Exod. iii, 5], suggests the proper moral bearing of man; he must put away from himself all that bears upon itself the character of the common, the unholy, the dross of earth. The duty of sparing, as relating to the sacred, is not a mere non-doing, but, like every other form of this duty, it is a self-restraining out of regard to the higher right of the sacred object; a sparing from mere indifference would be sinful.

The objects of this sparing are: (1) The immediate *personal* revelations of God himself. Here there is no room for a mere passive bearing; here the mere non-doing, the mere not respecting the divine presence, is an offending of God himself; and moral sparing passes over at once into adoring reverence; here the declaration of Christ holds good: "He that is not for me is *against* me;" the not-concerning ourselves about God is a dishonoring of God.—(2) God's revelation and self-communication through his *Word* should be recognized as absolutely sacred, and distinguished in every respect from whatever is merely human and natural; it is disesteemed and dishonored by doubt, unbelief, and disobedience, and by trifling or irreverent use, by ridicule or neglect; the divine Word as sacred is to be treated entirely differently from the merely human; it calls for unconditional faith and reverent submission.—(3) The *name* of God [Exod. iii, 14] and other symbolical designations of God must be treated with sacred awe and sparing,—may not be associated with the common and thus subjected to irreverent use, may not be misused in sport, or frivolity, or for deception [Exod. xx, 7; Lev. xix, 12; xxii, 32; Matt. vi, 9]. A name is not a mere empty sound; it is the body of a thought; and as the human body is not an object of indifference for the spirit, and as to dishonor it is to insult the spirit, so also is a misusing of the divine name a dishonoring of God himself. In the awe of the Jews as to the pronouncing of the name of Jehovah, there lay a deep moral significancy, though indeed this peculiarity rendered also possible an outward evasion of the command itself. That the precept to revere God's name appears as one of the chief commandments of the Mosaic law, evinces its high moral importance. Where there exists reverential love, there the name of the beloved will not be desecrated by triflingness and frivolous sport. And what is true of the name is also true of all symbols of God, as, for example, in the Ancient Covenant, of the covering of the ark of the Covenant (the mercy-seat), of the pillar of fire, etc. In a more general sense every form of sin is a dishonoring of the name and image of God, inasmuch as man himself bears God's name and image in himself, and should therefore spare and respect these in his own person [comp. Rom. ii, 24]; and all morality may be summed up in the keeping sacred of the divine image in ourselves,—as expressed by Jehovah: "Ye shall sanctify yourselves and be holy, for I am holy" [Lev. xi, 44], or in the words of Peter: "Sanctify the Lord God in your hearts" [1 Pet. iii, 15].—(4) The *human organs* of divine revelation, the prophets and the called heralds of the divine Word in general, have a moral right to reverential sparing, though this sparing refers essentially not to them as men, but to God in whose name they speak. [Psa. cv, 15; Matt. x, 40, 41; comp. xi, 49–51; 1 Thes. v, 12, 13; Heb. xiii, 17]; the persecuting and killing of the prophets is frequently spoken of in Scripture as among the most heinous of offenses. Also in a sinless development of humanity all those would be regarded in the light of prophets of God, who, having attained to higher spiritual knowledge, should bear witness of divine truth; they would stand not strictly on an equal footing with those whom they should teach and train; and their recognition as divine messengers would beget a greater willingness to give heed to them. Wherever there is a really moral communion, there the ministers of God are honored; not to respect them is a sign of deep moral declension; but the deepest degradation of all is where they themselves do not respect their calling. No prophet of God was ever without moral self-denial and constant humiliation before God,— without the deeply felt consciousness of Moses: "Who am I that I should go unto Pharaoh, and bring forth the children of Israel out of Egypt?"—but also no prophet of God was ever without the sacred right to be recognized and respected as God's messenger, provided only that he be found faithful. —(5) All that relates to the *worshiping* of God,—the holy seasons, places, and things, are, as sacred, to be distinguished from the non-sacred, and to be honored accordingly, and not to be placed on an equal footing with that which serves only temporal, individual ends. The Sabbath is to be treated quite otherwise than the day of labor; it has a right to be respected, for it is God's day, set apart to his special service. Its celebration by actual divine worship is only one of its phases, the other is its being sacredly spared. Every thing is to be avoided on the Sabbath which disturbs the devout frame of the soul,—attracts it back to the merely earthly and sensuous, impresses upon it a mere every-day character. He who does not honor the day of the Lord, honors also not the Lord of the day. Holy places and things, being consecrated to heavenly purposes, should not be profaned to worldly entertainment and to merely temporal uses. Though we do not recognize any mystic power in a special consecration, yet we hold fast to the principle that holy places and things belong exclusively to the service of the Lord. God himself ordained, in the Old Testament, particular sacred things and a special consecration of them [Exod. xxv, *sqq.*; xxx, 22 *sqq.*]. Even as the "burning bush" [Exod. iii, 5] and the mount of legislation and the holy of holies in the temple were separated from all that was not sacred, so also is it with every place that is dedicated to the holy One [Lev. xix, 30]. The significancy of this setting apart, and the importance of this respecting of the sacred, increase with the actuality of sin.

Note. God cannot of course be an object of moral *forming* in the strict sense of the word. Though prayer is in fact a moral influencing of God, inasmuch as it finds hearing, still no change is thereby wrought in God, and that which is realized by the efficacy of prayer is not so much in God as in us and in the world. But in a remote sense we may speak of a forming of the *divine*, namely, in so far as God is expressed in sacred symbols and in sacred art, and in so far as, by our witnessings for God, the knowledge and love of God are implanted in the souls of men; all this, however, is in reality simply a forming of the finite and the human into an image of God, and not a forming of God himself.

II. THE MORAL ACTIVITY, IN RELATION TO THE MORAL PERSON HIMSELF.

SECTION CXIX.

(*a*) The duty of moral *sparing* is here the preserving of one's own existence and of its normal peculiarity and development, as prompted by a consciousness of the divine will, and hence also the warding off of all therewith-conflicting and disturbing or destroying influences on the part of nature or of the spiritual world. To this end it is necessary that in all things the true relation of the body, as a serving power, to the rational spirit, as the dominating power, be preserved, and that the image of God, which though originally inherent in man, is yet in need of fuller development, be preserved pure even in its corporeally-symbolical manifestation.

The moral sparing of one's self is the higher moral application of a law that pervades the entire totality of being. That which is cohesion in a nature-body, and the law of gravitation in the natural world in general, and the instinct of self-defense and of self-preservation in the animal world, becomes with man a moral duty. When man seeks to preserve himself, to ward off injury and death, out of mere natural instinct, his action is not yet moral; it becomes moral only when it springs from a consciousness that it is God's will,—that God has pleasure in our existence as his own creative work, that He has a purpose in us which we are morally to fulfill. Of a duty of self-destruction there can never be any possibility; and for a duty of entire self-sacrifice, of the giving up of life for the sake of a higher end, there is, in a state of sinlessness, also no possibility; otherwise the divine government would be in anarchy. God who gave existence to man wills also its preservation,—has willed it as a moral end, and not simply as a means to an end. Death is simply the wages of sin, and not a condition of virtue, save alone where on account of sin there is need of a sacrifice.

In a sinless state the duty of self-sparing is of easy fulfillment, partly for the reason that it corresponds to a natural law immanent in all living creatures, and partly because disturbing influences are conceivable only where they are occasioned by the fault of man himself,—for example, when he presumptuously exposes himself to such natural influences as he is not yet able to resist,—which is in fact possible seeing that, also for the unfallen state, the complete mastery over nature is presented as a condition yet to be attained to by moral effort. Also from the influence of spiritual beings an injuring of the moral person is possible, so long as the rational creature has not as yet attained to its ultimate perfection, so that here also there is place for the duty of watchfulness, in order that the diverse personalities that are as yet in process of development may not act hinderingly upon each other. And this duty of sparing watchfulness is still more increased when the moral person stands no longer in the presence of simply sin-free beings, but is assaulted by spiritual temptation, as in the case of Adam and Eve; here the duty of self-preserving sparing assumes at once the form of a positive warding off.—In the Scriptures the duty of sparing one's self, even in relation to the corporeal life, is presented as *per se* strictly valid; "no man ever yet hated his own flesh, but nourisheth and cherisheth it, even as the Lord the church" [Eph. v, 29]. Man is also to exercise this duty of sparing in view of his own possible sinning; in protecting his moral innocence, man protects also the image of God as created in him.

SECTION CXX.

(*b*) Moral *appropriating* is, as regards the moral person himself, directly at the same time also a moral *forming* of the person into a progressively more perfect expression of the moral idea,—into a personally-peculiar realization of the moral end; and in proportion as the moral person appropriates to itself its own self, puts itself into possession of itself, it accomplishes upon itself also a moral forming.

(1) Not the body is to appropriate to itself the spirit, but the spirit is progressively more and more to appropriate to itself the body, and to form it, and thereby also to form itself; hence the spirit alone is the appropriating factor, and the body is simply to *be* appropriated and formed. Even as nature stands to God in a twofold relation, namely, in that, on the one hand, God accomplishes his will *in it*, makes it *good*, and, on the other, reveals himself *through* it, makes it into his image, into an object of *beauty*, so also has the body in relation to the spirit the twofold destination of being its *organ* and its *image*; the former it becomes essentially by particular forming, the latter by *general* forming (§§ 109, 110).

(*a*) The body is formed and appropriated to itself by the spirit as its true absolutely subservient *organ*, in that (1) it is strengthened and rendered apt in accomplishing every service for the rational will, through the mediating and carrying out of all appropriating and forming action of the rational spirit as bearing upon the external world; (2) in that, in its sensuous impulses, it is held under the *discipline* of the spirit, and is never allowed to have an independent right for itself; in both these respects realizes itself the complete domination of the spirit over the body.

It is characteristic of the true moral nature of man, that he is capable, not merely, as is the case with the brute, of appropriating and forming external objects, but also himself. The brute is formed by nature, not by itself, and it appropriates to itself only nature, but not itself; but man in his first-given condition does not as yet really *have* himself, but must first learn to possess himself,—must attain to moral ownership of himself.

Man virtualizes his god-likeness primarily in this, that he glorifies God even in his body as the temple of the Holy Ghost [1 Cor. vi, 19, 20], and that he presents this body to God as a living, holy, and well-pleasing sacrifice [Rom. xii, 1.] The preliminary manifold dependence of the spirit on the body, and through the body also on external nature, is to be overcome and changed into spiritual freedom; the spirit is itself to make the body truly its *own* body, to appropriate it to itself as a moral possession, to form it into the perfect organ of the spirit,—in a certain sense, to create it spiritually. The original foreignness of the body to the spirit is to be overcome; its as yet partially-actual independence is to be broken; the body is to be thoroughly permeated by the spirit, and all that is *merely* objective and unfree in it, to be done away with. The dominion of the spirit over nature, which is set before it as a moral goal, is to realize itself first on its own nature, that is, on the body. That this is a moral task is plainly indicated by nature itself. The brute is much earlier self-supporting and mature than man, and needs no training in order to attain to its greatest skill; all the skill that man attains to he has to get by learning, to acquire by moral effort; and all learning is an appropriating through consciousness; man must in some manner first comprehend his body, before he can really form it and take it under his control; he who is spiritually dull usually remains also physically clumsy; man as coming from the hands of nature is the most helpless and most unskillful of creatures; all that he ever becomes is by the spirit,—by free moral activity; that his nascent life is much more helpless than that of any of the animals, is simply an incident of his high moral dignity. That which he has from nature is indeed good, but if it remains as mere unspiritualized, undominated nature, then it becomes for him evil,—becomes something of which he is to be *ashamed*. This rendering the body skillful is a personally-particular forming—a *working* of the spirit upon the body; thereby the spirit forms the body into its own true possession; it aspires to have it *for itself*, to have it entirely in its control. Herein consists also the true particular appropriating, the *enjoying*, of the body; man enjoys it when he has it fully in his power. This is the secret of the rich enjoyment of young persons, when, in free corporeal movement, in skillful playing, in skating, in rhythmical muscular action, etc., they feel themselves masters over their bodies; it is the consciousness of freedom, of acquired mastery; for, all consciousness of mastery is a feeling of happiness, and that, too, a *per se* legitimate one.

Man is to form and appropriate to himself his body in two respects; for as a spirit he stands to the outer world in the double relation of receiving and of influencing,—through the senses and through the organs of motion. The cultivation of the *senses* is more an appropriating than a real forming; the senses must first be brought under the control of the spirit; the seaman and the huntsman have not always a really sharper natural eye than others, but their seeing is more skilled,—they see many objects from which others may indeed receive exactly the same light-impressions, but yet not actually perceive them, for the reason that they *over*look them; seeing is an art, and many, though with open eyes, see comparatively little. An uncultured person hears, in a beautiful piece of music, little more than confused sounds, for the reason that he does not know how to hear. It is a moral duty of man to develop his senses to perfection, fully to appropriate them to himself, for they were given to him by God as channels through which to appropriate to himself the outer world; and it is unthankfulness to God for man to be willing to see and hear little or nothing in God's nature,—for him to have no open eyes for the glory of God as resplendent in creation, and no ear for the beautiful harmonies of nature and art. Rudeness and unculture are sinful in every respect, and hence also in respect to the senses.

The appropriating training of the *organs of motion* to vigorous skillfulness, not merely as a pleasure but also as a duty, is brought about under normal circumstances not so much by calculating art as by spontaneous natural activity; and it takes place chiefly during youth. While it was an error of many former educators entirely to neglect the training of the body to skillfulness and grace, still, on the other hand, there is danger of overestimating the worth of regulated gymnastics. The unnatural physical life of our city populations may render necessary a systematic process of corporeal exercise, notwithstanding its manifold unesthetic and even repulsive joint-wrenchings; but where the young people can have scope for indulging in more natural and frolicksome muscular recreation, regular gymnastics are doubtless quite superfluous; the learned cramming of overcrowded schools needs them indeed as a sanitary complement, but it is dangerous to substitute mere medicine for daily bread. It is a morbid condition of society, when that to which nature itself prompts us has to be made a school-requirement.

The complete subordinating of the sensuous impulses to the *discipline* of the spirit, that is, the training of the body by the spirit to *temperateness* in respect to all sensuous enjoyments, and to such *activity* as is necessary to its being a proper organ for the spirit, is also, at the same time, an appropriating and a forming; the members are to be formed into "instruments of righteousness unto God" [Rom. vi, 12, 13]. Paul represents the complete dependence of the body on the moral spirit as a dependence, not on the merely individual spirit, but on the spirit as morally subordinating itself to God. Man, as consecrated to God, is not to permit the *per se* legitimate caring for his body to become a fostering of the sensuous desires [Rom. xiii, 13, 14], but is strictly to subordinate the nurturing of the body and the indulgence in sensuous enjoyments to the rational purposes of the moral spirit, so that they shall simply be means for the spirit and never ends, in themselves [Luke xxi, 34; Rom. xiv, 17; Eph. v, 18; 1 Thess. v, 6; 1 Tim. iii, 2; Tit. ii, 1 *sqq.;* 1 Pet. iv, 7, 8]. Temperateness, however, does not imply the taking of the least possible quantity of food and drink, nor indeed indifference to the sensuous pleasures of the table; this would in fact be unthankfulness toward the goodness of God who has prepared for us also this pleasure; it does, however, require the observance of that measure which is conditioned on the needs and health of the body, and on the properly understood social relations of the person. Excessive indulgence is not only a degradation of the person himself, but also uncharitableness toward the destitute.

SECTION CXXI.

(*b*) The body is to be formed into an *image* or *symbol* of the rational spirit,—to become a revelation of the spirit in the external world; that is, it is to be shaped into an object of *beauty*, into a spiritualized expression of the moral personality. This takes place: (1) immediately,—in that the body, without the express and conscious activity of the person, is formed into a true expression of the morally-cultured spirit; (2) mediately,—in that the body, which though *per se* possessing the highest nature-beauty, is yet not to remain in simply that state, is formed by means of a spiritually-expressive characterizing *adornment* into an expression of *artistic* beauty,—into a symbolical expression not merely of the spiritual in general, but also of the personally-moral character in particular,—and in that, with moral carefulness, it is kept free from whatever would present it in the light of an object that is disesteemed or given over to natural unfreedom, and cast off by the spirit,—the virtue of *cleanliness*. Adornment, both under its positive and its negative phase, is a moral duty, not merely out of regard to others, as the true moral presentation and revelation of self to others, but also out of regard to the moral person himself.

The natural perfection of the body is not yet the true,—is to be exalted from natural beauty to spiritual. As the spirit exists primarily only in a germinal form, hence the body cannot, from the very beginning, bear the full impress of the same; the spiritual expression of the body is at first not that of the personally-formed, but only of the as yet impersonal, spirit in general. The expression of the countenance becomes really spiritual, truly beautiful, only by and through a personal character-development, which is, in turn, reflected back from this personal peculiarity. The spirit must already have behind it a moral history, before it comes to expression in the features. A general beauty without character, is meaningless; a personally-spiritual beauty is winning and magnetic. The body becomes truly beautiful only through the complete appropriating of the same by, and for, the spirit; and the true secret of beauty consists in a genuine spiritual and moral culture. Where falseness has not yet gained firm foothold, there the countenance is the mirror of the soul; and, for the skilled look, even disguising falseness is transparent. There lies at the basis of "physiognomics" a deep truth; but this truth is not expressible in definite words and lines. It is not by mere chance that for certain historic personalities, such as those of Christ and the more prominent of the apostles, certain very definite forms and casts of countenance have found their place in Christian art, and by which every one recognizes them at first glance. The true character-expression of the cultured body is, in some sense, spirit-imbued,—is sensuous and super-sensuous at the same time; neither words, nor outlines, nor even the photographic pencil of nature, is capable of reproducing it, but only the spirit-guided hand of the artist; spirit is recognized and grasped only by spirit; no photograph of a spiritual, character-imbued face attains to the fidelity of an artistic portrait. In a sinless state, the beauty of the spirit would necessarily reveal itself in beauty of body. So also must it have been in the case of Christ,—and the erroneous notion that for a time prevailed in the early church, to the effect that in Christ there had been no physical comeliness, was soon dissipated by the correct consciousness of Christian art. The heavenly soul of Christ must have depicted itself in his countenance [comp. Psa. xlv, 3]; and the reason why the children approached Him with glad confidence and shouted: "Hosanna!" is doubtless because of a direct impression which Christ's person made upon them; children have a wonderful capacity for reading character in the external appearance. Female vanity, in laying such great stress on corporeal beauty, is guilty simply of applying to sinfully-perverted reality, the thought, that is correct for the unfallen state of humanity, namely, that beauty of body is evidence of a beautiful soul. The moral task in relation to this culture of bodily expression, is, happily, not an immediate intentional forming of the body, but rather the moral forming of the soul, which then, in turn, of itself impresses itself on the body.

The *ornamentation* of the body, including the exclusion of all uncleanliness, is a very important moral duty, and one that is very definitely emphasized in the Scriptures. On the subject of nudity and clothing, there has been, both from the moral and from the artistic stand-point, much disputing. Greek art, in its golden age, represented some of the gods nude: at a later period, when it had stooped to the service of worldliness rather than of religion, it expressed itself predominantly in the nude. Still, however, only such gods appear nude as represent a certain degree of moral and spiritual unripeness or sensuousness; Jupiter, Juno, Minerva, appear almost always draped; for spiritually-developed and historical characters, also among human beings, nudity was an artistic impossibility. This suggests the true law in the case. Nudity represents merely the naturally-beautiful, not the spiritually-beautiful, merely the human in general, not the personal in particular,—is that which is alike in all persons, not that in which they spiritually differ. That portion of the body which does not express the merely general, that is, the countenance, is, in fact, uniformly left free of clothing. The very sense for the morally-spiritual gives even a stronger expression to the personal through the medium itself of clothing. Who could bear the thought of a nude Cæsar or Homer! Christian art rejected the nude, for the good reason that it had spiritual characters to represent. Moreover, mere nudity is artistically beautiful only in the form of lust-repellent, colorless sculpture; in painting it becomes licentious and, therefore, un-beautiful. It is a very false opinion, that clothing really conceals beauty; clothing, as an expression of the spiritual, as a free artistic creation, is in fact the higher beauty. This appears very clearly when man is represented not as an individual, but in groups; a bathing-place, swarming with nude figures, presents assuredly no beautiful spectacle, even if they were so many Apollos; precisely where man appears in his higher truth, namely, in society, there a beautiful scene is presented only by the help of diversified, character-expressive clothing. It is true, clothing is beautiful only where it is really expressive of a character, whether of the nation or of the person. The slavish copying after journals of fashion, is evidence of a want of sense and of character, and of a lack of esthetic perception.

Clothing did not first become necessary because of sin. The Biblical account implies only, that it became necessary prematurely, and for another than its normal reason,—namely, before the development of personal character had led to its invention as an adornment. The sin of the first pair effected only that the hitherto-innocent consorts felt, now, shame in each other's presence, and that clothing, the proper object of which is ornamentation, was turned into a garb of penance. Clothing was not the very *first* want of persons living as yet in the most primitive simplicity; nor was yet its lack the characteristic trait of the Paradisaical state; clothing would have become a moral requirement also in the unfallen state so soon as man had grown into families, and the riper character of parents appeared in the presence of children [comp. Gen. ix, 21 *sqq.*] The nudity of savages is not innocence, but shameless rudeness.

Animals do not decorate themselves, they are decorated already; man exalts himself above the animal by ingenious decoration. The tawdry ornamentation of savages exemplifies this, under a rude form; with them, the mere changing of the natural form is regarded as a beautifying; the notion of ornamentation is conceived under an essentially negative form; the unnatural itself is regarded as beautiful. There is a higher significance in the hunter's hanging about himself the skins of the bear or lion;—this is to him essentially a decoration of honor, a sign of his courage. Thus also, in the simpler forms of civilized life, it is an honor for a woman personally to weave and to prepare her own clothing and that of the family; it is natural for man to display his work, the fruit of his skill; but he also loves to manifest his spiritual idiosyncrasy under an esthetic form in the ornamentation of the body. Clothing and ornamentation in general, when of a normal character, manifest, in part, the general element, the natural peculiarity, and, in part, the personal peculiarity; hence in the style of the clothing we can to a certain extent recognize the personal character; the distinction between male and female clothing among all civilized nations has a deep moral ground [comp. Deut. xxii, 5]; and just as, on the one hand, it is usually foolish and vain for an individual to break entirely with a general national custom, so, on the other, it is evidence of spiritual imbecility to make one's entire outward appearance a piece of mere imitation, without personal peculiarity.

The Scriptures attach some importance to a befitting adornment, especially in its moral significancy. Jehovah himself prescribes a worthy garb for those who officiate in his worship [Exod. xxviii and xxxix; Num. xv, 38 *sqq.*]; a holy adornment becomes those who offer worship to the Lord [Psa. xxix, 2; comp. Exod. xix, 10; Ezek. xxiv, 17]. When Christ in his parable [Matt. xxii, 2 *sqq.*] characterizes the not putting on of the wedding-garment as a serious fault, he manifestly does more than allude to a mere worthless custom [comp. Gen. xli, 14]; and the apostle does not consider it unimportant to commend to the societies a becoming adornment [1 Tim. ii, 9, 10].

That *cleanliness* of body and of clothing is regarded not only in the Old Testament [Exod. xix, 10; xxix, 4; Lev. viii, 66; Num. viii, 6 *sqq.*; xxxi, 21 *sqq.*; comp. Prov. xxxi, 25], but also in all the higher heathen religions and in Islamism, as an important moral and religious duty, so that in fact a large part of the worship consists in washings, with direct symbolical reference to moral purification,—is a plain indication of the deep moral significancy of bodily purity. The sanitary interest is here merely incidental; the essential point is the outward expressing of the spiritual. Man is to bear, in his entire inner nature, as well as in his outward manifestation, a spiritually-moral impress,—is to be, in all respects, an expression of free self-determination, is to have upon himself nothing which has attached itself to him merely outwardly or fortuitously, as something belonging not to him, but to an extraneous nature-body,—is to be a purely spiritual creation. Uncleanliness is the expression of unfree nature,—of a dependent, passive belonging to mere outward nature, an evidence of self-abandonment, self-disesteem and dishonor, and is regarded among all cultivated nations as a symbol and actual indication of sin; it has never been any thing other than isolated spiritual perversions of humanity who have found an especial wisdom and greatness of soul in an open display of uncleanliness. Sensual pleasure-seeking, riotousness and moral degradation usually lead to corporeal filthiness; and it is a very wise principle of education in the case of the morally abandoned, and in missions among rude tribes, to place a very high value on bodily cleanliness. The precepts as to cleansing, in the Old Testament, are based on this ground; Christianity expressly declares carefulness about outward cleanliness as a virtue intimately connected with religion [Matt. vi, 17; comp. John xiii, 4 *sqq.*].

To the gracefulness and beauty of the physique, belongs also that manner of *movement* or bearing which answers to the spiritual character, to beauty of soul; the cultivation of skillfulness of movement leads directly to the culture of esthetical motion. The beauty of movement consists in the fact that it expresses the perfect mastery of the soul over the body, and thus presents, in the body, not merely the organ of the will, but also, through the element of the beautiful, an image of the self-harmonious spirit,—in youth an expression of heart-gladness, in age that of earnest dignity. The dance is esthetic only in youth, in the mature it is repulsive.

SECTION CXXII.

(2) Moral appropriating and forming, as bearing upon the *spirit* itself, that is, the moral striving of the spirit to have and to possess itself as its own moral product, takes place through conscious, free activity, although indeed in the unconscious nature of the personal spirit there exists an impulse in that direction. In so far as man is a rational spirit he has before him his own self as a moral task,—is to form himself into a moral personality, into a character; all non-advancement is here retrogression. This appropriating and forming relates to the spirit both as cognizing, as feeling, and as willing, and looks to the harmony of these three phases of the spirit-life.

It is only when the spirit makes itself into its own possession,—forms itself into a truly rational spirit, that it is a moral spirit. He who is only a product of other spirits, who allows himself passively to be molded *merely* by the spirit that for the time being prevails in society, is, even when this spirit is a good one, not yet morally mature, but is in moral nonage; he is not yet a person, not yet a character. What Christ says [Matt. xxv, 14 *sqq.*] of putting to use the talents received, holds good also of the moral endowments of man; he dare not leave them idle, but must put them to moral usury,—must mold himself by spiritual appropriation into richer self-possession. He who "has not,"—who leaves idle his received talent, who makes it not into a vital possession,— does not retain it even as an unproductive power, but loses what he already has, and for the simple reason that it is a general law that a life-power, if unawakened into activity, dies away and perishes; it is only in virtue of a vital progressive development that the spiritual can be preserved,— even as water is saved from stagnation only by motion. The state of innocence cannot be preserved by mere non-doing; moral indolence would let even the trees of life in Paradise wither away. By the leaving idle of that which is destined to development, man sinks to moral dullness and insensibility; the spiritual condition of savages is a manifestation of the consequences of burying the received talent.

The culture of self by the appropriation of truth, that is, the forming of self to knowledge and wisdom, is presented in the Scriptures as one of the highest moral duties, and it is inadmissible to limit this appropriation to merely religious and moral truth, though of course this is the principal thing (§ 104). God actually directed the first man to the acquirement of knowledge by the fact of his referring him to the objective world about him (§ 60), and in the fact that He made known himself and his will to him. But the knowledge of good *and* evil was forbidden to man, for the reason that a real knowledge of the latter was possible only by its realization; he was indeed to know what he should *not* do, but not to know of a *real* evil, and only a real entity can be truly known; but the woman sought after a wisdom [Gen. iii, 6] apart from true wisdom, and consequently fell.

Feeling is primarily of an immediate, involuntary character;

but man is not to be under the power of unfree feelings; he is rational only when he develops his feelings into *moral* ones,—brings them under the control of his rational knowledge and of his moral volitions. There is absolutely no place in the human mind or heart for any thing that is not morally willed or conditioned. Hence it is a moral duty to cultivate our feelings into moral integrity, so that they may never incur the liability of being reproached by the moral consciousness,— never, even involuntarily, entertain envy, and the like. In the ante-sinful state such feelings of course do not yet exist; but non-moral feelings become very soon sinful ones unless they become developed. And even the, as yet, uncorrupted feelings are primarily still in a crude state and in need of culture. The feeling of delight, and hence of happiness, rises with the increase of culture; the first human beings could not be so happy in their first days as they could have been after further moral development. They too were liable to have morally false feelings. It is true there was as yet nothing immoral before their eyes which could have become an object of immoral delight; but they had, before them, themselves as in need of further development; hence if they had felt perfectly contented in this state of need, instead of thirsting after a higher perfection, this feeling would have been immoral. On the other hand, they were capable of feeling displeasure at the divine,—as in fact actually occurred in view of the divine prohibition. And the pleasure which Eve felt in the words of the tempter was already decidedly immoral, seeing that it implied a will *not* to follow the will of God, and was essentially the fall itself.

But feeling must be formed not merely as to its quality, but also as to its degree of liveliness. If only the more prominent phases of good and evil make an impression upon us, while the less prominent ones pass before us unnoticed, then our moral feeling is obscure and obtuse. The fact that feeling, like the bodily senses, is affected at first only by the stronger impressions, implies of itself the duty of making it *sensitive*— sensitive even for the most delicate features of the godly or the ungodly. And this can be brought about only by a constantly increasing growth in knowledge,—by an attending to whatever takes place within and without us; we must prove all things and hold fast to the best, the good, and that too not merely as knowledge but also as the possession of our heart, as our delight and joy.—Our feelings, as moral, stand not outside of, but also under our will. The notion that the heart cannot be commanded, is absolutely immoral,—is an assertion of man's irresponsibility. Natural feeling does indeed precede the will, but moral feeling is, under one phase, determined by the moral will [§ 93]. It is *not* left to the hearts of children whether they will or can love their parents, they are *bound* to love them; and the same is true of wedlock-love, of our love to our calling, to our rulers, to our country. The first promptings of feeling are as yet extra-moral, but in that by this first excitation the will becomes free and is set into activity, it then in turn directs its activity also upon the feelings and the affections.

That *willing* is in harmony with knowing and feeling, is primarily strictly natural; in man, however, as distinguished from the much earlier self-possessing animal, this agreement is primarily only approximative; the will must be *exercised* in order to be sure of itself; man must first learn how to use it. There is need of a moral will in order that the will may become moral. This has all the appearance of a vicious circle, but it is not; the fact is, I must *in general*, and as a principle, have a will always to follow the truth, in order that, *in particular*, I may actually form my individual will morally, and make it subject to recognized truth. The spirit is willing but the flesh is weak; this is relatively true also in a normal development of mankind; this flesh is, however, not merely sensuousness, but also the spirit itself, the will, in so far as it has not as yet become veritably free. The will of the spirit must become something which it is not, as yet, from the very start,—truly free; and it is free only when that feebleness, which is primarily merely a sort of clumsiness, is overcome,— when the spirit is not only in general willing to do God's will, but also shows in each particular case the same unwavering willingness. That which, in a state of sinfulness, becomes a self-conflicting double will [Rom. vii, 15 *sqq.*], exists also in the ante-sinful state, at least in so far as to constitute a difference between the will as purely individual and the will as truly rational, God-consecrated, and self-denying. The former is not to be done away with, but to be harmoniously subordinated to the latter; the will must be so formed as that we can say at every moment: I will, and yet not I, but God who dwells in me. The will should not be a willful will, but must be molded into an *obedient* one,—into obedience to the divine will, which, in virtue of our love to God, becomes at one with our own will. In obeying, man distinguishes indeed his own will from God's will, but he subordinates his will, not lothfully but in loving willingness, to the lovingly-appropriated divine will,—transfigures the former, more and more, by his love of the latter, so that finally there are no longer two wills, but only one,—and that, not in virtue of any destruction, but simply in virtue of love, not by violence but through freedom,—by following the example of Christ in the constant practice of the principle: "Not my will, but thine be done" [Luke xxii, 42; Matt. vi, 10; John v, 30; Psa. xl, 8; Jer. vii, 23; Matt. vii, 21; xii, 50; 1 John ii, 17; Heb. xiii, 21]. Every moral will must say with Christ: "My meat is to do the will of him that sent me" [John iv, 34]; obedience is the food of the soul,—forms and strengthens the will to an increasingly freer and holier manner of willing. Only those are the children of God who are led by the spirit of God,—who permit themselves freely to be guided by Him, who will only in and through Him [Rom. viii, 14].

Hence also in the forming of the will we have to distinguish between the quality and the degree. A will may in fact be good in quality, may aim at the good and detest the evil, and yet be lacking in strength and in steadfastness,—may shrink before difficulties; it may begin well and yet not bring to perfection; good resolutions do not necessarily imply a truly good will; in fact, the road to hell is said to be paved with good resolutions. He who has a good will only at first, but does not really carry out any thing, is as yet unfree in his will,—has it not under his control, and is yet a moral minor; he does not actually will at every particular conjuncture that which he wills in general. Hence it is man's duty to place his will entirely under the dominion of moral reason, to mold it to freedom, in order that in particular cases it may not offer resistance to good resolutions in general,—in a word, that a will of the flesh may not oppose itself to the will of the spirit.

III. THE MORAL ACTIVITY AS RELATING TO OTHER PERSONS.

SECTION CXXIII.

(*a*) The moral *sparing* of others consists in a real recognition of their *moral personality*, and hence of their personal independence, freedom, and honor.

(α) Man's personal independence and freedom, which are the expression of his morally rational essence, may be limited by others only in the interest of higher moral ends, namely, either in order to *train* the as yet morally and spiritually immature toward real freedom, or in the moral interests of the moral whole or society.—(β) The personal *honor* of our fellow-man is preserved when we recognize and treat him as a morally-rational being called to God-likeness and God-sonship, and hence as capable of, and entitled to, moral communion with us,—when we do nothing toward him which is inconsistent therewith,—which would stigmatize him as non-moral, or, undeservedly, as immoral and irrational; this is the duty of *respecting* our neighbor, and as implied therein of respecting the personal dignity of man in general,—the duty of sparing and protecting the *good name* of our neighbor.—(γ) From these two duties follows the duty of a sparing respect for whatever *appertains* to our neighbor,—belongs to him as a possession, is his property in the broadest sense of the word, that is, whatever he has a right to call *his own*,—and hence a positive avoidance of all action whereby it would be damaged or alienated from our neighbor.

Even as our personal morality does not consist in undisciplined arbitrary discretion, but in the controlling our own will by the will of God, so also there is no moral influencing of our fellow-man without a limiting of his individual will, of his individual liberty, and that too in the very interest of his higher personal freedom. The child cannot be educated without that in many respects limits be set to its, as yet, unripe, unintelligent will; in the person of the educator it is confronted with the principles of moral order under which it is to bow its individual will; it is in fact an essential part of the duty of sparing the personality of the child, that it be not allowed to grow up in rudeness. As the child is related to its parents, so is the individual person to the moral whole. He whose calling it is to govern, must confine the liberty of the individual within the order of the whole,—must in some measure limit it in order that all may become truly free; in an organized moral community it is each member's duty to co-operate in the realization of moral order, and hence to hold within bounds both his own will and the will of others. Hence the moral sparing of others is never of an unconditional character, but finds a limit in the duty of moral culture; but within this limit the duty of sparing becomes all the more imperative. The limiting may never be such as to reduce the object to a mere will-less creature of arbitrary discretion; the right of the object of education or guidance to be an independent moral personality with a moral purpose of its own, may never be ignored. He who is as yet morally a minor may never be treated as if he were always to remain such,— never as a mere means to an end,—but he must be treated as having an end in himself. A slavish education is sinful; despotic government is immoral, whether exercised by a single individual or by a minority-crushing majority. Whatever apology may be made for slavery in a sinful world, in the sphere of pure morality it is absolutely anti-moral.

The sparing and respecting of the personal *honor* of others, appears among the chief commands in the Old Testament [Exod. xx, 16; Lev. xix, 16], and is presented also in the Gospel as one of the most essential of duties [Matt. v, 21, 22]. My neighbor has upon me a claim to respect for his honor, for his *good name*. Man is not a mere isolated unit, but a vital member of a moral whole; the personal honor, the good name, of each is the moral bond which holds together the community; he who has lost respect in society stands outside of the scope of its common-life,—is a broken-off leaf soon to wither away.—The sparing of the *possessions* of others [Exod. xx, 15, 17; Lev. xix, 35, 36; Deut. xxv, 13 *sqq.;* xxvii, 17; 1 Thess. iv, 6] is only a special phase of the sparing of the person of others. In his property man creates for and about himself a little world which as the product of his labor, belongs to him, which he calls his earnings, and for which he has consequently a moral right to recognition and respect on the part of others.

SECTION CXXIV.

(*b*) The moral *appropriating* and the *forming* of others are, in virtue of the mutual moral relation of men to each other, always associated together in a normal state of things,—each being and involving at the same time also the other; and both take place at the same time in the moral *act of love.* In active love toward his neighbor, man brings about also love toward himself, for the beloved person becomes united to, and appropriated by, him who loves; the active love of one's neighbor is therefore an appropriating and a forming at the same time, both in respect to the neighbor and in respect to the loving person himself. The exercise of love breaks down the antithesis of individual persons, but at the same time respects their moral rights and moral independence.

It is noteworthy that in the Scriptures we never read of the love of *mankind,* but always of the *love of neighbor;* [Matt. vi, 14, 15 is only a seeming exception to this, as here "men" stand in contrast to God]. Christ's love to us is indeed called love to man or to the brethren, but never love to neighbor; but *our* love to man in general, and not merely to our Christian brethren, is always called love to neighbor. In this very circumstance the moral relation of men to each other is directly indicated. My fellow-man does not stand before me as a mere isolated individual, but as one who, by God's will, is near to me,—who belongs to me for my full love, belongs to me so intimately that there ought to be nothing strange or uncongenial between him and me. In love, my neighbor becomes mine, and I his; hence love is a mutual appropriating; and by the fact that I thereby enlarge both my life-sphere and his own, it is at the same time a mutual forming. Love seeks not merely the welfare of the other, but also his love. In the act of love I form the other, in that I impart myself to him as loving, and that too in my moral character; I rejoice him and exalt his moral life, in that I stimulate him to reciprocal love. At the same time also I exercise a formative influence on myself, in that by this communion I am myself exalted and promoted in my spiritually-moral existence,—in that I spiritually appropriate to myself an other spiritual being.

The law of love is presented by Christ as the highest of all commands, and love of neighbor as the substance of all moral duties toward our fellow-man [Matt. xxii, 39, 40; John xiii, 34, 35; xv, 12, 17; comp. Rom. xii, 10; xiii, 8–10; Gal. v, 14; Eph. v, 2; 1 Thess. iv, 9; 1 Cor. xiii, 1 *sqq.;* 1 Pet. i, 22; iv, 8; 1 John iii, 11; James ii, 8; Heb. xiii, 1]. All fulfilling of duty toward our neighbor is an exercise of love; when not so it is but deception; that which springs not of love, is not only morally worthless, but also immoral, because counterfeit. Love 'is the test of true God-sonship [1 John iv, 12, 13], "for love is of God, and every one that loveth is born of God and knoweth God" [1 John iv, 7]; human love is thankful reciprocation for *that* love which first loved us,—is true religion [James i, 27]; and love to God must necessarily manifest itself also in love to the beloved of God [1 John iv, 20, 21; v, 1, 2]. The precept of love to neighbor is presented even in the Old Testament as a chief duty [Lev. xix, 18], and is expressly extended to non-Israelites [verse 34; Deut. x, 19; Micah vi, 8; Zech. vii, 9]; what a contrast this forms to the boasted "humanitarianism" of the Greeks to whom every non-Greek was a right-less barbarian! Thou shalt love thy neighbor "as thyself;" this is not a mere comparison of two parallel forms of love,—both are at bottom but *one* love; a truly moral love of one's self as a moral personality, necessarily manifests itself also as love to other moral persons through whom in fact one's own rational being is heightened; true love of neighbor is also at the same time true self-love. This holds good even of the false love of neighbor; every one seeks, in some form, friendship and love, and feels himself unhappy in isolation; hence our Lord says: "If ye love [only] them which love you, what reward have ye? do not even the Publicans the same?" [Matt. v, 46, 47; comp. Luke vi, 32]. If now even a false love of neighbor is at the same time a love of self, how much more so is the true love of neighbor!—not however, of course, in such a sense as that I love my neighbor only for my own sake, for that would be self-seeking, but in the sense that I love my neighbor for God's sake, and in this love of God exalt at the same time my own moral life, and find in the love of neighbor true moral enjoyment.

The symbolical expression of mutual union in love is bodily touching, especially the giving of the hand [2 Kings x, 15; Gal. ii, 9], and in a higher form the *kiss*, which evinces a more intimate equality of love the more it is reciprocal; the kiss on the forehead or cheek is rather the sign of a condescending and more distant love, the kissing of the hand that of a reverential love, the kissing of the feet that of a humbly submissive love [Luke vii, 38; Isa. xlix, 23], the kiss on the lips that of a mutual, confidential, intimate love, and hence especially expressive also of sexual love. In the Scriptures the kiss appears as the sign of love between parents and children [Gen. xxvii, 26, 27; xxxi, 28, 55; xlviii, 10; l, 1; Exod. xviii, 7; Ruth i, 9; 1 Kings xix, 20; Luke xv, 20], between brothers and sisters and relatives [Gen. xxix, 11, 13; xxxiii, 4; xlv, 15; Exod. vi, 27; Ruth i, 14], between friends [1 Sam. xx, 41], as an expression of homage [1 Sam. x, 1; Psa. ii, 12; Luke vii, 38], and as an expression of love in other respects [2 Sam. xx, 9; Matt. xxvi, 48 *sqq.*; Luke vii, 45; Acts xx, 37]; hence it is also a symbol of reconciliation [Gen. xxxiii, 4; 2 Sam. xiv, 33; Luke xv, 20]; and the fraternal kiss was, in the early church, a general custom

[Rom. xvi, 16; 1 Cor. xvi, 20; 2 Cor. xiii, 12; 1 Thess. v, 26; 1 Pet. v, 14.]

SECTION CXXV.

Active love is a self-impartation of the subject to the object,—an imparting of what is one's own to another in order to exalt his life. Hence it manifests itself in service-rendering, in benefiting; all moral community-life is a reciprocal service of love; every act of love is a sacrifice. Sympathizing love imparts every thing which is dear to it:—(*a*) It imparts its own *spiritual* possessions in order thereby to promote the spiritual life and the spiritual possessions of the other, and this, in virtue of an honest and truthful self-communication. To this communication corresponds, on the part of the object, the answering and accepting love of *confidence*, that is, a willingness to let himself be formed by the appropriation of the spiritually-communicating love of his fellow,—a being receptive for self-revealing truthfulness. (*b*) Love imparts also its *material* possessions, and is hence a devoting of our personal productive forces to the aid of the needy, in the fulfillment of the duties of charity and personal assistance. In imparting and devoting itself, love acquires a right to the reciprocating love of the other,—to *thankfulness* in heart and act.

Love imparts lovingly to the beloved that which itself loves; only that in which I myself have pleasure, can I lovingly impart; for this reason every true act of love is a sacrifice, and a sacrifice that is not hesitatingly and stumblingly brought; love makes it easy; but every sacrifice must be made to God; only he who practices love for God's sake brings a proper offering. To do good and to communicate is expressly declared in the Scriptures as a God-pleasing sacrifice [Heb. xiii, 16]. The mite of the poor, when offered in love, avails more than the rich gift of the thoughtless spendthrift; in fact he who does not morally love his legitimately-obtained possessions, cannot in the nature of things make therefrom a sacrifice.

Christ gives as the determining rule for our conduct toward our neighbor the general formula: "All things whatsoever ye would that men should do to you, do ye even so to them, for this is the law and the prophets" [Matt. vii, 12]. Hence true self-love is the pattern and measure of love to neighbor; our own rational striving shows us what is the striving of others, and ought to put itself into harmony with the latter; that which I would acquire for myself as a right upon others, ought first to be a duty toward them. By this rule Christ implies, at the same time, that love begets answering love, and hence reverts back upon him who exercises it. This is a practical life-rule in answer to the question: How shall I exercise love in each and every particular case? and it gives as the answer: Just as I should wish that it should be done to myself,—a very safe rule, provided always that my own moral consciousness in general is not beclouded, so that I should no longer know what would really serve to my peace. The precious is purchased only by the precious,—love only by love. All love seeks to serve; love of neighbor is ministering love. "Whosoever will be great among you, let him be your minister, and whosoever will be chief among you, let him be your servant, even as the Son of man came not to be ministered unto, but to minister, and to give his life a ransom for many" [Matt. xx, 26 *sqq.*]. Christ's love, the highest pattern, is itself the highest love-service, and has brought the greatest sacrifice; all love to God is a service of God; all neighbor-love is a God-serving in the service of the neighbor. "Let no man seek what is his own, but every man what is another's" [1 Cor. x, 24]; love to self must not become a separating of ourselves from others, nor a self-seeking using of them; self-seeking must be sacrificed in order to attain to true self-love in the love of neighbor. "Remember the words of the Lord Jesus, how he said, It is more blessed to give than to receive" [Acts xx, 35]; giving makes happier in the very love-act itself, and, though a sacrificing, is yet at the same time a receiving, an enkindling of reciprocal love, an imitating of

God and of Christ who out of love gave all; it is more blessed than receiving,—not that we are simply to give acts of love, and not also thankfully to receive them,—for he who cannot, out of love, receive, is unable also to give out of love, and he who, because of pride, will not receive, *gives* in fact only out of pride; but that kind of receiving is not blessed and does not render blessed, which is not willing also to *give*, but only to *have*, and in which the person regards only the bestowment as such, and not the love which makes it,—inclines only to possess the gift, but not to recognize the love and to reciprocate it in love. The moral person receives also gladly, out of love, from love, not however for the sake of the gift but for the sake of the giver,—desires indeed to receive love, but only for the reason that he himself loves. The giving of presents is a universally recognized sign of love, even where the moral consciousness appears under its rudest forms [Gen. xii, 16; xlv, 17 *sqq.*]; there is no love which does not seek to impart itself,—which would not gladly offer liberally, for the delight and enjoyment of the other, that in which the loving one himself has delight and enjoyment, and thus prove itself genuine by sacrifice [Gen. xxiv, 22, 53; xxxii, 13 *sqq.;* xlii, 25; xliii, 11; xlv, 22 *sqq.;* 1 Sam. ix, 7 *sqq.;* xviii, 4; Prov. xviii, 16]. Among certain rude tribes it is customary for friends to interchange names, as is, in fact, the case with one of the parties, even now, in Christian marriage; this is also a love-offering.

Communicating love imparts indeed all that it has, but it does not give away all; the spiritual possession grows in imparting itself. The communicating of one's own spiritual possessions is the exercise of *truthfulness*. The rational spirit has, in virtue of its own duty of spiritual appropriating, an absolute right to truthfulness in the self-communications of others, though indeed not an unconditional right to the communication of *all* that is known by others. Love admits of no falseness; and though there may be things in the life, even of the righteous, especially inner states, which may not and should not be communicated indiscriminately to every one,—for example, to the as yet morally immature,—still, this silence is essentially different from falsifying. In the Scriptures truthfulness is based on love; "speak every man truth with his neighbor, for we are members one of another" [Eph. iv,

25], that is, because we are united as vital organs to a single moral body,—belong to each other, should be transparent to each other. "To this end," says Christ, "was I born, and for this cause came I into the world, that I should bear witness unto the truth" [John xviii, 37]; this is true of Christ also in his character of Son of man, and hence also of all men; now Christ came into the world out of love, and out of love he bore witness to the truth. Truth is the good, the divine, as relating to spiritual communicating. Whatever exists is for the personal spirit, and each personal spirit exists for all other personal spirits,—must be perfectly transparent to them, in so far as sin throws into it no shadow, in order that spirit in general, the essential nature of which is to unite the separated, may attain to the truth [Matt. v, 37; comp. Job xxvii, 4; Zech. viii, 16; Psa. xv, 2; xxxiv, 14; Rev. xiv, 5]. Where sin is not yet predominant, but love prevails, there truthfulness is easy and natural; it becomes difficult only where sin predominates.

The formative influencing of others through the living-out of a moral character is to be regarded simply as a phase of the truthfulness of loving self-communication, and not as constituting a special duty of giving a *good example* [Matt. v, 14–16; Rom. xiv, 19; xv, 2; Phil. ii, 15; iii, 17; Titus ii, 7; 1 Pet. ii, 9, 12, 15; comp. 1 Cor. iv, 16; xi, 1; Phil. iv, 9; 2 Thess. iii, 7]. No one may wish to be moral *in order to appear* moral; that would be downright hypocrisy; but also no one should desire to conceal that which in his character is truly moral; this would likewise be untruth. But in order to the formative influencing of others through moral self-manifestation, it is of course not enough simply to be inactive, simply as it were to let one's self be contemplated, but there is requisite, in view of the diverse characters that are to be influenced, a selection of special manners of self-communication; as bearing upon children the manner must be other than with the morally mature; from this, however, it does not follow that this self-impartation is to sink to a mere self-complacent display of self,—an intentional presentation of self as a moral pattern, in any respect whatever. This would be, even in a saint, a violation of becoming humility,—a tempting of hearts from Him who alone is the perfect type of holiness.

Spiritual self-communicating, even when perfectly truthful, is not *per se* of a moral character, for, in view of the limitedness of men as individual persons, it is in fact a direct necessity; for this reason, perfect solitude is so great a torment; the recluse endures his freely-chosen solitude solely because he is engaged in a continuous spiritual self-communicating, namely, to God in prayer; a non-praying, unpious solitary would either be suffering the severest punishment or would be spiritually deranged. Self-impartation may even be sinful, as in purposeless, thoughtless gossip; it becomes moral only when it is a practicing of love. Loving self-communication seeks not its own but that which is another's. Falsehood is hatred, is lovelessness; where true love is there falsehood is impossible; hence the deep pain occasioned by falseness on the part of the beloved one.

From the fact that truthfulness is an expression of love, it is entitled to answering love from the other party, to a ready welcoming, to *confidence*. It is true, confidence in men is generally presented in the Scriptures as deceiving [Psa. cxviii, 8; Jer. xvii, 5, 6, etc.]; here, however, the question is only as to an unpious confidence which builds not upon God but upon man, and of the state of sinfulness in general. But where sin is not yet in the mastery, there mutual confidence is the necessary antecedent condition of all moral communion, and a necessary out-going of love. Distrust paralyzes love. The truthful have a moral right to confidence in their word; confidence is the reverse side of truthfulness. Even as Christ uniformly required faith and confidence in himself, because he was the Truth, so may every one who is of the Truth lay claim to confidence; hence confidence is not a discretionary state of the mind, but a moral act. The little child that was proposed to the disciples as a moral type, is such also in respect to trust and confidence.

The more outward form of self-imparting through *service-rendering* [Gen. xxiv, 18 *sqq.;* xxxiii, 12, 15; Exod. ii, 17; Deut. xxii, 1 *sqq.;* Matt. xxi, 3; John xii, 2; xiii, 4 *sqq.;* Acts xxviii, 2; Gal. v, 13; 1 Pet. iv, 10; Heb. vi, 10; xiii, 16, etc.] which, on the supposition of a state of sinfulness, includes in itself also beneficence, is not as yet in the unfallen state a showing of pity, for misery does not exist save in a state of sin; but there is always need of mutual assistance so long as the last degree of perfection is not yet reached, and hence there is always also the duty of helping, through the imparting of our own forces and means,—of mutually complementing our possessions which largely vary according to the personal peculiarity of the possessors.

Love is in its very nature communion-forming,—calls for the love of the other. And unreciprocated love presupposes sin. Love gives itself over, but it does not give itself away; it desires to find itself again in the beloved, even as light never shines without being reflected. The loving reflection of love, namely, love as the fruit of love, is *thankfulness*. He to whom thankfulness or unthankfulness is indifferent, has no love; even the Lord himself wept over Jerusalem when it spurned his love. The warmer the love, so much the more sensitively is felt the chill of thanklessness; only a taking refuge in the love of God can assuage this pang. But only he is entitled to thankfulness whose love is itself humble thanks to the loving God; without this the pretended right is simply presumptuous self-seeking. The moral worth of thankfulness and the despicableness of thanklessness are recognized even among the rudest tribes, as in fact even in brutes thankfulness is manifested by brightened looks; and hence Christ represents this duty as valid even among the heathen,—as instinctively commending itself to the natural consciousness, and as also practiced by man in his natural state [Matt. v, 46; Luke vi, 32, 33; comp. Exod. ii, 20; Josh. vi, 22 *sqq.*; 1 Sam. xv, 6; 2 Kings v, 16, 23; Ruth ii, 10 *sqq.*; Luke xvii, 16; Acts xxiv, 3]. But only love has a right to thankfulness; a benefit which does not flow from love, which merely seeks thankfulness, does not deserve thankfulness, for it is inwardly false.

SECTION CXXVI.

At an equal stage of spiritually-moral maturity, men are related to each other as mutually-forming and appropriating each other to a like degree; but the more there is a difference in this maturity, so much the more predominates on the part of the morally higher-developed the formative influencing, and on the part of others the appropriating. However, the right and duty of formative influencing on the part of the morally less-developed never sinks to zero;—even the as yet morally immature inevitably exert a measure of moral influence upon the morally higher-developed and upon the totality of society.

A complete moral equalization of all men as to their moral influencing of others would be an irrational reversing of all moral order, a dissolving of all historical life into unorganized individual units. Children never sustain to their parents a relation of perfect equality; their relation to them is always rather appropriating than formative; the resistance of children to the higher moral validity of the parents is regarded among almost all nations as a flagrant outrage, and reverence for age as a high virtue. But society at large is a moral whole, and here also the higher-advanced have and exercise naturally a guiding and an educative influencing-activity over and upon the others, and the totality has a higher validity than the individual. The higher-developed moral individual sustains to the morally-immature the right and duty of educative influencing; a perfectly holy man would enjoy *per se* a right to spiritually-moral dominion; and for this good reason, and not simply in virtue of his being the Son of God, is Christ our legitimate Lord. Nevertheless the right and duty of moral forming never sinks, even in case of the most immature, to absolute nothing; childish innocence has disarmed many an evil intent; the direct impression of guileless confidence, of unsuspicion, strikes the malicious purpose with shame. The pious simplicity of the faith-word of a child has often proved a heart-stirring awakening for vain wisdom-boasting unbelief.—Also toward the moral community, the individual sustains the right and the duty of moral influencing, though in a normal development of the community-life this influencing would give place very largely to appropriating; moreover it varies according to the varying social stations of the individual.

IV. THE MORAL ACTIVITY AS RELATING TO OBJECTIVE NATURE.

SECTION CXXVII.

(*a*) The moral *sparing* to which nature, in virtue of its essence as God's perfectly created work, and as an expression of the divine love and wisdom, has a right, requires that man, in the exercise of the moral dominion over nature to which he is called, regard this, its divine phase, with due respect,—that he avoid all purposeless and wanton changing or destroying of natural objects, and that, on the contrary, he exercise toward nature a considerate love, especially in its higher manifestations, by preserving them in their peculiarity. The duty of considerate sparing rises in proportion as the nature-creature comes into actual relation to human life, and enters into the sphere of his moral activity as a helping factor.

Moral love to nature is thankfulness to God who gave it to us for moral enjoyment and for moral dominion; to man, as pure, God gave not an uncongenial and fear-awakening nature, but a Paradisaical nature. God loves nature as he made it, and from its bosom God's creative love beams out toward us, and he has even impressed manifold natural suggestions of the moral upon it; Christ himself requires respect for nature, for the heavens are God's throne and the earth is his footstool [Matt. v, 34, 35], and it is in virtue of this religious conceiving of nature that there can be moral duties also toward nature (as against Rothe, *Ethik*, 1. ed., iii, § 866). With the exception of the Indians, who adore nature as the revealed divine essence itself, no people has manifested so high a respect for nature as the Israelites; the legislation of the Old Testament surpasses all other systems in a considerate sparing of nature. Domestic animals especially are placed under the sparing protection and care of the law [Prov.

xii, 10]; the mouth of the threshing ox is not to be muzzled [Deut. xxv, 4]; on the Sabbath cattle, also are given rest Exod. xx, 10]; and in the Sabbatical year both cattle and beasts are to pasture on the fallow lands [Exod. xxiii, 11; Lev. xxv, 6, 7, in the original text]; the beast of another that falls under its burden, or loses its way, is to be helped [Exod. xxiii, 5; Deut. xxii, 1 *sqq.*; comp. Matt. xii, 11]; animals may not be castrated or otherwise maimed [Lev. xxii, 24; even the crossing of animals of different kinds is, in high moral recognition of the rights of nature-creatures, forbidden [Lev. xix, 19]. With the greates tenderness of feeling, a merely symbolical cruelty is not allowed; "thou shalt not seethe a kid in its mother's milk" [Exod. xxiii, 19; xxxiv, 26; Deut. xiv, 21]; it makes the impression of cruel mockery when the milk which is destined to nourish the young is used in connection with its death. Under the same category falls the prohibition of killing the calf, the kid, and the lamb, on the same day with its mother [Lev. xxii, 28], and of taking an incubating mother-bird at the same time with the nest [Deut. xxii, 6, 7]. The touching account of the care of God for the animals at the time of the deluge, is an emphatic illustration of the moral sparing of animals as it should be exercised by man; God includes also animals in his covenant with Noah, and promises to spare them [Gen. ix, 10, 15]. Christ himself illustrates his own relation to the body of believers in a gracious picture of a shepherd loving his flock [John x; comp. Matt. xviii, 12, 13].

The piety-inspired careful sparing of whatever contributes to the *nourishment* of man, is so natural an expression of the moral consciousness that it prevails among almost all, and even barbarous, nations. Christ sanctions this significant carefulness [John vi, 12]. This sparing has essentially a symbolical meaning,—is an evidencing of thankfulness for the good gifts of God,—a thankfulness which suffers not that these gifts of love be destroyed in wanton thoughtlessness and in purposeless waste, or contemptuously thrown away.

SECTION CXXVIII.

(*b*) The moral *appropriating* of nature is either of a purely spiritual, or of an actual character.—1. *Spiritual* appropriating consists, in addition to the legitimate striving after the highest possible knowledge of nature considered as a manifestation of divine power, love and wisdom, mainly in the *reflective* contemplating of nature in its symbolical suggestiveness of the moral,—God having implanted in it natural symbols of the moral.

The thoughtful, moral contemplating of nature is at once of a pious and of a poetical character;* it is not a mere play of the fancy, it is veritable reality. Nature is not moral, but it is the work of *Him* who is himself perfect morality. Nature as created by the holy God must necessarily reflect this holiness as from a mirror; it is the high and mysterious charm of nature that it is not *mere* nature, but that everywhere the Spirit whispers out of its bosom and broods over its expanse. Nature reveals to us not only God's creative power, wisdom and glory [Rom. i, 20; Job xxxvii, *sqq.;* Psa. xcvii; civ; cxi, 2; cxlvii, 8 *sqq.*],† the heavens not only declare God's glory [Psa. xix, 1 *sqq.*], but also God's love is made known to us in nature [Matt. vi, 26 *sqq.;* Acts xiv, 17], and the bow on the clouds [Gen. ix, 12 *sqq.*] and the bespangled vault of the skies are symbols of the divine faithfulness [Gen. xv, 5]. But the moral consciousness finds still more than this; the phases of beauty that are perceived in nature are suggestions of spiritual beauty. It is not a groundless fancy when the mind discovers moral ideas symbolically suggested even in plants; we feel at once the kindredness of impression upon the sensibilities that is made by a delicate rose and by modest virginity, by a violet and by childlike humility, by an oak and by firmness of character. And the fact that animals so frequently directly remind us of human moral qualities, is simply evidence that the holy creative

---

* Compare: Zöckler, *Theologia naturalis,* 1859.
† *Bridgewater Treatises,* vol. 9; Köstlin, *Gott in der Natur,* 1851.

Spirit rules in them and discovers to us; in that which is merely natural, embryonic premonitions of the moral. The ant, the bee, etc., are natural emblems of the virtue of industry [Prov. vi, 6]; it is God who causes them busily to care for a common want,—who works in them in order to speak to man an unmistakable word of exhortation and instruction. The care of birds for their young, the fidelity of the dog and of the horse, are manifestations of a deeply suggestive character in nature. The quiet gentleness and the patient sufferance of the lamb are applied as types even to Christ [Isa. liii, 7; John i, 29, 36; 1 Pet. i, 19; Rev. v, 6, and elsewhere]; Christ himself uses the dove as a symbol of uprightness of heart [Matt. x, 16]. The animal-fable has something of the mystical in it and contains deep truth. The attractive and convicting element thereof is this inner mysterious fact, that something of the divine rules in the animal, and looks out upon us,—a moral element unconsciously immanent in nature itself; and that which appears in the brute as a type of human sin, is more than a mere fancied resemblance,—is in fact the root of that which in man actually becomes sin, whereas in the animal it is simply a normal limitedness.

SECTION CXXIX.

(2) The *actual* appropriating of nature-objects for *nourishment*, and thereby at the same time for sensuous enjoyment, involving the destruction of living natural objects,—rests upon the moral right of man *over* nature; and the limitations to the enjoyment of the nature-objects which serve for food, lie less in the nature-objects themselves than in the degree to which they are used and in the moral state of the person, as also in the thought of the morally-becoming. Also the flesh of animals is allowed to man for food, and hence also the killing of the same for such purposes, although in connection therewith all cruelty and all wanton levity is to be avoided. The chase is moral only in this sense, and not for diver-

sion.—As drink man is permitted to use not only the strictly natural fluids, but also such as are prepared by skill, including the vinous; it is simply their misuse for inebriation that is immoral.

What things are *per se* appropriate as means of nourishment, is not a moral but a physiological question. Although for the state of sinfulness, the disciplinary law of God required man also in this sphere to distinguish between clean and unclean, and forbade to him a number of *per se* appropriate means of nourishment, still this law of limiting discipline had no validity for humanity while as yet unstained by sin. Here are applicable the words of Christ: "Not that which goeth into the mouth defileth a man" [Matt. xv, 11; comp. Titus i, 15; Acts x, 15; Rom. xiv, 1 *sqq.* 20; 1 Cor. x, 25 *sqq.*]. It is not the object *per se* that renders an article of food sinful, but the disposition of the eater, the manner of enjoying it,—namely, when one forgets God in the sensuous, forgets his own moral dignity in the pleasure, aims not at the satisfying of the want, but only at the enjoyment, and does not observe the measure prescribed by the purpose of nourishment.

The admissibility of *flesh-food*, though very clear from a physiological stand-point, has yet been contested from a moral point of view. Asceticism has in all ages laid great stress on abstinence from flesh; the Indians reject flesh-food unconditionally, inasmuch as, in consequence of their Pantheistic philosophy, they regard the slaughtering of animals, otherwise than for sacrifice, as a blasphemous outrage.* The Manichees (and Essenes?) abstained likewise from all flesh. The rejection of flesh-food in seasons of fasting has less an objective than an inner ground. According to St. Jerome flesh and wine were originally not allowed, and were first permitted after the deluge, but they are not permissible under Christianity.† Paul mentions similar views [Rom. xiv, 2]. Jehovah expressly conceded to man after the deluge also animals for food [Gen. ix, 3], whereas in the blessing after crea-

* See Wuttke's *Gesch. des Heident, II, p.* 466 *sqq.*
† *Ep.* 79 *ad Salvin.*, I, *p.* 500 *; ed Vallars.; adv. Jovinian.*, t. I, pp. 267, 342.

tion [Gen. i, 29] there is mention only of plants as food; from this circumstance some have inferred that, previously, flesh-food was not in fact allowed; but we find no trace of a previous prohibition, and we can discover no reason for a change; rather would there lie in the progressive corruption of mankind a reason for a limiting of former rights; God's direction to Noah has in fact all the appearance of an express confirmation of a former right; and the privilege conferred at creation, of ruling over the fish of the sea, etc., would hardly have any significance if it did not also include the right to eat them. Abel brought offerings of the firstlings of his flock and of their fat [Gen. iv, 4]; now as it was uniformly that which was most precious to man that was offered as a sacrifice, hence it is probable that flocks were kept also for the sake of flesh-food, to which in fact the "coats of skins" [Gen. iii, 21] seems to allude. Were flesh-food simply a concession to sinfulness, which in fact would have no comprehensible reason, it would certainly not be prescribed in connection with the Passover and with sacrifices, and above all Christ himself would have abstained from it, whereas we know that the contrary was the case [Matt. xi, 19; comp. Mark ii, 19; John ii, 2 *sqq.*; Matt. xxvi, 17 *sqq.*]. Paul declares abstinence from flesh as a weakness of faith [Rom. xiv, 2; comp. 21; 1 Cor. x, 25]; to Peter animals are expressly offered in a vision for food [Acts 11 *sqq.*], and animals are spoken of as destined to be slaughtered [2 Pet. ii, 12; Deut. xii, 15, 20]. It is true man can live without flesh, and he certainly has reason not needlessly and out of mere wantonness to multiply the destruction of animals; still, however, as it is grounded in the very constitution of nature that animals serve for food to each other, hence it must be allowable also for man to take food for himself out of the animal kingdom. And should there seem to lie in the killing of an animal something inconsistent with the original peace between man and nature, and with man's instinctive feelings, and should it be inferred therefrom that it is only the changing of the original relation of things, as alluded to in the blessing upon Noah, that rendered flesh-food morally possible, —still the force of this difficulty will vanish so soon as we reflect upon the very ancient, pious, and significant custom,— wide-spread even among heathen nations and suggested in the laws of Moses [Lev. xvii, 3 *sqq.*],—namely, of slaying the nobler animals in general only for purposes of *sacrifice*, and of receiving back the flesh, thus consecrated to the Deity, only out of His own hand. In regard to the primitive usage it is most probable, therefore, that before the deluge the devout children of God partook indeed of flesh-food, but only of animals offered in sacrifice, and that too only seldom, as indeed pastoral people in general use but little flesh-food. Noah might, in view of the sensuality of the perished world, have doubted the propriety of flesh-food, and hence God sanctions it expressly.

It is indeed not to be denied that in the practice of the slaying of animals in general there lies a moral danger; it tends to blunt our feelings of natural compassion; and it is not a mere morbid sensibility, that makes it repugnant to some persons, *e. g.*, to wring off the head of a dove; moreover it is a well-known fact that those who are engaged for the most part in the slaughtering of animals are liable to become hardened and cruel; it does not follow from this, however, that the slaughtering of animals for food is *per se* wrong, but only that the manner of the slaughtering is not a matter of indifference,—that it should be done with the least possible suffering, and that not every animal is equally appropriate therefor. It is in fact repugnant to our moral feelings to slaughter such domestic animals as by their fidelity to and fondness for us, have become in some respect our home-companions; it has the look of treachery on the part of man,— of a betrayal of the confidence which the animal had placed in him, in a word, of a breach of faith. The iron necessity of our evil-fraught actual condition may excuse it; but it is surely not the proper relation of things; and the fact that the general feeling of almost all cultured nations has a horror of the butchering of dogs and horses, man's most faithful companions, has its foundation surely not in any notion of the unwholesomeness of their flesh, but in a very legitimate moral feeling,—a feeling the disregarding of which is no mark of a special refinement of culture. Much more natural, and less questionably morally, is the killing of wild animals, and of such animals of the flock as have not as yet stood to man in a close relation of confidence. We cannot here as yet discuss in full the subjects of food and drink.

SECTION CXXX.

(*c*) The *formative* working upon nature, the shaping of it into an organ for man, is at the same time also an exalting of nature into the service of the moral life, and hence a forming of it into an expression of the human spirit,—an educating of nature whereby it is raised above its immediate naturalness, and is made to receive the impress of human action, of spiritual *discipline*. Man *ennobles*, spiritualizes, nature, and makes it into his spiritual possession, into his freely-formed home,—and in forming nature he appropriates it at the same time to himself.

If the dominating of man over nature,—to which God expressly called the first man [Gen. i, 28; Psa. viii], and which still holds good in a somewhat modified manner even in the state of sinfulness [Gen. ix, 2, 3], and which is promised again in the fullest degree for the yet to be recovered perfect state [Isa. xi, 6 *sqq.*],—is not to be regarded as a mere figure of speech, then it must also imply a forming of the same. Man forms nature into an obedient instrument of the spirit, and gives to it a spiritual, historical impress. Nature, in its wild state, stands to man in an unhomelike, not to say hostile relation,—it is only in its form as shaped and disciplined by his skill that he feels at home. God gave nature to man as a theater for his moral activity, but man is not at liberty simply to sport with it, simply to admire and enjoy it,—he should really rule over it; but all ruling is at the same time an appropriating and a forming. Man is to make of nature something which as yet it is *not*,—is himself to form it into a spiritually-molded home for himself. This forming of nature is either a forming of it into a *useful object* for the individual, and hence in the service of labor (§ 109), or a forming of it into an image of the spirit, into a thing of beauty, into a *work of art* (§ 110). A hill-side cavern is not a dwelling-place for man; his home-protection, he must construct for himself. If even the bird builds its nest in a way of its own, so that it bears an impress peculiar to the bird, how much more must man spiritually shape nature into a home for himself! Of course the forming of nature does not consist in an abuse of it,—*e. g.*, in a forcing of trees to be square, in cropping the tails of horses and the ears of dogs,—but in the further development of the natural beauty and perfection already existing in nature. The cultivated rose is more beautiful than the wild one; the improved fruit tree is better in many respects than the wild-growing one; the domesticated animals have become in many respects quite other and more perfect creatures than they were in their wild state; they have attained not only to higher soul-capacities, but also to a nobler and stronger physique; the wild dog and the wild horse cannot in any respect bear favorable comparison with those which have been cultivated by man. The fidelity of these creatures,—which indeed they show almost exclusively toward man, to whom they attach themselves much more closely and affectionately than to their own kind,—is an evidence of the normal dominion of spirit over nature, and a positive ennobling, and is the thankfulness of the animal for its culture.

The task of overcoming the wild forces of nature that stand in the way of individual human life, and of subjecting them to the discipline of the spirit, is a powerful stimulus to moral activity; and they are in fact, in virtue of the divine creative plan, perfectly overcomable by the rational spirit,—if not always by the individual, yet at least by the collective, spirit. Though it is not true that all nature-objects exist *merely* for the outward use of man, nevertheless they are in fact *for* man, in a still higher sense,—for his moral delight, for spiritual enjoyment, for the service of the moral life. The dominion and discipline which man can and should exercise over the animal world, does not in the original purpose imply that he is to surround himself in his domestic life with animals of every sort, but it does imply that he ought not (as, however, has actually taken place) to acknowledge them as a power over against himself, and before which he has to tremble, and against which he can secure himself only by strategy and deadly violence; on the contrary, he should rise to a consciousness of his all-sufficient dominating power over them; but to destroy is not to dominate. That nature-creatures should become to man a torment, a plague, a death-bringing danger, and that man in the interest of his self-preservation should have to carry on a war of extermination against a large portion of them,—all this is, according to the Scripture view, a consequence of the disturbance of the harmony of creation; hence, as it is a result of sin, we cannot as yet, here, treat of it. Even in the fallen state, however, we can still discover clear traces of the true relation of things; even the lion and the tiger cannot bear the steady, fearless look of man, and they throw off their natural awe of man only after having tasted of human blood. Man can and may, however, actually realize his dominion over nature, only when he permits himself to be ruled over by the holy Originator and Lord of nature.

CHAPTER VI.

THE FRUIT OF THE MORAL LIFE AS MORAL END.

SECTION CXXXI.

The end of moral action, as willed by man as moral, is identical with the end of God in man's creation; in this action man wills perfectly to realize in himself the image of God,—to develop himself in reality as a *good* being, and thereby to realize the good in general. In so far as the good is a fruit of moral action, it is not a something exterior to man, but inheres in him,—is his *possession*, which, as incorporated into the morally-formed essence of man himself, and as thenceforth inseparable from him, is a *property* or quality of his person. In so far as the good is the property of man, it is his *moral estate*. Hence, as the end of the moral activity in general is the good, so is this end, for the moral man himself, the good as having become a moral estate.

The world is, with its mere creation, not as yet complete, but is charged with a task which is to be carried out by moral creatures themselves. Though it is true that all good is from God, still all good is not from Him immediately; but in man's case it arises through the free developing of that which was directly created. Man is himself to create good; though as a creature he is good, yet he is not good *in such a manner* as he is to become so; the image of God becomes complete in him only through his own moral activity; and he makes into a good entity not only himself, but also the world that comes into contact with him,—he creates a spiritual historical world which is itself good. To this good as created by himself he sustains quite other relations than to that which is directly given to him in his natural existence. To the first man much good was given, to which he had a right, and which he could call *his own*. This good, however, was simply placed upon him,—was as yet external to him, and not as yet identified with his spiritual being; he indeed *possessed* it, but it was not yet his *property*,—was not a quality of his. All that I have in my power, upon which I have an actual claim, is my possession. But the idea of property is higher; only that is my property which by moral action I have appropriated to myself, and which consequently essentially belongs to my personal life-sphere, as my free personal acquisition. A merely inherited property or power is morally a mere possession, while an estate or power that is acquired by labor or is morally developed, is a property; in it I have invested my labor, my soul, my will,—it inheres in me and in my self-created life-sphere, —is my enlarged personality itself. Hence property has always a moral element in it,—is moral fruit, is an acquisition. In the case of the first human beings, the possession of Eden would have become a property, only in virtue of their cultivating and caring for it. A moral property is inalienable; it may, as, for example, in the case of a work of art, come into the possession of another, but it remains the spiritual property of its author. A slave is the possession of his master; but consorts not only possess each other,—they appertain to each other,—each is the property of the other. Thus in so far as the good becomes and is a property, it is *a good*, a moral estate,—and hence it is such only as a fruit of moral action. The good as an outward possession may be lost; but when exalted into a moral property, it is permanent; to this Christ alludes when he says: "Lay not up for yourselves treasures upon earth," etc. [Matt. vi, 19, 20].

SECTION CXXXII.

The good to be attained to by moral action is, that perfection which answers to the divine creative intention,—on the one hand, the perfection of the individual person, and, on the other, that of the moral community; that is, it is in part a personal, and in part a common good. The two forms mutually condition each other, and stand with each other in constant and closest relation; but both are further conditioned on the moral communion with God which is aimed at by the moral activity, and which is the highest moral goal as well as the ground and essence of all creature-perfection in general; for God alone is the eternally-perfect good. The real moral life-communion with God, as distinguished from the merely natural, is consequently the absolute good, and hence the *highest good*,—that which is the source and condition of all other goods. In so far as individual man has the highest good as his moral property, he is a *child* of God; in so far as the moral community has this good inherent in itself, it is the *kingdom* of God, which rests on the God-sonship of its individual members.

The thought of a moral communion, and hence also of a moral common-good, is met with also in the extra-Christian world; the Republic of Plato was meant to embody it. But where the common ground of the personal good as well as of the common good, namely, communion with God, is lacking, there this thought is realizable only as a sum total of single goods, or only by the all-dominating despotism of the community-organism over the individuals, as in the system of Plato. A vital union of the two forms of good is effected only by the Christian God-consciousness. Some form of communion with God is enjoyed by every creature as such; this, however, is of a merely natural character, and needs, in the case of rational creatures, to be exalted to a moral character. As coming from the hands of nature man is not the child of God; he becomes truly such only by free moral love to God.

The question as to the highest good,—for the heathen difficult and in fact not truly solvable at all,—is, from an evangelically-moral stand-point, readily answerable. There is absolutely no good realizable or actually realized without standing in relation to God, without springing from God as its source, and hence none for man without personal life-communion with God [John xvii, 21; 1 John i, 3; ii, 5, 6] who is the perfectly good One in an absolute sense [Matt. xix, 17]; only he has the highest good who is rich toward God [Luke xii, 21; Psa. lxxiii, 25], and who has everlasting treasures in heaven [Matt. vi, 20; 1 Tim. vi, 19]. While heathen philosophers grope about in uncertainty as to the highest good, Jehovah reveals it in all simplicity and definiteness to the patriarch Abraham at a time when he was wavering in faith as to the fulfillment of the prophecies made to him,—reveals it in these words: "I am thy exceeding great reward" [Gen. xv, 1],—thou canst aim at and attain to nothing higher; and the highest blessing of the Old Testament is the "peace of God" [Num. vi, 26; Psa. xxix, 11]. This highest good man cannot have as a merely outward possession, as a mere gift,—he cannot have it from nature, but only as a morally-acquired property; even under the economy of redemption from sin, where not merit but grace prevails, faith which is in fact a moral work—is the necessary condition. The idea of a *kingdom* of God,—unknown throughout heathendom, but prepared for and anticipated in the Old Testament, and realized in Christianity,—presents the moral community as in full possession of the highest good, which now becomes, in turn, for the individual members (by whom it is enjoyed as God-sonship) the source of higher moral perfection. In virtue of life-communion with God the highest good bears the stamp of eternity, in the sense of endless duration; the life of the children of God is an everlasting life [Matt. xix, 16, 17, 29; xxv, 46; John xvii, 3; 1 John ii, 25, and other texts], and the kingdom of God is an everlasting kingdom.

I. THE PERSONAL PERFECTION OF THE INDIVIDUAL AS THE END OF THE MORAL ACTIVITY.

SECTION CXXXIII.

The personal perfection of the individual person is the realization and virtualization of God-sonship, that is, of the idea of man, and of the creative will of God as to man. The moral goal set before man, namely, the all-sided personal perfection of the human life-powers and of their manifestation, is, as a fruit of the collective moral activity, never fully and definitively realized during the temporal life, but is involved in constant progress, though at every stage of the truly moral life it is in fact relatively realized.

To be perfect is neither an improper nor an impossible requirement upon man; on the contrary, it is expressly presented by Christ and the apostles as the moral goal: "Be ye therefore perfect (τέλειοι) even as your Father which is in heaven is perfect" [Matt. v, 48]; "if thou wilt be perfect, follow me" [xix, 21; Luke vi, 40; 1 Cor. ii, 6; xiv, 20; Eph. iv, 13; Col. i, 28; 2 Tim. iii, 17; Heb. v, 14; James iii, 2]; the term τέλειος implies the contents of τέλος, that is, the purpose and goal of the moral life. This perfection of the creature is indeed, as compared with the divine perfection, of a limited character; such as it is, however, it really exists, in every case of normal development, from the very first moment on, and it steadily advances, keeping pace with every stage of the life-development. Christ himself, even as a child, is presented as a pattern, while as yet he was increasing in wisdom and in favor with God and man; that is, he was even as a child perfect, though this perfection was not yet that of the full man's-age of Christ [Eph. iv, 13]. Every moral being should and can be relatively perfect at every moment of its life; even the child is to be so in the manner of a child [1 Cor. xiii, 11]; and the final and true perfection is not a merely conceived and never-to-be-realized goal, for such would not be a goal at all, but it can in fact and should actually be realized by each and all. Christ as the son of man really reached this goal, and all who belong to him have, in virtue of their God-sonship, both the duty and the possibility of attaining to it [Phil. iii, 12, 15; 1 Cor. xiii, 10].

SECTION CXXXIV.

All moral attainments, and hence all the elements and forms of perfection or of the true good, are a moral possession, and hence a property. Every possession is an enlargement of the existence, the power and the life-sphere of the moral person, in virtue of moral appropriation,—is a breaking down of the limits of the original individuality, a uniting of the isolated existence with the life of the whole. Corresponding to the distinction between special and general appropriating (§ 104), and, from another point of view, to that between natural and spiritual appropriating (§ 101), the possession acquired by moral appropriating (which is at the same time necessarily also a forming) is, on the one hand, partly of a more external character,—bearing upon the individual as such and widening his life-sphere, and hence, as relating to others, of an exclusive character,—and, on the other, in part of a more inward, spiritual and, in so far, not merely personal, character, but, on the contrary, promotive of communion.

(*a*) The *outward* possession—legal property, temporal *means*—is, as the fruit of moral labor, a real and legitimate good, and hence also a legitimate end of moral effort, though it becomes at once sinful when it is made the end *per se*, the highest good itself, when it is placed above the inward possession and not rather vitally united with it, when the effort for it aims merely at the enjoyment and not also at the moral culture and the moral communion naturally involved in it,—when it does not become a channel of communicative *love.*

If appropriating is *per se* a moral activity, then is also the striving after temporal possessions not only a right but also a duty. Possessions distinguish man from the brute, and civilized man from the savage; the Diogenic form of wisdom is by no means very profound. Labor finds in possessions its normal fruit; possessions are labor as having become reality

The brute is possessionless because he does not labor. In property man ceases to be a mere isolated individual of his species; he creates for himself a world about himself which he can call his own; his property is the outward manifestation of his inward peculiarity. The fact that he who possesses much is also much regarded and esteemed in the world, is, indeed, often very hollow and baseless, though in reality it springs from the *per se* correct consciousness that possessions are the fruit of labor,—the result of moral effort. He who acquires nothing for himself passes in the world, not without reason, for unrespectable. Of a special virtue of possession-despising, as with the mendicant monks, there can, in the ante-sinful state, be no question; and even after the fall, possessions are presented as a perfectly legitimate end of moral effort, and their being increased as a special divine blessing. Cain and Abel possess already personal property; and the God-blessed possessions of the patriarchs occupy a very large place in their morally-religious life [Gen. xii. 5, 16; xiii, 2; xiv, 14; xxiv, 22, 35, 53; xxvi, 13, 14; xxvii, 28; xxx, 27, 30, 43; xxxi, 42; xxxii, 5, 10, 13 *sqq.;* xxxiii, 11; xxxix, 5; xlix, 25; Exod. xxiii, 25; Lev. xxv, 21; Deut. ii, 7; vii, 13; xv, 14 *sqq.;* xvi, 15, 17; xxviii, 3 *sqq.;* xxxiii, 13 *sqq.;* xxiv, 25; comp. 1 Kings iii, 13; Psa. cvii, 38; cxii, 2, 3; cxxxii, 15].

Property being the enlarged life-sphere of the moral person,—in some sense his enlarged personality itself,—the moral phase thereof lies not merely in its antecedent ground, namely, labor, but also in its moral use and application. To its *enjoyment* man has a moral right, as such enjoyment is the reward of labor; but to the exclusive enjoyment of it for himself alone he has no moral right, seeing that he is bound to other men by love, and love manifests itself in communicative distribution.

SECTION CXXXV.

(*b*) The *inner* possession, namely, the perfection of the personality itself in its essence and life,—perfectly realized in the person of the Son of man alone,—is,

(1) The perfection of *knowledge*, namely, *wisdom;* that is, that all-sided knowledge of God which rests

on a true love of God, and which in virtue of moral effort has become a true property of the person, and which consequently also constitutes a life-power determinative in turn of the moral life itself,—and hence involving also a knowledge of the being, essence, and end of created reality, especially also of one's own life (§§ 60, 104). As influencing the moral life, wisdom is necessarily also practical; and as taking into view the actual circumstances of existence and their application to the moral end, it assumes the form of *prudence*.

Wisdom is presented in the Scriptures as the first and most essential element of the highest good, and in fact always under its two phases, as a knowledge of the truth, and as power to fulfill it. It is not a mere knowledge in which man forgets himself in the object, not mere science, but a knowledge which merges the person himself into the life of the truth,—which fills the soul with vital, life-creating truth. The object of wisdom is not this or that particular truth, but *the* truth,—is the self-consistent complete whole. Knowledge is not yet wisdom; with scantier knowledge there may be more wisdom than with a richer knowledge; a much-knowing one may even be a great fool. Wisdom is essentially not world-science but God-science; it is, as a manifestation of God-sonship, never without a life in God,—is in its essence piety; without God-knowledge and God-fearing there can be only folly [Psa. cxi, 10; xxv, 14; Job xxviii, 28; Prov. i, 7; ix, 10]. Wisdom is more than knowledge and science, inasmuch as it always aims at unity, at the central point, at the whole,—always unites the person himself with God and with the All, both cognoscitively and actively; it is *moral* knowing. Its essence consists not in the compass and in the fullness of the knowledge, but in the harmony, the true foundation, the truth and the moral potency of that which is known. There is no wisdom, therefore, without constant moral effort; but also none which does not itself produce a moral life. Such wisdom is presented as the most essential element of the highest good, and to acquire it, as a high duty [Prov. ii, 2 *sqq*.; iv, 5 *sqq*.; viii, 11; xvi, 16; xxiii, 23; John viii, 32; xvii, 3; Acts xvii, 27; Rom. xii, 2; xvi, 19; 1 Cor. xiv, 20; Eph. i, 18; iii, 18; iv, 13; v, 10, 17; Phil. i, 9, 10; iii, 8; iv, 8, 9; Col. i, 9, 11; iii, 10, 16; 1 Tim. ii, 4; 1 Pet. iii, 15; 2 Pet. iii, 18; James i, 5], and the non-recognizing of the divine as deep guilt [Rom. i, 20, 21; iii, 11; 1 Cor. i, 21; 2 Tim. iii, 7; 2 Thess. i, 8]. Wisdom associates all knowledge with God, and uses it all in moral self-revelation,—is pious and moral at the same time,—goes back always to the primitive ground, and forward to the ultimate end; hence it leaves nothing in its isolation and separateness, but brings all things, man included, into relation to the whole, and the whole into relation to every part; it is knowing in its truly rational character; the fear of the Lord, it is wisdom.—As wisdom makes knowledge the full *property* of the person,—as it belongs not merely to the understanding but also to the heart, and is in fact intelligent love,—hence it is necessarily also active life,—begets love and works from love, awakens a striving to manifest the attained truth in the reality of life. A wisdom which does not generate life,—which remains locked up in the subject,—is folly [Deut. iv, 6; Prov. viii, 11 *sqq*.; James iii, 13, 17].

Prudence (φρόνησις, different from σοφία, Eph. i, 8) is indeed in the sphere of sinful humanity not identical with wisdom, and can even exist as a merely worldly quality apart therefrom; but where sin is not yet actual, this difference is merely formal. Wisdom, as essential rationality itself, embraces truth *per se* as a harmonious whole; prudence, on the contrary, takes into account actual reality with a view to bringing it into relation to the moral idea as embraced by reason,—in order to find for the moral idea its realization in each conjuncture, and the means thereto; hence it is simply wisdom as relating to specific real circumstances. Hence true prudence can neither exist without wisdom, nor wisdom without prudence, and moral duty involves both of them in inseparable unity. The harmonizing of prudence with open-hearted simplicity becomes difficult only in a world of sin. *Considerateness* and *circumspectness* are designations of prudence as applied in cases difficult of decision [Luke xiv, 28, 29], especially in so far as it guards against the promptings of over-rash feelings.

SECTION CXXXVI.

(2) The perfection of *feeling*, as a moral fruit, is the feeling of pure pleasure in the divine, and of unmitigated repugnance to the ungodly, and, as based on faith, the feeling of pure joy which springs from the consciousness of the morally-wrought harmony of one's own existence with God and with the universe. As relating to existence other than that of the moral subject, this perfection is perfect *love* as a power grown essential and inherent in the personality; in relation to the moral subject himself it is the perfect *bliss* of the child of God, the repose of the soul in God.

So long as the feeling of self is not yet reduced to full harmony with the love of God (§ 92), so long also is feeling, as relating to the godly and the ungodly, not pure and not decided. As the ear must first be made skillful by attentiveness and practice in order to be able readily to distinguish beautiful from discordant notes, so also must feeling, first be made sensitive by moral exercise in order to be able, at every moment, unhesitatingly to love and to hate at once in the right manner. Such decisiveness, such purity of feeling, constitutes an essential part of the perfection of the life in God, that is, of blessedness; blessed are they who are *pure* of heart; blessed they who find no occasion of offense in Christ and in the ways of God [Matt. xi, 6.] Mere joy is not yet blessedness; the merely natural pleasure in existence, even were it of a Paradisaical character, is not enough to satisfy the spiritual nature of man; only that which is morally wrought, or at least morally appropriated, renders blessed. Even a normal child rejoices more in its own playful creating than in mere eating and drinking. The nine Beatitudes of Christ [Matt. v] relate, all of them, to the moral, and not one of them to a mere state of enjoyment. All blessedness, however, is love, and true love is blessedness; but only morally attained love is true love; even love to God becomes truly blissful only when it is the expression of already-attained God-Sonship. The moral man feels blissful when he views the harmony of being not as simply immediately existing and as merely contemplated by himself, but as in moral freedom recognized, willed, and realized by himself,—namely, in so far as, on the one hand, those features in the objective world which are originally as yet exterior and uncongenial to man are overcome, and the dominion of man over nature realized, and in so far as, on the other, a spiritually moral world is brought into being with which the individual knows himself in moral harmony; but the consciousness of this double harmony produces loving blessedness only when it rests on the consciousness of a morally virtualized filial relation to God. True blessedness exists only in union with God; peace of soul only in the eternal.

That such blessedness is not simply an inheritance in the future but the destination even of the present life, is implied in the moral idea itself, as well as in the thought of the divine love. God has not appointed us unto wrath, but to obtain blessedness [1 Thess. v, 9]; "but whoso looketh into the perfect law of liberty, and continueth therein, he being not a forgetful hearer, but a doer of the work, this man shall be blessed in his deed" [James i, 25]; though this thought may hold good on the part of one redeemed by grace, only under certain limitations, yet it is unconditionally valid of man *per se* and as unfallen; with him moral activity is *per se* blessedness, and there is no blessedness without moral activity. "Blessed are they that hear the word of God and keep it" [Luke xi, 28],—keep it not merely in memory but in their heart, in love and in volition; "blessed are they that do his commandments" [Rev. xxii, 14].

SECTION CXXXVII.

(3) The perfection of the moral *will*, that is, the full moral freedom of self-determination as effected by wisdom and love, the perfect mastery over one's self, the completed possession of one's self, constitutes the fully developed personal *character*. As distinguished from all mere fortuitous character-forming,

the truly moral character is the copy of the divine holiness as attained to through free moral culture,— the moral law as become the real free property of man, the harmony of the human with the divine will as become a dominant power, a moral nature, so that consequently the willing and accomplishing of the ungodly becomes to man a moral impossibility,—so that the love to God becomes perfect *hatred* against sin. The constantly advancing development of the moral striving toward this *holiness*, constitutes the ever-progressive *sanctification* of the soul, the ultimate fruit of which is the perfect *freedom* of the will, and as contained therein the enjoyment of blessedness.

In that the moral activity becomes fact, that is, becomes a moral possession of the person, it transforms the original, as yet, undetermined will-freedom into a determined moral will-quality, into moral character. Character-formation illustrates clearly the nature of moral freedom. An, as yet, undetermined character has a much wider possibility of choice in single cases than a definitely shaped one; a characterless man is unreliable because his freedom has no moral determinedness, but is merely external freedom of choice. Character is reliable, and upon the degree of its firmness rests the confidence which it inspires; we know in advance with certainty how, in a definite moral conjuncture, such and such a character will choose. This is now surely no limitation of freedom, but rather its moral maturity. The freedom is all the more perfect, true, and mature, the more it is character-firm, the more it has moral determinedness; and the highest moral freedom is that where the person can no longer waver in any moral question, where it has become for him a moral impossibility to choose the immoral,—and this is the state of holiness. Holiness is related to innocence as morally-acquired good to ante-moral natural good—as moral property to mere possession.

Human holiness as a copy of the divine holiness differs from the latter in this, that with God holiness constitutes his essence itself, and the possibility of sin is not in any sense conceivable; whereas human holiness is simply a morally-acquired good, and presupposes the possibility of sin, which in fact it has morally overcome. God's holiness is eternal; human holiness is, in its true character, the goal of development,—depends on progressive sanctification, which advances from a mere non-willing of the sinful to hatred against it and to abhorrence of it. The moral requirement of complete heart-purity and holiness may not in any manner be lowered, as if a limited measure thereof were enough, and as if a lower requirement were to be made of feebly constituted man than, e. g., of the angels. According to the testimony of Christ, men are in fact to become equal to the angels [ἰσάγγελοι, Luke xx, 36]; and also in their moral essence they should and must not remain below them. Man ought (and the word ought expresses the fundamental condition of all morality in general) to become morally perfect, and hence holy. This requirement is fully maintained even in the state of sinfulness, where primarily, that is, before the completion of redemption, the entire fulfilling of the same was not possible. The legislation from Sinai places this moral requirement, as the fundamental idea of morality, in great prominence: "Ye shall be holy, for I am holy, the Lord your God" [Lev. xi, 44, 45; xix, 2; xx, 7]; and the apostles adopt the same words as fully valid also for Christians [1 Pet. i, 15, 16]. The utterances of the Scriptures elsewhere fully harmonize therewith [Eph. i, 4; iv, 24; 1 Thess. iii, 13; comp. Matt. v, 48; Luke i, 75; and other passages], and the fact that the faithful of God are so frequently styled "saints" is clearly an expression of their moral destination.

Man is originally innocent, but not yet holy; he is not, however, to remain merely innocent, but is to advance to real holiness. Man is created *in* innocence *unto* holiness. The mere unconscious retaining of the first innocence would be a lingering in the child-consciousness; and the going beyond it,—not of course in the direction of sin but only in that of conscious holiness,—was the true normal course; Christ's holiness was not mere innocence. As a morally-acquired *property*, holiness as distinguished from the mere *possession* of innocence, is a permanent quality, and constitutes the moral character itself of man; he for whom there is yet possible a single sinful moment, has not yet attained to holiness. There is not only a natural but also a moral *must;* and when the child Jesus says: "Wist ye not that I must be about my Father's business?" [Luke ii, 49], this is a direct reference to this moral "must" of a holy soul. Holiness is consequently not a quality of single actions, but it is character-peculiarity; not the single volitional act, the single frame of mind is holy, but the heart itself. This purity of heart is not a merely negative state, a mere non-presence of sin, for that would be only innocence, but it is a moral fruit, a morally-acquired power over sin, and hence where sin has once actually existed it cannot be attained to by a mere ceasing to sin, but only by ceaselessly militant santification. *Sanctification* (ἁγιασμός) is consequently by no means a merely negative bearing, even in the ante-sinful state, but is a positive forming of the will and heart unto holiness. The sanctification mentioned in the Scriptures [1 Cor. i, 30; 2 Cor. vii, 1; 1 John iii, 3; Heb. xii, 14, and other passages] designates of course only the putting off of existing sinfulness as taking place in virtue of redemption; but when Christ says of himself: "For their sakes I sanctify *myself*, that they also might be sanctified through the truth" [John xvii, 19], this self-sanctification of the holy One is indeed primarily to be understood of his giving himself in sacrifice, but it alludes at the same time also to the perfecting of the moral life-development of the Son of Man unto the plenary possession of morally-acquired holiness in his character as man; such sanctification is the duty of man as man.

Through progressive sanctifying culture of the will man becomes perfectly master over his heart, over his will,—the moral becomes *easy* to him, becomes his second nature, whereas his first nature is the as yet not morally formed one. The will of the person is now no longer different from the divine will, but it is, in full freedom, at one therewith; the divine will has fully become the inner essence and the vital power of the disposition of the person, not merely in general but also in particular, so that in each special case the will with unfailing certainty chooses the right,—even as a true artist possesses full mastery over his hand, so that it never introduces a false tone or makes a false stroke. Practice leads to mastery; and the morally-matured man is master over his own will.

It is only in this mastery that man is truly *free*, namely, in that he has then overcome every thing in himself which, as a morally-to-be-mastered material, was as yet different from the moral idea itself. But freedom is bliss; he who has become truly free in his will is thereby necessarily also happy. Master over himself, he is also at the same time master over all that is unspiritual, over nature; and in having put himself into complete and free harmony with God, he participates in the lordship of the absolute Spirit over nature. "The Father that dwelleth in me he doeth the works," says Christ in reference to his miraculous works—the works of the Spirit upon nature; "verily, verily," says Christ to his disciples, "he that believeth on me, the works that I do shall he do also; and greater than these shall he do" [John xiv, 10, 12]; for God who dwells in him, as he in God, the same does the works; having become free in God, man has nothing more either within or without himself which could prove a hinderance to the moral will of the rational spirit,—which would say, No! to the striving of the Holy Spirit; as an expression of true and complete freedom, and not as the caprice of the immature and unsanctified spirit, this promise of Christ holds good for all his faithful followers. The hard rind of unspiritual nature must be broken through, the longing of the vanity-bound creature must be fulfilled; nature must be "delivered from the bondage of corruption unto the glorious liberty of the children of God" [Rom. viii, 19–22]; all that is natural must be spiritualized, must be exalted into the complete untrammeled service of the free spirit; such is the freedom, such the blessedness of the children of God.

In the possession of knowledge, of purified feeling, and of the mastery of the will, as attained to by moral appropriating and self-forming, man becomes morally *cultured*, as distinguished from the as yet morally immature and crude man; and in such culture he is truly *free*. The very first man was called unto perfect culture, and it is quite the opposite of correct to conceive, with Rousseau, the first human beings as living in a state of happy barbarism. As far back as the Biblical account reaches we find even in the state of sin no trace of an actual cultureless barbarism. The fact that Adam was to till his garden was of itself an implication of his destination to culture, for barbarians never till the soil; Adam's sons appear, from the very first, as persons of culture with a definite savagery-excluding calling; Cain was a founder of villages [Gen. iv, 17]; and among his immediate descendants appear inventors of manifold articles of skill [Gen. iv, 21, 22]; and from that time forth we find traces of a progressive culture. The progenitors of the Israelites are by no means half-savage nomads; their wandering-about is only a temporary state of necessity, for they are in search of a home; and their entire form of life gives evidence indeed of great simplicity, but yet also of high spiritual and moral culture. True culture is always a fruit of *moral* effort, and a culture that aims at mere temporal enjoyment and profit is but a deceptive self-defeating counterfeit.

SECTION CXXXVIII.

(*c*) In that the morally-good becomes an acquired *possession* of man, his real *property*, it has become an essential element of his moral nature, and hence is not an inert state, but an active *power* generative of new moral life,—has become a creative, operative *disposition*, and is consequently itself *per se* a directly active motive to moral action. The morally-good has become *virtue*, which is accordingly, on the one hand, a good not innate and embraced in the nature itself of man, but a morally-acquired possession, and on the other a power generative in turn itself of the good.

"All Scripture, given by inspiration of God, is also profitable for doctrine, for reproof, for correction, for instruction in righteousness, that the man of God may be perfect, thoroughly furnished unto all good works" [2 Tim. iii, 16, 17]; the moral perfection attained to by the sanctifying activity is itself in turn a stimulus to the good, a capacitation, a skilledness and power for moral activity; such is the inner idea of virtue. Man as come into possession of virtue is no longer the original man possessed of merely naturally-moral power, but he is man as armed with morally acquired and hence heightened power. There are no innate virtues, but only innate capabilities of virtue. The merely natural man has moral freedom as a simple and as yet undetermined freedom of choice; the virtuous man has his freedom as exalted to a determinedness for the good; he has no longer an equally balanced choice between good and evil, but his morally acquired peculiarity of character inclines spontaneously to the good. Man can never merely *possess* virtue, he must let it be operative; a dormant virtue is none at all. Hence, varying from the usual view which distinguishes and contrasts goods and virtues, we consider virtue directly as a good. The contrasting of virtue as a power and of goods as a possession is inaccurate; all power is a good, and every good is a heightening of power; hence men of the world seek so zealously after earthly goods, as they thereby enlarge their power. That virtue is not a dormant possession, but strictly an operative power, does not make it differ essentially from all other goods; no real property exists merely to lie idle, no talent is to be buried; but it is to be put to usury and made constantly to acquire more. Money is a good; for him, however, who does not put it to use, it does not really exist; it becomes a real good only when it becomes a power, when it is employed in heightened life-activity. Virtue, however, is a much higher good than that which is given us directly and from nature, or as an outward possession.

In the New Testament the notion of virtue is variously expressed; ἀρετή [Phil. iv, 8; 1 Peter ii, 9; 2 Peter i, 3, 5] is not strictly virtue, but is rather the notion of the morally good in general. Usually the notion of virtue is expressed by δικαιοσύνῃ, in so far as this quality is a personal possession [Luke i, 75; Rom. vi, 13; Eph. iv, 24; v, 9, and other passages], also by ἁγιωσύνη [1 Thess. iii, 13], by ἀγαθωσύνη [Rom. xv, 14; Eph. v, 9], and likewise also by εὐσέβεια, in so far as the root of virtue rather than virtue itself is meant; for Christian virtue, χάρισμα is also used, as designating its resting upon divine grace. In the Old Testament the notion proper of virtue is wanting; under the predominance of the thought of the law and of right, the morally correct character is designated as "righteousness," in virtue of its answering to the law and claims of God; hence this is merely a designation of the form. Before the full accomplishment of redemption, the inner essence of virtue was neither fully realizable nor comprehensible.

SECTION CXXXIX.

Inasmuch as all moral motive consists in *love* (§ 91), and inasmuch as virtue, as a moral property, is also an actuating power, hence virtue is essentially *love to God*, and is consequently *per se* not multiple but single. In so far, however, as the relation of this one-fold virtue may be different both as to the moral person and as to the object, it appears under the form of a plurality of virtues, which, however, as merely different phases and manifestation-forms of the one virtue, are never to be entirely separated from each other, and can never exist alone. These diverse manifestation-forms of virtue may be reduced to four cardinal virtues:—(1) Moral love preserves itself for the object in its proper relation to it, and thus manifests itself in the virtue of *fidelity*.—(2) Moral love preserves the object in its moral rights, and hence in its legitimate peculiarity,—as the virtue of *justness*.— (3) Moral love preserves the moral subject himself in his moral rights, and hence at the same time within his moral limits, in that it places upon the moral activity of the same a definite measure,—the virtue of *temperateness*.—(4) Moral love preserves at once both itself, the moral object and the moral subject in their moral rights, in that it actively opposes all hinderances that stand in the way of it and of its realization,—the virtue of *courage*.

We do not adopt the Platonic classification of the virtues which has found its way into a large portion of works on Christian ethics, for it is only by violence that it can be accommodated to the Christian consciousness. The cardinal virtues which we adopt, result logically and naturally from the notion of love as a disposition of the soul; and it is, by no means, accidental that they correspond to the four temperaments. The so-called temperament-virtues are simply the natural germs of the real virtues. The virtue of courage corresponds to the warm or choleric temperament; that of temperateness to the cold or phlegmatic; that of justness to the quick or sanguine,—for sanguine persons are very receptive for whatever is objective, accepting it just as it presents itself, yielding themselves to it, doing it no violence; sanguine persons are very companionable. The virtue of fidelity corresponds to the melancholic temperament, which, directed inwardly and dwelling within itself, and largely closed to outward influences, is not easily led astray.—The four virtues are so intimately connected with each other that each contains within itself in some measure all the others. Temperateness is justness in so far as it restrains man from that which does not become him; it is fidelity in so far as it regards love to God and to God's will as having the highest claims, and does not allow the individual self to become too prominent; and it is courage in so far as it actively confines the unspiritual and the irrational within their proper limits. Justness is fidelity in so far as it preserves love for and verifies it upon the object; it is temperateness in so far as it respects every-where the measure and the limits of the moral person and of the object; and it is courage in so far as it carries out and vindicates the just. Fidelity is courage in so far as it asserts itself in the active overcoming of all hinderances; it is justness in so far as it manifests to the object only the measure of love which is really felt for it; and for the same reason it is temperateness. Temperateness and fidelity correspond to each other in so far as they both retain the moral person in a proper bearing in relation to the object; justness and courage correspond to each other in so far as they both resist all influences that are unfriendly to the moral. Temperateness and courage are purely *human* virtues in so far as both presuppose a creature-limit of the moral personality, and hence they can in no sense be predicated of God; fidelity and justness are also *divine* virtues [1 John i, 9] because they presuppose only a difference of the personal subject from the object, and a claim of the moral. The former two have in their manifestation a negating character,—presuppose an antagonism in which one phase must be made subordinate; the latter two bear a more affirmative character,—are an express recognition and carrying out of the moral rights of the object. Of a conflicting of the virtues with each other there is no possibility.

Of the cardinal virtues here presented, three coincide with the Platonic virtues; but in the place of wisdom our classification gives fidelity. With the Greeks the making of wisdom the fundamental virtue was quite consequential; for all the other virtues were a fruit of moral knowledge, but not of love. From a Christian stand-point, where the moral freedom of the will is conceived more highly and is not placed in so unconditional a relation of dependence upon knowledge as with the Greeks, and where, consequently, virtue inheres essentially in the *love*-inspired *will*, wisdom is indeed conceived as a high morally-to-be-acquired good, as the presupposition and attendant of all virtue, and is also in fact closely associated with love, (§ 135), but still it cannot be regarded as a virtue proper. The first and most essential manifestation-form of virtue as love is persistent love, namely, fidelity, which consequently cannot be classified under any one of the other virtues as a subordinate manifestation, but it must be placed at the head, as the virtue dominating all the others.

(1) *Fidelity* ($\pi\iota\sigma\tau\iota\varsigma$), thrown very much into the background in heathen ethics, for the reason that, there, the absolutely firm basis of all morality, faith in the true God, was lacking, comes in the Christian consciousness into the foreground. Human virtue, as lasting love, is an image of the divine fidelity, which is presented in the Scriptures as one of the most prominent of the divine attributes, and is almost always associated with love, grace, and mercy [Gen. ix, 9 *sqq.;* Exod. xxxiv, 6; Deut. vii, 9; ix, 5; xxxii, 4; 1 Sam. xii, 22; Psa. lxxxvi, 15; 1 Cor. i, 9; x, 13; 1 Thess. v, 24; 2 Thess. iii, 3; 2 Tim. ii, 13]. God's fidelity is loving grace; the fidelity of man is humble obedience, and is hence a manifesta-

tion of piety,—is, in ground and essence, fidelity toward the faithful God [Matt. xxv, 21; 1 Cor. iv, 2]; the holy walk of the Christian is summed up in the word: "Be thou faithful unto death" [Rev. ii, 10; comp. Psa. lxxxv, 11, 12; Matt. x, 22; Luke xvi, 10–12; 1 Cor. vii, 25].—True fidelity relates not to a mere idea, to a mere law, but to a spiritual reality, and chiefly to the personal spirit; love loves only a loving spirit. A merely conceived law cannot be loved; hence there can be no real fidelity to such, which is not in reality fidelity to the holy law-giver. Fidelity toward man is morally without anchor unless it is based on fidelity to God; for fidelity can be based only on a perfectly firm foundation. Fidelity to a creature in the absence of fidelity to God, would not be a virtue but sin. Fidelity is the truthfulness of love; a changing love is mere inclination, and is not moral; truth changes not, and hence also moral love changes not.—As relating to industrial activity in a temporal calling, fidelity appears as *diligence*, which is only then morally good, and hence a virtue, when it is a conscious persistence in our God-appointed moral task [Prov. x, 4; xii, 27; 1 Thess. iv, 11].

(2) *Justness* or righteousness is the constant willingness to the actual recognition of the rights of every moral personality, as well those of God as those of man; it is love in the fulfilling of the command: "Render unto Cesar the things which are Cesar's, and unto God the things that are God's" [Matt. xxii, 21],—the imitating of the righteousness of God which gives to each that which is his due. In the Scriptures justness or righteousness is one of the most important of the moral notions, and it appears even in its widest sense as the respecting of the *suum cuique;* it is a manifestation of love, and a never fully to be absolved debt [Rom. xiii, 8]; and in so far as it is a manifestation of reciprocal love it is *thankfulness* (§ 125). It is for the reason that justness lovingly fulfills the claims of God that it can lay claim to the essence of virtue in general; it is virtue in so far as virtue is a disposition of soul recognizing the claims of God upon us. Christ sums up all our moral relations to our fellows under the one head, justness, and makes of this, in its fuller sense, the fundamental idea of morality: "All things whatsoever ye would that men should do to you, do ye even so to them, for this is the law and

the prophets" [Matt. vii, 12]; this is not merely ordinary civil justice, but the higher,—that which is an expression of love. But all love seeks to maintain the harmony of existence, and hence the divine order of the world, that is, the rights of whatever truly is; and all human justness is a copy of the divine [Deut. x, 17, 18.]

Justness adapts itself to the differences of existence and of rights; God has different rights from those of man, and among men there exist, even in an unfallen state, different rights, according to their differing conditions and relations; parents have different rights from those of the children, governors from those of the governed; justness gives not to each the same, but to each-that which is his due [Rom. xiii, 7-9], and thus realizes the harmony of existence. Even toward nature there is a justness, inasmuch as nature, in virtue of its being good, has a claim upon the moral spirit (§ 127). Real justness therefore presupposes wisdom; its practice becomes difficult, however, only where the harmony of existence is already disturbed by sin. The Scriptures describe justness manifoldly in its single manifestations [*e. g.* Lev. xix; Job xxxi; Psa. xv; ci; Ezek. xviii, 6-9; Isa. i, 17; Jer. xxii, 3; Zech. vii, 9, 10; viii, 16, 17; Luke vi, 38]; the Decalogue itself is but a description thereof. That Christian justness or righteousness is not a merely human virtue but essentially a gift of grace, need here only to be mentioned in passing. As virtue simply and purely, it appears only in the person of Christ [1 John ii, 1, 29; Acts iii, 14; 1 Pet. iii, 18].

(3) *Temperateness*, the self-discipline of the heart, the σωφροσύνη of the Greeks, is presented in the New Testament in the narrower sense of ἐγκράτεια, while σωφροσύνη has, here also, only the more specific sense of modesty and irreproachableness of behavior [1 Tim. ii, 9; perhaps only in verse 15 in a somewhat wider sense], but the adjective σώφρων is used in a more general sense [1 Tim. iii, 2; Tit. i, 8; ii, 5]. Temperateness in the wider and full sense is the self-restraining of the subject within his normal moral limits, a subordinating of all self-seeking desires to unconditional obedience to the moral law, and hence, on the one hand, as relating to sensuousness, a controlling of the sensuous desires by the moral reason, and, on the other, as relating to the spiritual, a con-

trolling of self-love by love to God and to our neighbor,—a maintaining of the rights of the rational spirit in its true essence. That temperateness is at once also justness is self-evident; it is but another phase of the same virtue. Even as relating to the sensuous desires it is also justness, in so far as these are restrained within their moral limits out of regard to the higher rights of the spirit. Modesty, patience, and obedientness are special phases of this virtue; so also are shame, pudicity and chastity, as a keeping of sexual sensuousness within bounds, a subordinating of it to its higher moral conditions; shame and pudicity are rather the inner elements, the state of the heart, and chastity rather the outward manifestation; they are an expression of the fact that this sensuous instinct has absolutely no right *per se*, but only in the service of wedlock-love.—Temperateness presupposes indeed a difference and a *possible* antagonism between selfish desires (especially the sensuous ones) and the morally-rational consciousness, though not an actually-existing antagonism and opposition. In its manifestation it is more a negating virtue than justness, and yet its essence is very affirmative.—This virtue becomes most difficult where the individual energy stands forth most strongly over against general, rational right, and hence in the period of youthful vigor when the consciousness of personal strength and of self-will delights to cope with objective barriers, and seeks to cast them off as trameling fetters,—when the strongly self-conscious individuality delights to enjoy this consciousness, whether in the enjoyment of sensuous pleasure, or in that of unbounded freedom, or in that of will-assertion. Fidelity, justness, and courage are, for vigorous youth, much more easily attained to and preserved than the virtue of temperateness; but as all the virtues are only different phases of virtue in general, and as they are all connected with each other in a vital unity, hence the violation of one of them is necessarily also a violation of the others; intemperateness is, in every respect, *per se* also an infidelity, an unjustness and a cowardliness, and it leads directly to a further development of these vices.

(4) *Courage*, the moral readiness to combat against whatever opposes the moral end,—expressed by the Greeks by the more limited ἀνδρεία, and in the Scriptures by the higher and

more inward notion of παρρησία [Eph. iii, 12; 1 Tim. iii, 10, etc.],—is the being joyous and confident in the carrying out of the moral idea on the basis of hopeful faith [Matt. v, 12; Acts ii, 29; iv, 13, 29, 31; ix, 27, 28; xiii, 46; xiv, 3; xviii, 26; xix, 8; xxvi, 26; xxviii, 31; Rom. viii, 31 *sqq.*; 2 Cor. iii, 12; v, 6, 8; xii, 10; Eph. iii, 12; vi, 19, 20; Phil. i, 20; 1 Thess. ii, 2; Heb. xii, 3; Psa. cxviii, 5 *sqq.*]. The moral life of the Christian is a constant struggle [Luke xiii, 24; 1 Tim. vi, 12] as well against the outward hinderances of the moral life as also against the inner opposing desires and against carnal sloth and fear. Though both these forms of hinderance do not hold good in a strict sense for the unfallen state, still we must doubtless admit that there were relatively corresponding relations of a normal kind. During the development of man toward his ultimate perfection there constantly exists an, as yet, extra moral reality, namely, nature within and without him, which is to be brought within the dominion of moral reason, and which is, as extra-moral, also *per se* a barrier that is to be overcome by moral effort; however, it is not an active antagonism, and the effort does not involve suffering. Self-love, in itself perfectly legitimate, needs also to be brought into perfect subordination to the love of God, and the mastering of it requires conflict and courage. This "parrhæsia" is not mere feeling, not mere inward peace, but it is essentially a combat-courting courage, a persistence in the moral struggle in virtue of joyous trust in God. Absolutely sure of victory, it fears nothing and undauntedly carries out what it undertakes.

SECTION CXL.

In so far as God himself is the object of love, and in so far as, in the creature, the divine phase, the image of God, is brought into prominence, the above four virtues appear under a special form expressive of the essence of piety, as *piety-virtues*, which, however, do not stand along-side of the other virtues, but are in fact the highest and God-directed phase of the same. Fidelity as relating to God appears as moral *faith;*

justness as moral *devotedness* or pious *obedience;* temperateness as filially-pious *humility*, as child-mindedness; and courage as *hope* or *confidence*.

The piety-virtues, only partially corresponding to the so-called theological virtues, are the essence proper, the ground, the kernel and the crown of the virtues in general,—are neither super-ordinate nor co-ordinate to the four cardinal virtues, but are their essential substance and spirit itself.

1. *Faith*, designated in Scripture by the same expression with fidelity, is the loving response to God's fidelity to us, and, as an expression of our fidelity toward the faithful God, is a high moral requirement,—is a loving confiding of our own being and life to the faithful love and truthfulness of God, a holding-fast of love to God. Were faith a mere holding for true, then it would not be a moral requirement, and hence the possession of it not a virtue; as fidelity, however, it is a virtue (§ 113). Faith is reckoned to man for justness or righteousness [Rom. iv. 3; Gal. iii, 6], for the reason that, as fidelity, it is itself justness toward God, and the root and essence of all righteousness.

2. *Obedience* toward God, moral *devotedness*, ὑπακοή, is the inclination and willingness that God's claim upon us should be perfectly realized in our moral conduct, and hence that we should do that which, as God's creditors, we owe to Him [Rom. viii, 12]; we meet God's claim upon us only by perfect, voluntary and joyous submission to his will [Exod. xix, 8; xxiv, 3, 7; Deut. iv; xi, 1; xii, 1, 32; xiii, 4, 18; Jer. vii, 23; Luke i, 38; James iv, 7; 1 Pet. i, 2, 14, 22; comp. Gen. vi, 22; vii, 5; xii, 4; xxi, 13 *sqq.;* xxii, 1 *sqq.*]; the obedient are by that very fact the just [Hos. xiv, 9; Mal. iii, 18; Matt. xxv, 37; 1 John iii, 7]; obedience is the fruit of faith [Heb. xi, 8], the expression of the child-mindedness of believers toward the Father. The Son of man is the holy pattern of obedience [Rom. v, 19; Gal. iv, 4; Phil. ii, 8; Heb. v, 8; Isa. liii].

3. *Humility*, ταπεινοφροσύνη, the moral and reverential confining of ourselves within the limits fixed by God for us as creatures and for each of us in his special moral calling, is an absolute duty even of sinless man, inasmuch as the moral crea-

ture, as related to God, is and has nothing which is not to be recognized as depending upon God's support; hence it holds good also of the angels [Col. ii, 18], and of Christ as the Son of man in his subordination to God [Matt. xi, 29; comp. xx, 28; Phil. ii, 6–8; Heb. xii, 2; John xiii, 4 *sqq.*]. All moral humility is at bottom humility before God [James iv, 10; comp. Gen. xxxii, 10; Luke xviii, 14], even as the first sin consisted in a lack of humility; when humility before men does not rest on this ground, it sinks to abjectness and servile-mindedness; it is only in humility before God that man learns to harmonize humility before men with a proper respect for his own moral dignity. All humility rests on faith and is also obedience; its essence, however, is a keeping within bounds, a self-retention within our divinely-appointed position [Matt. v, 3; xxiii, 11; Luke xxii, 24 *sqq.*; Acts xx, 19; Rom. xii, 3, 16; Eph. iv, 1, 2; Phil. ii, 3; Col. iii, 12; 1 Pet. v, 5; James iv, 6]. Child-like humility aims not at high things, but only at the highest, which in fact are accessible only to child-mindedness,—retains always toward God its filial character [Matt. xviii, 3, 4]. Humility is a purely Christian virtue; to Greek ethics it was almost unknown (§ 21).

4. *Hope*, ἐλπίς, mentioned in connection with faith and love as a high virtue [1 Cor. xiii, 13], directs itself with firm confidence toward the highest good as the goal to be attained to, toward the idea of the good [Rom. viii, 24], and is not a mere expecting of a future happiness, but a joyful trusting faith-born confidence that God means it well with us, and will also actually enable us to reach our moral goal, provided we honestly strive toward it,—is, in a word, that moral courage in God that is sure of its victory, and that has consequently already overcome all inward obstacles to the outward victory; it is not merely an involuntary state of feeling, but a morally-acquired good. All hope is faith [Heb. xi, 1], but it is also moral self-surrender and child-like humility, for it expects the victory not from itself but from God. The hope that is fixed merely upon created things is vain and sinful; but moral hoping in God does not end in disappointment [Rom. v, 5], and all moral courage is based upon it [Psa. ix, 10; xxv, 2; xxxi, 15; xl, 4; lvi, 4 *sqq.*; lxii, 6; xci, 2; cxii, 7; John xvi, 33; Rom. iv, 18; v, 2, 4, 5; xii, 12; Phil. iii, 1; iv, 4;

1 Cor. i, 10; iii, 12, etc.]. God is a God of hope [Rom. xv, 13], because all hope is based on him, and relates to his *promises*. The word of the faithful God is the ground, the contents and the vitality of all true hope. Hope is a virtue belonging essentially only to the kingdom of God; among heathens only the Persians have as much as a darkly-groping hope; the Greeks looked but dismally into the future, and their ethics knows nothing of hope as a virtue; in the Old Testament, however, we meet with it almost on every page; it is the key-note of the religiously-moral life, constantly bursting out in inspired strains; the Christian's hope, as fulfilled in Christ, awakens and gives ground for new hope.

As all virtue whatever is a force and a motive to moral action, much more is this true of the piety-virtues. All moral action directs itself essentially toward a yet to be attained good, and which consequently exists primarily only in thought; hence the moral motive is not merely love to an existing entity, but at the same time also love to a, as yet, not existing one, to a merely conceived one, the realization of which, however, is, in virtue of our love to the truly existing primative ground of all morality, absolutely sure to us,—hence it is, essentially, *faith* in the living and truthful God, and *hope* of the realization of the highest good. In virtue of this pious believing and hoping, as springing from our love to God, fidelity in our temporal calling becomes joyous perseverance; and in our working for the spiritual and the eternal, it becomes enthusiasm.

Observation. The systematic development of the cardinal virtues has ever been one of the most weighty and difficult points in ethics. Plato was the first to present the four virtues, which were adopted by Sts. Ambrose and Augustine, and which then held sway through the entire Middle Ages and up to the most recent times; and to these were added and superordinated, without any clear connection, the three theological virtues (§ 31). The Greek classification of the virtues is, however, entirely unadapted to the Christian notion of virtue, as the violent construction of them, to which even Augustine had to resort, abundantly manifests; while with the Greeks the fundamental virtue was wisdom, in Christianity it is love, love to the loving, personal God; this love to God was entirely lacking to the Greeks, because with them its certain object was also lacking. Protestant ethics sought out, therefore, with a correcter consciousness, new paths, and that too from the very beginning (§ 37). The three cardinal virtues of Calvin: *sobrietas, justitia, pietas*, do not, however, exhaust the material, and they admit of no proper organic union, because *pietas* is not co-ordinate to the other two, but superordinate. Schleiermacher's cardinal virtues (§ 48): wisdom, love, discretion and perseverance, are, in spite of all the dialectical skill bestowed in their development, of a merely artificial character, and are least of all adapted to Christian ethics,—to which in fact he does not apply them; the Platonic virtues admit of a much more natural development. In the system of Schleiermacher, love is by no means presented in its full Christian significancy, least of all as love to God (which is in fact regarded as an unapt expression), but it is presented only as the "vivifying virtue, as working forth out of itself into the world, namely, into nature,"—as manifesting reason in its action upon nature; reason is the loving element, nature the loved; love to God is true only as love to nature (*Syst.* §§ 296, 303 *sqq.*); this is almost the very opposite of the Christian notion of love. C. F. Schmid accepts this classification under a more Christian form, without, however, developing it in greater fullness (*Christl. Sittenl.*, p. 528).—Most peculiar of all is *Rothe's* classification (*Eth.* 1 ed., § 645 *sqq.*). He gives two virtues of the self-consciousness or rationality, and two virtues of self-activity or freedom. (1.) Individually-determined rationality is geniality,—aptness for an absolutely individual cognizing, so that the same can absolutely be accomplished by no other person—the artistic virtue proper; to it belong courage, composedness, modesty, grace, sympathy, confidence, etc. (2.) Universally-determined rationality is wisdom—aptness for a universal cognizing, so that the same may absolutely be accomplished by every other spirit in the same manner; it appears under the forms of considerateness, impartialness, sobriety, instructiveness, benevolence, fairness, etc. (3.) Individually determined freedom is originality, the virtue which specifically qualifies for individual forming,—the social virtue proper; to it belong valor, temperateness, chastity, dignity, unselfishness, fidelity, etc. (4.) Universally-determined freedom is the strength which leads to a universal forming, that is, to laboring and acquiring,—the public or civic virtue proper; it appears under the forms of persistence, patience, self-control, eloquence, beneficence, magnanimity, etc.

II. MORAL COMMUNION AS A FRUIT OF THE MORAL LIFE.

SECTION CXLI.

All moral activity is of a communion-forming character, and all true communion is an expression of love,—in nature an expression of immanent divine love, in humanity, an expression of human love. The highest end of the moral life is indeed the full morally-acquired communion with God, but man, as an individual being placed in natural and spiritual relations to other creatures, fulfills his moral destiny not in an exclusive communion with God, but only in a communing at the same time with the children of God, and hence he has it as a moral duty to form this his relation to other men into a moral *communion*, without which his personal perfection cannot be reached. The most primitive natural communion is sexual communion, from which naturally arises the second form, that between parents and children; both forms are to be raised from the merely natural, to the moral communion of the family.

As all love presupposes some form of communion, though it be ante-moral and merely natural, hence the moral forming of this communion is not an absolutely new creating of a communion, but the spiritual exalting of one that already exists naturally. Though moral communion with God is the highest good, still this does not exclude, but includes, a communing with other rational creatures, for God is himself in communion with them. Mystical quietism is but a refined self-seeking, and conflicts with the essence of Christianity; for God did not create mere isolated beings, but destined them *for* each other; "it is not good," not in harmony with the moral destination of the race, "that man should be alone," for an isolated person lacks a very essential sphere of moral activity—that upon which he can not only (as in his relation to God) appropriate and obey, and not only (as in his relation to nature) dominate, but also, as relating to beings like himself, form and appropriate at the same time in mutual moral reciprocity. Without moral communion with other men morality cannot come to its full development; communion is not a mere inactive condition, but it is a productive good, a condition of new, higher morality. This of itself is a condemnation of the hermit-life; of such a life the Scriptures know nothing; solitude may indeed be salutary as a preliminary preparation for a calling that requires great collection of soul [Luke i, 80], as indeed the Son of man himself resorted thereto for a while [Matt. iv]; but the Sabbath-introspection of the soul cannot, as opposed to an active life among men, be made the exclusively-legitimate life. The recluse life, even where the severest discipline is exercised against the sinful nature, is an immoral renouncing of the moral duties of man toward his fellows, a dissolving of the kingdom of God into mere atoms, into mere isolated individuals, and hence it was utterly foreign to the earliest Church.

The communion of man with his fellows is primarily of a merely natural character; but man is to have in his whole being and nature, and above all in his spiritual nature, nothing which he has merely naturally received and not also morally appropriated to, and formed for, himself. The communion of the sexes, as well as that between parents and children, is primarily as yet extra-moral,—does not yet distinguish man from the brute; both forms of communion need to be raised to a moral character, otherwise they will sink to an immoral one; even parental love may be sinful.

(a) THE FAMILY.

SECTION CXLII.

Natural sexual love is, as a manifestation of the divine love ruling in nature, *per se* a type of moral communion, but it does not itself suffice to create this. The merely natural, and hence extra moral, element of the same is confined entirely to the unconscious natural inclination; the exalting of the mere inclination to real love is never an ante-moral or extra-moral process, but springs of moral determination; the actual accomplishing of the sexual communion should never follow upon mere natural love, but must, as a free act, be simply a manifestation of the already realized *moral* communion of the persons in virtue of moral love. Without this condition it is not extra-moral, but anti-moral, as an actual destruction of moral communion.

Sexual communion is the first possible communion, and hence has in nature its first incitation. As man was not an absolutely other and new creation but the divinely-animated nature-creature, so also is the first moral communion not one that was absolutely new-created by man, but a morally-exalted natural communion. Sexual love prevails throughout animated nature,—is its highest life-function, and, therefore, also the highest manifestation of the divine love as ruling in nature The flower develops in its sexual bloom its highest force and splendor; the brute has, in sexual love, the highest pleasure-feeling, that of a perfect, mutually life-unifying harmony with its like; it is the feeling that it is not a mere isolated unit, but a living member of a higher whole. It is not man's duty to suppress this life-manifestation, but to exalt it,—to raise the unconsciously-prevailing love of the animal into a conscious and moral love. Though in idea the same, the sexes are in reality different, mutually complementing each other to the full idea of man. The somewhat clumsy myth as to the original androgynous forms of humanity, as given in Plato's *Symposium*, is but a distorted echo of the thought, much more suggestively expressed in the Biblical account, of the formation of Eve from a rib of Adam.

Love, according to its inner idea, is not only preservative but also communicative, awakening new life and promoting it; hence the propagation of the human race is conditioned on the highest earthly love. All love is an appropriating and a forming at the same time. In sexual love the sexes mutually appropriate and form each other as natural beings, though in different degrees; the spiritually moral appropriating and forming must, however, precede the natural, as its moral consecration and conditionment; the reversing of this relation, the letting the moral and personal love simply follow the sexual communion, is morally impossible, as thereby the latter is degraded to a purely bestial, immoral character, and cannot become the starting-point of a moral communion.

A possession is moral only as property, that is, in virtue of its having been morally-acquired and appropriated; now the communion of the sexes is the complete giving up and appropriating of each party as the property of the other; hence when it is not a manifestation and fruit of an already-accomplished, morally-personal, spiritual unity,—of the appropriation of the persons as moral and hence as permanent inalienable property,—it is then not only not a simply natural action but an immoral throwing away of one's moral personality, an irremediable ruining of the moral personality of the other. Lost innocence is irrecoverable; mere sexual communion without moral love is a defamation. But moral love is in its very essence permanent; that which is by love appropriated to the person as property is inalienable,—can be destroyed only with the personality itself. Whoredom is not mere bestiality, but, as a moral self-abandonment, it is below bestiality; for the brute does not throw itself away. Even in the case of the first man, moral love preceded sexual communion. "And Adam said: this is now bone of my bones and flesh of my flesh; she shall be called woman, because she was taken out of man" [Gen. ii, 23 *sqq.*]. This is a child-like, natural expression of moral love, the full consciousness of the harmony and unity between man and wife; the wife is the man's other *ego*, belongs to him, is destined to him as property, as also he to her; she is of, and for, him. Hence to this expression of moral love joins itself, as a sequence, the further thought: "*therefore* shall a man leave his father and his mother and shall cleave unto his wife, and they shall be *one* flesh;" the becoming one in the flesh follows only from and upon the being one in spirit; they become one also sexually, because they have mutually recognized each other as joined in a personally-spiritual unity. The moral consciousness of the personal belonging of the one to the other, the free recognition of their mutually-possessing each other as property, is the indispensable antecedent moral condition of sexual communion. Without this moral condition, that which is the acme of the nature-life, the innermost center of nature-mysteries, the synthesis of all that is wonderful in nature-force, namely, the generative act,—which, as moral, is a sacred act,—becomes an absolutely immoral one, and sinks man toward the brute more than any other natural action.

SECTION CXLIII.

Moral sexual love being a love of the persons to each other, and the moral personality of the one being *per se* equal to that of the other in moral worth, and consequently also in moral rights, hence that giving up of the one person, as a complete moral possession, to the other, which is required by sexual communion, is only then possible when this surrender is a mutual one, that is, when the two persons belong to each other exclusively; and hence moral sexual love exists only in the *marriage* of two persons, in view of sexual communion and consequently of complete personal life-communion. Polygamy is morally impossible,—is but legally regulated whoredom, makes a real personal love-surrender, and hence marriage itself, impossible. For the same reason, marriage is morally indissoluble. Marriage is not a mere right, is not simply allowed, but it is a divinely-willed and expressly ordained moral communion, and hence the entering upon it is not a merely natural but also a religious action, which, standing as it does under the express promise of the divine blessing, is very naturally invested with a religious consecration.

The extra-Christian notion of polygamy absolutely excludes the moral essence of marriage; in it the woman is indeed the man's property, but not man the woman's; this involves a difference in the moral worth and rights of the sexes, which, from a moral stand-point, is impossible; for it denies the moral personality of the woman; and in fact, in polygamy, woman is only a slave. Of the polygamy of the Old Testament it is not here the place to speak. The primitive divine institution of marriage recognizes only the marriage with *one* woman, and the New Testament presupposes this throughout [Matt. xix, 3 *sqq.*; 1 Cor. vii, 2; xi, 11; Eph, v, 28; 1 Tim. iii, 2].

As marriage rests entirely on personal love to a person, hence it is not a mere legal relation; and as in it the persons belong entirely to each other,—are to each other a mutual property, the essence and strength of which is love,—hence to view marriage as a merely legal relation not only falls below the moral idea of marriage, but is *per se* immoral, for a contract-relation presupposes the non-presence of mutually-confiding love,—excludes a perfect moral life-and-body-communion, the reciprocal belonging to each other as a moral property; on the contrary, such a contract tends to raise between the two persons, as exclusively bent on their personal advantage, the separation-wall of distrust, and delivers the one consort to the other for mere stipulated service and use. As little as a contract-relation is conceivable between parents and children in their mutual family duties, just so little is it morally possible between husband and wife. Sexual communion when based on a mere legal contract is only respectable concubinage; it stands essentially on an equal footing with polygamy.—The generating of children is not so much the purpose as rather the blessing of marriage; its purpose is absolutely the fulfilling of moral love; marriage is and continues in full validity even where this blessing is wanting.

The legal principle that "the chief end of marriage is the generating and training of children," is consistent rather with a legalized concubinage or with polygamy than with the moral idea of marriage, and would in consistency require that barrenness be regarded as a perfectly valid ground for divorce.

For the simple reason that consorts belong to each other as moral property, marriage admits morally of no *dissolution*. A moral property is inseparably united with the moral peculiarity, and hence with the personal essence of the individual,—is, like this essence, inalienable. It is as impossible morally to dissolve a marriage as it is for a person to separate from his personal life, his peculiar character, and hence from his own self; and, as a violent internal anarchy of the spirit, namely, in insanity, is conceivable only in a sinfully-disordered state, so also is a dissolution of marriage conceivable only in a state of sinfully morbid disorder,—it is in fact an ethical insanity, a moral ruin of the two self-separating consorts. Christ affirms this moral impossibility of divorce [Matt. xix, 3–9], and bases his doctrine on this significant reason: "They are no more twain, but *one* flesh; what therefore God hath joined together, let not man put asunder." This is not two reasons but only one; God has joined together marriage in his primative instituting of it, that is, by his creative will, which established the essence of marriage to consist in the fact that the two consorts should be one flesh, one single absolutely inseparable life as to soul and body, even as every living body is a single inseparable whole, and any dissevering of it, the death of the same. The indissolubility of marriage is still more strongly emphasized by Christ by his citing the words of the Creator at its institution: "For this cause shall a man leave father and mother, and shall cleave to his wife, and they twain shall be one flesh." Man is *not* to abandon his father and mother with his love, though he may outwardly withdraw from them in order to build up a family of his own; but still more intimate than the bond between parents and children, is the bond between husband and wife, who mutually fully belong to each other. Now if the bond of love and unity between parents and children can never be dissolved without great moral violence, still less can the bond between husband and wife be morally dissolved. The unity of the "flesh" is not to be understood merely, nor even chiefly, of the bodily union, but alludes to the highest and perfect moral union of the whole life of both body and soul. A merely spiritual unity is designated by μία καρδία και ψυχή [Acts iv, 32], but husband and wife are also εἰς μίαν σάρκα [1 Cor. vi, 16; comp. vii, 4; Eph. v, 28 *sqq.*]. Adultery alone works divorce, and all divorce is in its moral essence adultery [comp. 1 Cor. vii, 10], and, as relating to the children, a ruthless annihilating of the family.

It is of high significancy that the Scriptures expressly affirm the divine institution of marriage, and give to moral marriage a promise of special blessing [Gen. i, 28; ii, 24; ix, 7; Matt. xix, 4; comp. Psa. cxxviii, 3; cxxvii, 3–5]. Hence marriage cannot in any sense be implicated in unsanctity or lowness, so as to be inconsistent with a truly spiritual and holy life; otherwise God, when he introduced woman to man as called to be holy, would have encouraged him to turn aside from his high destination, and Adam would have had not merely the right but in fact also the duty of declining this gift of divine love; the creation of the woman would really have been the first temptation. In a normal, uncorrupted state of humanity it is not only the right, but also the duty, of the morally and corporeally mature individual to live in this God-instituted state of marriage; it is not marriage itself but the particular choice of the consort that is left to the particular, personal preference of love. God's declaration: "It is *not* good that the man should be alone; I will make him an help-meet *for* him," distinctly implies that celibacy *per se* is *not* the better but the less good state,—as well for man, for he *ought* to have a help-meet, as also for woman, for her express destination is to be a help-meet for the man. Of the relations of marriage *after* the fall into sin, it is not here the place to speak.

The fact that in all not totally savage nations marriage is not constituted simply by the consent of the two persons, but by some sort of solemn and, most usually, religious ceremony, is a significant implication of the moral essence of marriage; and the importance that a people places on the religiously-moral consecration of marriage, is a pretty safe criterion of its morality in relation to the sexual life.

SECTION CXLIV.

The two consorts stand to each other, as moral persons, on an equal footing; they both find their union in a complete devoted love, and hence, in fact, in a loving, free subordination to the moral law. The consorts complement each other also in spiritually-moral respects; and it is only in respect to this harmony-conditioning complementing that the woman is in many things rather guided than self-determining. This, however, is not a real domination of the man over the woman as over a subject, but only a conditional super-ordination of the man as the actively-guiding unity-point of the common life. As a moral relation marriage rests on freedom, that is, on free mutual choice; consequently it presupposes the moral maturity of the two lovers. This freedom of choice, however, is not irrational caprice, but determines itself in view of the true life-harmonizing, reciprocally-complementing, personal peculiarity of the two parties, and receives its moral ratification by its being freely recognized on the part of the moral community, and primarily of the family.

But moral equality is not sameness. As the final destination of all moral beings is the same, hence a difference of the *moral* worth of the sexes is not conceivable [Gal. iii, 28; 1 Pet. iii, 7]. The inferior position of the female sex in all non-Christian nations is a sign of moral unculture, which even the Greeks did not entirely put off. The account of the creation of woman indicates her true dignity; taken from man's heart, she belongs to man's heart, and is not a slave at his feet; she is a part of him,—is not merely flesh of his flesh but also soul of his soul. The antithesis of sex, which is not of a merely bodily character, conditions indeed also very different moral duties; but these duties are absolutely equal in moral worth. The precedency of the woman in the interior of the family is in no respect less than that of the man in the civic sphere; and though, in virtue of this difference, the woman is, in many respects,—especially in those of the external, public life, that is, of the outward-directed activity,—properly subject to the man as the natural leader in this sphere [Eph. v, 22, 23], yet, as an offset to this, the man is in his turn properly dependent on the woman in the sphere of female activity; it is not to the credit of the man to dominate in the kitchen and nursery. Each rules, by the constitution of nature, in his own sphere; and it is perfectly in order for the woman, in her sphere, to exercise a determining influence on the man (§ 69). The historical tyrant-relation of the man over the woman is *not* the original and true one, and is inconsistent with true confiding love and with the dignity of womanhood, and is expressly explained in the Scriptures as a punishment for sin [Gen. iii, 16]. On the other hand, however, a certain guiding super-ordination of the man is the original and normal relation, and is in no respect a fruit of the fall; Adam was as guilty as Eve; sin was effectual only in changing the original normal subordination of the woman into a relation of *servitude*. Though the woman is, in more than one respect, the "weaker vessel" [1 Pet. iii, 7], nevertheless she is a "co-heir of grace;" and she has, though indeed another and peculiar, yet not a less noble moral life-task than the man; as the help-meet of man it is hers faithfully to preserve and foster that which the stronger and more independent-willed man actively creates. The strong vital initiative, the fixing of the goal, and the task of producing, are the work of the man; in this work the woman is to be for him, to aid him, to have him for the vital central-point of the activity peculiar to her [1 Cor. xi, 8, 9]. Though the woman had first sinned, and the man was thus led astray by her, yet the offended and sentencing God turns himself first to Adam, and requires account of him, and then afterward to Eve; Adam was in duty required to strengthen and dissuade the yielding and sinning woman, and not to let himself be led by her.

The contracting of marriage is neither a mere business-transaction nor a fruit of a simple falling in love; where moral love does not form the marriage, there it is desecrated. Hence marriages cannot be planned and brought about simply by parents, no more than can the parents practice virtue for their children; the moral must be accomplished by each for himself. The free personal choice that is absolutely necessary to marriage proper is not to be made arbitrarily or by hap-hazard; it aims essentially at the realization of the complete life-unity of the two persons, to the end of moral communion. This unity, and hence this perfect harmony, presupposes a difference and at the same time a similarity of the spiritually and bodily self-complementing persons. The difference consists in the normal spiritual and corporeal antithesis of the sexes in general, and, in particular, in the respective peculiarity of the persons, which finds, largely, in the opposite peculiarity its complement, and hence its moral satisfaction; a fiery, impassioned temperament is advantageously complemented by one that is gentle and calm. The similarity consists in the essential agreement of the persons, not merely in their moral and spiritual, but also in their physical peculiarities,—a similarity which can well exist in the midst of large difference. Without the similarity there would be no unanimity; without the difference there would be no mutual complementing, and hence no mutual attraction. The selecting for marriage is a *finding* of the complementing personality, and is free and unfree at the same time. There lies, indeed, in this finding, something of the mysterious, something which transcends the dialectical consciousness; and an anticipatory feeling antecedes, even in a normal state of things, the definite recognizing of the person; the matter should not rest, however, at the stage of mere feeling, but the person should at once exalt it to a rational consciousness,—should transfigure the ante-moral love-feeling into rational love.

The morally-rational character of the contracting of marriage is recognized by usages prevalent among all not utterly uncultured nations, and is guaranteed by the fact that it is not left to the mere discretion of the individuals, but is subject to the ratifying recognition of the moral community, and hence primarily of the parents concerned [comp. 1 Cor. vii, 37]. Though parents are not entitled so far to represent their children as to choose consorts for them, yet they are perfectly entitled to ratify the choice of their children by their approval.

SECTION CXLV.

Marriage as productive is the basis of the more extended *family*, which, like marriage, is not a merely natural but essentially a moral relation. The family members stand to each other either in the relation of equality, as husband and wife or as brothers and sisters, or in that of super-ordination and subordination, as parents and children. The relation between parents and children is the first *inequality* among men, and the presupposition and type of all other relations of super-ordination and subordination. Parents and children stand to each other in the relation of moral personalities, and hence also of mutual moral duties; parents have, in relation to their children, preponderatingly the duty of forming, and hence of educating, during the progress of which, however, the constantly and necessarily therewith-connected duty of *sparing*, rises gradually to greater prominence as the development advances, until finally it predominates, and the child has attained to its moral *majority*. As, however, in a process of normal development, the parents also constantly advance spiritually and morally, hence they always retain their super-ordinate relation to the children even as matured; their formative influence on the children can never cease, and never gives place to a relation of moral equality with them. The children, on their part, continue always, though not in a constantly like manner, subject to the parents in reverential *obedience*, which, however, as itself resting upon love to God, is ever also conditioned thereby.

The difference between consorts and blood-relatives rests on the difference between moral and natural communion. In both cases the communion is not only spiritually-moral but also corporeally-natural. With consorts, however, the bodily-natural communion rests on an antecedent moral communion; and with blood-relatives the moral communion rests on the precedent corporeally-natural communion; the former become corporeally one because they love each other, the latter love each other because in blood they are already one; the former proceed from an original state of separation, toward union; the latter tend from their original union to a state of separation; blood-relationship proper precludes sexual communion. The fact that relatives are bound to each other by especially close bonds of love [Gen. xiii, 8, 9; xiv, 14 *sqq.*; xviii, 23 *sqq.*; xxix, 13 *sqq.*; Exod. xviii, 5 *sqq.*; Ruth i; ii, 20; Luke i, 38, 40, 58; comp. Job xix, 13; Psa. xxxi, 12; lxix, 8], does not conflict with the more general love of neighbor.

In the family begins, now, moral society with all its normal differences. Husband and wife do not as yet constitute a society, for they are *one* flesh; nor do parents and children form one, for although they are one spirit, yet they stand to each other in the relation of super-ordination and subordination. Persons who are entirely alike, and who stand to each other in absolutely like relations, constitute indeed a multitude, but not a society; where there is no vital all-guiding nucleus, no throbbing heart for the body, no soul for the acting members, there there is no living whole, no society. Inequality, unlikeness, lies in the essence of every moral society,—not an inequality of the moral rights of personalities, but an inequality, a difference, of spiritually-moral position in and relation to society. Parents are the first princes, and true princes are the fathers of their people; *patres* was the title of distinction of the Roman senators; "elders" is used in a like sense for the leaders of moral society in almost all the free constitutions of antiquity and also of the church. Parents are the guides of their children by the grace of God, for children are a gift of divine grace [Gen. xxi, 1; xxv, 21; xxix, 31; xxx, 6, 17 *sqq.*; xxxiii, 5; Exod. xxiii, 26; Deut. vii, 14; Ruth iv, 13; 1 Sam. ii, 21; Psa. cxxvii, 3; cxxviii, 3; comp. 1 Tim. ii, 15]; therein lies the right as well as the duty of the parents. Guiding the children in God's name, standing in God's stead for them [Eph. vi, 1; comp. Lev. xix, 32], they have not only a right to reverential obedience, but also the duty of reverence-awakening training. Parental love is *per se* strictly natural, hence it is found even in the natural man [Gen. xxi, 16; xxxi, 28, 43, 50, 55; 1 Kings iii, 16 *sqq.;* Isa. xlix, 15; Matt. ii, 18; Luke xv, 21 *sqq.;* John iv, 47 *sqq.*], and consequently very much more so in the pious [Gen. ix, 26, 27; xxi, 11, 12; xxii, 2; xxiv; xxviii, 1–4; xxxvii, 3, 34, 35; xlii, 36 *sqq.;* xliii, 14; xliv, 22, 30; xlv, 28; xlvi, 30; xlviii, 10 *sqq.;* Exod. ii, 2 *sqq.;* 2 Sam. xii, 16 *sqq.;* xiii, 30 *sqq.;* xiv; xviii, 33; xix, 1 *sqq.;* Prov. x, 1; xv, 20; Jer. xxxi, 15; Matt. ii, 14; Luke ii, 35, 44; John xix, 25].

It is the part of parents to cultivate their children into morally-matured personalities; this is not merely a right of the parents, but also of the children, and hence, for the former, a duty; they are to impart to their children the spiritually-moral attainments of their own spiritual development, and consequently also those of humanity in general, so that the children shall not have to go through again, in the very same manner, the same absolutely new-beginning development as the parents, for this is simply the manner and characteristic of nature-objects, but that they may place themselves in the current of history, and learn and appropriate to themselves its spiritual results, and then, in their turn, carry them further forward. All spiritual forming of the, as yet, spiritually immature is an historical working,—an initiating of the, as yet, immature spirit into the current and working of history. Now, as the child is in fact to ripen on into a morally-mature personality, and yet from the start already *is*, both in essence and in faculties, a moral personality, hence the forming of the same by the parents is never a strictly exclusive influencing, and hence, on the part of the child, never a merely inactive receiving, but always also a spiritually-moral co-operating of the child, a constantly increasing initiative self-forming of the same, so that consequently from the very start there must always be united with the formative activity upon the child, also a *sparing* bearing toward it; and such a forming is in fact *education*.—Education,—which, as aiming at the moral goal, namely, harmony with God and with the totality of moral being, must always be at the same time a natural and a spiritual, a special and a general forming, directed toward bringing the child to God and to God-sonship [Gen. xviii, 19; Deut. vi, 7; xi, 19; xxxi, 12, 13; xxxii, 46; Psa. lxxviii, 3 *sqq.*; xxxiv, 12; Isa. xxxviii, 19; Eph. vi, 4; comp. Luke ii, 27],—is a characteristic manifestation of rationality; the brute needs no education, as it is never destined to become free and moral. All created beings are, in their essence, naturally good; but it is only by education that they become morally good, and truly rational and free. Wherever the morally uncultured and unmatured undertake to establish liberty, there it soon results in unbridled license, and, as an attendant thereof, in the coarse tyranny of the stronger. In the want and requirement of education are implied a recognition and admission that the entire true essence of the child is not conferred upon it immediately by nature, but must be first acquired by free spiritual acts, and that too not by merely individual acts, but by the spiritual appropriation of the already extant spiritual attainments of humanity,—by spiritual obedience toward the spiritually and morally mature. The child cannot educate itself, nor can it on the other hand simply *be* educated without its own moral co-operation; but it must willingly *let* itself be educated.

Reverence for parents, and, what is only another phase of the same thing, for the aged in general, is regarded by all nations, with the exception of the totally savage, as a sacred duty [comp. Gen. ix, 23]; and it is a sure sign of a deep moral corruption of the spirit of a people where there is a declension in the reverence of children for parents, and, in general, of youth before old age; and more especially so when this declension is not undeserved. In a morally-normal development-course of humanity it is absolutely inconceivable that old age should so deeply decline as to fall behind the wisdom and moral maturity of the youth; the superior wisdom and knowledge of divine and human things would, in virtue of the higher inner and outward experience, continue to be the imperishable possession of old age; and it belongs among the most distressing evidences of the sinful disorder of the human race, that in fact old age does frequently sink back to childishness, and needs to be taken under the guardianship of the children. If any one can regard this as the natural order of life, let him also regard as foolish and groundless the pain which every, not totally perverse, child's heart experiences at the sight of such a sinking of the gray head, before which it would fain only bow in reverence.

Children have, toward their parents, predominantly the duty of appropriating, which, however, gradually passes over more and more into a self-forming, though without ever entirely breaking off from the formative influence of the parents; and the sparing bearing of the children toward the parents can never, save under utterly corrupted conditions, be transcended by their formative bearing toward them. The formative influence of the children upon the parents, that exists indeed from the very beginning, can, even after they have become morally mature, assume only a secondary rank. This predominatingly-receptive relation of the children to the parents is that of filial *reverence* [Gen. xlv, 9 *sqq.*; Exod. xx, 12; Lev. xix, 3; Prov. xxx, 17; Matt. xv, 4; Eph. vi, 2], the outward expression of which is *obedience* [Prov. xxiii, 25; Eph. vi, 1; Col. iii, 20]. Christ himself is the pattern also in this [Luke ii, 51; John xix, 26].—Children, when entering into wedlock and establishing a new family, enter thereby indeed into a greater independence of the parents [Gen. ii, 24], but the bond between parents and children, the duty of the former to care for the weal and the honor of the latter [Gen. xxxi, 48 *sqq.*; Deut. xxii, 13 *sqq.*], and that of the children to show reverence for the parents, is not thereby dissolved.

The right of parents to obedience, and the duty of children to show it, are, however, essentially conditioned on the agreement or disagreement of the parental command with divine will, and can never become *per se* and unconditionally binding. For this right is not a merely natural but a moral one; the merely natural dependence of children on their parents extends, as with brutes, only so far as the state of actual helplessness and need extends; the moral dependence, however, is a permanent one that is never to be dissolved. The moral right of the parents to obedience rests on the fact that they do not represent their own individual will, but the divine will. And for this very reason the guilt of parents is so deep when they misuse their moral mission to educate in God's name, and lead the child away from God, placing their own sinful will in the stead of the divine will.

SECTION CXLVI.

Brothers and sisters sustain toward each other, in the same manner as consorts, though only in morally-spiritual respects, complementing relations; and their mutual love forms an essential element in the morality of the family-life; but this complementing is, because of the predominant like-character of the parties, never perfect and all-sufficient, and hence brothers and sisters naturally seek for complementing elements also outside of the family-circle. This form of love which passes beyond the merely natural communion and freely selects for itself the complementing personality, is *friendship*.

Also the mutual love of brothers and sisters is primarily of a purely natural character and requires to be exalted to a moral one [Gen. xxxiii; xxxiv; xlii, 24 *sq.*; xliii, 16 *sqq.*; xliv, 18 *sqq.*; xlv, 1 *sqq.*; l, 17; Exod. ii, 4 *sqq.*; Psa. cxxxiii, 1; Luke xv, 32]. Brothers and sisters can never personally complement each other to such an extent as that the need of friendship outside of the family-circle should not arise; they are originally too homogeneous, too similar, to render attainable that full harmony that both requires, and perfectly consists with, large difference. Brother and sister complement each other much more than brother and brother or sister and sister; and they in fact usually unite themselves more intimately with each other than do brothers or sisters among themselves; nevertheless there remains also here, and especially as spiritual maturity draws near, an unbridged chasm, and there is felt the need of a harmony more vital—one that is conditioned on a more strongly developed antithesis. It is not a loveless turning away from the family, but a strictly legitimate impulse, when the boy and girl seek after outside *friendship*. This does not interfere with the family-love, but heightens it. Friendship is an enlarged brother-and-sister love, or rather it is its complementing of itself outside of the family proper; it is brotherly love as resting upon purely spiritual affinity. Hence friendship is usually stronger in the period of transition from the original narrow family-circle into new and more independent forms of life; and on the establishing of a new independent family-circle it is usual for the friendship of the consorts with others to grow less strong, and for new friendships to be less easily formed; wedlock-love occasions an enfeebling of friendship; he who in youth has had true friendships usually turns out to be an affectionate consort; and friendship with persons of the other sex very readily develops itself into real sexual love, and is consequently not without its essential dangers.

SECTION CXLVII.

The necessity of the complementing of family love by friendship, indicates of itself the reason of the moral impossibility of *marriage* between *near blood relatives*. The instinct that prompts brothers and sisters to seek friendship outside of the narrower family-circle, prompts them also to seek for themselves consorts outside of the same. The requisite antecedent condition of marriage, a difference of the bodily and of the spiritual peculiarities of the persons, exists most feebly in near blood relatives; and marriage is, in its very essence, a free moral communion which does not spring from a natural communion, but, on the contrary, itself gives rise to this. As marriage presupposes a moral equality, and is a relation of homogeneous reciprocal love, hence it would be, between parents and children, a revolting crime, inasmuch as here the relation of reverence is insuperable; also, as between brothers and sisters, it is, for all save the second generation of the race, absolutely inadmissible, partly for the reasons already given, and in part because of that deep awe of the parental blood which holds good also as towards brothers and sisters. The antecedent moral presupposition of marriage is not filial or brotherly love, but friendship.

The obstacle to marriage as found in blood-relationship is one of the most difficult of ethical questions, not so much, however, because of any kind of doubt as to its legitimacy, as rather in reference to the moral grounds for this recognition, which in fact is almost universal and which prevails in almost all, even heathen, nations. With the adducing of mere outward grounds of fitness, such as the avoidance of near-lying temptation, very little is gained; also it is difficult to establish this prohibition, as a nature-law, from the practice of animated nature in general, for brutes do not observe it. The grounds lie deeper and are essentially of a spiritually-moral character. In the first place, however, a distinction is to be made between ascending and collateral blood relationship. Marriages between parents and children and within other ascending and descending degrees of relationship are an outrage even for our natural feelings in general [Lev. xviii; xx, 11 *sqq.*; 1Cor. v, 1 *sqq.*; comp. Gen. xix, 30 *sqq.*]. The insuperable relation of reverence between children and parents [comp. Gen. ix, 23] renders morally impossible any sexual mingling, inasmuch as sexual communion rests upon the closest confiding equality of the persons; whatever conflicts with filial and paternal love is absolutely immoral, and this would unquestionably be attendant upon sexual communion. The same is of course true of grand-parents and grand-children. The case stood originally somewhat different as far as regards marriage between *brothers and sisters;* in this respect there occur in the general consciousness some, though indeed very rare, exceptions. The Peruvians punished such marriages with death; and yet for political reasons they prescribed them for their ruling Inca. In the case of the children of Adam, God made an exception in the interest of the indispensably essential unity of the human race (§ 88). And the unconditional prohibition of such marriages could only come into force when the possibility of other alliances was fully realized. In the legislation of Moses, the sexual mingling of brothers and sisters was visited with anathemas and death

[Lev. xviii, 9, 11; xx, 17; Deut. xxvii, 22]; and as early as in the time of Abraham such marriages were utterly foreign even to the heathen consciousness, as is evidenced by the fact that Abraham, in order to protect himself, caused Sarah to pass as his sister [Gen. xii, 13; xx, 2]. (That Sarah was really Abraham's half-sister in the stricter sense is not proved by Gen. xx, 12, as the expression "daughter of my father" may also designate Terah's grand-daughter, and it is not improbable that she was the daughter of Haran, Abraham's brother, and that her earlier name Iscah [Gen. xi, 29] was exchanged for the title of honor, Sarai [my mistress, my wife]; in verse 31 she is called Terah's daughter-in-law, which would hardly be said had she been his daughter; and whatever the facts may be, the contracting of this marriage falls *before* Abraham's call.)

The most immediate ground for the inadmissibility of marriage between brothers and sisters lies in the fact, that though here the requisite likeness of disposition in the parties does exist, yet on the other hand there is lacking that degree of difference which is essential to a vital complementing harmony; brothers and sisters are entirely too homogeneous in their bodily and spiritual natures to give rise to a vital, fruitful, reciprocal influencing. Narcissus fell in love with his own image, and passed, for this very reason, for a simpleton; and brother and sister are to each other, each, the image of the other. No sensible man will select for himself as a friend one who is only his strictly-resembling second-self, but, on the contrary, such a one as, by his difference, will stimulatingly-complement himself; the same holds good of husband and wife; of these, because of their constant uniformity of life in marriage, it holds good in fact in a still higher degree. This explains also the well-known fact that an actual falling in love between brother and sister is among the rarest of occurrences, even under circumstances where moral corruption has taken deep root; (illustrated in the case of Amnon, 2 Sam. xiii, 1). To attempt to explain this natural phenomenon simply from the express law is inadmissible, and for this reason among others, because this law, as existing among all cultured heathen nations, can in fact be explained only from a natural conviction, and because this sentiment prevails even where in general no regard whatever is had to religious and moral laws. This reason, however, is not fully sufficient, because while indeed it has reference to, and accounts for, unhappy marriages, yet it does not explain why some marriages should be regarded as criminal; and, besides, in many cases, where only too great differences exist between brothers and sisters, it would not apply at all. A second reason for this inadmissibility reaches deeper, namely, that marriage as distinguished from a merely natural communion, must rest essentially upon a purely moral free choice and act; it exists in its truth only where it does not proceed from natural communion as developing itself into complete love, but where it first creates this natural communion; its purpose is to create love and spread it abroad, and not merely to affirm a love which is already strong from nature. Blood-relationship and marriage are two different moral ordinances and bonds, which are not to be intermingled with each other; marriage looks to the uniting of a previously existing antithesis by love, and not to the uniting or ratifying, a second time, of an already existing natural unity. It is because of this peculiarity that marriage forms the basis of *all* moral community-life, and must therefore express in itself the essential character of this life, namely, purely spiritual love. If the marriage of brothers and sisters were admissible, then the family would tend to hedge itself in upon its purely natural basis,—would grow up animal-like to a merely natural, but not to a purely spiritual, communion. There is need of the general dissemination of love, as St. Augustine remarks, and this would be obstructed by the possibility of marriage between brothers and sisters; and family self-seeking in narrow-hearted seclusion would become almost inevitable; marriage looks not merely to the uniting together of two persons, but also of two families. The moral development of a people as a whole imperatively requires this breaking down of the walls of family seclusiveness, namely, the non permission of the marriage of brothers and sisters; hence this prohibition is of high world-historical significancy.—The chief ground, however, and one which expresses itself chiefly in our natural feelings, is reverence for the parental blood which has passed from the parents over upon the children, and which calls for a respectful avoidance of fleshly-sensuous enjoyment. Man sees in his brother or sister not merely the image, but also the blood of his parents [comp. Lev. xviii, 9; vii, 8, 11 *sqq.*, where this thought is implied]; and the feeling of reverential awe and shame that springs from this consciousness precludes any feeling of sexual love. And in general the feeling of reverence is uncongenial to sexual love; and when, as not unfrequently occurs, a maiden has stood in a reverential relation to the man who offers himself to her as husband, there the transition from this feeling of reverence to that of conjugal love costs her a severe and poignant struggle.—Where sin has actually taken deep root, there arise other grounds for the inadmissibility of the marriage of blood-relatives. But we must confine ourselves here to the expression of the fundamental idea.

SECTION CXLVIII.

The family is a unitary vital whole also in relation to its moral *property;* it is not a mere sum of simply isolated persons of like name, but a body and a soul —a moral person with a common moral *honor* and a possession of its own, in which all the single members participate.

The family has as a living unity, also *one* spirit, a common moral life-purpose and a common moral peculiarity; the common life-purpose consists in the mutual promotion of the moral life in *one* God-inspired spirit; the common peculiarity is, spiritually, the moral *honor* of the family, and, outwardly, its temporal possessions. The moral acquirements of one family member, especially of the head, pass over to the whole family, and the deserts of the parents bear, in virtue of the divine order of the world, fruits of blessing for the children, and are rewarded upon them [Gen. xxvi, 4, 5, 24; xlix, 10, 26; Exod. xx, 6; Deut. v, 10; vii, 9; 2 Sam. ix, 7; xxi, 7; 1 Kings xi, 34; Psa. xxv, 13; xxxvii, 25 *sqq.;* cxii, 2, 3; Prov. xiv, 26; xvii, 6; xx, 7; Jer. xxxii, 18; comp. 1 Cor. vii, 14; Rom. xi, 16]; and the sins of the fathers are visited upon the children, and are for them a shame and a misfortune [Gen. ix, 25; xx, 7, 17 *sqq.;* xlix, 7; Exod. xx, 5; xxxiv, 7; Lev. xxvi, 39;

Num. xiv, 18; Deut. v, 9; vii, 9; 1 Kings xi, 39; 2 Kings v, 27; Job v, 4; xxi, 19; xxvii, 14; Psa. xxxvii, 28; cix, 9, 10; Prov. xi, 21; xvi, 5; Isa. xiv, 21; Jer. xviii, 21; xxxii, 18; Lam. v, 7; Hos. iv, 6; comp. Matt. xxvii, 25], and the sins of the children upon the fathers, as their disgrace [Lev. xxi. 9; Prov. x, 1: xvii, 25; xxviii, 7; comp. Deut. xxii 13 *sqq.*],—whereof we shall speak elsewhere more fully. The consciousness, deeply rooted in all cultivated nations, of a transmission of deserts, of a moral *nobility* of family-lines, has a profoundly moral basis; but this moral solidarity of the family is conceived even by the Old Testament more clearly and more distinctly than was ever done in any heathen nation. This is morally a very weighty thought. Man is made to feel that he does not live and act as a merely isolated individual, but, on the contrary, every-where and always as a member of a moral whole,—that the fruits of his actions, be they good or evil, pass over to those who *belong* to him and with whom he is morally connected, and hence that in sinning he commits an injustice not merely against himself, but also against *all* whom he calls his *own*. So the family is a divine ordinance, so is the solidarity of moral deserts and guilts such also; this is not injustice but sacred justice, for the simple reason that man is never a merely isolated individual. That which is true of the spiritually-moral property of the family is true also of the material property, and upon this rests the principle of inheritance.

(b) MORAL SOCIETY.

SECTION CXLIX.

Moral society is the family as enlarged by its own natural growth and by friendship, but which, in this enlarging, assumes also an essentially different character. Social communion differs from family-communion by the greater retreating into the back-ground of the natural unity and at the same time of free personal choice; society itself assumes an objective, and, in some sense, nature-character; and the place of natural and free moral love is supplied by *custom*, which becomes more or less an objectively-valid power over the individuals. It differs, furthermore, from the family in this, that it involves a communion of a far more general character, one that absorbs into itself the individual person far less, and requires and brings about a more interrupted and only occasionally-exercised moral intercourse of its members. The members of society sustain to each other the relation of *friendliness*, which is larger in extent, but feebler in inner quality and power, than friendship. That form of love which manifests itself in friendliness, and which consequently constitutes the moral essence of society, is the *love of neighbor*, which, as distinguished from more intimate love, does not elect its own object, and is not directed toward particular persons but toward man in general. Social communion realizes itself through mutual, spiritual and natural, *communicating*, of which the latter form is the expression and the medium of the former. Spiritual communication may, however, take place only within the limits conditioned by the family, and hence only with some degree of moral reserve,—should never become family-confidentiality.

The family throws itself open indeed, in a normal state of things, to and for, society, but it does not merge itself therein,—rather is it the uniform and indispensable moral basis and presupposition thereof; it is a morbid state of society that does not rest on the family, but rather throws it into the back-ground, and more or less assumes its place. Only the moral integrity and the deep-reaching moral nature of the family give to society moral vitality; without these elements society declines to selfish, enjoyment-seeking characterlessness.

Society cannot, from its very nature, require as large a personal giving up of individual peculiarities as does the family; it rests essentially on a greater independence of its individual members to each other,—gives greater scope to the equal right of the individuals to independent peculiarities, than is the case with unreservedly-confiding love or reverence; it is made up therefore strictly only of the truly independent, and hence of the spiritually and morally mature; minors should belong predominantly only to the family, and should not as yet enter society; premature ripeness for society damagingly affects not only the taste for family-life but also the moral character of the person; and the most common reason for the characterlessness of the fashionable world, is the too early supplanting of the family-life by society-life. In society the individuals stand less in a strictly personal relation to each other,—stand not in the relation of a special, personal love, personally complementing each other, but rather as the single members of a more extensive generality. Here each one sees and loves, in the other, not so much the special personality as rather simply a single representative of society as a whole. In order to the exercise of social virtue, not so much depends on the personal choice of the individual—on the fact that I have to do with precisely this or that, to me, congenial personality —as on the fact that the person be simply a member of human, of moral, society in general. Hence the members of society make also less demands upon each other for mutual devotion and confidentiality than the members of a family; in the place of such perfect, mutual self-devotion as the property of others, come tender deference, politeness, friendliness and complacency. Politeness, which has nothing in common with hollow-hearted pretense, is not shown to the person as such but simply as a member of society, and should not be confounded with a manifestation of friendship, as this regards only the person. Forms of politeness are an expression of love, of friendliness, of humble deference, to another; they are manifestations of honor to whom honor is due, and it is due to every upright man [Rom xii, 10; xiii, 7; 1 Pet. ii, 17; v, 5; and, for examples, see Gen. xviii, 2 *sqq.;* xxiii, 7, 12; xxxii, 4, 18; xxxiii, 3, 6, 7, 13, 14; xliii, 26, 28; xliv, 18 *sqq.;* Rom. xv, 14, 15; etc.].

The boundary lines between the family and society are very

delicate, but also very legitimate; and he who, from a misconception of this difference, oversteps these limits and demeans himself in society as in the family, that is, does not show that proper reserve which seeks not to press itself upon others,—in a word, he who shows himself over-confidential, is regarded, and rightly so, as indelicate, characterless, or impudent; and when the person so acting is a female, she is looked upon as unwomanly or shameless. French *gallantry*, for which, happily, we have no German word, is a treating of the female members of society as if they were family-members; it treats every maiden as if she were an affianced sweetheart; it manifests the appearance of love where neither its reality nor the design of realizing it exists; this is an immoral disintegration and invasion of the family by society, a breaking down of the limits between them. With the growth of gallantry the dissolution of the family usually increases also; and the gallant society-man usually is or turns out to be a very ungenial husband. That devotion, that full, mutual, spiritual self-communicating, and that confidentiality, which, within the family as well as within the bounds of friendship, are not only a right but also a duty, become sinful when shown to society at large. Hence the personal love that manifests itself in the family is less in compass, but greater intensity in, than that *love of neighbor* which extends to all members of society without exception, as well as also without choice, and which manifests itself in the equally generally due spirit of *friendliness* [Matt. v, 47; Gal. v, 22; 1 Cor. xiii, 4; Eph. iv, 2, 32; Col. iii, 12; 2 Tim. ii, 24; Prov. xii, 25; Ruth ii, 8 *sqq.*]. He who loves and treats the members of his family merely with the friendliness of neighbor-love sins quite as much as he who promiscuously treats any or every one he meets with as a personal friend or as a consort; and this holds good not simply and merely of society as sin-disordered, though of course the difference is here much greater than in a state of innocence. Christian neighbor-love is indeed designated as *brother-love*, and the members of the moral community are to regard each other as brethren, even as also Christ calls his disciples his brethren [John xx, 17; Heb. ii, 11] or his friends [John xv, 13, 14], but this must not be so taken as to do away with the difference between family-love and neighbor-love; but, on the contrary, it rather simply implies that the latter is a form of love that is to be shaped after the pattern of brotherly love proper. Society is to be progressively more closely allied to the family,—is to be more and more affectionately and intimately united together on the basis and after the pattern of the family; and the closer bonds of the family are not thereby relaxed but in fact confirmed. The Son of man who embraced entire humanity in his love, loved yet his disciples with a closer love than he felt for others; and even among the disciples there was one "whom the Lord loved" by pre-eminence —who lay upon Jesus' bosom; and also Lazarus was a special friend of the Lord [John xi, 3, 33 *sqq.*], although Christ's love to these persons was still always something essentially other than human friendship—the Friend never predominating over the divine Master.—Of the distinctions that naturally form themselves in every society, and hence of the classes of callings, we cannot as yet here treat, as their sharper separation springs of and presupposes a sinful perversion of humanity.

As, on the part of the moral person, love in society is more of a general and, so to speak, impersonal character, so also is this love met from without by the objective reality of the moral, not so much as personal love in a personal form, as rather under a general and impersonal form—as a merely spiritual power, as *custom*. Custom is indeed upheld by the individual members of society, but it does not proceed from them as particular single persons, but rather from the collective public spirit of the whole. Custom is a fruit of the moral life, not of the individual, but of the collective public; it is the virtue of society as peculiarly-constituted; and, as such, it has a right to be respected by the individual; and the duty of the individual to conform to custom cannot be limited by mere caprice, but only by the higher moral law itself and by the legitimate peculiar duty of the individual subject. It is not requisite, in order to entitle social custom to the right of being respected, that in each particular case a definite moral or other rational ground be readily adducible for its continuance; this is in many cases even impossible; and though, of course, the custom, if legitimate, must ever have its sufficient reason, yet this reason is not always a universally-moral one. A respectful deference for that which has become historical in society is a high moral duty, provided simply that society itself is not already morally perverted. The ebullient juvenile vigor of the intensely self-conscious youth gladly recalcitrates against the historical reality of society,—is loth to recognize for itself any other limits than such as are imposed by the general and, as yet, not historically-determined moral law. The moral law, however, is not of a merely universal character, but shapes itself in society into a particular historical form; moral society has the same right to the forming and retaining of a peculiar character as has the individual person; and as the individual is entitled to be respected and spared in his moral peculiarity, so is entitled also, and with still greater right, the moral collective whole [Gen. xxix, 26]. It is a sign of moral crudity when individuals disregard social custom in cases where it is not positively evil, and oppose themselves to it for the simple reason that they do not regard it as absolutely necessary,—as, for example, in the style of clothing and in the forms of social intercourse. It is true, each individual is entitled to his own moral judgment as to a custom, and an immoral or irrational custom may by no means be spared or conformed to; on the contrary, there arises here the duty of reformatorily influencing society itself. But of such a perverted state of things we are not as yet here treating. The proper moral respecting of custom is *good-mannered* or *becoming* behavior [κόσμιος, 1 Tim. ii, 9; iii, 2]. The female mind embraces the moral more as an expression of custom; the male more as that of the law.

As all communion of love is a mutual imparting, so is it also with social love; the basis and at the same time the moral limit of this imparting or communicating, is the family. The family throws itself open occasionally for society,—imparts itself to society, welcomes its members hospitably into itself. *Hospitableness* or hospitality [Gen. xviii; xix; xxiv, 31 *sqq.;* Exod. ii, 20; Lev. xix, 33, 34; Judges xix, 20, 21; Job xxxi, 32; Matt. xxv, 35; x, 41, 42; Luke xi, 6; Acts xxviii, 7 *sqq.;* 1 Pet. iv, 9; Rom. xii, 13; 1 Tim. iii, 2; v, 10; Titus i, 8; Heb. xiii, 2] is properly a virtue practiced not by the individual, but predominantly by the family. It is the occasional letting in of society into the family, the outward manifesting of the love that prevails in the family toward those who stand to us simply in the relation of members in society. It is only the family that can exercise true hospitableness—that can constitute a hospitable house; this manifests itself, even in our present so radically perverted state of society, in the fact that it is always the housewife who takes the lead of the guest-circle, and gives it the family-consecration. Hospitality is one of the first and most natural manifestations of neighbor-love, hence it is highly esteemed even among many uncultured nations; it exists always in its highest form where also the family is preserved in high moral integrity, as, for example, among the ancient Germanic races. It is a very special and important characteristic of hospitality, that it is not exercised merely toward friends proper, who in fact already belong to the outer circle of the family, but also, and historically even primarily, to strangers who are as yet not known personally at all, that is, to man simply in his quality of neighbor.

SECTION CL.

The recognition of the moral character of a person on the part of moral society, is his social *honor;* each and every one has, normally, a moral right to such recognition by every other morally honorable person, and should strive to obtain and retain it. The actual manifestation of personal honor, as a moral possession, is personal *dignity.* No honor is morally valid save in so far as it is, at the same time, honor before God. The moral society into which the individual is incorporated by virtue, on the one hand, of custom, by which he as well as the collective society is influenced, and in which he consequently recognizes the morality of society, and, on the other hand, by virtue of the honor which he enjoys in the eyes of society, and in which consequently *his* morality is recognized by the society, is for him his moral *home.*

Only he has honor who has acquired a moral character; the characterless is honorless. Honor is the reflection of the personal character in the consciousness of society,—is its recognition by the same. Honor is the reverse phase of love; only the moral man can rightly love, and in loving he thirsts also to be loved, and hence to be recognized in his moral personality by others; the immoral man as such is not loved, because he is not in the possession of honor. Though honor is based on moral character yet it is not identical therewith,—it is character as having become objective in the moral consciousness of society. God's honor is not his holiness and his divine essence themselves, but the recognition of the same on the part of rational creatures; and as God vindicates and seeks his own honor [Exod. xiv, 4; 1 Sam. ii, 30; Psa. xlvi, 10; Isa. xlii, 8; xlviii, 11; Ezek. xxviii, 22; comp. John v, 23; Rom. xi, 36; xvi, 27], so also the moral man seeks, and rightly so, his honor, but only such as is at the same time *honor before God*, namely, a recognition of his conduct and spirit as those of a child of God, and hence an honor which is at the same time the witness of a good conscience before God [Psa. iii, 3; lxxiii, 24; cxii, 9; John v, 44; xii, 26, 43; Rom. ii, 6, 7, 10, 29; v, 2; 1 Cor. iv, 5; 2 Cor. x, 18],—the pleasures of God in him who loves Him [2 Cor. v, 9; Col. i, 10]. In this sense honor before men and the children of God is a high good [Psa. vii, 5; xlix, 11; lxxxiv, 12; Prov. iii, 16, 35; viii, 18; xi, 16; xxi, 21; xxii, 4; xxix, 23; Phil. ii, 29], and to disesteem *such* honor is either to think unworthily or to be too high-minded.

Personal honor and social custom condition man's moral *home*. Society and country are only in so far a home as they are expressive of the spiritually-moral life of society. My fatherland is not where I am outwardly prosperous, but where I enjoy myself *morally*,—feel myself vitally at one with a moral community. Mere nature forms a sort of home only for the savage; a true home is of a spiritual character, and nature is such only as brought within the sphere of history, as transformed by man. It is at home that man enjoys his existence; the far-off is tempting mostly only for him who is as yet in process of development toward spiritual and character-maturity; the seeking of a new home is in normal circumstances less an affair of the single individual than of whole branches of a nation, namely, in cases of the founding of new colonies; but here in fact the moral home migrates along. To be shut out from one's home is properly regarded as a severe misfortune; the declaration that he should be a fugitive wanderer in the earth was the bitterest element in the curse upon Cain; among ancient nations banishment was the severest of punishments.

(c) THE MORAL ORGANIZATION OF SOCIETY.

SECTION CLI.

As single persons unite themselves into a family and develop in it a vitally organic life in common, so in turn society unites itself into a higher-organized copy of the family, into a society-family, into a homogeneous moral organism,—organizes itself into a real unitary life; social custom rises from being primarily a purely spiritual, impersonal power, and becomes a real personally-represented and actually self-executing power,—that is, it becomes social *right* as expressed in *law*, in which form morality becomes for and over the individual an objective reality and power, and is not a mere formula but is in fact embodied in and tested and executed by moral personalities. There is no law without a personal representative and executor of the same.

If at first view society appears as a mere falling apart of the family, as a loosening of the narrower bond of love and duties as existing in the family itself, as a dissolution of the family-generated collective spirit into mere independent individual spirits, as a freer-making of the single individuals,—and if it is nevertheless, at the same time, a necessary progress beyond the mere family-life,—still there can be no resting at mere society and social custom, but society must in turn in its further development return back to the fundamental character of the family,—must exalt itself to the ideal of the family and of its moral organism, even as the plant, when unfolded out of the seed into branches and leaves, in turn generates again in the fruit the original seed. This return of society to the family takes place not merely through the fact that society itself becomes the occasion to constantly new unitings of families, but essentially by the fact that it itself takes on the character of a family of a higher grade,—that custom itself (which rules in society only as a bodiless spirit) assumes full objective reality, attains to flesh and blood and vital force, so as to vindicate and execute itself against whatever individual will may oppose it. Social custom depends for its realization entirely on its favorable recognition on the part of individuals; it falls away powerless where it meets with extended resistance; but when raised to the state of social right or law, it can itself compel recognition in the face of such resistance,—can force its opposers to submit themselves to general rationality as incarnated in the law. Just as mere custom is society-virtue as sentiment, so is law society-*character*, with firm will-force for carrying itself out. Custom is, as it were, the heart-rich idealistic bride-state of public morality; right as enunciated in law is its marriage-state with the full earnestness of obligation; the former rests on the discretion of the individual; the latter binds the individual unconditionally and with the power of active compulsion. That is surely a very bad legal condition of society where right is accomplished *only* by coercion and fear; and the normal condition of society is that where the law is inscribed in, and a vital force of, every individual heart, and that, too, *as* law and not as a mere and, as it were, simply beseeching custom; and where it does *not* find free recognition, there it *should* not bow its head and suffer in silence, but it has been intrusted by God with the sword for the punishment of evil doers, and for the praise of them that do well [1 Pet. ii, 14; Rom. xiii, 1–4]. That would be a bad-ordered family where the father, as against his disobedient children, merely bewailed in inactivity,—where he should not virtualize his true moral love by palpable chastisement; and organized society has, as the higher-developed family, also the love-duty of coercion and penal chastisement. Morality cannot and ought not to have a merely subjective form; it should attain also to objective reality,—should become a power above the individual person, and that, too, not as merely conceived, but as having full reality; and this condition is realized only in the fact that right or objective morality is not a mere thought, a mere written code, but that it has its personal upholders and executors; this is not merely human order, it is divine order. —As the highest form of the moral community-life, positively-organized society cannot do away with the earlier stages, the family and society in the larger sense of the word,—but as it is itself based upon them, it must necessarily contain them within itself, and foster and promote them. A state which, as was the case with Plato's, swallows up the family is totally illegitimate and in utter conflict with the moral idea. That unlimited autocracy of the state which assumes to be the sole and absolute source of right is a heathen notion, and, within the Christian world, anti-moral.

SECTION CLII.

The difference, as necessarily existing in every moral communion, of the morally-advanced and the morally less-matured, and which finds its first expression in the relation of parents and children, forms also the basis of organized society. In this society the duty of forming, of guiding and of educating falls mainly to the former; that of appropriating and obeying, to the latter. The guiding rests entirely on morally-religious culture, and aims by general forming to make of society a moral art-work, a moral organism. The difference between the guiding or ruling ones and the guided and obeying ones, is therefore *per se* strictly identical with the difference between the morally and religiously higher-developed (the prophets and priests) and the as yet to-be-developed, namely, the general public, the body of society. In so far as the moral organism expresses the antithesis of priest-prophets and people-congregation in the sphere of religion, it is the *church;* in so far as it expresses the antithesis of the ruling and the ruled in the sphere of law or right, it is the *state.* In a normally constituted and absolutely sin-free society church and state are perfectly identical, and the moral organism appears as a *theocracy;* its definite popular form would be a fully developed *patriarchal* state. The religious and the legal commonalty in their perfect unity are the morally developed family; and as its inner law and essence are absolutely the moral law itself, which rules at the same time as a vital power in the hearts of all its members, hence the theocratically-organized religiously-moral society is the historical realization of the *kingdom of God* on earth, and its perfecting is the goal of all rationally-moral effort, of the individual as well as of society as a whole; and the spiritual and moral development of humanity toward this ultimate end forms *universal history.*

We have nothing to do here with the actual church and the actual state, which are both essentially conditioned on, and constituted in view of combating, sin, but with the ideal moral community-life which is free of all sin. The family continues to be the moral basis and the pattern. The inner difference between the guiding and the guided can, in a sinless state of things, be only of a very mild and a merely relatively valid character. In a perfect religious community all the mature members are of priestly character, are invested with the duty of spiritual guidance; and in a perfect civil society all the mature citizens participate in the spiritual and moral guidance of the whole; and the more perfect the collective development of all the members, so much the more does the fundamental relation of fathers and children retire into the back-ground, and assume rather the form of the gentler antithesis of the two sexes in marriage.

As in the normal family, religious and moral life are united, and the father is also the spiritual and priestly guide of the religious life, hence in the ideal social organism, church and state are simply one and the same thing; they are but two absolutely inseparable phases of the same spiritual life. All religion becomes social reality, and all social life rests on religion; the normal state is also a church, and the true church develops out of itself a corresponding social community-life, —as was seen in the early Christian church, and as, in recent times, the *Unitas Fratrum*, from a correct presentiment of the goal of Christian history, has partially carried out. That the father of the people should also be the chief bishop, is implied in the prototype of the moral commonalty; but whether in this particular the ideal is to be applied to the very unideal present reality of the world, it is not here the place to decide. The patriarchal state is the primitive manner of morally organizing society,—the one most nearly related to the family prototype; and the family-chief of the closely related tribe is at once its chief leader and its priest; he represents, however, not his single personal will, but the moral will of the whole, which is in turn itself a faithful expression of the divine will. For this simple reason the ideal form of the social state is necessarily and essentially a theocracy; for it is only in a vital communion with God that the rulers of the people have their right, their law, their power; and it is not the mere divine law that is the all-guiding factor, but the living personal God himself, who enlightens and guides his trusting children, and governs directly through his prophets and anointed ones. The divine right of a true magistracy is based on this idea, but is valid as a *moral* right only in so far as humble submission to God rules in the hearts of the rulers. The theocracy of the Old Testament [Exod. xix, 3–6; Deut. vii, 6 *sqq.;* xxxiii, 5; 1 Sam. viii, 6 *sqq.;* Isa. xxxiii, 22] is only a faint shadow of that which was to have been realized in sinless humanity, and of which as partially regained through redemption only glimpses are caught in prophetic vision [Isa. ii, 2; iv, 2 *sqq.;* ix, 6 *sqq.;* xi, 1 *sqq.;* xxxii, 15 *sqq.;* lxv, 17 *sqq.;* Ezek. xxxiv, 23 *sqq.;* xxxvi, 24 *sqq.;* xxxvii, 24 *sqq.*].

The mysterious phenomenon of the priest-king of Salem, Melchizedek [Gen. xiv, 18 *sqq.*; Heb. vii, 1 *sqq.*; Psa. cx, 4], like a reminiscence of a long-forgotten better age floating down into a totally different present,—perhaps the last scion of those who had remained faithful to the Covenant of Noah outside of the family of Abraham,—is in some respects the expression of a true theocracy as it exists in a higher manner only in Christ. With the Israelites royalty and priesthood were in fact separate; Aaron and David represent the two sides of the *one* theocratical idea; Samuel approximated this idea, but was more a priest than a king. The theocratical form of society was realized in Old Testament times only in its first beginnings, in the family-state of the patriarchs. The people of Israel was both outwardly and inwardly too little at peace both with the world and with God to be able to sustain a theocratical form of government; it is only in "Salem" that the Prince of Peace can rule.

The moral commonalty in its double form as church and state is, on the one hand, a complete preserving and virtualizing of the personal moral freedom of the individuals, in that the collective will, as manifesting itself in laws and in the government, is at the same time the will of the individual, and on the other, a real objective presentation of the moral idea with a determining power for and over the individual, but which acts as a limit to the freedom of the individual only when this freedom has fallen from its harmony with God into irrational caprice. In the ideal state all morality becomes right or law, and all law is a pure expression of morality. When this moral commonalty has become a full reality, then it is the kingdom of God as having attained to historical form and reality. The kingdom of God *comes* not, it is true, with outward show [Luke xvii, 20, 21], inasmuch as it exists primarily in the hearts of men; but when it has come into the hearts of men—when God has assumed form within them—then will also the kingdom of God itself take upon itself a form, and the collective history of the God-imbued portion of humanity (the true church) is simply this gradually self-developing form. As soon, however, as sin has entered into reality, then church and state at once fall apart, and dissolve themselves in turn into discordant and contradictory subdivisions, and the kingdom of everlasting peace becomes a plurality of kingdoms of endless strife. The moral or ideal destination of universal history is, to be the uniformly undisturbed evolution of the kingdom of God; to confound its criminal reality with the unclouded ideal, is to deny ethical moral truth. But universal history, in its pure and normal form, is the development of humanity as *unitary* (§ 88); of this humanity the statement would hold good in the most perfect manner, that "the whole earth was of one language and of one speech" [Gen. xi, 1].

GENERAL INDEX TO VOLS. I AND II.

Aaron *vs.* David, ii, 337.
Abel, ii, 231, 280.
Abelard, i, 205.
Abortion, in Greece, i, 66, 85, 119; as viewed by the Jesuits, 269.
Abraham, purpose of the call of, i, 157; his marriage, ii, 321.
"Accommodation," i, 260.
Achilles, i, 41, 63.
Adiaphora, i, 253; ii, 123.
Adornment, ii, 242.
Adultery, Jesuitical teachings in regard to, i, 266 *sqq.*; ii, 309.
Ænesidemus, i, 145.
Agrippa of Nettesheim, i, 281.
Ahura-Mazda, i, 60.
"Akosmism," i, 289.
Albertus Magnus, i, 208.
Alcuin, i, 200.
Allihn, i, 357.
Alsted, i, 248.
Ambrose, i, 191.
Amesius, i, 247.
Amiability, i, 106.
Ammon, i, 338, 360.
Amyraud, i, 247.
Andreæ, i, 248.
Androgynism, ii, 305.
Anger, i, 105, 108.
Angra-mainyus, i, 59.
Animals, ii, 202, 264, 267, 270.
Anti-hero-worship, of the Jews, i, 163.
Antisthenes, i, 72.
Apocrypha, ethics of the, i, 169.
Apollo, i, 63.
Apologia, the, ii, 44, 62.
Appropriation *vs.* formation and sparing, ii, 180; 186; sexual, 189; spiritual, 190; 214; 237; natural, 266.
Architecture, sacred, ii, 207.
Arnauld, i, 274.
Arndt, John, i, 249.

Arrian, i, 133.
Aristippus, i, 73.
Aristotle, i, 41, 89; relation to Plato, 92; works of, 92 *sqq.*; influence on the Middle Ages, 93; on the God-idea, 94; on virtue, 96; on the highest good, 97; on depravity, 102; on the virtues, 103 *sqq.*; on the contemplative life, 109; on the community-life, 110; on friendship, 111; on democracy, 114; on marriage, 119; on education, 120; on war, 121; *vs.* the Christian spirit, 124.
Art, ii, 205, 209; 271.
Art-works, ii, 184; 205 *sqq.*
Asceticism, Brahminic, i, 51; Buddhistic, 54; early Christian, 183; ii, 268.
Astesauus, i, 222.
Atheism, i, 52; of the Epicureans, 129; of La Mettrie, 320; 352 *sqq.*
Augustine, ii, 192; on grace and on the will, 193; on the principle of virtue, 194; on the four cardinal and the three theological virtues, 195; on the divine counsels, 196.
Autonomy, ii, 7, 9, 18.
Avesta, the, i, 59.
Awe, ii, 173.
Azorio, i, 256.

Baader, i, 342, 375.
Babylonians, the, i, 54.
Bacon, i, 303.
Balduin, i, 251.
Banishment, ii, 332.
Barnabas, i, 181.
Basnage, i, 248.
Basedow, i, 322.
Basil, i, 190.

340 INDEX.

Bauer, G. L., i, 152; Bruno and Edgar, 354.
Bauny, i, 257, 263.
Baumgarten, Alex., i, 298; Jacob, 325.
Baumgarten-Crusius, i, 361.
Baxter, i, 248.
Beautiful, the, i, 63; ii, 9.
Beauty vs. morality, i, 65; vs. the ethical, 80; ii, 242.
Becoming, the, ii, 210.
Bede, i, 199.
Beneke, i, 357.
Bernard, St., i, 206, 224.
Bertling, i, 325.
Besombes, i, 376.
Besser, i, 257.
Bliss, ii, 283.
Blood-relationship vs. marriage, ii, 320 sqq.
Böhme, i, 342.
Boëthius, i, 197.
Bolingbroke, i, 312.
Bona, i, 275.
Bonaventura, i, 224.
Brahma, i, 41, 42, 45; ii, 184.
Brahminism, i, 48 sqq.
Brandis, i, 107, 123.
Braniss, i, VII.
Breithaupt, i, 255.
Brothers vs. sisters, ii, 318.
Bruno, i, 281.
Buddæus, i, 324.
Buddhism, i, 41, 48, 52 sqq.
Büchner, i, 354.
Busenbaum, i, 257.
Butchering, moral influence of, ii, 268.

Cain, ii, 231, 285, 332.
Calixt, i, 250.
Calvin, i, 242; on the virtues, 243; ii, 301.
Cana, the marriage at, ii, 188.
Canz, i, 298, 325.
Caste, i, 49, 83, 120.
Castration, i, 269; ii, 265.
Casuistry, i, 199, 221, 250, 255.
"Categorical imperative," the, i, 330; ii, 33, 52, 83.
"Celestial kingdom," the, i, 45.
Celibacy, i, 188, 189, 254.

Chalybäus, i, 357.
Chase, the, and war, i, 121.
Chastity i, 181.
Childhood, ii, 69, 263.
Child-innocence, ii, 152.
Children vs. parents, ii, 313.
Chinese, ethics, i, 43; virtue, 46; marriage, 47.
Christ, the nature of his moral precepts, ii, 87; his comeliness, 243.
Christian ethics, i, 173, 328; ii, 1; threefold form of, 2.
Christianity, scientific impulse given by, i, 179.
Chrysostom, i, 190.
Church vs. state, ii, 335.
Chytræus, i, 242.
Cicero, i, 132, 149; on collision of duties, 150; 280.
Clarke, i, 306.
Clavasio, i, 222.
Cleanliness, ii, 242 sqq.
Clemens Alexandrinus, i, 186.
Clothing, ii, 245 sqq.
Collins, i, 310.
Collision of duties, i, 150; ii, 136, 292.
Commands vs. prohibitions, ii, 124.
Communism of Plato, i, 84; of the Stoics, 141.
Community-life, the, i, 82, 110, 220; ii, 76, 302.
Compassion, Buddhistic, i, 53; 286.
Concini, i, 376.
Concilia vs. præcepta, ii, 113.
Concubines, i, 65; ii, 307.
Condillac, i, 314.
Confession, ii, 223.
Confidence vs. distrust, ii, 261.
Confucius, i, 44.
Consanguinity, ii, 155.
Conscience, i, 339; ii, 99 sqq.
Considerateness, ii, 282.
Consorts vs. blood-relatives, ii, 313.
Constance, the Council of, i, 260.
Contemplative life, the, favored by Aristotle, i, 115; by St. Victor, 224.
Continence, i, 108.
Contract-marriage, ii, 307.
Corporeality, ii, 60.

INDEX. 841

Courage, i, 103; ii, 291, 292, 296.
Counsels, the, i, 196, 215, 242.
Culture vs. savagery, ii, 288.
Creation, to be completed by the creature, ii, 274.
Crell, i, 281.
Crüger, i, 325.
Crusius, i, 299, 326.
Cudworth, i, 306.
Cumberland, i, 305.
Culmann, i, 375.
Custom, ii, 325; vs. law, 333.
Customariness, i, 21, 348.
Cynics, i, 72.
Cynics vs. Cyrenaics, i, 73.
Cyprian, i, 189.
Cyrenaics, i, 73.

Damascenus, John, i, 198.
Damiani, i, 200.
Danæus, i, 247; ii, 57.
Dance, the, ii, 247.
Dannhauer, i, 251.
Darwinism, ii, 154.
Daub, i, 344, 351.
Death, Epicurean view of, i, 138; ii, 67.
Dedekenn, i, 352.
Decalogue, the, ii, 28.
Deism, i, 302, 312.
Depravity, i, 38, 42; Plato's explication of, 78, 79; Aristotle's remedy for, 114; 123.
Descartes, i, 282, 288.
Determinism, i, 282, 293.
Devotedness, ii, 298.
De Wette, his works, i, 37; 360.
Diana, i, 264, 270.
Diderot, i, 319.
Dignity, ii, 330.
Diligence, ii, 294.
Diodorus, quoted, i, 57.
Diogenes, i, 74; ii, 279.
Dionysius the Areopagite, i, 198.
Discretionary, the sphere of the, i, 155; ii, 122.
Distrust, ii, 261.
Divorce, i, 85; vs. barrenness, ii, 308.
Dogmatics, vs. ethics, i, 22 sqq.; the presupposition of ethics, 180; ii, 31.

Domestic animals, ii, 264.
Dualism, i, 60, 62, 63, 87; Stoic, 133; Schellingian, 341 sqq.
Dürr, i, 250.
Duns Scotus, i, 217; ii, 85.
Dunte, i, 251.
Duties, the, i, 296; all duties are duties to God, ii, 148.
Duty, i, 345; ii, 336 sqq.; vs. right, 139.

Eberhard, i, 298.
Ebionites and Gnostics, i, 185.
Ecclesiastes, the Book of, i, 168.
Eckart, i, 225; ii, 20.
Eden, ii, 51, 275.
Education, Platonic, i, 84; Aristotelian, 119 sqq.; ii, 198 sqq.
Egyptian ethics, i, 55 sqq.
Egyptians, the, i, 54; ii, 191.
Elvenich, i, 357.
Empirical ethics, i, 28.
End, the, sanctifies the means, i, 260; ii, 179.
Endemann, i, 326.
Endurance, Buddhistic, i, 53.
Enthusiasm, ii, 173; vs. the ideal, 174; 206.
Epictetus, i, 132.
Epicurean view, of the highest good, i, 129; of pleasure, 130, of right and wrong, of religion, of death, of the universe, 129–131; ii, 55.
Epicureanism, principle of, i, 128 sqq.; realistic, 142; vs. Christianity, 143.
Epicurus, i, 128.
Equanimity, i, 105.
Erasmus, i, 279, 281.
Erigena, i, 201, 223.
"Eros," i, 79.
Escobar, i, 257.
Ethics, defined, i, 13; Harless' and Schleiermacher's definition, 15; Platonic, 79 sqq.; Aristotelian, 93 sqq.; Epicurean, 129; Stoic, 141; Old Testament, 151; Christian, 173; heathen, 177; vs. dogmatics, 180; Patristic, 181; mediæval, 199; Protestant, 235; Reformed vs. Lutheran, 244

sqq.; Roman Catholic, 255, 375; Spinozistic, 281; Leibnitzian, 290; Wolfian, 292; Lockean, 303; materialistico-French, 314 sqq.; Kantian, 327; Fichtean, 338; Schellingian, 342; Hegelian, 345 sqq.; Schleiermacherian, 361; Rothean, 371; classification of, ii, 23–34.
"Eudæmonia," i, 97, 109.
Eudemonism, i, 328; ii, 176.
Eve, ii, 103, 249.
Evil, i, 13, 42; Plato's view of, 78; origin of, 156.
Example, ii, 86, 260.

Fables, ii, 267.
Fairness, i, 107.
Faith, i, 153, 212; ii, 10; vs. knowledge, 12; 215; as a virtue, 298.
Fall, the, in Persia, i, 60; true nature of, ii, 166.
Falsehood, i, 85; ii, 192 sqq.
Family, the, in China, i, 46; in India, 51; in Greece, 85, 110 sqq.; in Israel, 165.
Family-honor, ii, 323.
Fatalism, i, 115.
Fear of God, ii, 89.
Feder, i, 301.
Feeling, ii, 13, 49, 98, 159, 249; its perfection, ii, 283.
Fénelon, i, 276.
Ferguson, i, 312.
Feuerbach, i, 351.
Feuerlein, i, 37.
Fidelity, ii, 293.
Fichte, i, 338; his moral canon, 339; J. H., 358.
Fischer, i, 358.
Filliucci, i, 257.
Flatt, i, 360.
Formation, ii, 180, 198 sqq.
Frederick the Great, i, 320.
Freedom, i, 38; true, ii, 280.
"Free love," i, 85.
Friendship, i, 111 sqq.; Christian, ii, 318; vs. friendliness.
Fulbert, i, 200.
Future life, i, 41; Egyptian view of, 57; Aristotle's view of, 95; why not prominent in the Mosaic law, 161 sqq.

Gallantry, ii, 319, 327.
Garve, i, 301.
Gassendi, i, 314.
Gellert, i, 300.
Genettus, i, 272.
Gerhard, i, 252.
"German Theology," i, 229.
Gerson, i, 228.
Gifts, i, 125; ii, 259.
Giving, ii, 258.
Goal, the Chinese, i, 44; the Brahminic, 49; the Buddhistic, 53; the Persian, 60; the Platonic, 91; the Aristotelian, 96; the Mosaic, 154; the Christian, 174; 220; ii, 7, 24, 30, 149, 274.
God, the basis and measure of the moral, ii, 9; his free immutability, 85; 145; 232.
God-consciousness, the, ii, 80.
God-fearing, ii, 172; vs. God-trusting, 173.
God-likeness, i, 77; ii, 164.
God-worship, ii, 276.
Gonzales, i, 262.
Good, the, i, 13, 40; among the Chinese, 42; among the Greeks, 43; among the Indians, 47; according to Plato, 77; according to Aristotle, 96; according to Peter Lombard, 206; ii, 5, sqq.; vs. the moral, 10; three phases of, 91.
Gossip, ii, 261.
Grace-saying, ii, 188.
Graffiis, i, 272.
Grecian, the, his unseriousness, i, 67; his presumption, 68; his virtues, 293.
Gregory, of Nyssa, of Nazianzum, i, 190; the Great, 198.
Guion, Madame, i, 276.
Gutzkow, i, 362.
Gymnastics, ii, 241.

Habit, i, 99; ii, 290.
Hales, i, 208.
Hanssen, i, 325.
Happiness, ii, 175.

INDEX. 343

Harless, i, XII, 22, 374; ii, 28.
Hartenstein, i, 357.
Hatred, ii, 161 *sqq*.
Heart, ii, 101.
Heathen ethics, ground-character of, i, 38, 177; ii, 175.
Heathenism, i, 39, 64, 86, 155.
Hebrew ethics, i, 156.
Hegel, his view of ethics, i, 20; 345; on State and Church, 349.
Heidegger, i, 248.
Helvetius, i, 314.
Hemming, i, 242.
Hengstenberg, i, VI.
Henriquez, i, 256.
Hellene, the, i, 64 *sqq*.
Help-meet, the idea of, ii, 309.
Herbart, i, 356.
Hermaphrodite, ii, 75.
Heroic virtue, i, 108.
Heydenreich, i, 336.
Highest good, the, i, 97, 159, 161, 176, 209, 365; ii, 6, 43; 276.
Hildebert, i, 204.
Hirscher, i, 376; ii, 117.
Hobbes, i, 304.
Holbach, i, 321.
Holiness, ii, 285, 286.
Home, significance of, ii, 331.
Honor, ii, 183, 253.
Hope, i, 212; as a virtue, ii, 299.
Hospitality, ii, 196.
Human flesh, the eating of, i, 270.
Humanism, i, 279.
Humanity, i, 38, 121.
Hume, i, 311.
"Humanitarianism," i, 66, 121; ii, 255.
Humility, i, 175; as a virtue, ii, 298.
Hunger, ii, 187.
Huss, i, 231.
Hutcheson, i, 310.

Ideal, the, *vs.* the real, ii, 82.
Illuminism, i, 302, 322, 327, 337; ii, 20.
Image, the, of God, ii, 37, 42.
Immortality, ii, 51.
Incarnation, conditional or unconditional, ii, 86.
Incomprehensibility of God, ii, 44.

Innocence *vs.* holiness, ii, 285.
Intercession, ii, 224.
Irenæus, i, 185.
Isenbiehl, i, 376.
Isidore, i, 190, 198.
Islamism, i, 171.
Israel, the world-historical significance of, i, 157 *sqq*.

Jacob, i, 159; L. H., 336.
Jacobi, i, 342, 344.
Jansenism, i, 273.
Jealousy, ii, 196.
Jerome, i, 192.
Jesuits, i, 256 *sqq*.; their Pelagianism, 260; their moral laxity, 264; on equivocation, 266; on adultery, 268; ii, 178.
Jocham, i, 376.
John, of Salisbury, i, 220 *sqq*.; of Goch, 231.
Jovinian, i, 192.
Judaism, i, 171, 282.
Judas, i, 343.
Judith, the Book of, i, 171.
Justin, i, 186.
Just mean, the, i, 45; of Aristotle, 100.
Justness, i, 81, 106; ii, 294.

Kähler, i, 361.
Kant, i, 324, 327; his ethical works, 329; his canon of morality, 330; criticised, 333; his second canon, 334; ii, 22, 39, 44, 52, 83; on prayer, 222.
Keckermann, i, 247.
Kiesewetter, i, 336.
Kingdom of God, the, i, 156; ii, 276.
Kiss, the, significance of, ii, 356.
Klein, i, 344.
Knowledge *vs.* faith, ii, 12.
König, i, 251.
Köstlin, ii, 266.
Krause, i, 344.

Labor, ii, 203, 271.
Lactantius, i, 191.
La Mettrie, i, 320.
Lampe, i, 248.
Lange, S. G., i, 338.

Latin theology *vs.* Grecian, i, 193.
Law, ii, 90.
Laymann, i, 257.
Leibnitz, i, 278, 290; his theodicy, 291.
Less, i, 257, 326.
Liberality, i, 104.
Liberum arbitrium, ii, 45.
Life-stages, ii, 67.
Ligorio, i, 375.
Lipsius, i, 281.
Lobkowitz, i, 271.
Locke, i, 303.
Lombard, Peter. i, 206.
Love, Platonic, i, 99; Christian, ii, 213; *vs.* hatred, 161 *sqq.*; *vs.* fear, 172; *vs.* happiness-seeking, 176; a duty, 178; 201, 257.
Luther, i, 235; ii, 109.
Lutheran ethics, i, 244.

Magic, ii, 157.
Magnanimity, i, 105; portrayed by Aristotle, 124 *sqq.*
Majority, i, 168; civil *vs.* moral, ii, 70.
Malder, i, 272.
Mandula, i, 271.
Manichees, ii, 268.
Manliness, i, 81.
Manu, the Laws of, i, 48.
Marcus Aurelius, i, 133.
Mariana, i, 269.
Marriage, moral presuppositions of, ii, 304 *sqq.*
Masculinity, ii, 75.
Marheineke, i, 37, 146, 352.
Marriage, Brahminic, i, 51; Grecian, 66; Platonic, 85; Aristotelian, 118; Stoic, 140; Israelitic, 165; early Christian, 181; "irresistible aversion" in, ii, 169; Christian, 310 *sqq.*; requires diverse qualities in consorts, 321.
Martensen, i, 358.
Martin, i, 376.
Materialism, ii, 61.
Maxim *vs.* law, ii, 133.
Maximus, i, 198.
Mehmel, i, 341.
Meier, i, 250, 299.

Meiner, i, 37.
Melanchthon, i, 236; his works, 237; on will-freedom, 239.
Melchizedek, ii, 336.
Mengering, i, 251.
Mexicans, the, i, 43.
Michelet, i, 351.
Middle-way, the, i, 100.
Minority, ii, 68.
Miracles, i, 158.
Moderation, ii, 189.
Moral element, the, of an action, ii, 178.
Morality, Chinese, i, 50; Buddhistic, 52 *sqq.*; Persian, 62; Grecian, 63; Socratic, 70; Platonic, 79; Israelitic. 154; Christian, 174; Patristic, 181; Hegelian, 347; ii, 8; *vs.* religion, 15; centrifugal, 17.
Möller, i, 344.
Mohammed, i, 172.
Moleschott, i, 354.
Molinos, i, 275; ii, 20.
Monasticism, beginnings of, i, 183; 200.
Monkery, ii, 280.
More, i, 306.
Morus, i, 326.
Motive, general nature of, ii, 159; 179.
Moses, i, 164.
Mosheim, i, 15, 326.
Müller, i, 351.
Mummies, significance of, i, 57.
"Must" and "should," antagonistic, i, 14; ii, 90; 167.
Mysticism, i, 198, 224, 231, 273, 275, 341; ii, 18, 20.

Name-giving. ii, 39.
Name-interchanging, ii, 260.
Narcissus, ii, 321.
Natalis, i. 272.
Nationalities, ii, 73.
Naturalism, i, 144; Greek, 122; Epicurean, 129; 288.
Nature, its destination, ii, 156; duties toward, 264; symbolism in, 266; abuse of, 272.
Navarra, i, 265.
Neander, i, 37.

INDEX. 345

Nebuchadnezzar, i, 58.
Neighbor-love, ii, 254.
Neo-Platonism, i, 144, 147; Pantheistic, 148; mystical, 149.
Nicole, i, 274.
Nimrod, i, 58.
"Nirvana," i, 40.
Nitzsch, i, 24; F., ii, 58.
Nobility, ii, 324.
Normality, moral, ii, 286.
Nudity, in art, ii, 244.

Obedience, ii, 298.
Objective morality, i, 86.
Official morality, ii, 78.
Old age, ii, 68.
Olearius, i, 251.
Ontology, Chinese, i, 44; Brahminic. 48; Buddhistic, 52; Egyptian, 55; Semitic, 57; Persian, 59; Grecian, 63; Platonic, 78; Aristotelian, 94; Epicurean, 131, 142; Stoic, 133, 142; Hebrew, 153; Neo-Platonic, 201; Spinozistic, 282; Leibnitzian, 290; Kantian, 329; Fichtean, 338; Schellingian, 342; Hegelian, 345 *sqq.*
Opera supererogatoria, i, 234.
Origen, i, 187.
Ornamentation, ii, 244.
Osiander, i, 251.
Osiris, i, 56.

Palmer, i, 29, 374.
Pain, ii, 60.
Pantheism, Indian, i, 47; Neo-Platonic, 147; mediæval, 198; of Erigena, 201; of Eckart, 225; of Spinoza, 282; of Fichte, 337; of Schelling, 341; of Hegel, 346; of Strauss, 352; ii, 47; moral tendency of, 81 *sqq.*; *vs.* prayer, 222.
Paradise, i, 45; true significance of, ii, 197; 212.
Parents *vs.* children, ii, 313.
"Parrhæsia," ii, 297.
Pascal, i, 274.
Patuzzi, i, 376.
Peace, ii, 163.
Pederasty, i, 141.

Pelagianism, i, 260, 279.
Pennaforti, i, 222.
Peraldus, i, 219.
Perazzo, i, 272.
Perfection, moral, i, 278.
Perkins, i, 248.
Pericles, i, 65.
Personal honor, ii, 330.
Peru, ii, 121.
Petition, ii, 224.
Pharisaism, i, 136, 232.
Philosophical ethics, i, 16, 27; *vs.* theological, 28; 355.
Physiognomics, ii, 243.
Piccolomini, i, 256.
Piety, i, 81; ii, 15; *vs.* morality, 147; 170.
Pietism, i, 252, 337.
Piety-virtues, the, ii, 297.
Plant-sparing, ii, 184.
Plato, i, 75; his works, 76; on the virtues, 81; on the state, 82; on caste, 83; on property, 84; on divorce, 85; on religion, 91; on reading Homer, 92.
Play, ii, 128.
Pleasure, i, 109; Epicurean, 130.
Plotinus, i, 147.
Plutarch, i, 151.
Polanus, i, 247.
Politeness, impersonal, ii, 326.
Polygamy, ii, 306.
Pomponatius, i, 281.
Pontas, i, 272.
Porphyry, i, 147.
Prayer, i, 177; ii, 147, 218; Kant on, 222.
Predestinarianism, i, 242, 273.
Presentiment, ii, 226.
Prierias, i, 222.
Priest *vs.* layman, ii, 334.
Proclus, i, 147.
Probabilism, i, 255, 261.
Property, Plato on, 84; ii, 279, 280.
Prophecy, ii, 226.
Proverbs, the Book of, i, 167.
Prudence, ii, 282.
Pyramids, the, significance of, i, 57.
Pyrrho, i, 145.

Quesnel, i, 274.
Quietism, i, 273, 275; ii, 18, 303.

Race, the human, its unity, ii, 153.
Radicalism, i, 346.
Rationalistic ethics, i, 37, 322, 324; ii, 22.
Rationality, ii, 6; *vs.* morality, 9; 41.
Raymond of Toulouse, i, 230.
Reynauld, i, 257.
Reason, i, 329; the practical, 331.
Recluse-life, the, ii, 303.
Redemption, progressively revealed, i, 166.
Reformation, the, i, 232, 233.
Reinhard, i, 360.
Religion *vs.* morality, ii, 15; centripetal, 17.
Repentance, i, 286.
"Republic," the, of Plato, i, 82; criticised, 290; ii, 276, 334.
"Rescuer" of the-Persians, i, 61.
Reservatio mentalis, i, 255, 266, 271.
Resurrection, the, ii, 66.
Reusch, i, 325.
Reuss, i, 326.
Reverence for elders, ii, 316.
Right, three stages of, 291 ; 345, 347; *vs.* duty, ii, 139; *vs.* law, 332.
Rixner, i, 250.
Rodriguez, i, 257.
Roman philosophy, i, 149.
Rothe, i, XII, 9; on the scope of ethics, 18; 25, 30; on heterodoxy, 31; criticised, 32 *sqq.*; 359; on church and state, 372; ii, 10, 21, 24; on conscience, 104; 110, 129, 168, 264; on the virtues, 301.
Rousseau, i, 37, 280; his ethical views, 317 ; 222.
Rudeness, ii, 184.
Ruisbroch, i, 228.

Sa, i, 265.
Sabbath, the, idea of, i, 155; ii, 212 *sqq.*
Sacrifice, ii, 218 *sqq.*
Sailer, i, 376.
St. Victor, i, 224.
Sakya-Muni, i, 52.
Salat, i, 245.
Sales, Francis de, i, 275.

Sanchez, i, 257.
Sarah, ii, 321.
Sanctification, ii, 285, 287.
Savages *vs.* history, ii, 191.
Scavini, i, 376.
Sartorius, i, 24, 374.
Satanology, i. 344.
Savonarola, i, 231.
Schleiermacher, i, XII, 317; on Spinoza, 290; 361 *sqq.*; ii, 24 *sqq.*, 39, 63, 110, 129.
Scholling, i, 280; his ontology and ethics, 341–344; ii, 47.
Schenkel, i, 337; ii, 107.
Schenkl, i, 376.
Schlegel, i, 362.
Schliephake, i, 358.
Schmid, i, 336; J. W., 338; O. F., 374.
Schmidt, i, 338.
Scholasticism, i, 200, 203.
Schopenhauer, i, 358.
Schubert, i, 325.
Schwarz, i, 360; ii, 24, 141.
Schweitzer, ii, 58.
Self-culture, ii, 248.
Self-love, false *vs.* the true, i, 175; *vs.* God-love, ii, 165.
Self-mortification, i, 50, 274.
Secret-keeping, ii, 193.
Seneca, i, 132; on suicide, 139.
Senility, ii, 71.
Senses, the, ii, 63.
Service-rendering, ii, 261.
Servile-mindedness, ii, 185.
Sex, ii, 74; in nature, 304.
Sextus Empiricus, i, 145.
Sexual relations, Jesuitical teachings as to, i, 266.
Shaftesbury, i, 308.
Shame, i, 106; ii, 239.
Sin, its historical origin, i, 156; Christian view of, 176, 215.
Sismond, i, 264.
Sirach, the Book of, i, 169; ii, 46.
Skepticism, i, 144 *sqq.*; ii, 13.
Slavery, Grecian, i, 66; Aristotle's apology for, 117 ; ii, 152.
Sleep, i, 14.
Smith, i, 311.
Snell, i, 336.
Socinianism, i, 281.

Socrates, i, 65, 69, 70, 72; *vs.* his wife, 72; advances made by, 127.
Solidarity, ii, 324.
Solon, i, 66.
Sparing, ii, 180; its objects, 183; 232, 252.
Speculation, theological, i, 30.
Spener, i, 252.
Spinoza, i, 31, 278; his *Ethica*, 281; *vs.* Calvin, ii, 47.
Stackhouse, i, 326.
Stahl, i, 358; ii, 130.
Stapf, i, 376.
Stäudlin, i, 36, 338.
Stapfer, i, 324.
Stattler, i, 376.
Steinbart, i, 323.
Stirner, i, 354.
Strauss, i, 352.
Strigel, i, 242.
State, the Chinese, i, 47; the Platonic, 82; the Hegelian, 345, 349.
Stoicism, i, 131; *vs.* Epicureanism, 132, 145; errors of, 141; *vs.* Christianity, 143, 182.
Stoic view, of virtue, i, 131; of the life-goal, and of the norm of truth, 133; of the good, 134; of religion, 136; of compassion, 137; of death, 138; of suicide, 139; of marriage, 140.
Suarez, i, 257.
Subjectivism, i, 144.
Suicide, i, 139.
Summæ casuum, i, 222.
Supererogatory works, i, 234; ii, 114 *sqq*.
Supralapsarianism, ii, 46.
Symbolical forming, ii, 209.
Symbolism, ii, 206.

Table-luxuries, ii, 189.
Table-pleasures, ii, 241.
Talmud, the, i, 171.
Tamburini, i, 257.
Taste, ii, 195.
Tauler, i, 226; on three kinds of works, 227; ii, 20.
Temperaments, the, ii, 71; four of them, 73, 292.
Temperateness, i, 81, 104; ii, 291, 295.
Tertullian, i, 187; on marriage, 188.
Thankfulness, ii, 262, 294.
Thanksgiving, ii, 223.
Theological ethics, i, 21, 27; *vs.* philosophical, 35; as a distinct science, 247; 250, 359, 371; ii, 1.
Theocracy, the, in Israel, i, 166; ii, 335.
Theosophy, i, 30, 341, 375.
Thomas à Kempis, i, 229.
Thomas Aquinas, i, 208; on the will, 209; on virtue, 211; on the virtues, 212.
Thomasius, i, 298.
Tieftrunk, i, 336.
Titans, the, i, 64.
Tittmann, i, 326.
Tollner, i, 326.
Tolet, i, 256.
Tournley, i, 376.
Trendelenburg, ii, 107.
Trust, ii, 173.
Tweston, i, 364.
Typhon, i, 56.
Tyranny, of man over woman, ii, 311.
Tyrant-murder, Jesuitical code of, i, 269.

Unitas Fratrum, ii, 336.
Unity of mankind, ii, 152.
Utilitarianism, ii, 203.

Vatke, i, 351.
Vasquez, i, 256.
Vedas, the, i, 48.
Venial sins, i, 188, 265.
Vergier, i, 275.
Virginity, ii, 190.
Virtue, Brahminic, i, 49; Chinese, 50; Platonic, 77, 81; essence of, 207; 339, 366; ii, 177, 274; New Testament, idea of, 290.
Virtues, the cardinal, i, 195; 207, 239, 243; four chief, 290; the Platonic, ii, 292; different classifications of, 300.
Vogel, i, 338.

Vogt, i, 354.
Volition, ii, 250.
Voltaire, i, 28; superficiality of his ethics, 319.
Von Eitzen, i. 248.
Von Henning, i, 251.

Waibel. i, 376.
Walæus, i, 247.
Waldenses, the, i, 231.
Weber, Dr. A., i, VIII.
Wedlock-love, ii, 121.
Werner, i, 376.
Wickliffe, i, 231.
Will, the, the sphere of the moral, ii, 10.
Will-freedom, i, 14; in Aristotle, 96; threefold, 206; 209, 224, 239, 335; ii, 13, 45, 84.
Wirth, i, 357.
Wisdom, i, 81, 107; practical, ii, 133; true, 286.

Wisdom, the Book of, i, 170.
"Wise men," the, i, 69.
Wolf, i, 278, 292 *sqq*.
Wollaston, i, 308.
Womanliness, ii, 75.
"Woman's rights," Plato's view of. i, 86; the author's view of, ii, 310 *sqq*.
Worship, i, 369; ii, 215.
Writing, the art of, ii, 191.
Wuttke, sketch of his life and works, i, VII; his confessional position, VIII; his life-task, IX; his relation to Hengstenberg, X; character of his ethics, XII; scope of the same, 35.

Youth, prone to revolution, ii, 329.

Zeno, i, 131 *sqq*.
Zöckler, ii, 266.

www.ingramcontent.com/pod-product-compliance
Lightning Source LLC
Chambersburg PA
CBHW020227240426
43672CB00006B/440